# GENTLEMEN
## *of the* WOODS

# GENTLEMEN
## *of the* WOODS

MANHOOD,

MYTH, *and the*

AMERICAN

LUMBERJACK

Willa Hammitt
BROWN

UNIVERSITY OF MINNESOTA PRESS
MINNEAPOLIS
LONDON

Frontispiece courtesy of the Minnesota Historical Society

Maps on pages xxxiv–xxxvii by Rhys Davies

Published by the University of Minnesota Press
111 Third Avenue South, Suite 290
Minneapolis, MN 55401-2520
http://www.upress.umn.edu

ISBN 978-1-5179-1245-1 (hc)
ISBN 978-1-5179-1757-9 (pb)

A Cataloging-in-Publication record for this book is available from the Library of Congress.

Printed in the United States of America on acid-free paper

32 31 30 29 28 27 26 25 24      10 9 8 7 6 5 4 3 2 1

# CONTENTS

Introduction: The Cost of Cheap Nature    vii
A Note on Sources    xxxiii
Map of the Northwoods    xxxiv
Map of the Lumberjack's Playground    xxxvi

PART I. IN THE WOODS    1
ONE. Bull Cooks and Walking Bosses: Camp Life in a Booming Industry    3
TWO. "His Flesh Hung in Tatters and Strings": The Violence of Nature    40
THREE. On Greenhorns and White Men: Skill and the Boundaries of Race    61

PART II. IN TOWN    83
FOUR. That Restless, Roving Spirit: Itinerancy and Resistance    85
FIVE. "Such People May Invade the City": Tramp Scares and Skid Rows    111
SIX. Five Hundred Drunks in the Street: Snake Rooms, Sprees, and Saloons    138

PART III. IN MEMORY    161
SEVEN. The Only American Hero: Reinventing the Lumberjack    163
EIGHT. Papering over a Wasteland: Creating a Corporate Myth    184
NINE. The Passing of the Pines: Buying and Selling Legends    204

Conclusion: The Stories We Still Buy    231
Acknowledgments    235
Notes    239
Index    295

# THE COST OF CHEAP NATURE

An hour's drive north of the Blandin Paper Factory, up Highway 46, lies a section of the Minnesota State Forest known as the Lost Forty. There's a dirt path that winds through enormous pines, some up to five feet in diameter. On the forest floor, it's cool—the sun barely filters through the thick branches. The trees tower over a hundred feet above your head, and even straining, it is hard to see their crowns. Over a century ago, a hapless surveyor took a bad measurement and never fixed it. He claimed a 140-acre lake lay over these trees, which meant no one could buy them. They are a mistake, a clerical error. And they are nearly all that is left of the Northwoods.[1]

By the time of my earliest summer memories, the transformation of the Northwoods of Michigan, Wisconsin, and Minnesota, from old-growth forest to second-growth tourist site, was complete. Once a boundless sea of pines, northern Minnesota is now less than 2 percent virgin-growth forest. When my great-grandfather August arrived from Sweden in 1882 and worked his first seasons as a lumberjack in the Minnesota pines, the logging industry was just coming into its height. By the time my grandmother was born in 1902, the industry was nearly done eating up and spitting out the land, leaving a territory scarred by fires and poverty. The woodsmen built Chicago, Minneapolis, St. Louis, and Detroit in the process. And more than fifty years before I was born, the Civilian Conservation Corps began the long work of turning the barren cutover back into a pristine forest.

When I arrived as a child, there was no sign any of it had ever happened. On Deer Lake, "the lake of changing colors," my siblings and I swam and fished off the dock of my grandparents' house, in a lake we believed to have been untouched.

Three lumberjacks fell timber with an axe and a crosscut saw near Grayling, Michigan, circa 1880. Courtesy of Library of Congress.

Researching this book, I came across the mention of a lumber camp on its western shore and an outbreak of smallpox among settlers on its east. There is now no trace of either. On the rivers of the Northwoods, pleasure seekers' canoes glide over sunken logs. The land shows few scars from its past.

Instead, the lumber industry is remembered as semimythical. The lumberjacks tourists encounter in statues, billboards, and festivals littered across the Northwoods do not wield chainsaws or use machines. They are not forces of industry, but old-timey, sentimental figures who could coexist with the popular conception of untouched wilderness. At my Northwoods girls' camp, we took our group names from Anishinaabe words for the colors of the rainbow. But on Saturday nights the camp director would stand in front of the fire and ask us to throw in a "key log" to thank someone who made our week better. A key log, we were told, was the log that broke up a logjam. We were asked to imagine ourselves the inheritors of two traditions: Anishinaabe and lumberjack. Both, to the eyes of a ten-year-old girl, were romantic, almost mythological figures.[2] Like centuries of Anishinaabe life, the lumberjacks' presence in the Northwoods is still presented to tourists and summer visitors as part of a distant past, existing only in the historical imagination.

Of course, those visitors are—I am, as I write this—still on Anishinaabe land. The Anishinaabe quite obviously still live and work and claim their rights here. But the continued production of romantic, stereotypical images of Indians is one way of erasing this reality, and the ugly history of Indigenous oppression at the hands of white Americans. Similarly, if less disturbingly, lumbering continues to this day on cultivated tree farms, and loggers are still a thriving workforce. All the trees we see today are second growth. But all that does nothing to dispel the aura of romance around old-time lumber camps.

A family vacationing in the scenic Northwoods of Wisconsin in the 1950s might well have stopped at Historyland, a state-sponsored living history park. There they could have visited two exhibits: an industrious lumber camp filled with men in checkered shirts; and an Indian village, complete with teepees and men and women in "traditional" dress.[3] These two idealized versions of the Northwoods—one the site of labor taming the wild frontier, the other as a "natural" landscape inhabited by "natural" Native Americans—were, to midcentury Americans, two sides of the same coin, two complementary parts of the same imagined past. Nor is this relegated to the 1950s. It is part of a century-long story that continues to evolve. Today just miles from a functioning lumber mill you can visit an "authentic duplicate of . . . that by-gone era" "when rugged men and tough animals fought the bitter cold and heavy snow to harvest the mighty forests of Northern Minnesota." The gift shop features "Pottery, Dolls, and Handicraft from the Chippewa Tribes," as well as turquoise from New Mexico.[4] The fact that the Anishinaabe still live here, that I write this on Anishinaabe land, is seemingly irrelevant. As is the continuing presence of the lumber industry. The myths overshadow the history. The past, we insist, ought to stay in the past.

This book only proposes to explore one of those myths: the industrious camp full of wholesome jacks. Beneath the second-growth memories of Historyland and Paul Bunyan are the stories, the culture, and the memory of thousands of real men.

The lumberjacks of the Northwoods were part of one of the largest environmental transformations in American history. While lumbering had been afoot in Michigan since the 1840s, it was only in the 1880s that it came into what historian Thomas R. Cox called the "full flowering." Everything that came before the Northwoods was "but prelude to what unfolded on the St. Croix and Chippewa, at Cloquet and Beef Slough, along the Menominee, and in scores of places related thereto." All the lumbering that followed, all the conservation policy and forest management, the entire logging of the Pacific Northwest, "was heir to what took place in the upper reaches of the Mississippi drainage."[5]

The scale of Northwoods lumbering is hard to exaggerate. It was a result not merely of industriousness but of an accidental and perfect triad of environmental circumstances, commercial demand, and evolving technology. The lumbering of the Northwoods seemed, to those who witnessed it, almost predestined by nature. Not only was the land heavy with soaring white pines—many more than four feet across—but it was laced with waterways. One of the white pine's greatest virtues, for the thousands of lumberjacks who arrived in the Northwoods well ahead of the railroads, was that it floated. The rivers and lakes of the region could easily carry the wealth of the land to market.

Moreover, when the Northwoods opened to lumbering, the timing could not have been better. In the late nineteenth century, the American West was experiencing an unprecedented population boom fueled by new opportunities and heavy waves of European migration. The great trees of Wisconsin, Minnesota, and Michigan became the buildings of Chicago, Minneapolis, Detroit, and St. Louis.[6] Just eight years after lumbering began in Minnesota, the Homestead Act helped drive the need for timber across the West. A blooming network of railways allowed lumber to be carried increasingly far from sawmills. And the rails meant that the unprocessed logs could be shipped farther as well: small-scale mills of the early lumber days shut their doors as the Northwoods lumberers increasingly shipped their logs to enormous mills in centers like Duluth and Saginaw. And the jacks grew more efficient. In the last two decades of the century, lumber camps

Wannigans, floating bunkhouses and cook shanties, on the Mississippi River in Minnesota, circa 1880. These boats traveled with the men as they worked the river. Courtesy of Anoka County Historical Society.

also replaced their even-toothed saws with a crosscut saw that worked at a vastly quicker pace.

The results were awe-inducing and devastating. Trees came down faster than anyone imagined. In 1847, Daniel Stanchfield, a land scout working for a Maine lumber company, traveled to Minnesota's Rum River Valley. Upon returning, he reported, "seventy mills in seventy years could not exhaust the white pine I have seen."[7] Thirty years later, the abundance of the Northwoods still seemed unconquerable. Richard Griffin, an ex-jack, remembered being overawed the first time he came to Minnesota. "As I stood upon the brow of Embarrass Hill on the old tote road leading from Mesaba station west," he recalled, "one of the grandest sights I ever looked upon was in view, a veritable ocean of pine." Griffin, like Stanchfield, saw the forest as "inexhaustible, enough to last for ages." But he would live to see that, "within the course of very few years not to exceed fifteen, this great forest was laid bare, leaving only a few scattering stands of pine in patches here and there."[8] Lumberjacks tore through the forest with a speed and recklessness that was unimaginable by the 1930s, when the Civilian Conservation Corps began to introduce sustainable logging practices and replant the great Northwoods. In just over six decades, the logging industry reduced a forest that had covered tens of millions of acres to open plains and rotting stumps. The Northwoods became a tinderbox. Fires raged across the landscape in the 1910s and 1920s. The largest—the Cloquet Firestorm of 1918—burned nearly fifty communities to the ground and ravaged a quarter of a million acres. The story of the lumberjack's work was, in the eyes of one who saw it, both "an epic and a tragedy."[9]

The massive endeavor of cutting the Northwoods took thousands upon thousands of men. In the beginning, they came from New England stock, men who had worked the camps in Maine and New Hampshire, New York and Pennsylvania. Some came from Canada: French and Anglo-Canadians who had worked the great forests of Quebec and Ontario. Anishinaabe and Menominee men worked across the region. There were Germans and Irishmen among the Yankees, French immigrants, too. Eventually they came from Norway and Sweden, and finally eastern Europe and Finland.[10] Some were farmers' sons, and some were farmers themselves in the summer. Here and there were educated men, men who had fallen on rough times and needed money to support their families or, rarely, to pay their tuition. But most were illiterate and poor men who carried most of the possessions they owned with them.

In the early years, it was possible to make quick money, to move up the ranks, to really make something of oneself. Most owners in the 1850s and 1860s were small-time farmers, or "jobbers." They were men clearing their own land, buying from the government, or stealing from Anishinaabe or Menominee land. An early camp took very little capital to set up: a single bunkhouse for ten or twenty men and the horses or oxen that the farmer himself owned. "Do not get the idea," warned William Bartlett, a man who lived in Wisconsin timber country from the 1870s through his death in 1933, "that in the early days a few wealthy lumbermen grabbed up most of the good timber. There was enough for all, and everybody went after it."[11] Men came from farming and mercantile backgrounds; some were common laborers. Many had extraordinarily little formal education and began with little to no capital. But as time wore on, the chance for a lumberman to pull himself from poverty diminished.[12]

By the 1880s and 1890s the prospects for the average jack were bleak. Frederick Weyerhaeuser and Daniel Shaw bought up thousands upon thousands of acres of prime pine land. While many of the barons began as poor men themselves, they offered few opportunities for new men to follow in their footsteps. Large camps of eighty or more men took formidable cash, or equally formidable debt, to establish. Buying vast tracts of land and specialized equipment took yet more wealth. In an even more profound shift, lumber barons in the 1880s began to trade in social capital.

Loggers stand in the barren cutover near Biwabik, Minnesota, circa 1892. Photograph by George A. Newton. Courtesy of the St. Louis County Historical Society, Archives and Special Collections, University of Minnesota Duluth.

The lumber industry was not nearly as concentrated in the hands of a few men as steel or oil, but it was nonetheless the domain of dozens, not hundreds, of lumber barons. In the cities of the Northwoods these men gathered in rarified neighborhoods and formed fraternal societies. They shared business interests and culture, while the camps were remarkably heterogeneous in national origin: of the 131 most prominent lumber barons, over a hundred were from American-born, English-speaking Yankee stock. Within these networks, lumbermen negotiated boom contracts and river rights.[13]

The average jack did not join the brigades of the lumber barons, but instead was most closely related to the swarms of wandering itinerant laborers who built the railways, manned the farms, and worked the mines of the booming West. When money was scarce during the panics of the mid-1890s, "jacks were glad to take what they could get," but even when the economy improved, lumberjack Jesse H. Ames recalled that "the workers in logging camps were always among the most poorly paid workingmen."[14] The pay the men made varied by role and by year. Throughout the 1880s and 1890s, the heart of the period covered in this book, lumberjacks made an average of thirty dollars a month. Those at the bottom of the pay scale were road monkeys and bull cooks. Road monkeys were among the least skilled workers in camp—they helped ensure the roads were clean for the sleighs.[15] Bull cooks were "chore boys," although in many camps the role was fulfilled not by a young boy but rather by an elderly jack made unsuitable, by injury or simply age, for other work in the camp. At the top of the pay scale were the most skilled workers: the clerk, the foreman, and the cook. The cook could make fifty dollars or more a month, double the pay of a road monkey. But these elite jobs were hard to get—they were reserved for literate men, and few of the jacks were.

So the regular jacks worked. Without much hope of promotion, they worked all winter. They walked scores of miles from camp to camp. The jobs, the pay, and the conditions were much the same, but they followed better cooks, fairer management, or slightly better working conditions. In the spring, they went on the spree, drinking their earnings and taking what jobs they could for the summer. For many, even most, lumbering was the job of a few winters: a job to supplement farm income, or to bring money home to their parents. Some had the good sense and opportunity to save money or educate themselves, moving on to better work in towns or their own farms. But for some it was a way of life. Men worked in the camps for ten or twenty winters, until they couldn't work anymore.

Yet this, a poorly paid itinerant worker with little hope of promotion, is hardly what we imagine when we think of lumberjacks. The advertisements for bespoke camping gear, the cartoons dancing the lumberjack's ballet, even the man on our paper-towel packaging all pass on a very different image: that of a cheerful woodsman, at once both more powerful than nature and at one with the woods, who is eking out a meaningful existence working deep in the forests.

What we remember, and how we imagine our past, is neither accidental nor incidental. The past is, by its very nature, too much out of which to make meaning. There are too many individual stories, experiences, and memories to be of any use. Nor do events have immediately apparent meanings. On January 7, 2021, it seemed clear to many Americans that there had been an attempted coup at the U.S. Capitol, but over the months that followed, we watched in real time as opposing forces worked to impose a narrative on that day, a narrative that would have national and criminal implications. In our current climate of fake news and contested narratives, this all seemed clear enough: people were battling to create a story out of January 6 that would support their current politics.

Yet when events recede further into the past, we can lose this clarity of understanding. We are so often taught that history does not lie, that the fact are facts, and that the past is in the past, that we are trained to overlook the clear fact that someone, somewhere, has been making stories out of events, imposing meaning, and

A booster publication in 1891 promoting the Menominee Iron Range began with an appeal to investors from the lumberman and the miner. Courtesy of Library of Congress.

promoting ideas and narratives that are useful to support their politics.[16] Moreover, when these stories come to us not through textbooks but through more emotional means—the stories of our parents and grandparents, the immediate emotional impact of film, the seemingly passive memorial landscape of statues, tablets, and street names—we do not approach it with a critical eye. We take these things in and make them part of ourselves. We quote funny movie lines, cry at moving scenes, often allowing these stories to bypass the critical part of our brain that might ask why, exactly, we're meant to feel sorry for Scarlett O'Hara.[17]

Over the past several decades the field of the history of memory has exploded as historians continue to examine the way the past is remembered, forgotten, and fabricated. Recent works, most notably Adam Domby's *The False Cause*, have pushed beyond tracing the way politically powerful groups asserted their own dominant memories to exploring how cultural memory has been built on outright fabrications. These histories of memory have focused primarily on political power and political aims in the aftermath of cultural trauma. For good reason, historians have focused on major ruptures in which differing memories have had concrete political and military consequences: the American Civil War, World War II, and the creation of the Israeli state.

In this book, I turn my attention not to a dramatic moment, but instead to seeing how those same mechanisms operate on a quieter level in parts of our lives we might not consider influential, or even worthy of manipulation. I examine a different form of power, and a different set of players: not politicians and nation-states, but corporations, local boosters, and chambers of commerce.

Not all of us have equal access to creating cultural memories, and to promulgating them. As novelist and critic Viet Than Nguyen argues in *Nothing Ever Dies*, "memories are not simply images we experience as individuals, but are mass produced fantasies we share with one another," and, as such, "are not only collected or collective, they are also corporate and capitalist."[18] For a message to be carried and shared broadly, it must be disseminated widely and effectively. And that takes money. It also makes money: nostalgia in all its forms is an enormous industry and has been for almost a century. Modern technologies of mass consumption have become one of the central ways we learn about history, whether it be through the open-air living history museum, the historical film, or the advertising images we are bombarded with every day. Americans consume nostalgia for pleasure and comfort, as a distraction from modern life and a way of affirming values and identity. As Gary Cross argues, "Modern people discovered inexorable change and tried to get the past back as a possession."[19] And they used the very modern technologies they were trying to escape to get the past back through road trips to "untamed wilderness," visits to re-created logging camps, and hours of watching Paul Bunyan cartoons.

Memory, then, is produced and consumed like any product: it is manufactured to meet demand, and to fill the needs of its consumers. For most of the twentieth century, neither plantation museums nor presidential homes nor Colonial Williamsburg featured slaves.[20] The uproar and backlash when Monticello introduced Sally Hemings as a central figure in Thomas Jefferson's life alone put those worried about profit margins on edge. Slavery may well have been part of the history, but it was not the memory consumers sought.

Unpicking the connections between capitalism and cultural memory is a difficult task, not because these memories are obscure, but rather because they are pervasive. As Micki McKelya's *Clinging to Mammy* showed, stock figures like the Mammy are so central to our thinking, and so deeply entrenched in consumer culture, that it is difficult to step back far enough to see them objectively. Moreover, these memories are not simple creatures in and of themselves. Cultural memories often have overlapping or even contradictory meanings.[21] The lumberjack certainly did: for half a century he was both the famed lout of the woods, a canker sore on the social body, and a gentlemanly hero of true masculinity. Today he is the hypermasculine, working-class modern man embodied by both timbersports champions and the folksy fiddlers who provide the entertainment at those very same championships.

Understanding these connections forces us to reconsider the lumberjack, gaining enough critical distance to see him not as a folksy hero, but as a member of the working class.[22] Doing so strips him of his romance in order to engage more directly with him as a producer of capital, and as "cheap nature" ripe for exploitation in and of himself. But I also consider lumberjacks on a closer, archival, intimate level as actual people. Many at the time saw the jacks as a resource to be exploited, flattening them to something closer to the logs they cut than to individual humans. In many histories, this is how workers appear: grist to the mill of industry. Even sympathetic renderings often view workers like lumberjacks as passive actors, victims of growth. But reducing them to another exploited resource concedes the logic of capitalism as an almost inevitable, natural process whereby workers and nature lose in order to pave the way for the eventual triumph of capitalism.[23]

Fundamentally, it is impossible to explain the period from 1850 onward in the Northwoods without acknowledging that capitalism was one of, if not the, defining forces at work. I make no attempt to deny that reality but am not interested in tracing enormous forces in the abstract. This book is unapologetically focused on the workers themselves and on a defined geography. As historian Bryan Palmer notes, workers' voices and resistance are, in the grand scheme of the history of something so giant as capitalism, "aligned as an endnote to the elaborations of capital's circuits, in which what rises and falls seldom does so in ways that either give workers voice or allow them vibrant visibility." That vibrant visibility gives needed detail to a field that tends toward global analysis.[24]

Detailed study of the actual men involved knits together the divide between histories of capitalism, environment, labor, and gender, since in this case all of those are different lenses for examining the same man—different angles, but a single subject. More importantly, looking at the lumberjacks carefully forces us to question some of our most basic assumptions about how capitalism works. The men who worked in the Northwoods did not adhere to capitalism's imperatives to aspire to be "small capitalists," because many did not aspire to either family or the accumulation of wealth. The history of Anishinaabe resistance to the lumber industry also helps in doing something that is difficult, almost to the point of impossible, for those who grew up immersed in capitalism: it de-centers and de-normalizes it. We often view capitalism as an inevitable process unfolding from the first moment land is valued as a tradeable commodity and proceeding through a series of steps until we reach the modern financial institution.

In this linear progression, anyone not participating in capitalist economies is labeled "precapitalist," hinting that theirs is not a rejection of capitalism, but just an insufficient awareness of its power.[25] But the Anishinaabe were far from precapitalist, or even proto-capitalist. Instead, they engaged with the system in a manner that undermined capitalism's basic assumptions. If capitalism depends on the rise of individuals as economic units, then the use of "private" land or commodities as community resources is not a pre- or quasi-capitalist choice (with all the condescension that comes with that language) but is instead the proposal of an alternative system of value, one that is unconcerned with individuals as economic units. This is not to say that the Anishinaabe, or the Euro-American lumberjacks, for that matter, were able to entirely resist capitalism. As Palmer puts it, "men and women do make their own history, but not entirely as they please."[26] But if the people who lived on the land could not proceed entirely as they pleased, neither could the capitalists.

The greatest resistance to the commodification of the Northwoods did not come from a rational actor at all: rather, it came from the "cheap nature" that investors, with the enthusiastic support of the state, hoped to harvest and commodify. The Northwoods resisted exploitation with a wiliness that makes them seem nearly animate. From the offices of financiers and emerging timber barons, the landscape of the Upper Midwest was a rational grid, written neatly on Public Land Survey maps. These maps, with their tidy township lines and straight edges, were meant to open up the land to investment and aid the transition from Native land, to public land, to private property. But lines are not straight in nature. The men sent to physically survey this land for investors, timber cruisers, spent weeks struggling to follow map lines and find out what these paper squares *actually* contained. Camping in the winter in the Northwoods, working in small teams, exhausted men often found themselves unable to find markers left by surveyors and lost precious time to the tedious tasks of just staying fed, alive, and warm.[27]

Even here, at the very first step, the Northwoods refused to comply. It took armies of workers, and vast stores of capital investment, to organize the land and open it for exploitation. And once it was wrestled into compliance, disaster struck. Fires claimed thousands of lives and burned down the investments of timber barons, small farmers, and middle-class city dwellers alike.[28] Cheap nature, then, was not particularly cheap. Attending to the way that geography and environment shaped and flaunted the ambitions of timber barons forces us to focus on the role of place—messy, detailed, uncontrollable place—in the history of the economy.

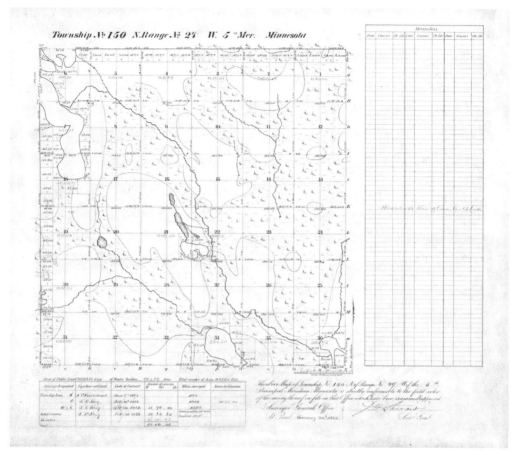

The surveyor error on this 1883 Public Land Survey map meant that a portion of Itasca County, Minnesota, wasn't logged. It remains today the last remnant of old growth forest in the Northwoods. Courtesy of General Land Office Records, Bureau of Land Management.

Speaking of place, I focus specifically on the Northwoods states of Michigan, Minnesota, and Wisconsin. Lumbering was, of course, a national endeavor. Lumberjacks worked in the Americas from the seventeenth century onward, first in Maine, and then steadily along what historian Thomas R. Cox has termed "the lumberman's frontier." There was heavy lumbering in the pine barrens of the South during the same late nineteenth-century years as the Northwoods lumbering. Perhaps the most spectacular lumbering, at least as far as novelty photographs are concerned, occurred in the early twentieth-century in the giant redwood forests of the Pacific Northwest. But none of these compared in scale to the giant project of lumbering the Northwoods.[29] Moreover, there is good reason to believe that the mythic lumberjack, the one represented by Paul Bunyan and red-and-black-checkered mackinaw coats, came directly from the Northwoods. After exhaustive research, Michael Edmonds concluded in *Out of the Northwoods* that Bunyan, at least, originated in the region.[30]

The Northwoods form a distinct region that, while in the Midwest, is not exactly of the Midwest. For anyone who has lived there, or anyone who has studied the region, the Midwest is defined mostly by its refusal to hold together. People argue endlessly about which states are in the Midwest at all: Iowa, certainly. But Nebraska? Michigan? I have regularly heard people from Ohio claim to be from the East Coast and Oklahoma claim to be Midwestern. And none of these states have much in common with one another. But more than any other parts of the Midwest, the Northwoods seem to hold together.[31] They have historical, cultural, and environmental similarities that cross state lines. While our understanding of what made the Northwoods so odd has changed over the last two centuries, that they *are* odd has remained a fixed assumption among both the residents of the lake states and their historians. The key distinguishing features of the Northwoods in popular and historical imagination, for my purposes, are these: they are vast, and they are separate from the plains. Together, these two characteristics have formed a long-lasting impression, in both the historiography and popular literature, that the Northwoods are somehow impenetrable.

The sense of space, of vastness, that characterizes the Midwest seems amplified in the Northwoods. For the first century and a half of settlement the Midwest was not seen, as it often is today, as an area of meek conformity, but rather of enormous possibility. The Midwest loomed, enormous and unsettled, as a land of almost limitless prospects. Rutherford B. Hayes hoped that, in the Midwest, "we *can be*, for all the purposes of every-day happiness, precisely what *we could wish* to be." The great evangelical preacher Lyman Beecher saw the Midwest as God's own valley, a place where true paradise could be formed. For many, as for Beecher, that possibility was tied to what was seen as the vast emptiness of the land; it was, fundamentally, malleable territory.[32] By the late nineteenth century, Frederick Jackson Turner had essentially handed the title off to the far West, but the Midwest had long thrived as the frontier of American possibilities. And nowhere was that possibility more tantalizing than in the unexplored Northwoods.

While the vast potential of the Northwoods made an excellent canvas for imaginative storytellers and mythmakers, the separation of the Northwoods from the southern prairies was equally necessary for the creation of the mythic versions of the lumberjack. Lumberjacks did not follow the same settlement patterns as their neighbors to the south. While the economy of the logging industry tied the

River drivers, sometimes called "river pigs," wearing distinctive caulked boots, photographed in Maine by Samuel W. Sawyer, circa 1867. Courtesy of the Smithsonian American Art Museum, 1994.91.168.

Northwoods to the Midwestern plains, the culture of the loggers was quite separate. The drive for wood in Chicago and across the exploding Midwest tied the Northwoods ever closer to the regional centers of milling and the national centers of lumber distribution. That wood created an industry, and that industry created a class of itinerant laborers who did not fit neatly within dominant settlement patterns of the region. Plains immigrants settled, as often as possible, in ethnically homogeneous farming communities.[33] These workers, and their movement, fit outside historians' and contemporaries' dominant images of the Midwest. The cosmopolitan blending of ethnicities and the development of a dedicated working class, especially a floating working class not tied to families, was not solely an urban phenomenon. Rather, networks of itinerant lumberjacks created cultural ties across the Northwoods that were dictated by the environmental constraints of their industry. The requirement to move on as new areas were clear-cut, combined with the method of resistance to management most commonly used by jacks—"voting with their feet," that is, leaving conditions that did not appeal to them—were mother and father to a way of life that was, quite literally, hidden in the woods.[34]

Among the pines, men and women imagined anything could happen. The trees, according to the jacks themselves, were populated with agropelters and hodags, jackalopes and snipes. In the popular imagination, the woods were full of not only fantastic beasts but also thieves and criminals. Some stories are hard to verify: while several women's rights campaigners claimed that young girls were taken prisoner and used as sex slaves inside the lumber camps when they ventured alone into the woods, exhaustive research shows no reliable corroborations for the story. Others, however improbable, are true: a man named James Strang did, indeed, set up with a group of Mormon dissenters on Beaver Island in Lake Michigan and declare himself king, funding his kingdom by raiding passing boats. The sum of these truths and half-truths was this: in the minds of the good citizens of Gilded Age Wisconsin, Michigan, and Minnesota (as well as in the minds of their earliest historians), the Northwoods were a place where anything could be—and probably was—true.[35]

The first two parts of this book follow the lives of the lumberjacks as they moved between the urban and semiurban enclaves of the Midwestern frontier and the vast hinterlands of the Northwoods. A lumberjack's year was defined by a round of work and wandering that took him from town to country, and linked cities and backwoods throughout the region. This network of itinerancy drew together jacks throughout the Northwoods, helping create a coherent culture within a class of workers. One year in the life of a single jack might take him between camps, into several urban areas, and across state lines. The most salient feature of nearly all jacks' lives was motion—the constant moving from town to town, job to job, and camp to camp.

Their working year began in late September. When the summer faded and the harvest ended, the jacks gathered in the cities. They flowed into Bridge Square and the Gateway district of Minneapolis, the Sawdust Flats of Muskegon, the Catacombs in Bay City, or the Cribs of Duluth. They stayed in lumberjack flop hotels or came into town to register at the employment office—slave markets, they nicknamed them. At the employment office, an agent would pay for their ticket to hop on a train headed north. They wore thick boots and woolen socks, heavy flannel shirts and checkered mackinaw coats. They trudged along railroad tracks or hopped a ride on cars. They followed tips and joined up with other men they met walking. No matter how they came, they were all headed to the same place. Winter was coming; it was time for the lumberjack's year to begin: the men were headed to the woods.

Take, for instance, the year of 1888–89 for Euclid J. Bourgeois. Euclid was a young man taking his first chance in the woods, and so had decided to travel with his father. In late September, the two Bourgeois men headed north to work in a lumber camp. Along the way, they encountered another camp owner who offered Euclid a job as a cook. Euclid knew a bit about bread baking from his father, who had learned to be a baker in Boston before he headed to Wisconsin to make his fortune in the woods, and so he accepted the position. First though, he detoured to visit Henri LaBeouf, a lumber camp cook of his acquaintance, to get a sourdough starter. Euclid then traveled on to the north fork of the Flambeau River north of Eau Claire, Wisconsin, to begin work.[36] Euclid's job as a cook afforded him respect and a substantial paycheck. Cooks could make or break a camp. The living and working conditions in the camps were uniformly dismal, and so it was the quality of the food that kept men from leaving a camp, or encouraged them to return. Some men were known to follow cooks from camp to camp, staying loyal not to their employers, but to the men who fed them best.[37]

Euclid held his position at camp for a month or so. One afternoon he switched jobs with his assistant, or cookee, and made the daily lunch run himself. Leaving his assistant Felix to tend to the fire and the bread that was rising for supper, Euclid himself loaded up the swing-dingle: a heavy, wooden sled that was part of standard kitchen equipment. The walk from the camp where men lived to "the cut" could be up to a mile, and work in camp was from "see" to "no-see"—sunup to sundown. Men breakfasted in the dark, walked in the hazy hours of early dawn, and worked until twilight when they trudged back through the gloom to eat their dinner after darkness fell. To save time and money, foremen sent steaming vats and

Itinerant laborers pass the time at an unemployment bureau in Bridge Square, downtown Minneapolis, circa 1908. Many followed the railroads to find work in the lumber camps or further into the wheat fields of North Dakota. Courtesy of the Minnesota Historical Society.

hearty pies to the men, rather than having them lose an hour to come back to camp for their lunch.

Euclid hooked the swing-dingle to the horses and headed into the woods. When he returned, an hour or so later, his "assistant was sleeping and the bread dough was all over; . . . if there had been a floor in the shack [he] could have saved some of it," but the cook shack, thrown up quickly for a winter's work, had only dirt. Euclid was fired.[38]

Throughout the winter the men rarely stayed still. They followed leads to better working conditions, better bosses, or better cooks—voting with their feet. Despite their deep isolation in the backwoods, far from urban centers and, often, far from railroads, camps had a constantly rotating labor force. Finding oneself unemployed, without transit in the rural backwoods of Wisconsin was not all that unusual. Leaving the camp, Euclid trekked eighty miles back to Fifield, where he spent the rest of the winter as a hotel chore boy. By the time the ice melted and the

The 1886 log jam on the St. Croix River contained an estimated sixty million feet of timber. Successfully breaking jams of this size and living to tell the tale required not only skill but a good amount of luck. Courtesy of the Minnesota Historical Society.

rivers began to run again in spring, he found that he had had enough of the hotelier's wife, who "was poison." He quit.

The very next day, Euclid heard that the water was high, and the next stage of logging had already begun. Spring was magic in the logging world: those who witnessed the grand drives down the arteries of the Northwoods never forgot the site. Thousands upon thousands of logs clogged the Eau Claire, the St. Croix, the Mississippi, the Muskegon, the Chippewa, and dozens of other rivers. Lakes were filled with enormous rafts of logs being pulled along by steamboats. Around corners and rapids, log jams could stretch out of eyesight, and the groaning of the wood under pressure could, it was said, be heard miles away. Outside Eau Claire, Stillwater, Muskegon, Cloquet, and dozens of other towns, boom companies set up enormous reservoirs where logs—each stamped with the mark of the camp that cut it—waited to be sorted and sent to the mills. From there, they would be refined and shipped off to Chicago, St. Louis, Omaha, and other booming Midwestern cities.

The process of directing the logs, of keeping them moving over obstacles, and of climbing out on the creaking mounds of lumber to unpick jams was "the drive," and among both jacks and witnesses it was the most exciting part of the year.

At only seventeen, with a slight build and a hotel chore boy's uniform, Bourgeois did not make a promising river pig. But timing was of the essence, and by the time he found the head of the drive, it was getting on in the morning and many of the potential workers "were taking another drink, which might have been costing [their employer] another man." The foreman took young Bourgeois.

Once he was hired, Bourgeois rushed back into town. It was too late in the season for him to buy "driving shoes," the caulked boots specially created for the difficult work of scrambling over moving logs. So Bourgeois took a friend's boots to the shoemaker instead and managed to convince him to "detail a man for each shoe to rush the soles and calking." Installing the spikes would keep Bourgeois alive on the river. By noon his shoes were ready, and Bourgeois had packed his "turkey," the small sack in which men carried their necessary personal possessions. Borrowing a horse and buggy from a friend in town, Bourgeois drove the four miles to the landing and began the log drive.

For the next ten days he was paid $2.50 a day—top dollar in the logging industry. After finishing this first drive, he joined another drive at Sailor Creek, and then yet another at Squaw Creek. He quit each drive as the water ran out and the logs became mired, waiting for heavier spring rains to move them on their way. After Squaw Creek, Bourgeois managed to work the last twenty days of spring at a camp in Fish Trap, where the foreman continued to log past the end of the usual season.

Summer, when camps were closed, was the dead season. Jacks disappeared back into the itinerant workforce from which they were drawn. While census bureau estimates of loggers tended to assume a year-round annual wage based on lumberjacks working summers in the sawmills, few other records corroborate this. Some jacks returned to the farms from which they came. Some worked in the mills. Some took odd jobs in the cities. And many "grassbacked" as hired farm hands on the plains.

Bourgeois filled his summer with a series of odd jobs. He fished on the Brule River and took the fish to Duluth, Minnesota, to try to sell them. Duluth was a bustling city, and he found a job there at the St. Louis Hotel until the stove blew up and ruined the kitchens. He took up a brief job cruising—looking for good timberlands—near Ely before heading out to Grandin, North Dakota, to work on a farm, haying. Here he would have made, on average, between one dollar and two a day, plus housing.[39] After the harvest, he returned to Minneapolis, where he "found a lot of idle boys," and spent three weeks blowing through the one hundred dollars he had made in North Dakota with them. Come the fall freeze, he took a job as a cookee. Over a dozen jobs and almost a thousand miles later, he finished his annual round, right back at the camp he had first been walking toward the winter before.

Parts of a lumberjack's round might vary year to year, or man to man. John Sirotiak spent his summers not on farms, but in Minneapolis, building roads, though only after first stopping over to spend a few days in the "sporting establishments" of Duluth. His friends, all Slovak immigrants like Sirotiak, followed. Come fall, they would leave their street crew behind and find their way back to the hiring offices of Duluth.[40] Abraham Johnson spent his summers working as a farm hand on the prairies of Minnesota.[41] John Emmett Nelligan worked in sawmills.[42] But come November they would always find their way back to the woods.

In their own day, by those who lived among them, the lumberjacks were no heroes; they were barely tolerated. But beginning in the late nineteenth century, they became a source of fascination to those who had little direct experience of the woods. Journalist Meridel Le Seur and critic H. L. Mencken took an interest in lumberjack language. The lumberjack's image was reproduced in countless advertisements, books, and posters. The lumberjack of that time is still with us today, whether in the form of "lumbersexuals" wandering the streets of Brooklyn or in that of the Brawny Man on a roll of paper towels. He is manly, authentic, and natural. His masculinity is secure and simple. There is a reason that Monty Python's "Lumberjack Song" strikes audiences as hilarious: of all the men in all the world, the lumberjack is among the least likely to "wear high heels, suspenders, and a bra."

The lumberjack is a multifaceted character, at once the epitome of turn-of-the-century manhood and a brawling, dangerous hooligan. Like the cowboy, he embodies both a desire for adventure and violence and an emphasis on the overarching importance of moral restraint. But unlike the cowboy, the jack is not always the good guy. In fact, one of the difficulties in uncovering and understanding the lives of these men is that their memory is shrouded in not one, but two strains of mythology. Beginning in the 1880s, two sets of ideas about jacks emerged, at times contradicting and at others reinforcing one another. The third section of this book explores their roots, their uses, and their lasting, pervasive impact on the region and the nation.

The first is deeply positive—it is what I refer to as the "gentleman of the woods" mythology. It came from a romantic, nostalgic image of the lumber camps: a vision of them as places that were small and homespun, nostalgic and cozy. The men lived together in a world of hard work and egalitarian values. As John Nelligan, a former lumberjack, put it, lumberjacks were "rough in dress and speech and manners, gaining their livelihood by the hardest kind of manual labor, living and loving and laughing crudely, still they were gentlemen."[43] This version of the jack was carefree, with an honesty and authenticity bred of a well-ordered life working hard in the deep woods. While he happily indulged in manly vices, he was ultimately moral—he might drink to excess, but he would never offend a lady. He and his foreman were like father and son: eating, sleeping, and working side by side. Paul Bunyan is the epitome of this version of the jack—a giant among men, rambunctious but ultimately harmless.

The other myth—less well-known today, but equally salient in its time—was of the bad jack, the men who were "so filthy and had such disgusting habits that one might have thought they had been brought up in a pig pen."[44] The men of this myth were carriers of diseases and lice. Some saw them as a disease in and of themselves: like locusts, they would descend on towns to drink and whore every spring, leaving irreparable damage in their wake. This understanding of jacks was also tied to an exaggerated image of the camps as places of filth and iniquity. When this version of the jack was not in the camps, he refused any home at all. Vast networks of itinerancy and seasonal employment meant that this reprobate enjoyed none of the sanitizing, moralizing influences that came from a steady domestic life.

Throughout the 1880s and into the early twentieth century these two myths—the good and the bad—flourished side by side. But, of course, the truth is the jacks were neither wholly gentlemen nor total degenerates. They were complicated men who created a unique culture in the context of a quickly changing industry. Theirs was a culture that glorified risk and reward, one that balanced the incredible dangers posed by their work with a celebration of skill. In drawing the lines around who was and was not a "real" lumberjack, the jacks policed their membership and contributed to their own image—an image that navigated the tricky lines between the loaded categories of "savage" and "civilized." Within the restraints imposed on them by geography and economics, they managed to find ways to assert their manhood and rights as laborers. The lumberjacks created a rich culture, but one that has been wiped out by time and glossed over by mythology. Unraveling not only what these myths were, but also whose interests they ultimately served allows us to see lumberjacks with new eyes and to understand how men outside of the camps distorted the jacks' histories and lives for their own objectives.

American interest in the development of folk culture hit a fever pitch in the early twentieth century. In many ways, this was part of a broader Western trend: from the Romantics onward, Europeans grew intensely interested in the "folk" and the "authentic" histories of their lands. As empires broke into nation-states, historians, writers, and artists revived folkways, with varying degrees of accuracy, to help justify and explain the character of these new countries. But American folk culture

Lumberjacks line the crowded bunks at a Backus-Brooks lumber camp north of Grand Rapids, Minnesota, circa 1900. Courtesy of Superior National Forest.

required a whole other level of commitment. It required deliberately deciding who the "folk" was to begin with, and then ferreting out any scrap of tradition that might be made into their lore.[45] For Americans in the early twentieth century, the "folk" became synonymous with workers, particularly rural workers whom the middle and upper classes had previously relegated to the outskirts of respectability. These men and women, but particularly men, were seen as a pure, preindustrial folk who were rapidly being quashed by industrial growth.[46]

The full flowering of nineteenth-century lumbering neatly coincided with this moment of overwhelming nostalgia in the elite classes of the eastern cities. As historians from Jackson Lears to Gail Bederman have persuasively argued, the Gilded Age in America was defined (as, indeed, many eras of radical change and modernization are) by a longing for an authentic past. In American culture, that past was often a space that was not just historical, but geographical. When Americans sought to recover lost ideas, they looked to where the past seemed to still be alive: the West. Moreover, when the census declared the frontier closed in 1890, middle-class Americans began a curious transformation: now that they felt the wild was no longer accessible, it became an object of overwhelming fascination.[47] For the myth of the cowboy, this meant the Wild West of Buffalo Bill and Deadwood. But for the lumberjack, this meant the place where lumbering was flourishing—the Upper Midwest. When eastern magazines like *The Atlantic* and *Harper's Weekly* wrote about the great and mighty lumberjacks, they sent their journalists to neither Alabama nor Maine, but to Michigan and Wisconsin.

This mighty lumberjack was the memory that won out, and the confluence of corporate and local interests caused lake staters to embrace the mythic lumberjack as their own, mapping a myth that was developed in the magazines of the urban East onto the landscape of the Northwoods. After the collapse of the extractive lumber industry in the Northwoods, timber companies were left with their reputations in shreds and enormous tracts of wasteland to dispose of. When it became clear that farming would not be a sustainable use of the land, colonization companies set up by the major lumbering concerns turned instead to tourism. Promoting the image of the folksy, friendly lumberjack as a corporate emblem served as a powerful mechanism for promoting tourism, and an equally powerful facelift on a large-scale extractive industry.

Left with degraded land and in need of new revenue streams, both local boosters and tourist bureaus gratefully embraced this image of the jack. In festivals across all three states, small towns celebrated the lumberjack not as exploited laborer or degenerate itinerant, but as an authentic piece of folk culture, an antimodern hero fit for the modern world. Lumberjacks were repackaged and commodified as a way to engage with America's past without having to leave behind the modern comforts of air-conditioned resort cabins and paved highways. But claiming that tourists would have access to virgin wilderness meant writing out some of the lumberjack's story—the new lumberjacks came out of the woods swinging an ax, but left the actual forests intact.

When there was nothing left of great Northwoods, the men followed the work, moving on to the Pacific Northwest. Their stories were told and retold, turned into advertising campaigns and cartoons, monuments and theme parks. But amid this larger-than-life mythology, the memory of the men themselves—the hard up men and farm boys and new immigrants who worked in the woods—was lost. What lived on was the memory of a man in a checkered shirt, smiling and leaning on his ax, welcoming you to town. This version of the jack, and stories told about him, served

Program for the first annual Paul Bunyan Exposition in Brainerd, Minnesota, 1935.
Courtesy of the Crow Wing County Historical Society.

the industry and the local economy; they have been propagated by comics, movies, tourist brochures, and statues.

My mother took my first picture with Paul Bunyan when I was four years old. In the photograph, I'm sitting in his hand. This particular Paul was a statue in Akeley, Minnesota. Since then, I have had my picture taken with a dozen Paul Bunyans, yet I grew up knowing little of the actual men who cleared the woods, including my own great-grandfather who first found work in this country driving logs outside Duluth. While the mythic lumberjack is celebrated and caricatured, used for festivals and advertisements, found everywhere from World's Fair pavilions to Disney movies, the historic lumberjack is all but lost. But beneath the storytelling, there were thousands of men who stripped the Northwoods of her pine, men who have been left out of the cartoons and the caricatures. It is their story I tell here.

6

# A NOTE ON SOURCES

To tell the story of the lumberjacks, this book ranges over a broad geography and several decades, using a wide array of sources. Much of this project is based on two sets of oral histories: the first carried out in the 1930s by the Works Progress Administration (WPA), and another in the 1960s by the Forest History Society. Unfortunately, both these sources are obscured by myth and memory. Those who recorded the history of lumberjacks were often guided by their own assumptions, whether it was the act of editors shoehorning Paul Bunyan into a lumberjack's memories, or interviewers asking leading questions (e.g., "A lot of these men had farms, didn't they? They'd just work winters in the woods?").[1] This does not mean that these are not valuable sources, but they require reading that goes against the grain of memoirs and oral histories, weeding out the romanticism and mythology.

I have filled out the context of camps with newspaper articles from the 1880s through the 1930s, government records, record books from camps, and letters and journals from lumberjacks. Quotations from these sources are reprinted exactly as they originally appeared. The two most well-used memoirs of lumberjacks, John Nelligan's *A Lumberjack's Life* and Stewart Holbrook's *Holy Old Mackinaw*, have been invaluable in establishing the general activities of a camp.[2] In all of this work, I have stayed close to the Northwoods of Minnesota, Wisconsin, and Michigan, because these woods directly produced the lasting cultural legacy of the lumberjack.

Saws, axes, and workboots in the foreman's quarters of a Forest County, Wisconsin, logging camp, 1937. Photograph by Russell Lee. Courtesy of Library of Congress.

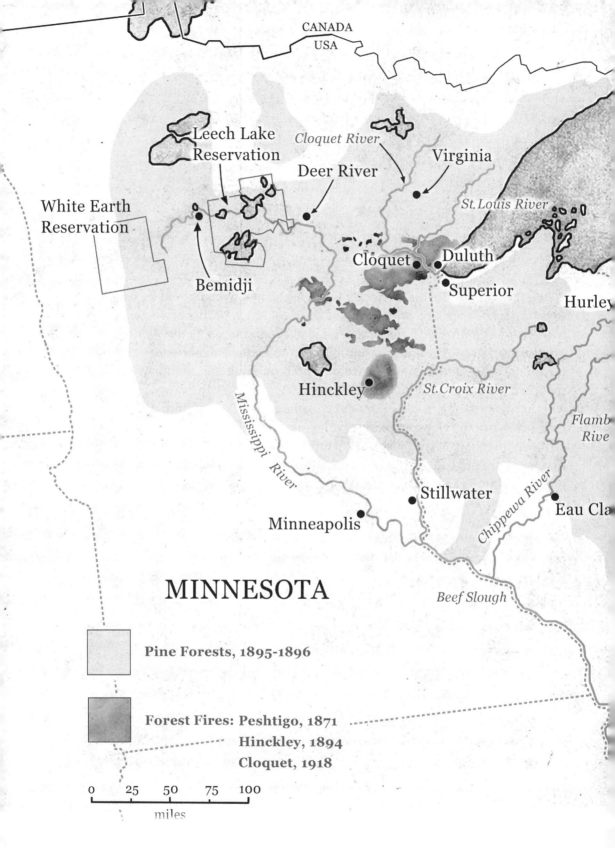

CANADA
USA

Leech Lake
Reservation

*Cloquet River*

Virginia

Deer River

*St. Louis River*

White Earth
Reservation

Cloquet

Duluth

Bemidji

Superior

Hurley

Hinckley

*St. Croix River*

*Flamb
Rive*

*Mississippi River*

Stillwater

*Chippewa River*

Eau Cla

Minneapolis

**MINNESOTA**

*Beef Slough*

Pine Forests, 1895-1896

Forest Fires: Peshtigo, 1871
Hinckley, 1894
Cloquet, 1918

0    25    50    75    100
miles

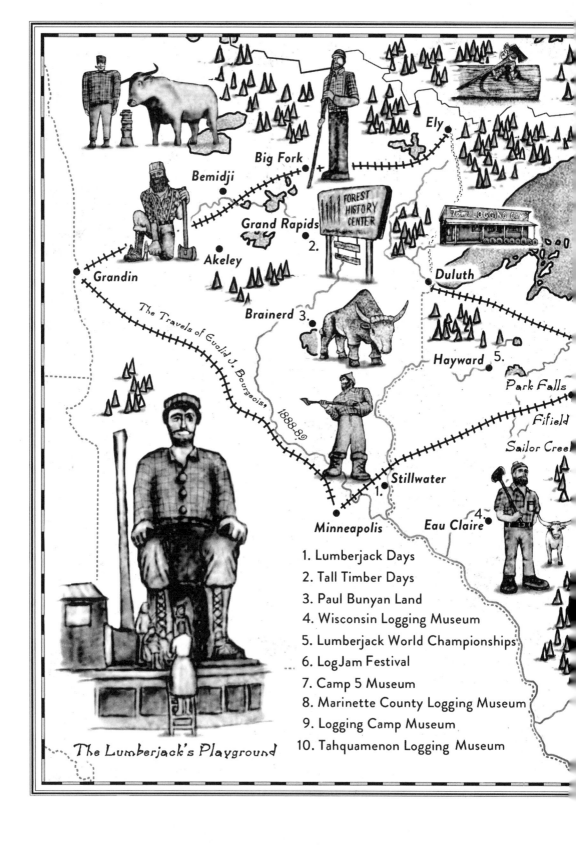

Ely

Big Fork

Bemidji

FOREST HISTORY CENTER

70th LOGGING CAMP

Grand Rapids

2.

Akeley

Duluth

Grandin

The Travels of Euclid J. Bourgeois

Brainerd 3.

Hayward 5.

Park Falls

1888-89

Fifield

Sailor Creek

Stillwater

1.

Minneapolis

Eau Claire

4.

1. Lumberjack Days

2. Tall Timber Days

3. Paul Bunyan Land

4. Wisconsin Logging Museum

5. Lumberjack World Championships

6. LogJam Festival

7. Camp 5 Museum

8. Marinette County Logging Museum

9. Logging Camp Museum

10. Tahquamenon Logging Museum

*The Lumberjack's Playground*

11. Jack Pine Lumberjack Shows
12. Lumberjack Festival
13. Hartwick Pines Logging Museum
14. Lumberman's Monument
15. Lumberjack Festival
16. The Old Town Lumberjack Festival

PAUL BUNYAN'S COOK SHANTY

Newberry
10.

Seney

sh Trap

nocqua

Laona
7.

Rhinelander

9. Menominee

8. Marinette

sinee          Hodag

PAUL BUNYAN
LUMBERJACK
MEALS
ALL YOU CAN EAT OPEN 7 AM

Mackinaw City   11.

12.
Wolverine

Grayling
13.

Alpena

Oscoda

14.

15.
Farwell

16.  Lansing

04389 THE LOGGERS

# IN THE WOODS

One winter in the late 1870s, Sophronius Stocking Landt found himself in possession of eleven tons of butter. The young Wisconsin businessman, delighted by low prices, had been a little overeager in purchasing his fall stock. Without a hope that anyone locally would need that much butter, he bought a ticket on the Wisconsin Central Railroad to travel 120 miles due north, deep into the Northwoods. Landt was headed for the camps.

He arrived in Knowlton, Wisconsin, just after dark and disembarked alone onto a moonlit platform. Pine boughs cracked in the cold under the weight of winter snow. Looking around, he saw no town beyond the platform, just the dark silhouettes of trees. He turned to get back aboard, but "the train started up immediately." He "concluded that [the town] must be on the other side," and so waited, stamping his feet for warmth as the train pulled off, heading further north, into the forest. But "when the last coach passed it revealed nothing but dense woods." Landt tentatively crossed the tracks and saw "the roofs of a few houses some distance away" and a footpath leading toward them. Trudging toward what he assumed was the village, he found "a sawmill and a few houses . . . but not a soul around."

Everyone had gone to the woods.

He returned to the tracks and walked along them, holding his "grip for companion," for eight miles to Mosinee, comforting himself that he was "equal to the emergency." In Mosinee, he found an inn that would put him up for the night. The next morning, he headed out to the woods to join the men.[1]

The Northwoods of Wisconsin, Minnesota, and Michigan at the beginning of the lumbering period were an isolated and, to early white colonists, uniquely

Lumberjacks pose atop a massive felled tree near Grayling, Michigan, circa 1883. Courtesy of Library of Congress.

impenetrable place. While mapped out in neat squares on the survey maps of the investors who bought pinelands, they were, in reality, difficult for European settlers to traverse and sparsely settled. In the imaginings of the plains residents to their south, they were full of terrors: rumors persisted into the twentieth century of forts filled with stolen girls and trees full of mysterious creatures. The one way to navigate them—the road timber cruisers looking for pines took—was by the paths of the people who had inhabited them for several centuries: the Menominee, and the Ojibwe and Odawa Anishinaabe.

In less than a century the woods were gone—only one stand of virgin white pine stood in all of Minnesota—and all but a few small reservations had been wrested by treaty or violence from Native American hands. The first part of this book tells the story of that incredible transformation. That century changed the ecology and economy of the lake states in ways that would make them unrecognizable to those who had lived there in the 1820s.

At the heart of this transformation was a work force that, at times, swelled to the tens of thousands: the lumberjacks. In their own day, they were known mostly as shanty boys or loggers, and they created a rich and vibrant culture that spread across the region. In response to their violent and precarious work they developed their own ideals of manhood that resisted the middle class's urges to practice restraint and propriety. Instead, these men celebrated risk and lauded the skills required to survive the woods. Their paths from camp to camp, and from camp to town, were the arteries and veins of industry. Along with the men, stories, traditions, workways, and ideas circulated through the woods.

# ONE

# BULL COOKS AND WALKING BOSSES

## CAMP LIFE IN A BOOMING INDUSTRY

"As we look back, in the light of our experience, we wonder, that
with such warning so little heed was paid to the imminent danger
the people were in, and by the fact one more illustration is given of
the old truth, that men become so accustomed to great peril, that it
loses its terrors."

—William Wilkinson,
*Memorials of the Minnesota Forest Fires in the Year 1894*

Returning from a visit to a cousin in Duluth in 1894, Mrs. E. N. Saunders boarded a
train headed for Minneapolis. As the passengers rolled out into the open country
near Cloquet, they noticed that "the air all around us was of a bright lemon color, or
what the ladies would call canary," but, assuming the railroad workers knew best,
they "suspected no ill." Yet within minutes they "rushed into the fire." On either
side of the train, the air "glowed blood red with the light of flames through which
could be seen the spectral outlines of the doomed trees." As they proceeded, the
sky went from red to black and the distant flames became "great flaming balls of
fire and sheets of flame whirling, rising, charging, retreating and dancing in fren-
zied mirth." Suddenly, men, women, and children appeared, "rushing to the train
out of the fire; dusty, scorched, breathless, full of terror, half-blinded." An engineer
informed them that the bridge ahead was out. The train reversed, slowly, through
the flames. Glass shattered into the carriage. One fragment "fell upon the neck of
Engineer Root and cut a dark blue gash near his jugular." Soon the train itself was
alight and came to a halt. Passengers stumbled out, protecting themselves with wet
clothes, occasionally "falling on the grass to let the fire sweep over." Mrs. Saunders

and some fellow passengers found a bog where they sat, crouched in the muddy water for eight hours, knowing that "within a hundred feet of [them] there were the burned bodies of people who had vainly sought to escape."[1]

The horrific fire that Mrs. Saunders's train journeyed through was the Great Hinckley Fire. By September 1, 1894, the fire had claimed at least 418 lives, although later estimates put the number closer to 800. Ninety-nine are merely listed as corpses, too charred to be identified by either features or belongings. But Hinckley was not the first, nor certainly the last, of the great firestorms of the Northwoods: in October 1871 the Peshtigo Fire tore through Wisconsin, killing at a minimum 1,500 people in a single day. Two days later, some two hundred or so miles to the south, Mrs. O'Leary's cow kicked over a lantern, and Peshtigo's horror was quickly eclipsed by a much more dramatic Great Chicago Fire, but Chicago had a comparatively modest death toll of three hundred. Peshtigo stands, to this day, as the deadliest fire in American history. These firestorms raged across the Northwoods with growing intensity toward the end of the nineteenth century and into the early twentieth. For the cities in the "cutover region," the region left clear-cut or nearly clear-cut by the lumber industry, they became a reality of life. No sooner did one begin to fade into memory than another took its place.

Cities like Duluth became adept at harboring the refugees that fled infernos in smaller towns. In 1918 Bart Foss, a young man working in Duluth, wrote to his mother about the "terrible fire" that had burned Cloquet, Moose Lake, and dozens of other communities to the ground. "The refugees," he told her, "began coming in about 5pm . . . women with babies in their arms and only half dressed some of them with their hair burned and hands burned." For two days refugees poured into Duluth and Superior, Wisconsin, just as they had in 1894. Foss told his mother, "I thought the world was surely coming to an end."[2]

In a way, he was right: the Cloquet Firestorm was the last of its kind. The white pine industry was shutting down. For nearly a century, timber had been slashed down at an astonishing rate, and capitalism had left its scars on the land. Between just these three fires—Peshtigo, Hinckley, and Cloquet—2,600 people lost their lives and over two million acres, an area half again the size of Delaware, burned.[3]

These fires were a direct result of the relentless force of industrial capitalism upon the landscape of the Northwoods. The drive for speedy lumbering and the maximization of profits created a multimillion-acre tinderbox. Popple (the generic lumber-industry nickname for not only poplars but any other small trees) were hacked down and left to wither in an effort to extract pine. Huge piles of pine were left to dry, often within easy reach of the loading platforms for trains, and therefore within easy reach of any sparks that might fly from the wheels of passing

The 1918 Cloquet Firestorm devastated the town of Cloquet, Minnesota, and the surrounding woods. Photographs by T. J. Horton. Courtesy of Cloquet Forestry Center Records, University of Minnesota Libraries.

locomotives. The race for profits proceeded at a dizzying pace, with little attention to the firm, Victorian virtues of sober restraint and responsible shepherding of wealth. Instead, like in the agricultural landscape of the upper South, profits were put above all. And, as with the dust bowl, all it took was one long, hot, dry summer to spark a disaster.[4] An 1895 book memorializing the deaths of the victims of the previous year's firestorms lamented the unusually dry weather and speedy winds that caused the fire to rage out of control. It even criticized capitalist profiteers who made "calamity a means of gain." But it never described the fire *itself* as an act of man. Instead, the author insisted that the trouble with fire is that it wasted lumber that could otherwise be used to house the growing population.[5] It was only in retrospect—only years after men and women had watched winter nights glow red with flames and seen their communities reduced to ash—that residents of the Northwoods expressed their astonishment that the industry could have been so reckless with its planning, so greedy for its profits, and so blithe with risk.

The sweep of the lumber industry across the Northwoods was astonishingly fast. As one lumberjack recalled years later: "Everything was a race—cuttin' the timber, haulin' the logs, swampin', everything."[6] By the 1930s, many ex-lumberjacks were lamenting, as John Emmett Nelligan put it, that "it was almost a crime against Nature to cut it." But as he recalled, "we lumbermen were never concerned with crimes against Nature. We heard only the demand for lumber, more lumber, and better lumber."[7] For those of us who grew up far from the Northwoods, the flowering and withering of the lumber industry in that region might not be as familiar as images of men standing by thirty-foot stumps in the California Redwoods. But the Northwoods lumber story was, if less visually dramatic, a yet more incredible story of extractive ruin than that of the Pacific Northwest. In 1835 an entrepreneur named Norman Little took up residence in Saginaw, Michigan, and opened the Northwoods' first commercial timber operation; by 1929, the Virginia and Rainy Lake Lumber Company in Virginia, Minnesota—the largest white pine lumber company in the country—closed its doors.

Contemporaries understood that what was occurring was unprecedented in American history. A *Harper's Weekly* profile on lumberjacks in 1889 noted that "few persons who are not in some way actually engaged in the lumber business have any adequate idea of the magnitude of the industry. . . . which, as the scientists tell us, is rapidly changing the face of nature and the very climate of our country."[8] And while that particular article summed up the resulting transformation as "picturesque," some saw it in more dire terms. But these naysayers were almost unilaterally ignored: As early as 1867, Increase Lapham and the Wisconsin State Forestry Commission he headed produced the *Report on the Disastrous Effects of the Destruction of*

A GLIMPSE INTO THE FUTURE: THE LAST TREE.

The clear-cutting brought by Minnesota's logging industry inspired an editorial cartoon in the *St. Paul Pioneer Press* in 1901 showing a lumberjack stampede toward the last pine in the state. Courtesy of University of Minnesota Libraries.

*Forest Trees.* In it, Lapham called for measure in deforestation and vaguely encouraged tree planting instead. The legislature ignored him. In neighboring Minnesota, the first call for stewardship of the land and a slower pace of lumbering was made even earlier. In 1860, Minnesota's first governor, Alexander Ramsey, used his inaugural speech to make a plea for more careful stewardship of the state's land.[9] He, too, was roundly ignored. By 1901, the *St. Paul Pioneer Press* was running a satirical cartoon that showed several desperate jacks, fully dressed in plaid, flat caps, and mackinaw boots, running through a field of stumps toward one, single, towering pine. "A glimpse into the future," the caption read, "the last tree."[10]

That "last tree" (or nearly last, since one stand of forty acres remained in Minnesota) fell only a few decades later. In the process, Wisconsin, Michigan, and Minnesota had been effectively clear-cut. Millions of acres had burned in devastating fires. Immigrant homesteaders now attempted to eke out a living on sandy soil best suited to the towering pines that came before. In less than a century the industry had changed the nature of the Northwoods—completely and irrevocably. A new, and different, place had emerged at the hands of the lumber barons.

Later mythology would often remember the lumber camp as a small operation with low starting costs and a closely knit crew, something akin to the woods' version of a romantic band of cowboys. But that mythology had as little to do with the height of lumbering as the mythos of cowboys had to do with their reality. That myth was not entirely disconnected from reality—the early logging of the Northwoods largely happened in small, family-run camps. But by the turn of the century, that picture had changed entirely. In place of a camp made up of family and a few laborers treated as family, the Northwoods were dotted with highly structured and stratified large-scale camps, consisting of up to 150 men from dozens of ethnic and racial backgrounds whose lives, ambitions, and futures were shaped by the structured theft of Native land and the attempt to turn that land into profit.

In Park Falls, Wisconsin, the post office is adorned with a dramatic mural. Above and around the postmaster's door, the entire wall is covered in huge men fighting. Over the clock one man has another in a headlock, and both are wallowing on a riverbank, locked in a fight that neither appears to be winning. To the right of the door, a man shoves a caulked boot into the head of another who is pinned beneath him, driving a peavy hook (the long, straight tool with which lumberjacks broke jams) into his chest. Across the top of the wall men are spilling out of boats, tumbling over walls, and generally doing their very best to kill one another. The mural is called *Lumberjack Fight on the Flambeau River*. And while the heavily muscled bodies and particularly gory fighting methods it depicts are the romantic imagination of a WPA artist, the actual battle it depicts is very real.

Park Falls sits on the Flambeau River, one of a dozen smaller tributaries to the Chippewa, which itself empties into the Mississippi at the Minnesota border. This basin, cutting a diagonal across the richest pinelands in the state, was the heart of Wisconsin logging. In fact, the very position of that borderline between Minnesota and Wisconsin was determined on the question of who would control the river: whoever controlled the upper reaches of the Chippewa controlled the logs that floated down it—and that timber was worth a fortune. Vast stands of white pine lined the streams and tributaries that fed into the river, and in the years before effective logging railroads, the river was the only means of moving the logs to market. And from the early 1850s, the fate of those logs had been in the hands of the citizens of Eau Claire, Wisconsin.

A small city settled by those associated with the lumber industry, Eau Claire had, as of the late 1860s, no major lumber company. Instead, half a dozen mills

*Lumberjack Fight on the Flambeau River,* a mural painted by James S. Watrous in 1938 in the post office of Park Falls, Wisconsin, depicts a violent brawl said to have occurred in 1888 at the junction of the north and south forks of the Flambeau River. Photograph by Tom Parker.

processed the logs of dozens of small logging camps; some of those who worked the spring lumber drives on the rivers remembered working for a dozen or more companies, sometimes two or three in a single year. The camps that populated the river in the 1860s were largely still "State of Maine" camps, small concerns with a couple dozen men on their payrolls. These men worked throughout the winter to cut and clean trees, stacking their logs in piles along the shores of the Chippewa and its tributaries.

During the spring breakup, each company would leave that winter's cut sitting in piles by the riverbank. As the ice melted, the most romanticized part of the lumbering year began—the annual river drive. Men in caulked boots that went up to their knees and red sashes around their waists began their long journey down the river.

These were the river pigs, the possessors of the most dangerous job in lumbering. As they passed a camp, they would roll that camp's logs into the river, so that by the time they reached Beef Slough, a few miles upriver from Eau Claire, the river was seething with a tangled mess of logs. It was not unusual for river drives to pick up millions of board feet of lumber, stored in mammoth logs, sometimes six feet in diameter. The size of the drive is hard to fathom: photographs of log jams show what appears to be a giant pile of jumbled toothpicks, with men the size of ants standing among the mess.

But just as dozens of camps contributed their logs to the drive, half a dozen different mills had bought their cut. To sort all this out—to make sure that the correct camp got credit for their logs, and the right mill got the lumber they had purchased—it was necessary to build a boom. A boom is essentially a storage area, a side of the river separated out by a giant string of logs that acts as a gateway. When the boom is shut, logs cannot get by. They would be stored while they were sorted by the log mark that each camp pounded with an iron brand into the end of their logs.

In Eau Claire, timber was king. And to make the most of it, the citizens grouped together in 1866 to buy all the land around Beef Slough, a wide, calm spot on the river where it would be easy to remove logs from the main current and sort them for delivery to the appropriate mills. They did not, in fact, need the boom yet; the number of logs did not justify it. But as they watched logging camps mushroom across the upper Chippewa, the town's citizens realized that controlling the logs at a key point in the river would, eventually, be necessary—not to mention lucrative. It was a good, solid plan. It seemed likely to work. But the small businessmen and local investors who made it were unaware that they were about to play against competitors far out of their league. They were about to meet the first of the great timber barons.

In the summer of 1867, major investors from New England, Ohio, Iowa, and the newly booming Twin Cities created the Beef Slough Manufacturing, Booming, Log Driving and Transportation Company. The men who put this together were removed not only geographically, but economically and socially from the small-town business interests of Eau Claire, Wisconsin. Some were timber barons who had already made fortunes in the woods of New England, but others, like Ezra Cornell, founder and benefactor of the eponymous university, were rising captains of industry. They were men who had never worked in the woods themselves or even on the farms of the lake states, but who knew a safe investment when they saw it.

The only thing standing in the way of their making a fortune out of the rich pine lands of the upper Chippewa was their inability to find a place to build an adequate boom. There was only one suitable spot, and it was already owned by the small business owners of Beef Slough. This was, of course, exactly the situation the mill owners in Eau Claire envisioned when they pooled together to buy Beef Slough. What they did *not* count on was how overmatched they would be by the competition. It seemed to go well that first year: the barons of the Beef Slough Company attempted to build a boom on the land in the summer of 1867, but the Eau Claire investors sued and won a court order halting the construction. But their luck would soon run out.

By the summer of 1868, the Chippewa was no longer the peaceful logging river of the early 1860s, or even of the summer of 1866 when the Eau Claire investors built their boom. The drive grew exponentially, and by early summer the logs had reached the Eau Claire investor's boom at Beef Slough. The Eau Claire men, eager to ensure that all the logs floating down in the Chippewa would be milled in Eau Claire itself, rather than bypassing the town on their way further downriver to the larger mills in Stillwater and Rock Island, had closed the boom and refused to let any logs at all pass. In retaliation, the Beef Slough Company had sent mercenaries in the middle of the night to cut the boom and release all the logs. In the ensuing confusion, they were said to have stolen millions of board feet of lumber. The Eau Claire men again closed the boom and refused to allow logs past.

It was at this point that Bruno Vinette, a Canadian logger who had been working the Wisconsin woods for fifteen years, undertook a pleasure trip up the Chippewa River. When he arrived in Eau Claire, he found the town in a state of high alert and "badly torn up in mind." The men of the city had armed themselves for battle: "revolvers could be seen in the pockets of the lumberjacks and pike poles and cant hooks were carried about much as soldiers would carry guns, for attack and defense."

The night of Vinette's arrival was the battle of Beef Slough, a brief but violent bout of fighting in which "many were permanently maimed" and a dozen or so ended up in a hospital. When Vinette awoke at about four o'clock he looked out to see that "sure enough the river was alive with logs," which the Eau Claire men had been forced to release. The logs tumbled down through the churning waters of the Chippewa, right past the mills of Eau Claire, to the huge mills of the Mississippi— mills owned by titans of industry hundreds of miles away. It was the first pitched battle between small manufacturing and large industry in the Northwoods. Industry had won.[11]

Vinette had stumbled on the Chippewa at a moment of drastic change in the logging industry of the Northwoods. Beef Slough marked the entrance of major industrial logging into the region, backed by wealthy financiers, and carried out over a wide region. Timber logged in Minnesota, Wisconsin, and Michigan might now be milled in Illinois, or even further down the Mississippi. The battle of Beef

Slough also marked the entrance of the most influential lumberman of his, or perhaps any, era: Frederick Weyerhaeuser. One of the founders of the Beef Slough Company, Weyerhaeuser would expand his empire to include vast swaths of the Northwoods, before moving on to be the driving force of Pacific Northwest logging. While his company towns would define the landscape of Washington and Oregon, it was in the Northwoods that he cut his teeth. With the entrance of Weyerhaeuser and the other men who would come to be known collectively as the Timber Barons, the era of the small camp was quickly ending.

For the first thirty years of logging in the Northwoods, entry costs were extremely low. The government saw it as necessary that the land be cleared and sold it at low prices.[12] And when land could not be bought, it could always be stolen, with or without the government's aid. This was the era of great land-grabs, and the very nature of the lumbering called for speed. As each territory organized, a period of chaos allowed the enterprising lumberer to clear-cut state- and Anishinaabe- or Menominee-owned lands without paying. Once territorial and then state governments tightened restrictions of state-owned lands, white settlers soon discovered that the state would be more than happy to aid in their theft of Native-owned woods.[13] The faster men acted, the more they could steal before any authority stepped in to mediate. As a contemporary recalled in 1897, "Nobody attached any blame or shame to stealing pine timber—at least, in pine country no one did. And that for a good reason, indeed; they all did it . . . either in person or by deputy, all 'swiped'—that is the correct phrase for the act—if a chance presented itself."[14]

Even before Minnesota was legally open to settlement, loggers had begun to cut away at the edges of Anishinaabe land. For the men who engaged in this theft, the Anishinaabe were almost criminally negligent of the capital tied up in their trees. The men who engaged in land theft not only did not see their actions as a crime, but understood themselves to be engaged in a positive action.[15] They were clearing the land of trees to open it for farming, and in the meantime releasing the vast amounts of money tied up in those towering trees.[16] In fact, as Benson points out, the removal of lumber made land so much more desirable to agricultural settlers that loggers stealing timber from government land could "actually have been able to convince themselves that logging public land was a commendable act."

But, of course, this was the view from the side of settler colonists—not from those on whose land the trees were. The trees of the Northwoods are, in Anishinaabe

River drivers sort logs into brailing pockets at Beef Slough, near the mouth of the Chippewa River in Wisconsin, circa 1880. Photograph by Gerhard Gesell. Courtesy of the Wisconsin Historical Society, WHS-25748.

culture, the glory of the Gitchi Manito (Great Spirit) whose existence guarantees both shelter and life to every member of the Anishinaabe community. That community includes not only members of the Anishinaabe but any inhabitants of the woods, all of whom—from deer to the wind to the trees themselves—are expressed in Anishinaabe language as fully animate. While Euro-Americans saw the woods as an obstacle to be removed, the Anishinaabe understand the Northwoods to be a fundamental part of their community.

To stop here, simply noting the different understandings of the roles of the woods and lamenting the loss of lands, is to criminally oversimplify the story and rest our understanding on racist views of the Anishinaabe as a premodern people, swindled by market capitalists who outwitted them. That version of events is plainly ridiculous: by the time logging came to their lands, the Anishinaabe had long since embraced a mixed economy and had long encounters with white capitalists. For two hundred years, Lake Superior bands of Anishinaabe had participated in the fur trade, creating a complex negotiation with European market systems. This was not simply becoming quasi-capitalist but rather, as anthropologist Laura McLeod argues, mixing two forms of economy. It was only when facing outward toward white settlers that the Anishinaabe engaged with market economies. From the inside these trades were simply a different use of a community resource to continue to support the community itself.[17]

With the arrival of lumbering in the Northwoods this system was put under enormous strain. The resources of the woods themselves were exploited far more aggressively by white settlers than fur had been, and the Anishinaabe had a much more difficult time maintaining their community economy in the face of the overwhelming tide of market capitalism that arrived with lumberers and increased in pace when logging shifted from land-clearing to extractive industrial capitalism. Even where the land remained nominally Anishinaabe, the trees that grew on that land were much harder to protect. In addition to the practice of simply lumbering reservation land and apologizing (or, rather, not apologizing) later, several treaties, thefts, and regulations gradually forced forest resources out of community hands. From the opening of timberlands to the end of the nineteenth century, the Anishinaabe lost most of what they had left to federal policy. The U.S. government increasingly worked to use lumber resources to force the Anishinaabe into agriculture and a full engagement with capitalism.

Toward the end of the nineteenth century, the federal government played two more cards in an attempt to force assimilation into the market economy: in 1873 the Supreme Court ruled in *United States v. Cook* that the Anishinaabe could only lumber their own lands if they intended to farm them afterward. In other words, the government attempted to simultaneously enforce assimilation while ensuring that the Anishinaabe did not become active competitors in the lumber market. Sixteen years later, the Nelson Act (1889) divided much of the remaining forested land into allotments and sold them to lumber interests.

In the face of this, the Anishinaabe resisted the onslaught of fraudulent lumbering in a huge variety of ways, from attempts in the western portion of the White Earth Reservation to enforce the Nelson Act provisions that only Indigenous labor was to be used in lumbering Indigenous lands, to physically occupying and marching across land to stop timbering, as members of the Leech Lake Band did in 1901, to legal recourse. Each succeeded to varying degrees, although the legal rights of the 1837 treaty were not restored to the Anishinaabe until *Minnesota v. Mille Lacs Band* (1999). But while historians have documented many of the ways that the Anishinaabe resisted incursions on their land, little work has been done to analyze that resistance from within the lumber industry, and specifically at the site where the White Earth Tragedy—and the wider denuding of Anishinaabe resources—took place: the lumber camps.

Yet, despite widespread resistance, Native American–owned lands were quickly opened to industrialists in the late nineteenth century. This was especially true because even when they were nominally protected, Native woodlands proved to be ripe country for theft and fraud on the part of Indian agents. The career of W. A. Mercer serves as an impressive testament to the impunity with which Indian agents were able to exploit the timber resources of the Northwoods tribes. Mercer came to the Leech Lake Reservation in Minnesota after having been transferred from LaPoint Agency in Wisconsin where he had been caught indulging in timber speculation.

The Leech Lake Band protested the appointment but were told by the commissioner that he would be tried on probation. In Leech Lake, Mercer was overseeing "dead and down" operations, in which trees that had been blown over during the year were logged, hauled, and sold from Indian land. In March 1901 the *Minneapolis Journal* reported that the commissioner had received reports from Leech Lake Indians that green timber (the still growing resources) had been logged. Mercer responded that he had immediately shut down the operators who were carrying out green lumbering. The *Journal* defended Mercer, who claimed that he was "thoroughly earnest in stopping all infractions," but that it was "almost impossible for him to give his exclusive attention to logging operations." The commissioner eventually came to claim that it "does not seem possible to get rid of the timber on the Chippewa reservations without some sort of a scandal." They agreed to sell off the green timber to the highest bidder and declared the case closed.

Loggers ready a horse-drawn sled near the Leech Lake Reservation in 1906. This photograph was taken during a period of many years of dispossession of Anishinaabe logging rights by the federal government. Courtesy of the Edward A. Bromley Collection, Hennepin County Library.

From the Anishinaabe point of view, matters were far from over. In April a delegation visited Governor Samuel Van Sant to complain that they were certain Mercer was responsible. The *Journal* sent an investigator to the woods, who discovered that green timber was, indeed, being cut by unscrupulous contractors. The paper, however, concluded that Mercer should be absolved from any blame and had "administered the law as strictly as possible." He then went on to advocate for changed laws, while defending his position as a perfectly responsible agent. The statewide papers took his side, calling the White Earth Anishinaabe, who planned to "march . . . around the lake for the purpose of preventing the removal of from 15,000,000 to 20,000,000 feet of pine logs," "desperate and hostile in their intentions towards the whites around the lake on the White Earth reservation." While the Anishinaabe did not march, they kept up a campaign throughout the spring for a rescaling of their logs as their cause dropped slowly out of the headlines and the commissioner assured them that "the Red Men have No Cause for Alarm." In October, the Leech Lake Band were paid $150,000 for the green timber cut (a mere $640,000 less than a later rescale showed the timber to be worth), and shortly thereafter Mercer left his post with high commendations from the commissioner to return to the army where he had an "enviable record."

It was only two years later, after one of the subcontractors disputed their suit, that the truth came to light: Mercer had, thoroughly unsurprisingly, in fact known about and negotiated all the fraudulent contracts. In trial it was reported that when witnesses had reported the cutting of green timber, "Mercer 'just laughed.'"[18] By the time the verdict came down, Mercer was serving, once again, as Indian agent, this time on the Uintah Reservation where, *The Tomahawk* (the newspaper of the White Earth Reservation in Minnesota) wryly noted, "there was no pine timber to be stolen." Despite being found guilty, he retained his post. Shortly thereafter, presumably as a reward for his faithful service, Mercer was appointed the new principal of the Carlisle Indian Industrial School.[19]

In contrast, the Menominee story of preservation appears rather remarkable. While the Anishinaabe lost almost complete control of their community resources, Menominee reservation land was not nearly as aggressively logged. They were able to maintain their land through a series of decisions on the part of both the Menominee and white colonists that tipped the balance in Menominee favor. To begin with, their land was not viewed as particularly valuable farmland, and railroads never penetrated the Menominee reservation during the time it was logged. There was also a misdirected but lucky act of benevolent paternalism: Agent Jennings, the Bureau of Indian Affairs agent who believed that logging could be part of a sustainable mixed economy for the Menominee and encouraged Menominee control of timberlands. The Menominee agreed: their General Council held a meeting in 1888 in which 139 members agreed to take on the provisions of the Dawes Act under the assumption that the government would also give them "an equal share in the Timber of Timberlands." Moreover, while the lands were logged, the Menominee stringently resisted the presence of white loggers on their land, who they argued weakened the morals of the tribe. As a result, the Menominee managed to maintain many of their resources.[20]

Yet, even here, the BIA did everything in their power to free up the forests for destruction. In 1917 *The Tomahawk* railed against the "scientific management" of Menominee woods that had focused solely on efficient market gains. Rather than managing the community carefully, "the Indians were deprived of any voice in the cutting and sale of their timber." Only the most valuable hardwoods had been cut, leaving behind pulpwood trees. Not only, *The Tomahawk* argued, had this failed spectacularly to protect their community, instead serving to dissipate their resources, but it also served the tribe poorly financially: their net gain, *The Tomahawk* claimed, had dropped from $2.5 million over a "few years" to a system that "barely paid overhead charges."[21] The result of schemes like Mercer's, as well as the more "legal" theft by treaty, was that at times the reservations of the Northwoods found themselves unable to legally come up with enough lumber from their own land to serve their own needs.[22]

As the government stripped the Anishinaabe and Menominee of their treaty rights, opening more land to lumbering, the camps in which men lived changed drastically. For many years, the idea that lumber camps were small, family-run affairs endured both in popular memory and, often, in the historiography itself. The myth of the egalitarian camp did have roots in the reality of early logging practices in the Northwoods. For the first few decades of lake state lumbering, primitive technologies and a haphazard land policy both allowed for easy entry into the industry and kept lumbering in a preindustrial state. Even as late as 1870, a full 20 percent of the mill owners in Saginaw, Michigan's lumber capital, had a capital investment of less than five thousand dollars.[23] Without paying for land, the cost of entry into logging was within reach of most simple farmers. All that was needed was a few men to help and a simple hut in which to house them. In fact, the most striking difference between early and late lumbering in the Northwoods was the site of labor. The logging camp underwent enormous evolution from the 1840s to the 1910s. By the twentieth century, the camps had transformed entirely from primitive shacks to multibuilding sites where status was clearly demarcated by separate living quarters.

For the first thirty or forty years of lumbering, men lived in what were nicknamed "State of Maine" camps. This style of camp was imported, along with the earliest Northwoods jacks, from New England. State of Maine camps were extremely simple affairs. They rarely employed more than a couple dozen men, if that, and were housed in a single building. Two long bunks ran along each side of a log cabin where the men slept like sardines under a single, long wool blanket. The cabin was built low, with a pitched ceiling that ran almost to the floor, to conserve heat and money. In the middle of the camp was a large, open fire. A hole above served as a chimney. The space was dark, smokey, and above all, smelly. Men had few or no washing facilities, and some were known to put on their long underwear in December and never once remove it until camp broke up in the spring. The smell of drying sweat and body odor mingled with the scent of the cooked beans that served as the primary staple of the men's diet.

Nᵒ 2
In Camp.

In 1864 this high-ceilinged log hut served as both kitchen and sleeping quarters for a crew in the State of Maine–style camp of Elias Moses on Tibbets Creek, a feeder stream of the Rum River in northern Minnesota. Courtesy of the Minnesota Historical Society.

Some small camps persisted as late as the 1880s. In 1878, Euclid J. Bourgeois, a man who would one day be a jack but was at that time only eight years old, was taken to visit a camp by his father. In his memoirs, written in the 1920s, he gives a vivid description of what he saw:

In the fall of 1878 my father took me along to his camp on Main Creek, which had its outlet in the Jump River. At the camp I saw a chimney built of round sticks covered with clay, cooking pots hung on a swing crane, and bread cooked by reflectors before an open fire. The camp houses were low because the floors were dug a foot or so below ground. Split, hollowed-out basswood logs placed like half-tiles were used for the roof. They were chinked with moss. A few panes of 8"x10" window glass let in a little day-light, and the night light was a rag in a tin basin of tallow. This was called a bitch and was properly named, judging by what I heard about them. The men slept in a row in one long bed, packed like sardines and covered with one long blanket made according to the number of sleepers. The food consisted of salt beef and pork and beans. Vegeta-bles must have been limited because of keeping, and there could not have been many sweets because these were scarce years later.[24]

While this camp was less primitive than the earliest camps, by merit of having both a chimney and a window, it is nonetheless still easily recognizable as a State of Maine establishment.

The portrait of camps as pictures of American ingenuity and homespun sim-plicity where true merit won out were popular with eastern readers as early as the 1880s. In 1892, Arthur Hill wrote a long piece for *Scribner's Magazine*, aimed at middle-class urban readers in the East. After his loving description of "simple" shanty boys he concludes, "It is from these plucky shanty boys that most of the great lumbermen of the country have been developed. First they worked as com-mon hands; then they were chosen to run a camp. Out of savings they bought a few teams and went to jobbing, putting in timber on contract for others, then they bought and lumbered timber on their own account, and finally with a large capacity came large enterprises, great lumber mills, logging railroads and finally great fortunes."

Hill even goes on to give a grand example of his theme: "The veteran lumberman and politician, Hon. Philetus Sawyer." He describes Sawyer as "a young 'bull-puncher' in a Wisconsin logging camp" who eventually became a congressman, then a senator. Hill honors his "humble" roots by claiming that "his 'haw' and 'gee' were as good and guiding in Washington as Wisconsin." What Hill does not include in this description was that Sawyer was educated and married with a child before he ever came to the camps.[25]

Hill's article is only one of many that promote the myth of the simple lumber-man made good. The mythology of the egalitarian lumberjack was widespread throughout the Upper Midwest, and eventually the country, by the 1910s. This myth insisted that the camps were places where men were treated as equals, where snob-bery and division did not exist, and—as an offshoot of this—where men who worked hard could "make it." These ideas are powerful confirmations of the widespread ideologies of meritocracy circulating in the United States at the time. In dime novels and magazines, Gilded Age Americans told themselves again and again that the elite had risen from the ranks of the common man.[26] And the idea of a self-made lumber baron was particularly appealing. As avatars for white muscular manhood, their success in the market was seen as confirmation of the fundamentally meritocratic nature of American capitalism. If lumberjacks could succeed, then capitalism was, indeed, rewarding all the best qualities a man could possess.

The appeal of the myth of an egalitarian lumber camp and an open market in which simple men could become barons was so overwhelmingly powerful that it has even taken root in the historiography. In 2008, for instance, Adam Tomczik argued that while "the larger logging industry, like the American economy generally, grew increasingly monopolized, rationalized, and mechanized . . . the day-to-day activities and culture of loggers in the lumber camps of Maine and Minnesota remained comparatively stable from the 1840s into the 1930s. The men and their camps were a final bastion of the traditional workplace in America."[27] This view of the lumber camp as a site of traditional labor practices, combined with the occasional insistence among historians that the industry never truly centralized, supports a romantic view of the nature of lumberjacking.

It is a view lumberjack enthusiasts strongly support. Modern lumberjack games, played at fairs across the country and occasionally televised on ESPN, are purposefully portrayed as the continuation of a long-standing, traditional skill. Combining chain saw carving with pole shimmying, these games ignore the massive changes in the industry that make modern logging look nothing like its nineteenth-century counterpart. The images of a traditional, male skill surviving into the twenty-first century untouched are romantic but misleading. They gloss over the massive changes that occurred in the 1870s through 1920s—changes that led to lumber camps where class structure was apparent and rigid.

Yet by 1878, this type of camp was becoming increasingly rare due to huge changes in the industry. Starting in the 1860s, but picking up speed in the 1880s and 1890s, the logging industry of the Northwoods experienced an unprecedented boom. New technologies allowed for the trees to be felled and milled with greater efficiency, and the ceaseless migration of settlers to the new metropolises of the West created an insatiable demand for the Northwoods' lumber. There were clearly fortunes to be found in the trees, but as logging grew increasingly industrialized, it became clear that those fortunes would fall into the hands of the few, and often into hands far removed from the Northwoods themselves.

In the woods, the biggest change in technology was the invention of the alternating tooth crosscut saw. Before this innovation, trees had been felled by crosscut saws with regularly spaced teeth. A jack would first judge based on the shape of the tree as well as its surrounding environment in which direction the cut tree would be most likely to fall. He would then use an axe to mark a notch in the tree. Then he and his partner cut using a two-person crosscut saw, jamming wedges into the gash as they went to prevent the massive weight of the tree from pinching their saw and holding it in place. The problem was that with a saw featuring evenly spaced teeth—like modern handsaws—the teeth would quickly become jammed with sawdust. The long saw would then need to be dragged out of the tree and cleared of sawdust before the jacks could continue their work. On trees up to five or six feet in diameter, this process added an enormous amount of work and lost the jacks valuable daylight. The new saw had irregular teeth, alternating one sharp tooth with a small trough and then a smaller tooth. The space between teeth prevented sawdust from filling in the teeth and jamming the saw. It was a seemingly small innovation, but saved lumberjacks hours of work, allowing them to fell more trees in a single day.

The second innovation in the woods was more basic still: from the late 1850s onward horses began to replace oxen as the primary domesticated animal working in the woods. Horses have an agility that oxen lack—they can turn tight circles and cross one leg over the other to avoid obstacles and maneuver in crowded spaces. After a tree was felled and stripped of its branches, it was cut into regular lengths. Finally, a jack would chain the logs to a "go-devil," a V-shaped primitive sled, that was harnessed to a working animal who pulled the log out of the heart of the forest to a place where it could be stacked and moved to the riverbank. Throughout the eighteenth century and into the middle of the nineteenth century, oxen were the preferred animal for performing this task. Replacing oxen with horses meant that lumberers were able to remove logs from denser forests; they were no longer limited to only those trees most easily accessible.

Outside the woods, technological advances in milling and transportation, coupled with westward migration, created more demand for lumber than clusters of State of Maine camps—even ones equipped with new saws and horses—could possibly meet. The railroads, drivers of change wherever they reached, revolutionized the logging industry. The first logging railroads arrived in Michigan in the 1860s but were not in widespread use in the region until the turn of the century. Logging railroads removed what had been the single greatest limitation to the lumber industry: water. For centuries, river drives or rafting logs across lakes constituted the only reasonably sane method of bringing timber to market. But with railroads, logs could be hauled from areas distant from the water, opening vast new tracts of land to the lumberjacks' saws. In fact, between rivers and rails, so much land could be covered that only one virgin forty-acre stand of white pine still exists in the state

Two jacks use a crosscut saw on a massive felled tree at Thomas Foster's lumber camp in Tuscola County, Michigan, circa 1880. Photograph by J. A. Jenney. Courtesy of Superior National Forest.

of Minnesota. That it survived is an accident: an incompetent surveyor marked the stand as a lake, and no one was able to buy the rights to log it.

But perhaps the greatest driving force in the ramping up of the logging industry was not the technology that enabled greater numbers of logs to make it to market, but the demographic changes that created a market that simply could not be oversupplied. Throughout the second half the nineteenth century, the new metropolises of the Midwest boomed. While this growth was slowed by the Civil War, the Union army's demand for lumber kept the mills whirring. But nothing could have prepared the market for the sudden spike in demand when, in 1871, the great city of Chicago burned to the ground.[28] With enormous demand and the technology in place to meet it, it is hardly surprising that the farmer-foreman hiring out a dozen local boys to chop some trees did not survive the century. There was no way that model of industry could satisfy the market.

That small-scale loggers could not keep up with this demand was hardly pertinent, though, because as the lumber industry boomed, small-scale producers had

Lumberjacks pose with the tools of their trade while skidding a large log with the help of four oxen at Mud Creek, east of Mora, Minnesota, circa 1892. Courtesy of the Minnesota Historical Society.

less and less access to the woods themselves. While it may have been easy enough to thieve land from the edges of a reservation that was newly settled, or to add a few acres to the edge of your plot, skimming a neighboring farm's lumber, it was not such an easy proposition to steal lumber when your neighbor was, say, Ezra Cornell. In the 1860s, the timberlands of Minnesota, Wisconsin, and Michigan experienced an almost unprecedented speculative frenzy. Much of this came from the man who eventually grew to be the king of Northwoods lumber barons: Frederick Weyerhaeuser.

Weyerhaeuser was a passionate speculator who claimed his only mistake was "not buying pine trees whenever offered." He and others, including Daniel Shaw, quickly accumulated vast tracts of land. By the 1880s they began to formalize their stranglehold on the timber industry. While up until then transportation and land deals had been carried out on an as-needed basis, in 1888 the biggest producers expanded the Mississippi River Logging Company to include the Chippewa Lumber Company, essentially tying up all movement of timber along two of the main arteries of the Northwoods into a single cooperative. By 1889 Weyerhaeuser also controlled the St. Croix boom, putting another river under his ownership.[29]

Out of the frenzy for speculation, what emerged across the 1870s and 1880s was a creature entirely unlike the farmer-foreman of yore. The investors who built the white pine industry, the investors who brought it from a small-scale enterprise to a workforce of thousands, were rarely lumberjacks. As the industry grew, logging was increasingly carried out in networks of camps. These networks of camps were either owned by the lumber company or by contract loggers. Overseeing companies hired "walking bosses" to oversee groups of camps. These large corporations often also directly hired the foremen of camps. The foremen then contracted out workers separately. As a result, the foreman, walking boss, and sometimes other high-level employees were company men. They were sent from cities and hired based on extensive experience.

Under this system, the young lumberjack making good and working his way to foreman was increasingly implausible. More and more often even foremen had full high school educations, and those who oversaw several camps or ran the companies had college degrees. For a poor lumberjack who left school at thirteen or fourteen to begin working winters in the woods, opportunities were limited. Instead, ownership concentrated in the hands of a new class of men. Some were owners already, men who had become wealthy in the pine lands of Pennsylvania and Maine and were eager to turn their modest wealth into fabulous fortunes. This was the era of the lumber barons.

Lumber barons behaved not like lumberjacks made good, but as wealthy men in an age of outrageous wealth. By 1900 Duluth, Minnesota, had the most millionaires per capita of any city in the United States. A drive along its bluffs still demonstrates the fabulous wealth of the lumber and iron barons who built opulent homes overlooking Lake Superior. John Esse, a former lumberman, remembered that baron Daniel Shaw "set himself aside in a park from everybody else." At the same time, the lumber towns of the Northwoods developed "skid rows"—neighborhoods for itinerant jacks that were as separated as possible from the lumber barons. Nor was it possible any longer for men of small means to find their way into the industry.[30]

The lumber barons came to be seen by many at the turn of the century and in the first decades of the twentieth century as a class that lived off the backs of poor laborers. When, in 1911, a farmer's daughter was accidentally shot by the state militia in a scuffle over land that was flooded by a logging company, the newspapers erupted in fury not at the militia but at the lumber barons. The militia was only there because her father had refused a summons to court to defend himself against the Chippewa Log and Boom Company, which the *Eau Claire Leader* called a "cruel lumber trust," accusing the state of backing "those of a mighty 'money power'" against the "rights of a poor man."[31]

A train from the Brainerd & Northern Minnesota Railway transports a load of logs at Walker, Minnesota (named for lumber baron Thomas Barlow Walker), in 1896. Courtesy of the Edward A. Bromley Collection, Hennepin County Library.

The connection between the state and lumber barons was no coincidence. Several prominent lumbermen rose to enter government, and the connections these men formed served to cement their position at the top of the industry. Russell Alexander Alger, for instance, utilized government connections to build an essentially private railroad through the Upper Peninsula of Michigan, giving him nearly exclusive access to several lumber markets. As his wealth grew a county on the peninsula was named after him, and he was eventually elected governor of the state.[32] As former lumberjack John Esse remembered, "they did what they were told to do, what the tycoons themselves had in mind, nobody knew except the impression was that they were taking the best of the stuff out there."[33]

As the industry grew, their need for cheap, expendable labor expanded. As Jason Newton argues, the lumber industry maximized profits by exploiting not merely the cheap nature of the woods, but the equally cheap nature of the lumberjacks themselves. Industrial logging required industrial wage workers, valued not for their skills but for their ability to turn cheap nutrition into cheap muscles, and cheap muscles into profits.[34] Laborers were sought not for their particular skills, even though the work they were doing was highly skilled, but for their cost. The result was the creation of camps consisting of a small management class of educated company-men, and a large underclass of itinerant workers.

For those not born into wealth, education was the only possible way to rise through the ranks and go from laborer to company man. C. E. Blakeman, a lumberjack who left school at twelve, frames his memoir around the opportunities he was denied due to his own semi-illiteracy. Blakeman became a trapper at twelve, and at sixteen, in 1878, he decided to go to the camps to "earn a man's wage."[35] But almost immediately upon arriving in camp, he discovered that his lack of education would hold him back from opportunities for advancement. Two weeks into his work in the woods the foreman approached Blakeman's team of lumberjacks, looking for a second scaler. The work of a scaler was infinitely preferable to that of a lumberer. His job was to measure the trees as they were felled and estimate the board feet of lumber contained in each giant log. His wages were higher than that of a feller, his work less laborious, and his living conditions—in a small, better-heated cabin with the foreman—infinitely preferable. But while Blakeman, "understood good and rotten timber well, [he] had no ability with figures." So he stood "mentally kicking himself for having shunned the schoolroom" while another man took the job. Blakeman chafed knowing that a promotion is "what he gets for having something in his head," while Blakeman had his strength "in [his] legs and arms like an ox." From then on, whenever he saw the new scaler working with a pencil, that one phrase returned to haunt Blakeman: "like an ox."[36]

Others echo Blakeman's conviction that it was education that differentiated between boss and worker. John Nelligan, a lumberjack who worked in the Michigan woods from 1870 to the 1890s, found himself on the other side of the educational divide. In 1874, following a winter's work in the camps and a spring on the log drive, Nelligan enrolled in the Green Bay Commercial Business College. He had decided that after five winters in the woods he was "fairly well-versed in the practical side of the logging business, but . . . needed more education in business methods." As a result of taking this one summer to "improve [his] sadly neglected education," Nelligan went on to work as a foreman and then walking boss of several camps. He also saw those who spent that summer with him go on to successful careers and independent wealth.[37]

Those on the other side of the educational divide were equally aware of its role in separating workers and stifling promotion. Horace Glenn, a middle-class, native-born youth from Minneapolis spent a single winter in the camps in 1901 to earn tuition for the University of Minnesota. In one of his first letters home to his family

Two Michigan loggers use a crosscut saw on a downed tree while the scaler *(far right)* measures the length of the cutting and estimates the number of board feet the log will yield. Courtesy of Library of Congress.

he describes with disgust the enthusiasm his fellow lumberjacks display for the *Police Gazette*—the only news in camp. Glenn had brought several magazines with him to the camps and notes that when one of his bunkmates picked this novel item up, he put it down without recognizing what it was and said, "oh, it is only an advertisement." They are, Glenn decided, "the most utterly illiterate, ignorant savages that I have ever encountered." He complains that in addition to being illiterate, ignorant, and vulgar, they had no intention of bettering themselves. "Their sole ambition," he claimed, "and only idle recreation is to drink whiskey and blow their stake in the shortest possible time."[38]

Glenn was certain that his coworkers' vulgarity, violence, drunken behavior, and lack of ambition were direct results of their lack of education. In a letter from January 1901, two months into his winter in the woods, he told his parents that he "now

Jacks slept in cramped quarters on bunks lined with straw. Reading material in camps of the 1880s was scarce, and literate lumberjacks were equally rare. Courtesy of the Edward A. Bromley Collection, Hennepin County Library.

[recognizes] more fully the value of a good bringing up and schooling. If I ever become a legislature or statesman," he decided, "I shall see that a rigid compulsory education law is enacted and enforced in the back woods." It becomes clear, through his letters, that the feeling is mutual. "I am looked upon," he complained, "as a sort of stuck-up dude, because I wash my feet once a week and use a handkerchief." While he believed that he could "honestly say that [he is] the intellectual superior of the whole lot of men in this camp by a large margin," he also noted, warily, that he "[makes] no boast of these facts about camp."[39] For good reason—men like Glenn appeared with targets on their backs. They hardly needed to draw attention to it.

Perhaps the surest sign that lumberjacks were aware of the divide within the camps that education created was the special glee they reserved for making a fool of well-educated men. This is especially apparent in the hazing of new arrivals into camps. All new lumberjacks were potential prey for pranks, but signs of a middle-class background or education made hazing even more likely. "If he came there wearing tailor-made clothes," one jack explained, "a white collar and a necktie to match, was a loud, boastful talker, and showed signs of superior education and culture that settled it; he was their goat for the 'initiation.'"[40] Pranks often revolved around embarrassing new lumberjacks for their lack of practical knowledge. They would be handed a cant hook, told it was a peavy, and sent, cant hook in hand, to ask the foreman for a cant hook. Others were forced to incur the wrath of cooks by being sent to request "luxury" items, such as fresh fruit or meat, that were never available in camp.

These largely harmless pranks were designed to prove to a new lumberjack that while he "might be equipped with an education far superior to the average Lumber-jack and feelings pardonably proud of such good fortune," he nonetheless "lacked experience, native wit, and a good supply of common sense."[41] Of course, some-times the animosity went beyond harmless pranks. Horace Glenn, whether or not he was boasting of his "superior intellect" was, by February, writing home that he "licked one of them last week, and licked him bad, & I get so mad sometimes that I could whip a dozen if I had to."[42] For those who did not have the education to find their way out of the lowest ranks, the whole industry seemed rigged. As Martin Kuarala, a jack who worked in the Upper Peninsula at the turn of the cen-tury, recalled, "They were a down-trodden segment of society of the time, despised generally and pitied by people of good will and understanding. It was like lifting oneself out of the mire by the bootstraps—impossible for most."[43]

By 1900, even outsiders could and did detect a strict class divide within camps. The division seemed particularly noticeable to those who came from outside the working classes. While few men of means ever visited the camps, those who did pointed to a strict hierarchical structure, with distinct class divisions, in which foremen and workers were fundamentally divided. Rollin Lynde Hartt, a middle-class travel writer from the East, wrote a description of the camps for *The Atlantic* in 1900, depicting a clear divide between middle-class management and the distinctly working-class laborers. "Law" within the camps, he said, "proceeds from the 'office' where dwell the superintendent and his mate the bookkeeper, who wear white col-lars and maintain a tablecloth. Minor heroes, the foremen, enforce their edicts."[44] He describes foreman and bookkeepers often eating separately from their men, maintaining a level of middle-class refinement unheard of in the bunks.

Lynde Hartt's account is corroborated by a series of letters published in 1914 by the *Alpena News*. Nominally from an "old-time lumberjack" they described the

A pair of lumberjacks engage in a playful fistfight for the camera at a Cutler and Savidge camp in 1894. Fighting was banned, but boxing was a popular pastime in the lumber camps. Courtesy of Loutit Library, Grand Haven, Michigan.

conditions and life in Michigan camps in the 1890s.[45] The *Alpena News*'s old-time lumberjack echoed Lynde Hartt's descriptions of camp as a strictly hierarchical setting divided as much by class and educational attainment as by actual rank. This correspondent's camp is a place filled with unhappy, downtrodden workers and cruel managers. "Any time between 8 and 10 o'clock at night," he wrote, "the teamsters and landing men came trailing in, after a hard day's work of from 15 to 18 hours, some singing as if they were enjoying a picnic, others growling and cussing their luck in not being born rich; and many quaint and witty things were said on such occasions even by those who keenly felt that they were being unjustly treated."

According to the *News*'s correspondent, "those who keenly felt that they were being unjustly treated" were, well, nearly everyone. He describes a camp structure strictly divided by rank. At the top stood the foreman who was "not selected because of his genial character or his sympathy with the laboring classes." Instead, the writer claims, "A foreman who became too popular with men working under him, even though they did more and better work than that [*sic*] the men in other camps, lost his prestige in the main office and eventually lost his job."

Beneath the foreman was the scaler (the man in charge of measuring the day's cut), who was also divided not only by rank but by class from the men below him. "The scalar in those days," the *News*'s correspondent wrote, "was the most important personage, in and about the lumber camp—in his own estimation!" While the correspondent begins by mocking the scaler's airs, it is clear that, at least in the mind of the old-time lumberjack, those who worked for the scaler genuinely admired him. The scaler was

> looked up to as a man of superior education and culture. He wrote love letters for the boys who could not write and all disputes growing out of arguments in the camp, on questions of religion, politics, history or literature, were submitted to the scaler for his decision. The scaler's social standing in a lumber camp was similar to that of Washington Irving's "Country Schoolmaster" in Sleepy Hollow.

Another jack wrote of the scaler in his camp in the winter of 1899/90 that "most important and dignified [was] the head scaler, it was like sin for a swamper to speak to him."[46] As with the foreman in Lynde Hartt's account, the scaler was separated from the men not only by his education, but also by his refinement.

In practice, the camp's hierarchy translated to a physical separation. "The scaler," the correspondent wrote, "did not sleep in the men's camp, nor yet in the cook camp. He was provided with a little camp of his own, called 'His Office,' equipped with appropriate furnishings and a library."[47] If the scaler did, indeed, have his own camp or cabin in Alpena, this was a very rare setup. But almost universally, the scaler, like other men of learning, did live separate from most men. In most camps he lived with the foreman either in the camp office or in a room adjoining it.[48]

These higher-wage workers, and the lumber barons for whom they worked, were deeply aware of the divides within camps. At the very top, lumber barons grew increasingly concerned that the men under their care would be morally uplifted. In line with Gilded Age ideas about management, timber barons saw themselves as paternalistically responsible for their workers' well-being, and for the Americanization of the immigrants.[49] W. H. Laird, one of the largest owners, exhorted his fellow lumbermen to give their men "good reading matter in trying to interest them in living better and more manly lives." They would also invite "sky pilots," or wandering preachers, to come to camps and encourage their men to adopt Christian morality. Every few Sundays in season, the men would give up their day of rest to have one of these preachers encourage their moral behavior, often within the private space of their bunkhouse.[50]

Frank Higgins addresses a group of lumberjacks in a camp bunkhouse, circa 1910. Higgins was a well-known clergyman, or sky pilot, who traveled the camps preaching salvation to jacks. Courtesy of the Minnesota Historical Society.

While foremen and overseers consciously created a delineation of space that marked the boundaries of management, this process was not one-sided. As the industry became increasingly differentiated along class lines, lumberjacks became increasingly protective of their own working-class spaces. Violent initiation games, teasing of outsiders, and hostility toward management combined to make the bunkhouse into a space that was specifically working class. Entry and acceptance were based on a newcomer's demonstration that he could participate in the shanty boy values of violent independence and could carry out the craft. Once a jack was accepted as a member of the bunkhouse community, his inclusion was total—and his acceptance in other bunkhouses as well as lumberjack areas in town, like saloons and brothels, was virtually guaranteed.

The space that jacks were allowed to call their own was not, in and of itself, a highly desirable one. Bunks were notoriously unpleasant during the height of Northwoods lumbering.[51] Up to one hundred men would sleep in a single cramped space, in bunks that lined the sides. The beds were, typically, what were called

33

"muzzle loaders," in which the men crawled in from the foot. During the early days, conditions were so cramped that if one man rolled over, they all did. Bunkhouses were also dark. Before electrification, kerosene lamps and the flickering stove alone lit the bunkhouses. Toward the end of the century windows became standard, but even then the windows were small—glass was expensive, and camps were built to be cheap.

Above all, bunkhouses smelled. The men worked up a sweat that would soak through several layers of long underwear and heavy wool socks. At the end of the day, the men would hang their damp, sweaty socks over the fire to dry, while peeling off all but the bottom layer of clothing. Some men infamously never took off this bottom layer of long underwear all winter, and few men had options to bathe more than once a week. As the clothes dried, they created a steam that one reporter claimed was "so heavy that our blankets were wet and you could hardly see across the room." The putrid stench of up to a hundred unwashed men sleeping amid a mist created by their own steaming socks belied description and perhaps belies imagination.[52] Yet this was their space, and they protected entrance to it. When those who did not belong, such as the "walking bosses" sent by major lumber companies, appeared in camp they were "generally regarded with no friendly eyes by the lumberjack fraternity."[53]

The bunkhouse was occupied by a separate class of people, workers who often defined themselves in opposition to the foreman. For instance, in describing the boss-loader, a highly skilled worker in charge of balancing loads on sleighs, the *Alpena News* correspondent called him "a 'sucker,' employed to do the foreman's 'dirty work.' The term 'sucker,'" he goes on to explain, "in a lumber camp was a synonym for 'scab' in a labor union." Here the divide between bosses and workers is clear.[54]

At the very bottom of the pile was the chore boy. Chore boys, or "bull cooks" as they were most often called, were too young, too old, or too disabled to work. While those who were elderly or physically disabled from work in the woods were treated with a good deal of respect, the young boys and mentally disabled men who often occupied the position were treated with derision. It was on this figure that the *Alpena News*'s correspondent heaped most of his derision. "The Chore-Boy," he wrote,

> was an interesting character, who felt that upon his shoulders rested weighty responsibilities. He was a sort of an "office devil" about the premises, but he posed as the "autocrat of the lumber camp" and many time proudly remarked: "If I didn't understand my business I wouldn't be here!" In such democratic surroundings where the "boys" had no use for autocrats, quite naturally, the chore-boy was the most unpopular

A jack reclines to receive a Sunday afternoon shave from the chore boy in the bunkhouse of Dells Lumber Company Camp 1, east of Winter, Wisconsin, January 1908. Note the wheel for axe sharpening on the left. Photograph by Melvin E. Diemer. Courtesy of the Wisconsin Historical Society, WHS-1963.

and best cussed man in the camp, with the possible exception of the foreman, who was gently referred to as the "Nigger-driver," when he wasn't listening.

But the majority of men in this hierarchical version of camp were neither despised nor foolish, but merely downtrodden. They did not have even enough power to indulge in petty tyranny. Instead, in the picture the old-time lumberjack creates, they are nearly enslaved. When describing rising well before dawn, the correspondent writes, "It was on such occasions while turning out in the darkest hour of the night to prepare for breakfast, that peculiar ideas on questions of sociology and the rights of man puzzled his brain. . . . He might be excused for defending highway robbery or gambling as an honorable occupation, compared with the slavery of the lumber camp."[55]

The *Alpena News* columns stand out for their unusual vitriol. Even during the height of lumbering, in the 1890s, it is rare to find articles tinged with bitterness.

By 1914, the year of Paul Bunyan's birth as a folksy, cartoon spokesman, it was un-heard of. Yet his letters reflect many realities that showed up in other accounts. For all that lumberjacks told and retold the stories of small-time jacks who became prosperous lumbermen, it was incredibly rare for self-made lumbermen to rise to the top of the industry. In her study of the development of the lumber industry in Michigan, Barbara Benson points out that most owners were native-born, and many came from wealth.[56] As the lumber boom went into full swing, in the 1890s, the lumber industry became increasingly centralized. By the end of the decade, Weyerhaeuser, Shaw, and other timber barons owned nearly all the fully integrated logging operations.

By the 1880s, lumber camps had settled into a pattern across the Northwoods. The lumberjacks awoke before dawn to the sound of the Gabriel horn or the call of "day-light in the swamp." The chore boy and the cook woke earlier to stoke fires and begin the breakfast. By five it was time for the lumberjacks to pull their socks down from lines over the stove, and pull on thick canvas pants and heavy flannel shirts. These they wore over woolen long johns, which some men wore, without ever re-moving them, from November to spring. If the camp was keeping pace with their contract, the men were allowed Sundays for rest and washing. By all accounts, the first was a more popular pastime than the second.

The men, usually around seventy but sometimes as few as twenty and up to two hundred in the largest operations, trudged in the darkness to the cookshack where they took their seats in silence, out of tradition, respect, or fear. Cooks, as perhaps the most important members of camps, were notorious for their tempers. Since men would happily walk away from a camp that served bad food, cooks were the second-best paid people in camp (after the foreman) and allowed to reign with an iron fist. Any sign of disrespect was met with the possibility of men being summar-ily removed from the cookhouse or worse. While Arthur Hill reported in *Scribner's* that, "short of needed rest, [the cook] becomes sometimes a little irritable," Alton Van Camp more disturbingly remembered that "he wasn't supposed to talk at the table. Not only wasn't supposed to, he didn't dare. . . . You started talking the cook would take a cleaver and start right down your way."[57]

In silence, the men ate sweatpads (pancakes), logging berries (prunes), and cold-shuts (donuts) off thin metal plates, washing them down with swampwater (tea) and blackjack (coffee). Metal utensils clanged and clattered in lamplight, men speaking only to call out for more food when a bowl went empty. They were allowed fifteen minutes for the meal. Then, in the watery light of a winter dawn, just as the sun reached the horizon, they walked out into the drifts of snow to begin their day.

The cook for Camp No. 2 of the N. B. Shank Company near Biwabik, Minnesota, sharpens a carving knife while preparing a meal in 1913. Photograph by William Roleff. Courtesy of the Minnesota Historical Society.

Writing of the romantic image of dozens of men, gaily dressed in red flannel, walking into a crisp winter morning, their breath rising in clouds, Horace Glenn told his mother in 1901, "walking 2 or 3 miles behind a string of Swedes is something impossible to a person with a delicate nose. . . . It is an odor which comes only from generations of unwashed ancestors and no man can hope to acquire it in a lifetime without the aid of heredity." Just two weeks earlier the same young man told his parents that his Roundhead (Scandinavian) compatriots were "the most disgusting, dirty lousy reprobates that [he] ever saw." But, he assured his parents, while there were "probably fifteen white men [there] and sixty Swedes . . . those fifteen keep them so they don't dare to say their soul is their own."[58]

Here in the camps, men of different backgrounds and races mixed. And they did not find it to their liking. Lumber camps were one of the places that defied the tendency of midwesterners to seek cultural isolation.[59] The Midwest in general, and

37

Old show bills, minstrel posters, and vaudeville pinup art plastered the walls of the mess hall dining room at the August Mason lumber camp near Brill, Wisconsin, in 1902. A trio of fiddlers provided evening entertainment. Courtesy of the Minnesota Historical Society.

northern plains in particular, were settled by culturally and geographically distinct groups. Because there was so much space, groups were able to separate themselves. Like in industrializing cities where immigrants divided into ethnic enclaves, midwestern immigrants divided themselves by village. But unlike in cities, the geographical isolation of plains farmers meant that they avoided even the casual brushing up against one another that would naturally occur in cities. The Midwest, then, attained such an odd and persistent patchwork of ethnic identities into the third or fourth generation of Americans because the vastness of the prairies allowed them the space to do so.

Lumberjacks existed outside this structure. They had no small ethnic enclaves to return to. In their ambling way, they tied woods to towns, and towns to cities. At the same time, they created lines of flesh, friendship, and enmity between races and cultures that were otherwise isolated on the plains. As the industry expanded toward its height at the turn of the century, the culture of the lumberjacks became increasingly distinct. When men came into camp, they found themselves in the presence of a vast array of ethnicities and races. Anglo-American jacks encountered several European ethnicities as well as the Anishinaabe, whose land they were often illegally lumbering. Walking out from these camps, the men faced one of the most dangerous professions in American history; during World War I, lumberjacks had a higher casualty rate than soldiers. Returning at night they negotiated the boundaries of belonging, defining hierarchies within a world that the lumber barons saw as a homogeneous mass. While lumberjacks survive in memory as a jolly, cohesive culture of tall tales and manly feats, the next two chapters explore that culture in detail, using it as a window into working-class ideals of manhood, Gilded Age understandings of race, and the contentious relationship between an extractive laborer and the nature in which he worked.

# "HIS FLESH HUNG IN TATTERS AND STRINGS"[1]

## THE VIOLENCE OF NATURE

Come all of you true lumbering boys
Wherever you may be
I'd have you pay attention
and listen unto me.
Don't leave your aging parents;
Stay at home if you can;
And if you're forced to leave your home
Stay away from Michigan.

—"The Ballad of Harry Dunn"

In December 1880 a small notice in the *Motley Register* of Little Falls, Minnesota, described a "serious accident" in the woods. A dead tree had been lodged between the branches of another. Two lumberjacks had been working to fell the living tree. They had likely taken the usual precautions: checking the lean of the living tree, assessing the direction of the wind, and finally notching the trunk on the side where, they hoped, the tree was least likely to fall. Two men would then have begun to cut, dragging a six-foot crosscut saw between them back and forth across the gargantuan trunk, driving a wedge in to keep the weight of a fully grown white pine—some as high as a twenty-story building—from pinching and trapping their saw, encouraging it to fall away from them. But a dead tree is unpredictable. The weight of its rotting trunk throws off the delicate balance. If lodged in the upper branches, its deadly weight is well out of sight, hidden by fifty or a hundred feet of canopy. There was no possible precaution they could have taken. The two men were killed.[1]

The men who cut the Northwoods were part of one of the greatest (and most violent) acts of environmental restructuring in American history—and the reckless-ness, danger, and violence that characterized their relationship with the woods was mirrored in the culture they created. Surviving in the woods meant facing the daily, and very real, risk of death or injury—putting oneself at the mercy of nature with only wits and skill as armor. It was this reckless violence, the seemingly callous disregard for life, that became a central tenet of the masculinity of lumberjacks. The day-to-day work of a lumberjack was defined by his need to willingly engage in violent risk. This unrestrained vigor and relish for risk translated into a concep-tion of masculinity that enshrined violence and recklessness as the core pillars of working-class white manhood.

Deadly mishaps in the woods were so common that most were not reported even as local news items. The particular accident described in the *Motley Register* would have been intimately familiar to lumberjacks. One tree lodging in the branches of another—a "widowmaker" in jack parlance—was as commonplace as it was deadly. But coming across a widowmaker was not the only way a jack could be killed or maimed in the course of his day.

The level of threat depended on your job: road monkeys, the men who rode in front of sleds laden with as many as thirty logs, each of which weighed a ton or more, had a particularly hazardous occupation. Prized for their agility rather than strength, they were more often than not the youngest men in camp, some as young as fifteen, and among the lowest paid workers. Something as simple as fro-zen manure in the tracks of the sled could make it come to a sudden halt, causing thousands of pounds of logs piled behind him to slide forward and into the neck of an unfortunate road monkey who was not agile enough to leap out of harm's way. At the other end of the scale, top loaders, some of the most skilled and highly paid workers, stood atop pyramids of logs, settling loads onto sleighs. Each log was wrapped in chains tied to horses on the opposite side of the sleigh. When the horses started forward, they dragged the log up a ramp toward the top loader. If the horses went too fast or, worst of all, spooked, it was nearly impossible for the man to save himself. The numbers added up quickly.[2]

Local hospitals, most often run by Catholic religious orders, developed a system of hospital tickets as a form of makeshift insurance for the men. Toward the be-ginning of the lumber season, when all the men had been hired on for the season, nuns from hospitals would travel camp to camp, selling tickets. Once purchased, a ticket was good for a year, admitting the holder for treatment should an accident occur. By spring, the hospitals would be full of convalescing men. Men who saved nothing for farms, education, clothing, or books often put aside enough to buy a hospital ticket. There were few things a lumberjack could be as sure of as the likelihood of his own injury.[3]

But nothing caused as much damage to human flesh as the "break up" that came in the spring. When the winter snows melted, ending the logging season, the cut had to be floated downriver to the mills. The river drive was both the most dangerous and highest paid work in the lumber season. Logs, which had been stacked by the river all winter, were pushed in as the ice began to break. From there a crew of "river hogs" began a process memoirists tend to describe as picturesque, but might just as easily be described as horrifying. As thousands of logs drifted downriver, the river hogs were tasked with keeping the drive moving. And so, in the inevitable case of a jam, it was their job to walk out onto the churning mass of logs and break it.

This was highly skilled work. At a bare minimum it meant spending up to sixteen hours a day either in icy snowmelt up to their hips or balancing on top of a log. Men greased their legs under their clothes with lard to stay warm. But there is only so much lard can do. Fighting frostbite, they took on incredible physical feats. Frank A. Johnson, a lumber scout, recorded in his 1871 diary that men would ride a single log for up to two or three miles, keeping careful balance.[4]

When a jam occurred, the work grew exponentially more arduous and difficult. With thousands (if not millions) of logs floating on the icy, rapid current, these jams could be enormous. The largest spanned miles. Toward the front, where the combined pressure of millions of logs was at its strongest, jams could tower ten or even twenty feet over the river, multistory jumbles of wood. The groaning caused by so many logs could be heard miles away, and lead to up to thirty hours of straight work—often fortified only by whiskey. Men headed out onto the jam armed only with peavies, simple tools of long wooden sticks with a metal spike on the end, to break it—testing and moving logs near the front, searching for a key log that would loosen the flood of timber.

Exhausted, clumsy with cold, the men had to trust their intuition and skill to ensure they were not in the wrong place when the jam broke. John Nelligan remembered seeing a man run out onto a jam just as it broke, "for no reason at all." He and the other jacks watched as the man "was swept over the falls in a grinding, crashing mass of ice cakes and great sticks of timber. There was, of course, no doubt in our minds about [his] fate, for [they] were sure that no human being could live in that inferno of ice and wood and water."[5] To be in the wrong place meant, at the very best, a mangled leg. But more often it was a death sentence—pushed under the mass of moving logs, men were lucky if they were knocked unconscious before drowning.[6]

No.3059 **ST. MARY'S HOSPITAL,**

WARD
CERTIFICATE
$9.00

SISTERS OF ST. BENEDICT,
20TH AVE. WEST AND 3RD ST.

Duluth, Minn., Jan 19th 1895

This Ticket Entitles Mr. _____ upon

payment of NINE DOLLARS, to admission, medical and surgical treatment, medicine, subsistence, and nursing at the Hospital at any time during One Year from date hereof, in consequence of injury or sickness hereafter received or contracted, disabling him from manual labor, subject to the conditions endorsed hereon, and signed by him.

☞ On entering the Hospital Three Dollars will entitle a ticket holder to a private room.

EXPIRES _____  BY _____  B. F. Forrister

NOT TRANSFERABLE.  AGENT.

## CONDITIONS.

It is understood that insanity, contagious, infectious, venereal diseases or injury existing before the date of this ticket, or arising from the use of intoxicating drink, or fighting, are excluded from the Hospital Benefits under this contract.

This ticket is not transferable, and any person using it, other than the one named thereon, will be prosecuted and the ticket cancelled.

Signature _____

A hospital insurance ticket from 1895 for St. Mary's Hospital in Duluth. These tickets were sold to lumbermen in northern Minnesota by Benedictine sisters such as Sister Amata Mackett, who traveled to their camps. Courtesy of St. Scholastica Monastery Archives.

Fanciful illustrations that depicted the dangers of river work captivated readers of *Harper's Weekly* in 1887.

As at the cut, the fact that the work was deadly did not affect the jacks' willingness to engage in labor. When Arthur Hill, an eastern reporter, covered the spring drive for a local color piece in *Scribner's,* he was stunned by the constant threat of danger. "Death," he wrote, "constantly walked by the side of them on the river and made its frequent appearances in the most casual and unexpected ways." But rather than changing their work habits to avoid it, the jacks accepted death as a natural part of their work environment—in fact, Hill decided, it was because death "was so casual that it was treated almost callously." No matter the dangers,

the drive had to go on. No mere human misfortune or agency could stop it. Not even death could stop it. A slight miscalculation, a slight misstep and a man might disappear beneath the logs on which he had worked. The body was recovered at once if possible. The work went on. Jaws set a little harder, eyes blinked away moisture which might distort vision and prove fatal, feet stepped a little more carefully, and that was all.[7]

Lumberjacks worked the constant presence of death into the fabric of their culture. Their games, songs, and stories orbited around macabre themes. In some instances, death was treated casually, or, as Hill would have it, callously. For instance, river hogs played a game in which they stood on either end of a log and tried to roll the other off. They called it "kill"—an appropriate name given that the skill to stay atop a spinning log could well save a worker's life. Even when the danger was clear, foremen fretted that men did not take the threat of death seriously. Josephine Grattan, wife of the foreman of a camp in Michigan, noted regularly in her diary her husband's concern about the safety of the men. Getting new labor in from distant markets was difficult, and foremen were aware that without careful diligence—something lumberjacks seemed loathe to exercise—the men could easily hurt themselves. Grattan complained that despite her husband's admonitions, "the men new to this dangerous work will not exercise due care as they should. They play and tease, 'horseplay' on the river, the older men call it."[8]

But while horseplay may have been callous, the men took death more seriously in their songs, especially eulogies to a dead jack. Some of these were extremely local—when Earl Clifton Beck set out to capture the songs of Michigan shanty boys,[9] he discovered a few that were sung only across a few counties. Others, like the tale of Young Munroe who died in "The Jam on Gerry's Rocks, or the Ballad of Young Monroe," show up in compilations of lumber songs not only throughout the lake states but also in the Pacific Northwest. The men eulogized in these ballads were stand-ins for hundreds of others. While each song purported to be about a single gallant individual, their singing makes clear that they were about men, not a single man. One song sung throughout Michigan, with likely roots in the Maine camps, included, in the thumb of Michigan, these lines:

> Jimmy Judge was this young man's name,
> I mean to let you know;
> I mean to sound his precious name
> Wherever I do go.

In the Upper Peninsula, this theoretically self-same young man was honored as "Jimmie Jot."[10] For those singing, he could have doubtless been any number of names—the names of men they had lost to the rivers or woods.

All the death ballads follow a set of simple conventions. "The Jam on Gerry's Rocks," as the most well remembered and frequently sung of these ballads, includes nearly every standard convention of a lumber ballad addressing death. After

A massive log jam on the St. Croix River between Minnesota and Wisconsin became an attraction in 1886 as locals posed for photographs among the felled pines. Courtesy of the Washington County Historical Society.

calling the "true-born shanty boys" to "pay attention and listen unto me," the narrator introduces our young hero, "a young shanty boy, so tall, genteel, and brave." Youth, beauty, and bravery were the essential elements for any tragic death in the woods. Jimmy Whalen, the hero of another, was told by his foreman, "you're young, you're smart, you're active"; in "'Twas on the Napanee" the hero is "a brave and comely youth," and Harry Dunn is "a fair young man." Their youth and beauty come to be important only later, when their mangled bodies are retrieved. For them to be as ugly as they will be in death, they needed to be beautiful in life. Their bravery is always, however, central to what comes next.

In the second verse of "Gerry's Rocks" comes the jam itself, "logs . . . piled up mountain-high." While lumber balladeers occasionally commemorated death in the woods themselves, as in the beautiful "John Robertson" or the somewhat satirical "The Kid," the majority focused on dramatic deaths on the river. Not only did the river drive have a higher mortality rate than woods work, death there also came more suddenly, more violently, and, it would seem, more picturesquely.

Monroe is next required to do something that carefully treads the line between boldly brave and spectacularly stupid. This, again, is a standard element of the eulogy ballad. There is always a job that needs to be done, and it is always, for some reason, remarkably dangerous. If the jam itself does not seem threatening enough, an element of superstitious fear is added. In "Gerry's Rocks," there is both a terrifying jam, which "we could not keep . . . clear," and the added horror of the jam occurring on a Sunday, when lumberjacks typically refused to work. So when Monroe calls to "Turn out, brave boys; your hearts are void of fear," many of the lumberjacks "hid from sight / For to work on jams on Sunday they did not think it right." Our hero, Monroe, refuses to recognize such superstition. As a foreman, his utmost obedience belongs with the job. In those songs that concern regular lumberjacks or river hogs, their obedience belongs with the foreman, as in "The Old Tamarack Dam" when, as a dam broke,

> we rode her down to dead water
> Our foreman cried, "Boys, all obey."
> Not a man in that crew but could ride her;
> Not a man in that crew was afraid.

And then, calamity: the forces of nature overcome the forces of man, and obedience to the job leads to the heroic and tragic death of the lumberjack. Young Monroe had "not rolled off many logs" until he turned to warn his men that "you boys be on your guard: that jam will soon give way." Almost immediately "the jam did break and go / And it carried off those six brave youths, and their foreman, young Monroe." While songs about death in the camps could take several verses to describe the exact accident, in ballads concerning death on the river, little more detail was ever given of how things went awry—little was needed. A jam came, always, with the threat of sudden death. Or as the ballad "James Whalen" put it: "For death is like an arrow; it's ready to destroy / The Pride of many a father's heart, likewise a mother's joy."[11]

The rest of the boys then rush to the river to find Monroe. As when hats went around for injured men in camps to collect donations, lumberjacks took pride in their care for their fellow jack. After Monroe and his men are carried off, the rest of the men "to search for their dead bodies to the river they did steer." When the men finally reach him, they find Monroe utterly transformed, "crushed and bleeding on the beach."

In one of the earliest known photographs of a log drive in the Upper Midwest, lumberjacks from the Elias Moses lumber camp use jam pikes and peavies to maneuver logs down the Rum River, circa 1863. Photograph by Benjamin Franklin Upton. Courtesy of the Edward A. Bromley Collection, Hennepin County Library.

This transformation, from man to carcass at the hands of nature, runs through the many woods ballads; it is here, in understanding and describing the terrible power of nature over their lives, that lumberjacks depart sharply from the language of mastery that characterized Gilded Age middle-class discourses on masculinity. Working-class men understood that, like their economic fates, their bodies were not their own. But for those who worked in extractive industries, this awareness could never be far below the surface. While mastery of self relies on the idea that the mind can control the body, lumberjack ballads focused on the body itself—its frailty as well as its strength.[12]

Lumberjacks drive logs over the falls of the Apple River in Wisconsin, circa 1865. Photograph by Benjamin Franklin Upton. Courtesy of the Minnesota Historical Society.

These ballads frankly acknowledge the terrible power nature had to transform men. In their dramatic deaths, they not only lost mastery of their bodies, but became something less than human. If the self was the power to restrain and master the flesh, then the bodies described in lumberjack ballads have lost their selves—they have become merely flesh, destroyed by the powerful forces of nature. In "Old Tamarack Dam," the body that is retrieved is unrecognizable as human: "Every bone in his body was broken / And his flesh hung in tatters and strings." In "The Death of Harry Bradford," the scene is more gruesome still: "His ribs were broke, his back was broke, his legs were broke also; / And his brains they lay beneath the deck in the cold and bloody snow." Often the handsome appearance of the lumber-jack, established in the first two stanzas, is brought back for contrast, as in "On the Beau Shai River," where

> 'twould break your heart with pity
> When they brought him out on shore
> For to see such lovely features
> Where the rocks had cut and tore.[13]

Songs like "The Jam on Gerry's Rocks" were among the most popular of the lum-berjack tradition—sung often enough in camps that hundreds of versions were recorded by folklorists. By telling this story to greenhorns, and repeating it among themselves, lumberjacks acknowledged the terrible power of nature over their lives and bodies. Self-mastery was, in this context, a mindless exercise—for it was all too clear that their selves were subject to forces well beyond their control.

Even without injury, the woods loomed as a horrifying source of danger and vi-olence. Being surrounded by miles of trees, many taller than the tallest buildings any men had seen, effectively separated the men from the outside world. Illness in camp could be a death sentence. While men could get a ride out on supply sleighs, and did so when injured and going to the hospital, it was often days if not weeks be-tween sleigh runs into the nearest towns. Those trips, easily up to thirty miles, took at least a full day of exposure in subzero temperatures. It was not an easy trip, nor one taken lightly. Yet men walked through the woods constantly.

Lumberjacks, especially in the early days of Northwoods lumbering, were part of a culture that understood the woods—untamed, dark, and wild—as a sign of barbarity, their cultivation a signal of the march of progress. To the early nineteenth-century American mind, forests were associated with brutishness, darkness, and barrenness. Early American settlers associated the wilderness with biblical ideas of Jesus cast forth into the wilderness: untamed land was the enemy of civilization and the march of progress. Gustave de Beaumont, who visited Mich-igan in 1831, when Saginaw was little more than a collection of huts, wrote that an American "who lives in the country spends half his time fighting his natural enemy, the forest; he goes at it without respite. . . . The absence of trees is the mark of civili-zation, as their presence indicates barbarity."[14]

While American attitudes toward nature and the wild would undergo a sea change across the nineteenth century, it is clear that at least the initial lumberers saw the woods not as a place of innocence away from industry, but as an uncon-quered danger to be tamed and cleared in the name of civilization.[15] John Nowlin, a

Stories and songs repeated in the camps as entertainment also served to educate young jacks about the dangers of the woods. "A Logger's Camp at Night" was published in *Harper's Weekly* in 1886.

lumberjack who came from upstate New York to work in the woods of Michigan in the 1840s, later wrote that "the grand old forest was melting away . . . the light of civilization had dawned on us. We had cleared up what was a few years before, the lair of the wolf and the hunting ground of the red man."[16] The notion of the woods as wild, untamed, and dangerous colored the lumberjacks' every day as they labored in the woods.

This vision of the woods shot through the heart of lumberjack lore and mythology. Their stories and songs expressed both the danger inherent to their jobs and their discomfort with the woods. While many songs recounted the terrible deaths that occurred in the woods, and games mimicked the physical danger that came from lumbering, it was in tall tales that the woods emerge as a character unto themselves. Later, especially in early twentieth-century Paul Bunyan stories, the lumberjack emerged triumphant as a conqueror of nature. But for those who lived in the camps in the height of lumbering from the 1860s through 1900, the woods were not easily conquered. Stories often fell into one of two categories: tales of heroic adventures that the lumberjacks had supposedly had himself, or tall tales.

Tall tales were a central part of the experience of camp life. During evenings and on Sundays, storytelling and the singing of songs were the central forms of entertainment for lumberjacks. Men would gather and sit on the long benches that ran down either side of the bunkhouse, known as the deacon's seat. From here, they took turns spinning tales. Stories traveled camp to camp with the itinerant lumberjacks, some becoming common legends. Comparing stories from Minnesota to those from the Upper Peninsula of Michigan, it is clear that men who never physically crossed paths still shared the same oral tradition. For new lumberjacks, these stories were a form of initiation, a statement of the values, traditions, and boundaries of the lumberjack community.[17] In many of the tales, the woods were full of perils both natural and supernatural.

Many tall tales revolved around a set of supernatural beings that dwelled (just out of sight) in the trees. There was the agropelter, who hid in darkness among the upper branches of the pines, and with his long arms (sometimes only two, occasionally up to six) threw branches, pinecones, and sometimes stones down at men below. There was the hodag, with a spiny back, lethal tail, and sharp teeth in his fur-covered, horned head. He dwelt in the shallows of rivers, terrorizing and occasionally eating lumberjacks.[18] There were ghosts and spooks as well as the very real dangers of bears, wolves, and, of course, freezing to death. These stories were often brought out for the benefit of "greenhorns," or novice lumberjacks. Willis Ward, who worked the Michigan camps in the 1890s, remembered that among many pranks, "one was to create fear among novices about savage animals supposed to abound in the forest." He recalled that when a greenhorn questioned the existence of the hodag, as he had never seen one in a zoo, he was assured "that they were so savage that they could not be captured alive and besides they only came out after dark."[19] Old-timers would then hide in the dark woods as men made their way back to camp, howling and barking, seeing if they could force the greenhorns to break into a run.

These are games, stories, and jokes—no lumberjack took seriously, at least after his greenhorn days, the idea that the forest was full of these mythical creatures. But they are revealing nonetheless. They display an attitude toward nature that is distinctly unlike later, romanticized images of the lumberjack as a man who was one with nature: a man who came out of the woods himself. They also differ sharply from the idealization of the natural world promoted by middle-class intellectuals in transcendentalist circles a quarter century earlier. This was not wilderness as tonic. The lumberjacks saw, instead, the wilderness as a thing to be conquered for capital gain—and as a threat to be tamed. Above all, in the lore and songs of lumberjacks, nature was a source of constant danger. Violence for lumberjacks in

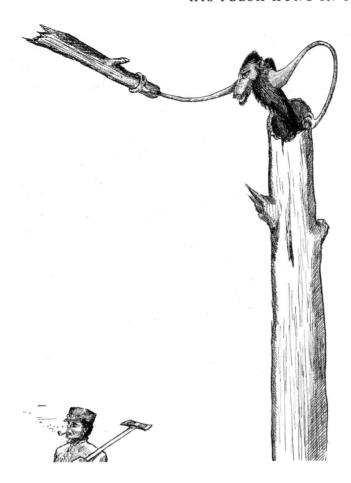

The "agropelter," one of the fearsome beasts rumored to stalk unsuspecting jacks in the Northwoods, as illustrated by Coert du Bois and published in *Fearsome Creatures of the Lumberwoods,* a publication from 1910 by William Cox, Minnesota's first state forester and commissioner of conservation.

the winter came, first and foremost, from the woods and rivers themselves. Nature constantly threatened to quite literally unman them; their songs, especially, focused with fierce intensity on the possibility of not just bodily harm, but bodily destruction. Set against a hegemonic middle-class masculinity that prized self-possession and self-restraint, the lumberjack's intense awareness of how little control they had over their bodies and lives created a unique understanding of masculinity, risk, and violence. The almost total divergence of their masculinity from middle-class ideals describes a gendered class divide that was nearly impenetrable.

That lumberjacks were so willing to engage in risk and chance—whether it be by riding the river or gambling in saloons in town—was a part of an ongoing dialogue between risk and control in late nineteenth-century American life, one whose contours were shaped by class and conflicting ideals of masculinity.[20] In *Something for*

*Nothing,* his history of gambling in America, Jackson Lears explores the history of this dichotomy. While tracing the culture of control to a Protestant impulse for de-mystifying the world, he points out that the vernacular culture of chance was never fully wiped out in America. In constant tension with the myth of the self-made man was the potent character of the confidence man—a trickster who made his fortune not by hard work but by luck. Chance and luck were tied to an understanding of the world as fundamentally unknowable, controlled by forces beyond the rational mind that could not be influenced by self-controlled striving. Gambling, chancing it, and engaging in risk were only a short step removed from the mysticism of animism and fortune telling. Those who continued to gamble, to engage in confidence games, and to take risks were in many ways openly defying the dominant cultural imperatives of the time. To understand the vital importance of risk in the culture of aggressive manhood among lumberjacks, it is necessary to outline the ideals of dominant, middle-class masculinity in the nineteenth century. For it was in their embrace of risk and chance that lumberjacks differentiated their culture of working-class, rural, aggressive manhood most severely from the ideals of the middle class.

Embracing risk rejected everything the respectable middle-class man stood for in the Gilded Age.[21] In the late nineteenth century masculinity revolved around two sets of ideas that, while seemingly contradictory, reinforced one another. One set of ideals valorized the tough, market-focused achiever of the Gilded Age city. As entrepreneurs, professionals, and shopkeepers found themselves increasingly successful in the marketplace, and coalesced as a solid middle class in the antebel-lum era, a code of ethics for marketplace engagement emerged in advice manuals and religious texts aimed at young middle-class men. These books stressed the vital importance of total honesty and ceaseless effort. Marketplace interactions in northern cities now took place among men who knew little or nothing about one another. In this bewildering new context, a man's honesty and ceaseless effort to-ward virtuous commercial success took on paramount importance. This honest man was set against the "confidence man," a trickster who used false pretenses for financial gain without honest work. The masculine achiever worked ceaselessly, tirelessly, and honestly to improve his reputation and his fortune.[22]

This idealized striver existed beside another ideal: an inward-facing man locked in battle with his own sins and licentiousness. Any pleasure of the flesh was both sinful and, when indulged, a sign of weakness and effeminacy. Focusing particular attention and energy on adolescent boys, pamphlets, lecturers, and religious lead-ers in the mid- to late nineteenth century encouraged a strong ethic of self-mastery. While this self-mastery was intended to inculcate humility and virtue, it was not, in fact, necessarily opposed to the ethics that governed marketplace behavior for

CAMPING IN THE WOODS

Even while "roughing it," men of the Gilded Age were often depicted as having refined tastes, as in this 1863 lithograph by Currier & Ives, *Camping in the Woods,* "Laying Off." Courtesy of the Whitney Collections of Sporting Art, Yale University Art Gallery.

middle-class men. As historian Anthony Rotundo explains, "By calling for such total self-control, the ideal of the Christian Gentleman demanded a conquest of the inner environment much like the conquest of the outer environment for which the Masculine Achiever called."[23]

Together, these strands of masculine ideals created a code of conduct and gender ideal built to navigate an increasingly urban and competitive marketplace. For, despite these ideals' widespread cultural dominance, they were firmly rooted in the unique economic experience of the middle class. Market interactions and urban environments protected the body of the middle-class man from risk. Advice centering on the control of the self—on the curbing of appetites, protection of reputation, and diligent application to capital gain—assumed that the body itself was safe and could be controlled. In addition to basic safety, these codes of masculinity rested on the assumption that economic gain was possible. While risk of failure was inherent, risk of death was not—and while success was not guaranteed, it was at least possible. The quickly changing economy of the late nineteenth century undermined the economic underpinnings of this brand of manliness, causing what has been identified by scholars as a crisis in masculinity in the Gilded Age. But at the time that lumberjacks in the Northwoods developed their own, working-class masculinity they did so against the backdrop of a culture that emphasized self-control, self-mastery, and, in many ways, self-preservation above all else.[24]

In this culture, by engaging in risk, whether it was by gambling in saloons or riding the logs, lumberjacks were flying in the face of the culture of restraint and self-control that formed the basis of late nineteenth-century manliness. The ideal white, middle-class man was a creation of his own willpower. By controlling his appetites, by restraining his worst impulses, he reaffirmed his own sense of self.[25] In contrast, the aggressive masculinity of the lumberjack rejected this restraint. In the eyes of middle-class observers this rejection of self-mastery walked the line between quaint and pathetic. The middle classes of the nineteenth century saw working-class men as, in the words of historian Carol Srole, "brutish or hypermasculine."[26] It is easy for historians to do the same; they have all-too-often analyzed working-class masculinity from this position. But what appears to be savagery and license from the viewpoint of the middle classes looks entirely different from the perspective of a man whose own life was on the line.

For a lumberjack, nothing could be more natural than the rejection of mastery. After all, he was more aware than most of the untamed and fundamentally untamable nature of wilderness. The most careful risk assessment could not stop a widowmaker from destroying a man's life. A jam could bring death without warning, and without reason. A culture of control was predicated not only on the mastery of one's self, but also the attempt to master risk of all kinds. In acknowledging the woods' power over life and death, in imbuing the trees with personalities, creatures, and caprices of their own, lumberjacks were embracing an irrational world—the power of nature, luck, and chance over their lives. Here, lumberjacks stood apart from many of their working-class peers. Factory work was inherently dangerous, almost ludicrously so. But by the late nineteenth century, the Knights of Labor and other unions had begun to demand safety as part of labor organizing.[27] No such movement emerged among lumberjacks until the 1917 strikes.

The middle-class masculinity that encouraged self-mastery and the prescriptive literature that promoted it assumed that the spoils of hard work were just economic rewards. In the early days of lumbering across the lake states, while land was still free—or, rather, easily stolen—and entry costs low, work could, and indeed did, result in economic success. Early owners often began as loggers. But as the industry

Dice, a game of chance, played in the bunkhouse at Joe Dunning's Camp 2, forty miles north of Grand Rapids, Minnesota, circa 1903. Courtesy of the Minnesota Historical Society.

grew, this fluidity disappeared in the 1870s and 1880s. Larger owners began to consolidate their holdings. America's industrial barons quickly became millionaires, and instead of identifying as, and living among, lumbermen, they began to divide by class. Lumber barons lived next door to railroad barons and hobnobbed with the owners of the mines that operated across the iron ranges. Increasingly, even the higher paid positions in camp required the trappings of class, be it education or an introduction to an owner. For the average lumberjack, often an immigrant, illiterate, or both, there was little hope of economic advancement. With risk built into the everyday texture of their lives, there was little reason for a lumberjack to practice self-mastery. As Lears argues, "to court grace, luck and fortune through serious play is to circumvent what passes for common sense and seek to spring the trap of the predictable."[28]

When skill cannot save a man from death, when work does not lead to reward, and when the caprices of a natural world whose violence was as unpredictable as

Camp horseplay for the lumberjacks of the Morgan Lumber and Cedar Company near Foster City, Michigan, included a greased pig competition, circa 1915. Courtesy of Dickinson County Library, Iron Mountain, Michigan.

it was severe rules a man's life, luck and risk take on a special power.[29] The rational self-mastery of the middle classes was irrational for a lumberjack. Even skill only went so far in the face of a raging flood, falling tree, or explosive fire. For a lumberjack, the fate of his body was outside his control.

No song better illustrates the lumberjack's understanding of luck and violence than "The Wild Mustard River." The song's origins are nearly impossible to trace. The tune is "When You and I Were Young, Maggie," a song first popular in the late 1860s, which puts at the very least a cap on its earliest origin date as the 1870s. Earl Beck, who collected the song in his book of Michigan lumber songs, traced it back to either Wisconsin or a river near Atlanta, Michigan, in the upper half of the Lower Peninsula, which was logged in the 1880s. Alan Lomax, the most thorough recorder of lumberjack songs, notes only that it was a popular lumber song when he recorded a version in 1938. But, unlike most other songs, it appears in compilations from more than one state and appears to have enjoyed a popularity on par with "Gerry's Rocks."

A lumberjack tests his skill and navigates the rapids near the Kilbourn Dam on the Wisconsin River at Wisconsin Dells, circa 1886. Photograph by H. H. Bennett. Courtesy of the Wisconsin Historical Society, WHS-4270.

The song is an argument for the power of natural violence over human endeavor—despite skill, luck, and effort, the river would ultimately win. It focuses on the story of Johnny Stile, who had "worked oftener than any other." He was the best of the best, "reckless and wild," and the narrative tells us that "on the river there was none any better."[30] Here Johnny is given all the attributes of the best lumberjacks: he was reckless, wild, and willing to take on risk for gain. Moreover, he had something more elusive: skill. Because he had worked "oftener" than anyone, he was the best. He was, in short, the man least likely to be taken down by the force of nature.

But the song makes clear that neither his skill nor his experience were the deciding factors in his fate—but rather his luck at the hands of nature. On the day the river was flooded from the reservoir, "his luck went against him." His foot caught in a jam, and he was pulled under into the raging current. The structure of the song emphasizes the vital role luck played: the first three verses exist only to set up both the danger of the river—whose water came "rustling and rolling"—and the skill, experience, strength, and bravery of the hero. The fourth verse then begins with the turn in luck, the description of the accident, and the force of the water that took him under as it ran "a-howling."

The rest of the song follows the standards of other songs like "The Jam at Gerry's Rocks," although it is a particularly gruesome example. The men spend an hour working, "till sweat down [them] poured," to find Johnny's body. Finally, they find the corpse. The powerful lumberjack is undone by the violence of the river. When they pulled the body out of the water, "it looked like our Johnny no more." Skill, strength, and an agile and accomplished self and body were completely destroyed: "his flesh was all cut up in ringlets / And rolled out as flat as your hand." The jacks lay him to rest, and "hold peace here on this earth for his body," a body once vital and filled with skill, energy, and the muscular strength that the middle classes would come to valorize. Here lumberjacks behaved similarly to other working-class men of the late nineteenth century who found their manhood challenged by an economy that left little chance for promotion. Cattlemen, as historian Jacqueline M. Moore has noted, also defined their masculinity as "a balance between risk and calculation."[31] For those working in the dangerous extractive industries of the West, there was little more for which to hope.

The lumberjacks who came to work in the Northwoods entered a world of risk and violence, and took part themselves in one of the greatest acts of environmental violence. As they shaped their understanding of their bodies and deaths, they created a culture that celebrated bravery and skill. For many, it was their only choice, for as "The Ballad of Harry Dunn," the ballad that began this chapter, told any jack who might hear it sung one night around the stove:

> There is many a wild Canadian boy who leaves his happy home
> And longing for excitement to Michigan will roam;
> But in less than three weeks after a telegram will come,
> Saying "Your boy was killed in the lumbering wood, and his body we'll
> send home."[32]

But nature's capricious cruelty was not the only form of violence that shaped the lives of these men. Far off in the Northwoods, away from the towns, lumberjacks took violence on as a core part of their identity.

# THREE

# ON GREENHORNS AND WHITE MEN

## SKILL AND THE BOUNDARIES OF RACE

Halfway through their tour, visitors to Minnesota's Forest History Center in Grand Rapids encounter a spirited sketch. For thirty or so minutes they have followed their costumed interpreter as he tells them all about life in a turn-of-the-century camp, and at this point the guests have likely met the cook and maybe the ink-slinger (the camp clerk). Outside the sawyer's hut, families, couples, and restless children sit down on long wooden benches to hear how, exactly, the men of the Northwoods loaded logs onto sleighs. As the audience listens, one jack explains the process—which involved chaining the log to horses and then having them pull it up an incline. The log rolled up toward a man who stood balanced precariously atop the logs: the top loader. His job was to ensure that when the log reached the top of the pile, it was settled into place securely enough to stay there.

But just at this point, several more interpreters come rushing up, interrupting and asking for the guide's advice. Eldon Marples, the camp's very best top loader, has suffered a terrible accident and died. You see, the ground crew was made up of a couple of greenhorns, and they didn't know the difference between throwing a Saginaw and a St. Croix. When they were meant to hold back the wide end of a tapered log, they held back the narrow end instead, causing the log to roll out of control and hit Eldon. As the men begin to debate where to store his body until it can be returned to his widow in town, two men rush by carrying a wooden gurney with work pants and a flannel shirt laid out on it: looks like the log got him good.[1]

Mike Robertson, a former jack who worked in the Red River Valley in the 1910s, remembered watching a similar event in person: an inexperienced top loader failed to settle a log properly—it slipped over the top of a pile, rolled down the other side, and crushed the leg of a fellow jack. But the man was neither a crushed suit of

In a staged photograph, a mock brawl breaks out in the bunkhouse of a Fletcher lumber camp near Onaway, Michigan, in 1901. Courtesy of the Besser Museum for Northeast Michigan.

clothes, nor was he joking. Undaunted by his broken bones, he "got up and killed the man that missed it just by stomping him to death with the caulks on his boots."[2]

Along with women and drink, fighting of all kinds was theoretically off limits to jacks in camp. But there were exceptions to the rule, and this was apparently one of them. Robertson passed no judgment: the top loader had failed to be a skilled worker, and while the response was, perhaps, surprisingly disproportionate, it was not uncalled for.

There were other circumstances where violence was allowed. It's not that being violent made a lumberjack into a man, or a man into a lumberjack. But it was a way of policing boundaries. In 1876 Francis Flynn, a lumberjack and Civil War Veteran, wrote home to his family that he "thought the soldier wer rough but they are good compared wit these fellows."[3] But, whether or not Flynn could see it, this roughness—the violence in which jacks regularly indulged—had a direction. Violence was not merely a pastime, but a way of enforcing authority and clarifying hierarchy.

"Every new arrival at camp was closely viewed and interviewed, by the boys," re-called Florence Tripp, years after he stopped working as a lumberjack in the woods. "When it was learned that this was his first experience in the lumber woods," he noted, "he became the object of special interest." This was because new jacks were ripe for "initiation." A new jack was walking into a world in which his standing was unclear. Among the workingmen the proof of dominance came, beyond anything else, from a proof not only of willingness to engage in risk, but of carefully learned skill.[4] In contests of strength and skill, of violence and risk, men within the camps used proof of manhood as a method of constructing a hierarchy.

Manhood was not defined by any one trait. Neither race, nor skill, nor reputa-tion alone made a man. But by looking through multiple lenses and seeking out the intersections of these traits, a clearer picture emerges; one in which jacks created not one but many hierarchies and reinforced them with violence.[5] If a man was ra-cially "inferior," violence was acceptable. If a man's skills were inferior, violence was acceptable. Exploring the way violence was used in the camps exposes a com-plicated set of ideas that combined nineteenth-century understandings of savagery and civilization (which have, most often, been explored as primarily middle-class preoccupations) with working-class valorization of violence and skill. Lumberjacks defined their manhood in the tensions between contemporary ideas of savagery, exemplified by a persistent interest in proving rough masculinity, and civilization, which they demonstrated through a mastery of learned skills.

The centrality of violence to working-class masculinity in the nineteenth century is well established, although scholars differ as to both its origins and its meanings not least because, especially with manhood, historians do not always agree on *what* they are analyzing or why. As long ago as 1996 Gail Bederman observed that "two types of 'men's history' are being written these days. One builds on twenty years of women's history scholarship, analyzing masculinity as part of larger gender and cultural processes. The other . . . looks to the past to see how men in earlier gener-ations understood (and misunderstood) themselves as men." Despite almost thirty years of scholarship, the story remains largely the same. As Bruce Dorsey wrote in 2012, echoing Bederman, "it seems that histories solely about men and groups of men show no signs of retreating into a bygone pioneer era of men's history."[6] This seems especially true in terms of studies that focus particularly on violence, in which the category of "masculine" is often taken for granted as a stable force.[7]

Assuming that "masculine" has a fixed meaning does not account for the use of gender to establish hierarchy and power within a homosocial world. Instead, it is helpful to draw on the frameworks of historians like Susan Lee Johnson, Lorien

Foote, and Martha Santos who conceive of gender in terms of power dynamics, in which masculinity is a way of creating and enforcing hierarchies.[8] For the lumberjack the use of violence was a way of establishing power and dominance over fellow lumberjacks in a place where other methods of establishing masculine prerogative were few and far between.[9]

Lumberjacks did not have access to many of the metrics by which men established their dominance in the nineteenth century. Mastery, either over one's self or over a family, was useless in a world where work could, and did, so routinely break the body. Moreover, especially during the years in which they actively lumbered, few jacks had any dependents. While recent histories have done excellent work in seeing men as full people who defined their identity as much by private as by public life, this is less pertinent to men who had nothing that could be accurately described as a private life.[10]

From the outside, in fact, lumberjacks seemed to have nothing at all upon which to base any claim to manhood. In fact, their status as itinerant laborers often marked them, in the eyes of their more settled contemporaries, as something somewhat less than men. Moreover, while artisan laborers based their claims to manhood on skill, lumber companies did not publicly affirm that their laborers needed any skills whatsoever. And, indeed, while some positions required previous experience, the majority of labor needed for camps was relatively unskilled, and men were able to learn on the job. For those just outside the camps, whether they were townspeople or labor recruiters, lumberjacks were part of a larger network of unskilled itinerant laborers, soon named hobos, who began to plague the country in the late nineteenth century.[11]

However, while their contemporaries understood lumberjacks as unskilled laborers, within the world of the camp skill was highly prized. The "worth and dignity" of a particular jack rested heavily upon his ability to navigate the dangers of his work environment, balancing carefully acquired skills against the bravado of engaging in high-risk activities. Negotiating this balance—showing that he was both willing to engage in risky behavior and had the skill to survive it—was at the heart of a lumberjack's expression of his manhood. Examining the use of violence within the homosocial worlds of lumberjacks exposes one of the most fundamental vectors upon which these itinerant laborers based their claims to masculine authority.

In writing about the use of violence in rural Brazil, Martha Santos conceptualizes honor as functioning through "the interplay of a man's conceptualization of his own worth and dignity and the social recognition or estimation by other members of his community."[12] The result of this is a preoccupation with reputation. This preoccupation is only magnified when the stakes are lower. While worth in middle-class milieus could be roughly measured by market value,[13] working-class masculinity and reputation rested on less immediately measurable qualities. As a result, even historians who have carefully studied working-class masculinity have had trouble differentiating among workers. Nancy Quam-Wickham's excellent study of masculinity within the western extractive industries carefully traces the importance of skill, and the valorization of skill in western folklore, as a fundamental building block for the "solidarity between workers." She allows that the social cohesion brought on by initiation rights and storytelling was tenuous, and even notes the gendered language in which men differentiated themselves from one another, but does not fully delve into the multiple ways in which extractive workers, including loggers, constructed gendered hierarchies that solidified racial, class, and skill differences among the men.[14]

The key to understanding hierarchies within the camp is to recognize skill not as a stable fact (as with someone who has the skill of computer programing), but as a category (as for someone who is considered a skilled programmer). Skill is, like gender often is, a way of demonstrating power. When a worker is considered skilled, and another not, that does, of course, denote a difference in ability to carry out certain tasks. But there is also an ideological component that becomes apparent when we consider *which* skills are valued and which are not. This is most obvious within sexual division of labor: there is not necessarily a difference in the physical abilities needed for cooking while holding a child compared with cooking while directing a sous chef, but one is considered a skill, the other not. Beginning in the 1980s, however, historians began to examine the ways in which skill related to gendered power relations even within same-sex working worlds.[15]

Sometimes the gendering of skill is obvious: in California mines, Mexican men were forced to do cooking and cleaning—feminine labor—by their Anglo-American counterparts as a way of enforcing a gendered hierarchy over who in the camp did "men's" work. This was not precisely true of the way lumberjacks worked. The cooks, perhaps for this reason, or perhaps for their outsized importance in camp life, were known to be particularly violent and domineering. There were, however, other roles to be taken on—playing women in dances, for instance—that were obviously feminine.

But even when the skills themselves were not particularly gendered, the way in which boundaries were enforced was. The men of lumber camps used violence to control the boundaries of skill. Since their manhood was tied to their reputations, and their reputations to their skill, it was vital to these men that their work not be seen as "unskilled labor" but rather as a highly skilled craft. The importance

While their socks dry from the rafters, young lumberjacks, or "greenhorns," sit along the "deacon's bench" in the bunkhouse of Ole Emerson's logging camp near Cable, Wisconsin, circa 1905. Photograph by Melvin E. Diemer. Courtesy of the Minnesota Historical Society.

lumberjacks put upon skilled labor is clearest in their treatment of "greenhorns," or new lumberjacks who had never worked in the woods before.

When greenhorns arrived in the camps they came in unproven. From the moment of their arrival their fellow workers impressed upon them the importance of learned skill within the lumber industry. In the evenings those sitting on the deacon's bench (the long benches that ran the length of the bunks) told the newcomers stories. Stories within camps largely consisted of inflated tales of derring-do and incredible feats of skill. As a "sky pilot," or itinerant preacher, recalled, "Here the man who can recount the 'toughest' stories concerning himself, and has figured in the most scrapes, is often considered the greatest hero."[16] Eventually, these tall tales translated to practical feats. Men staged attempts to stack logs as high as they could possibly go on a sleigh, creating enormous, unwieldy, and impractical loads, and then stood to pose by them. The pictures would often include a scaler (the man

A top loader stands high above the rest of his team on a stack of logs in northern Michigan, circa 1880. Show loads like this were not intended to be pulled but were instead photographed as proof of the loader's skill. Courtesy of Library of Congress.

in charge of measuring the logs) standing by with his scale to show just how high the pile went. Some stretch twenty or thirty feet up, and the largest weighed well above twenty-five tons.[17] These loads were almost unmovable, but the message they sent, of enormous skill and impossible strength, was unmistakable.

Tall tales and feats of skill (and occasional violent interruptions) impressed upon newcomers the importance of skill in the camp. But the place of greenhorns as inferior, emasculated, and unskilled workers was more practically and uniformly policed through games and pranks. Lumberjacks in the Northwoods remembered "fun" as a particularly violent pastime. John Nelligan, for instance, wrote about "sheep," a game in which one man would be bundled "tightly in a heavy blanket" and carried by two other jacks who would play the parts of the farmer and the sheep buyer. These two would then get into a staged argument about the "sheep's" weight. To solve it, "they would let it [the bundled jack] down repeatedly on 'scales.'

The 'scales' was a sharply pointed stick and the 'sheep' was always thrown onto the 'scales' in such a way that the point of the stick came into violent contact with the tender, rear central portion of his anatomy." There was also "jack in the dark, where are you?" which essentially consisted of beating a blindfolded jack until he got his bearings well enough to hit back, and many others.[18]

There are two key through lines to all these games: they were violent, and that violence was directed, almost without fail, against greenhorns. Greenhorns were the butt not only of violent games, but of innumerable smaller practical jokes. Leonard Costley recalled of his years in the woods that, in the evening when stories were being told, "the seat of honor for the fellows was this barber chair, and us young fellows, we couldn't get too close to them. We were kind of outcasts yet; we hadn't been let into the inner circle of lumberjacks."[19]

To become part of the lumberjack community, a new logger was required to prove himself. Greenhorns were generally made to endure some degree of humiliation or hazing to be considered a "real" jack. One of the more famous greenhorn jokes was of the jack sent back to camp for a cant hook—a piece of equipment used to load logs onto sleighs. The jack returns an hour later with an old ox who has no horns explaining that "it was the only thing I could find in camp that can't hook." One jack recalled a winter where they had been forced to shoot a horse that had broken its leg. Later in the winter, a jack broke his leg. That evening, the old jacks all drew straws and then approached a greenhorn, telling him to take one. When the greenhorn asked why they were drawing straws, an old-timer explained that it was to decide who was going to shoot the jack with the broken leg. He added that "the kid was gone at sunrise."[20]

At times the gendering of these roles—the dichotomy between the older, experienced jack and his hapless ward—was made clear. Maggie Orr O'Neill, who worked on her father's camps as a cook's aid (a "cookee" in lumberjack parlance) in the 1880s remembered that "we never went over and watched them dancing, but heard them." Instead, the jacks, normally the younger greenhorns, were forced to take on the women's part. They tied handkerchiefs around one arm or grain sacks around their waists to signify that they were the women, and "you'd see four couples getting up, all men, and dancing a square dance, someone calling off."[21]

All this emphasis on skill had a purpose. While many of the games seemed to do little more than earn a man a place in the brotherhood of jacks, it was also practically necessary to ensure that new jacks had the requisite amount of skill required for the job. Labor offices were perfectly happy to send unskilled workers into the woods, even though much of the work required high levels of skill. In the Scandinavian countries from which many jacks after the 1890s hailed, lumbering was not

An advertisement for E. K. Smith, Manufacturer appeared in the *Mississippi Valley Lumberman* in 1877. Pike poles and cant hooks were essential tools during log drives. Courtesy of the Minnesota Historical Society.

Lumberjacks use cant hooks to break a log jam on the St. Louis River near Duluth, Minnesota, circa 1890s. Photograph by Crandall & Fletcher. Courtesy of the St. Louis County Historical Society, Archives and Special Collections, University of Minnesota Duluth.

labor so much as a trade, passed down from generation to generation.[22] But in the United States, few lumberjacks came from generations of woodsmen, and many new laborers had no woods experience whatsoever. To protect against accidents, inexperienced men were often relegated to low-level, dangerous work without respect for several years. The task of "road monkey"—the man who rode ahead of loads of logs clearing the ice from the sleigh tracks—was particularly dangerous but required little to no actual skill. It was given to the young, agile, and unskilled, or occasionally elderly jacks who could no longer do other work.[23]

But sometimes, despite the hierarchy of jobs, inexperienced or unskilled men found themselves in positions in which skill was vital. When their lack of skill caused them to falter, the violence that was technically banned in camp was given not only a pass, but tacit approval, as with Mike Robertson stomping the unskilled top loader to death.[24]

When violence is viewed simply as an expression of "rough" masculinity, as a more-or-less natural side-effect of homosocial worksites and living spaces, the nuance of who uses violence against whom is lost. Violence in the camps was not random, but rather used as a way of enforcing gendered and racialized hierarchies based on skill. Skill, however, was only one way in which men measured their manhood. The line between who could and could not be considered skilled, and thus a full member of the brotherhood of lumberjacks, was complicated by contemporary understandings of race and ethnicity. The modern-day view of the Northwoods as blandly white should not overshadow the startling diversity of the Northwoods in the late nineteenth and early twentieth centuries. Anglo-American immigrants moved into the lands primarily of the Menominee and Anishinaabe (more commonly, at the time, known as the Chippewa). These nations had a long history of intermarriage with French-Canadian fur traders, adding to this diversity a métis culture in the Upper Mississippi valley.[25]

Through the 1880s and the 1890s, the ethnic picture of camps grew to be increasingly complicated with the arrival of massive waves of Scandinavian immigrants. Swedes, Norwegians, and Finns poured into the Northwoods, along with eastern European immigrants. These new arrivals joined earlier waves of Yankee settlers, large groups of French, Canadian, and German settlers, as well as the Anishinaabe population. And all found themselves working, side by side, in the woods.

Paul Buffalo, an Anishinaabe man who worked several winters in the woods, remembered working with all these groups. But, he said, employers generally assumed that the Anishinaabe worked best with Finns. Together in the woods they would work "just like horses."[26] It seems a small point, who worked best with an

Ojibwe man, but this parallel, Anishinaabe with Finn, workers with horses, begins to unlock something larger. It is a key to the fine-grained distinctions that jacks drew between ethnicities.

Using ideas of masculinity as well as concepts of civilization and savagery, jacks drew a line between who belonged and who did not. The Finns go with the Ojibwe, below the Yankees and the French. These differences were not mere preference, but an understanding that some ethnicities were fundamentally lesser and had not yet earned their place. As Yankee-born lumberjack Horace Glenn rather more pointedly put it: "There are probably fifteen white men here and sixty Swedes, and those fifteen keep them so that they don't dare to say their soul is their own."[27] For Glenn, and for many of the lumberjacks, some ethnicities simply were not white.

In the late nineteenth century, the ethnic makeup of the Northwoods across all three states changed dramatically. Enormous immigration from Scandinavia meant that by 1900, many counties in Minnesota were over three-quarters first- or second-generation Americans from Scandinavia. In 1890, the census recorded 478,041 Swedish-born persons in the United States, more than double the number in 1880 and up from 18,625 in 1870. Of these, more than two thirds were living in the lake states. The distinct similarities in climate, as well as overlapping agricultural and lumbering industries, made these states prime destinations for Scandinavians. Or as novelist Frederika Bremer wrote in her 1850s novel *Homes of the New World*, Minnesota was "a glorious new Scandinavia."[28] By 1916, a third of the population of Minnesota's Mesabi Iron Range, home to some of its largest lumbering operations, were Finnish born.[29] In the lumber camps of the Northwoods, these groups all came into constant contact—and constant conflict.

It is hard, from a modern perspective, to imagine something more "white" than a young, strapping Swedish immigrant. This is not just a bland statement on changing ideals of race: even within the majority of the United States by the early twentieth century Swedes were uncontroversially accepted. By 1924, immigration legislation was encouraging the desirable "nordics."[30] Most modern studies leave out any mention of Scandinavians as a group that had any burden of proving their whiteness. Jon Gjerde places Swedes and Norwegians among white people in his studies of European encounters with American ideas of race. His *Minds of the West* concludes that the continuing fixation on ethnic difference in the lake states comes from the extreme isolation of small farming communities in which even second- and third-generation Americans grew up speaking only Scandinavian languages and following extremely localized cultural traditions.[31]

Yet what this historiography misses are the more fine-tuned distinctions that occurred in camps, distinctions that suggest another source for the enduring popularity of making Swedes, Norwegians, and Finns the butts of jokes across the Northwoods.[32] For within the camps, it was clear that Scandinavians were, in the words of Horace Glenn "the most disgusting, dirty lousy reprobates that I ever saw."[33]

The hatred of Swedes, Norwegians, and eventually and most virulently, Finns shows up repeatedly in the historical record of the late nineteenth century in the Northwoods, as well as in the memories of those who worked as jacks or lived in the lumber towns. Francis Lunden, a Swede, remembered that it was from Finns that you learn to fight. Martin Kuarala, a second-generation Finnish-American, remembered Swedes and Norwegians as "hopeless alcoholics." Manita Kromer told interviewers that she remembered a "wild, weird character," a heavily drinking woman who, despite not being Swedish, earned the nickname "Swede Pete," because she "drank and cussed like a man," and, presumably, like a Swede.[34]

Swedes, Norwegians, and Finns were regularly made the butt of jokes in camp, either by one another or by native-born jacks. Songbooks are filled with mockery ("Ten thousand Swedes / ran through the weeds / chased by one Norwegian"), and when folklorist Richard Dorson went to write a complete folklore of lumberjacks he spent the better part of an article describing a Scandinavian caricature's accents, noting that the Scandinavian in a joke, "never pronounced *th*, but substituted d (de, dem, dey), or *t'* (mout', deat', teet'). His *t* frequently became d (sadisfied, pardner, oudskirds, gedding), and he used y for *j* (yust, yack rabbit)."[35]

These jokes could have a darker side. Horace Glenn's letters home from winters in camp display the violence that ran under these lighthearted tales. At his most benign he jokes with his mother that, given that few of them could read and even fewer cared to do so, "as you might imagine, the conversation of such people is highly edifying and instructive." In another instance he laments that every time he "consider[s] the way I am living . . . among such savages I can only come to the conclusion that I am a hopeless lunatic." But at times his rhetoric turns much darker. In February, after three months in the logging camp, he wrote that he "want[s] to hit them every time [he] looks at them."[36]

Nor was Glenn alone. In an interview with a folklorist, Alton Van Camp begins by recalling an old joke he liked. A bunch of loggers go over a waterfall, and the men on the bank yell "save the hats, let the Swedes drown!" Van Camp then fell into conversation with John Boyd, a jack who worked in the woods in the 1910s and was being interviewed alongside him. Boyd remembered that in his father's day, "Scandinavians had to have a cabin for themselves. You couldn't keep them in with any other group." Jhalmer Berg, an American-born jack of Swedish origins, recalled that in the evenings men would gather in "ethnical groups—there'd be Finns in one corner talking about there [*sic*] experiences and possibly Scandinavians in another." Among the groups, Berg remembered, "there'd be resentment" against the English and Irish who "had all the top jobs," while the Finns and others "had to do the heavy work."[37]

Grace Hale notes in *Making Whiteness* that even in the South where the boundaries of race, in our historical imagination, were strongest, whiteness still represented a "muddled middle."[38] This is perhaps even truer when the lens is narrowed dramatically. If, from a distance, the lumberjacks looked to be a homogeneous crowd of workers, from within their ranks there were differences that, while vastly less dramatic than those between Black and white in the Jim Crow South, nonetheless shaped how they understood their place in the camps, and in towns.

Whiteness as a category of analysis has come under increasing scrutiny of late, and for good reason. As pop culture has picked up on the term, those academics who saw it first as part of a rigorous analysis of cultural history have lost their taste for it entirely.[39] And it is true that far too much can be lazily chalked up to some vague sense of race solidarity. Yet, while the category of whiteness might trace its roots back to Marxism and antiracism, that does not mean it is the category's only use. As historian John Munro notes, removing whiteness from a Marxist analysis and looking at it through the lens of cultural studies does not necessarily render it a blank slate onto which historians can project just any old meaning they wish. Moreover, in an era in which the myth of "white" pasts and nationhood underpins so much of our politics, surely the study of whiteness is more, not less, relevant than ever before.

The category of "white" in the late nineteenth century was not a monolith divided along the explicit color-line of white and Black, but rather a contested category. As historian Eric L. Goldstein argues, "the black-white racial dichotomy has functioned in American history less as an accurate description of social reality than as an ideology."[40] The divides between groups we may now think of as all being white were not explicitly racial, even among those who could not claim full whiteness. But they were also not just the more benign interest in ethnic background displayed by white Americans today. In the deeply influential *Whiteness of a Different Color*, Matthew Frye Jacobsen insists that "we must admit of a system of 'difference' by which one might be both white *and* racially distinct from other whites."[41] Understanding these fissures between the racially white but ethnically different, unstable though they may be, helps us understand how the category of "white" was built. It also allows a window into the more minute hierarchies existing within working-class groups. It is not enough to just say that "people did this because they thought they were, or wanted to be, white." Peter Kolchin's critique that studies that focus

Many lumber camps were made up of a largely immigrant workforce. Here a crew of lumberjacks pauses for lunch in the woods near Walker, Minnesota, circa 1910. Courtesy of the Minnesota Historical Society.

exclusively on "common commitment to whiteness [are] so incomplete as to be totally misleading" is convincing, but tackling whiteness is one of many factors that can reveal nuance that a class analysis alone would miss.[42]

It is foolish to assume all immigrants wanted to immediately, and uncritically, be absorbed into the mass of white America. One of Goldstein's key contributions is to challenge a literature on whiteness that assumes that new waves of immigrants embraced and attempted to achieve existing ideals of whiteness. Looking at the lumber camps with this in mind helps us see just how new immigrants tried to become "white," but how they insisted upon keeping their ethnic identity at the same time. Indeed, it seems that through encounters with savagery and whiteness, the lumberjacks of the Northwoods, while positioning themselves as separate from "savages" were at the same time determined to protect some sense of difference and ethnic identity. Within the camp, jacks drew fine lines between ethnicities, creating an unstable hierarchy whose echoes can still be found in Northwoods culture.

The clearest window into the hierarchies between jacks who considered themselves white is to understand their attitude toward their only coworkers whom they did *not* consider white: the Anishinaabe. Chantal Norrgard and others have argued that Ojibwe in the camps were seen as startling anomalies that "contradicted popular beliefs about frontier development." But I have found little evidence to corroborate this assumption.[43] Rather, it appears that Euro-American loggers simultaneously accepted without question the Anishinaabe's presence in camps and used violence to demonstrate their dominance and ensure the Anishinaabe remained part of the woods that were being conquered, apart from the Euro-American conquerors. Anishinaabe skill ran counter to Euro-American understandings of the connections between skill, manhood, and civilization. In response, white loggers used violence to reinforce the boundaries between skilled civilized manhood and savagery.

For the Anishinaabe, work in the camps was part of a new economy in which community resources—the trees that were stolen by settler colonials—were returned to the community in the form of capital.[44] Forced into working in the industry by way of losing their access to natural resources, Anishinaabe loggers worked in every level of lumbering, though most actively cutting in the woods and working the river drive every spring.

Euro-American loggers were used to the presence of Anishinaabe loggers in camp, but treated them fundamentally differently from their immigrant counterparts. Rather than using violence, games, and skill to control hierarchies, Yankee and European immigrant loggers sought to keep the Anishinaabe on the outside of their system entirely. White loggers sought to control their presence through forcing them into the least desirable roles, denying skill where they saw it, and violently enforcing boundaries of skilled white manhood when they felt it was necessary.[45]

By late nineteenth-century American racial understandings, the various races of the world were essentially arranged frozen in time along different levels of evolution. White Americans conceived of Native Americans as being stuck in an earlier stage of evolution, closer to a primitive and wild state of man. For Euro-American loggers the wilderness of the woods and the "wildness" of its inhabitants was inextricably tied. The taming of one would lead to the civilization of the other. Failing that, the logging of one must, inevitably, mean the driving out of the other.

Lumberjacks were particularly invested in the process of civilizing and taming nature, because they themselves were seen as barely civilized to begin with. In the eyes of the settled, middle-class citizens of the emerging Northwoods towns, lumberjacks—with their violence, predilection for drink, and long stints in the woods—were something less than fully evolved. In the darkness of the woods, away from the bustling order of cities and domestic influence of families, jacks, both in the eyes of observers and in their own understandings, teetered on the edge of savagery.

In camps on the boundary of wildness, Native Americans were far from surprises: they were expected. I argue that Native Americans were seen in two distinct ways by white lumberjacks: either as a natural part of a logging camp, no more unexpected than trees, or—when found outside the camps—as an aspect of the natural "wildness" and danger of the Northwoods. Traits that were seen as choices or skills in white men were, for Native Americans, perceived as simply part of their racial identity. To the minds of those who had imbibed contemporary views about Indigenous Americans, since the Anishinaabe did not have to *work* to be light-footed on logs or agile in the woods, they also gained no prestige from these skills. Both visions constructed Native Americans as a natural part of the land, and both allowed itinerant workers at the bottom of the Midwest's class structure to define themselves as members of an evolving civilization fighting in the frontline against the savagery of the woods.

Euro-Americans had long defined their own civilization against images of Native Americans as both savage and noble. But both these images, the noble savage Rousseau praised or the threatening specter of frontier raids, linked Native Americans to the land from which they came. Native Americans were, to white colonial settlers, a creation of nature—wild, untamable, and fundamentally different from white men. As Robert F. Berkhofer argues in his classic study, for white men "the essence . . . of the Indian has been the definition of Native Americans in fact and fancy as a separate and single other," essentially "noble" or "savage." But the Native American who did not fit either—the Indian out of nature—was a problem for the white imagination. If a Native American appeared to be neither "noble nor wildly savage," he became instead the "third major White image of the Indian . . . degraded, often drunken . . . [exhibiting] the worst vices of both societies."[46] To contemporary white observers, the Indian without nature was not civilized; he was pathetic. As Ter Ellingson argues, the "savage" was noble only in imagination; when encountered by Euro-Americans in reality he was tethered to the political realities of the nineteenth century, in which he was, by definition, ignoble.[47]

This connection of Native Americans to nature, the construction of Native Americans as the very embodiment of wilderness, was strengthened by a growing understanding of civilization as an inherently biological concept. Civilization could

Three Ojibwe visitors, possibly from the nearby Leech Lake Reservation, at the Swan River Logging Company camp in Cass County, Minnesota, 1904. Photograph by E. S. Bruce, U.S. Forest Service Records, National Archives.

not be achieved by simply conforming to the behaviors of white men, because for late nineteenth-century Americans civilization was linked directly to race. Like skin color, Euro-Americans saw the capacity to be civilized as an inborn trait. Take, for instance, Tarzan, who leapt to life in 1912 after Americans had come to fully accept these concepts. While he was raised in the jungle by apes, Tarzan was, by birth, a white man. Despite his savage upbringing, the minute Tarzan came into contact with his first human woman, he showed sexual restraint. His capacity for "civilized" behavior was inborn—he did not need a civilized upbringing to learn it.[48] On the other hand, even when nonwhite men adopted every possible trapping of white civilization, they were more likely to be seen as caricature than civilized man.

Ideas of racial civilization grew out of an increasing scientific interest in the newly emerging field of ethnography. Early ethnographers followed on from large-scale Darwinian thought to see race not as diversity, but as a distinct stage in evolution, a stage that could be traced on the body. Mankind, they asserted, had evolved through a number of cultural stages, beginning with hunter/gatherer and ending in the present with the modern manufacturing societies. Thus, scientific racism took the form of cataloging the ways bodies appeared to betray their innate capacity for civilization as a sign of how far they had evolved.

In his *Types of Mankind: Or, Ethnological Researches* (1854), J. C. Nott noted that "lofty civilization, in all cases, has been achieved solely by the 'Caucasian group' . . . while . . . the *Barbarous* tribes of America have remained in utter darkness."[49] Ideas that attached capacity for civilization to biology came to a full flowering in the 1910s, when in an attempt to deny hunting land to those who were not "fully" Indian, lawyers with calipers descended upon the White Earth Band of Anishinaabe in Minnesota. Those who were "full-blood" were entitled to their reservation land. Those who were "mixed-blood" were not.[50] Full-blooded Anishinaabe might exist at the same time as métis relatives, but they were biologically trapped in an earlier stage of development.

The key word in Nott's taxonomy of races is "remained." It is not that the "*Barbarous* tribes" had evolved differently, nor that they had simply not been exposed to civilization. Rather, this new science concluded that they simply had remained in an earlier stage of evolution. By this way of thinking, Native Americans were not so much a different or even "backwards" or "barbaric" society as they were a stable past, in a very real way outside of time, against which modern Euro-Americans could measure their progress.[51]

Lumberjacks were nicknamed "jackpine savages" by contemporaries. They were men who lived their lives so far at the bottom of white class hierarchy that they were fundamentally outcast from society. So perhaps it is no surprise that they enthusiastically adopted the idea that they were intrinsically, by their very biology, more civilized, and more capable of civilization, than the Anishinaabe men beside whom they worked. Jacks saw the Anishinaabe they interacted with as a part of the woods, a savagery that they had come to conquer.

Understanding their ideas of race clarifies white lumberjacks' seemingly contradictory representations of the Anishinaabe who worked beside them in the woods. If traits that were seen as deficiencies of character—like the perceived laziness of Anishinaabe itinerancy—were part of their savagery then so, too, were their skills as lumbermen. But moreover, since their "savagery" was part and parcel with the wildness of woods, it was also a savagery that could be cut down, and one against which lumberjacks could measure their superior status as "civilized" white men.

Euro-American lumberjacks regularly worked side by side with Anishinaabe and occasionally Menominee lumberjacks. In fact, of the few records uncovered

Lumberjacks for the company of William A. Holmes & Son loading a narrow-gauge railway car east of the Michigamme River in Michigan, circa 1880. Among the crew is Tom King *(fourth from right)*, an Ojibwe logger from the Badwater Band. Courtesy of Dickinson County Library, Iron Mountain, Michigan.

documenting their experiences there, it seems that Native Americans were seen, within the camps, as natural, if not always especially welcome, coworkers. Paul Buffalo claimed that "in the logging camps they hired Indians and whites both; . . . it didn't make any difference. There was no discrimination. No. All worked together. All worked happily."[52] Euro-Americans also felt that this was the case. Alton Van Camp affirmed that he worked side by side with Indians, and that they were "good workers." But even as they affirmed the ease with which Indians worked in camps, most would immediately show that it was only in this one situation, as a lumberjack, that Native Americans were seen as natural coworkers. Van Camp himself noted, almost immediately after saying that he had had no trouble working with Ojibwe, that "most of them was pretty shiftless."[53]

But while Euro-Americans accepted that Native Americans were decent loggers, they were nonetheless uncomfortable with the idea that untrained savages could accomplish their highly skilled work. To establish their dominance over the men who worked beside them, Euro-American workers called upon ideas of skill, and used these ideas against the Anishinaabe. Euro-Americans had skills; the Anishinaabe had only natural predispositions. If what was bad about them was natural, so, too, was what was good. For instance, river work, of all lumbering labor, required the most dexterity. The delicate footwork required meant, for a logger, that a moment's slip would mean the difference between life and death. Native Americans were often remarked upon to be "naturally" excellent river men. Henry La Prairie, a famous Ojibwe log roller, not only worked in the camps, but also made a name for himself as a show burler. He and his brother would give shows of log rolling and participate in log-rolling competitions in Duluth to the delight of spectators. His agility and skill were attributed, by a local, to the fact that he, "like many of his kind," had these skills naturally.[54] Daniel Morrison, a logger who had worked on the Bad River Reservation, claimed that in those camps operating on the reservation itself, the highest skilled jobs went not to whites but to Indians who "being naturally expert woodsmen, proved themselves adept for these lines."[55]

In addition to being natural river men, Native Americans were also remembered as "beautiful loaders" who could pile the logs atop one another. This job, like the river work, required the same skills of light and delicate footwork from the man who stoop atop a teetering pile of logs, settling the loads into place.[56] While at first these ideas of skill seem to place Native Americans into the same category of skilled laborers as their Euro-American counterparts, the way they were constructed as natural outcomes of their racial identity instead served to separate the two groups. While Euro-American's achievements were seen as signs of skill and belonging, those of Native Americans were seen as an ethnic difference. Rather than being part of the group that arrived to clear the woods for civilization, Native Americans were a part of the woods themselves, skilled because the woods were in their blood. This understanding carried over into the language of Paul Buffalo, who remembered that Indians "look good in the woods."[57]

Euro-American lumberjacks combined ideas of skill and race to create a language by which they were no longer threatened by the presence of the Anishinaabe working beside them. However, these ideas had their limits, limits that are exposed by the often extraordinary violence directed at the Anishinaabe. John Nelligan remembered, "Indians and white men seldom got along very well on the drive," before going on to tell a story about how, after some Anishinaabe made fun of his men, they "didn't' waste any time with words, but went after them with fist and foot."[58] But most white memoirists were reluctant to recount anything beyond general antipathy for Indians. It is only by searching through the opinions of the Menominee and Anishinaabe that a true story of a struggle for dominance in which violence was freely used by white men as a tool becomes clear. The Menominee fought white men lumbering on their land because, they reported, white men raped and attacked Menominee women. Meanwhile a fur trader married to an An-ishinaabe woman reported that he was "sorry to see the coming of the whites, who he said were . . . wronging their women."[59] These are small windows into a world where dislike turned to violence—glimpses of the simmering threat of bodily harm that underpinned relationships between the Native Americans of the Northwoods and the men who colonized their land.

It is no surprise, under these circumstances, that Paul Buffalo's fellow jacks saw Finns as natural workmates for Anishinaabe, working side by side "like horses," or that Glenn saw them as "savages." The parallel was made even more clearly by a young consulate worker named Mr. Løvenskjold. In an 1890 report to the Norwe-gian consul Løvenskjold mentioned, among a laundry list of complaints about American treatment of Norwegians, that Norwegians were regularly called "In-dians."[60] In both instances, lumberjacks purposefully asserted the internal racial hierarchy by placing Finns and Norwegians side by side with those they considered incapable of civilization.

From a distance, it was all too easy to lump these men together. For the towns-people who endured the annual migration of lumberjacks to cities, they were all—ethnicity, age, and skill aside—pests. From the standpoint of a century later, many of these distinctions seem arbitrary: I laughed when my mother told me that she had been raised to never eat from a spoon in a house that kept its spoons lying flat, because that was how Norwegians stored them. But to the men *within* the camps these distinctions were key. Asserting who was and was not a "real" lumber-jack was a form of power, a way to establish hierarchies and to assert control over life in camp. That control, however, was limited. As logging industrialized and grew in scale, lumberjacks were soon to find out where the limits of their power lay.

PART II

# IN TOWN

When I drive up to the lake, I start in the prairies. The lower half of all the lake states are prairie. As much as they are defined by the craggy outcrops of the Upper Peninsula or the vast expanses of forest, these are places of low hills and grass. My great-grandmother is buried on the grassy slopes of a small cemetery in southern Minnesota, where the largest tree for a mile is the one she planted at the foot of her eight-year-old son's grave in 1916. It takes a few hours in a car, on Interstate 35, to get up to the woods.

A century or more ago it would have taken a train, and then from the train a walk of anywhere from one to twenty miles to get to the camps of the Northwoods. Yet the boomtowns that littered the forests were as much a part of the lumberjack's world as the camps themselves. As the men walked from place to place, they tied town to back country, linking the region together in economy, myth, and human geography.

Walking was at the heart of a lumberjack's independence, and it was his central weapon against the increasingly stratified camps: if he didn't like a boss, if he didn't care for the work, or simply if he wanted to, he could walk away. He could take his time-ticket and head into town to cash in his pay. Or he could walk on: there would always be more work within a day's walk. Come the summer he would walk back out of the woods, board the trains, and return to towns. Some men would then return home, to the civilizing influences of wife and family, and the honest labor of farming. But others, those that were permanent citizens of the red sash brigade, continued to wander: to hotel jobs and river drives, or to the fields of North Dakota to "grassback" as farm workers for the summer.

Lumberjacks pose for a studio portrait during their annual spree in a Northwoods lumber town, circa 1900. Courtesy of Minnesota Historical Society.

When they hit town, even those towns that were within the woods themselves, boom cities built off the back of the lumber industry's wealth, lumberjacks were not a welcome sight. Their arrival was a natural disaster, a seasonal danger tied to living so near the woods. Their itinerancy was a sign of their degeneracy, and their lack of interest in accumulating capital a sign of their weak morals and deficient manhood.

So they were herded into the Gateway in Minneapolis, Sawdust Flats in Muskegon, the Cribs in Duluth. Middle-class residents disdained and avoided these vice districts and saw them as blights at best, cancerous decay at worst. But within them, at the flop houses and lumberjack hotels, the saloons and the brothels, those jacks who remained itinerant year round reaffirmed their culture, using violence, drinking, and treating to rounds to express their values of camaraderie.

Memory and history cannot happen outside place. Regions are shaped by the memoryscapes that are impressed upon them: road names, neighborhood plans, and sites of victories and losses all tell a story of what happened there.[1]

I look at some of the same stories, the same landscapes twice. I first look at a place—the saloons and slum districts of the boom towns—through the eyes of middle-class observers who saw in itinerancy a moral threat. Itinerant workers were tramps, and a contagion to be contained. The urban plans of towns like Duluth, Muskegon, and Minneapolis reflected the mindset of those in power: districts were set out to contain jacks and quarantine them from the more respectable neighborhoods. Then, I reexamine these neighborhoods from the inside out. For it was in these areas that communities formed in the woods recongregated and created new rituals to enact their most deeply held values. By changing perspective, by switching viewpoints, it becomes clear how contingent and unstable the meaning of a place is. And it is that very instability that left the lumberjack's legacy and memory up for grabs.

# FOUR

# THAT RESTLESS, ROVING SPIRIT

## ITINERANCY AND RESISTANCE

The sheriffs of Koochiching, Beltrami and St. Louis counties last night reported that they were in control of the situation in the timber districts of their counties where armed I.W.W. agitators have been driving lumberjacks from their camps during the past two days.

—*Minneapolis Star Tribune*, January 3, 1917

Woodsmen Are Freed: . . . They were charged with coercion. It being alleged that they were members of the I.W.W. "rebel gang" that drove the working lumberjacks from their camps. Evidence was insufficient.

—*Brainerd Daily Dispatch*, January 5, 1917

Days after Christmas in 1916, ragged groups of men began to appear in the lumber town of Virginia, on Minnesota's Iron Range. They were walking out of the woods, carrying their few possessions with them. They were dirty and unbathed—few would have had access to a bath or an effective way of doing laundry for weeks, if not months. Some had been walking for a dozen miles or more, trudging through the heavy snows of a Minnesota winter. They came in the dozens, then the scores, and then the hundreds. By the new year, perhaps as many as two thousand men had emerged from the shadows of the woods—those numbers would swell by thousands more on January 1. The lumberjacks were, at long last, on strike.

The 1916 lumber strike, spreading from Virginia, Minnesota, across the Iron Range all the way to Bemidji, 130 miles away, has long been seen as an aberration.

When explained at all, it is assumed that the strike came from outside the industry—the result of Industrial Workers of the World (IWW) agitation and the geographical proximity of the camps to well-organized and strike-primed iron miners. This version of events is resonant with a long-standing historiography and popular memory in which the lumber camps of the Northwoods are remembered as a worksite nearly void of unrest. It is a version of events, though, that misreads the history of labor agitation and resistance in the Northwoods. When the first large-scale strikes broke out in 1917 and then again in 1937, they were not exceptions to a long history of quiescence, but rather culminations of a long-standing pattern of resistance techniques—most prominently, the lumberjack's use of his itinerancy as a method of protecting himself from exploitation.[1]

Nonetheless, while lumberjacks used a variety of methods to resist management and protect working-class spaces, the jacks themselves seemed curiously resistant to striking and unionizing. Of 114 lumber industry strikes between 1850 and 1906 in the Northwoods, only 18 involved the participation of unions. And, if 114 seems like a high number, it is worth noting that almost all these walkouts were from mills. While lumber mills were often grouped with camps by labor bureaus, their workforces were far from identical. The relatively urban and at least somewhat stable nature of mill work lent itself more easily to industrial organization.

Even the 1916 strike was not meant to happen. The IWW felt that the camps were not ready yet. Instead, IWW organizers slated the 1916–17 season as a time of preparation. They sent dozens of representatives from the Agricultural Workers Organization into the camps to live as undercover agents. They were not to tell anyone who they were working for, and would happily disavow any connection to the IWW and tear up union cards if questioned by bosses. But at night in the camps, while the push (foreman) slept in his separate quarters, they spread the word about international unionism. Over the early months of the season, bosses noticed that "One Big Union" fliers were appearing pasted to the walls of cook shacks. Silently, but surely, the power of the Wobblies was spreading through the camp.

As Christmas approached, the workers at the Virginia and Rainy Lake plant—at the time, the largest white pine mill in the world—began to agitate for shorter working hours. They organized under the leadership of two diametrically opposed men. The first was Charles Jacobsen, the official IWW secretary for the area. Jacobsen was a quiet, steady man who worked tirelessly out of his office in the Finnish Socialist Opera in Virginia to carefully coordinate union activities. Earlier that summer, he had worked to organize mine workers who spontaneously walked off in August. His union members were largely Finns, familiar with the ideas of One Big Union and comfortable working under Jacobsen's careful, bookish organization.

Jacobsen's counterpart was Jack Beaton. The two men shared a workspace in the Socialist Opera, but little else. Beaton dressed in a mackinaw and tall boots, carried a revolver at his hip, and spoke in the lingo of the jacks. He called himself "Timber Beast" and had worked for several winters in Wisconsin camps. Where Jacobsen was careful, Beaton was impulsive. Where Jacobsen worked to organize, Beaton worked to antagonize.

Under the spell of Beaton's hotheaded language, on December 24, 1916, mill workers met at the Socialist Opera and drew up a list of demands—a raise, eight-hour workdays, and no reprisals for union activities. Their plan was to present their demands and require a response by noon on December 27, or strike. Jacobsen attempted to stop the process. As a better, and more careful, organizer he understood Beaton's plan was rash and bound for failure. He attempted to have the IWW general secretary intervene, but even Big Bill Haywood's warning that a strike would be disastrous had no effect. The men, under Beaton's leadership, were too riled up to be dissuaded. On January 28, the millworkers struck.[2]

A large part of Beaton's swagger in the days leading up to the strike came from a threat he made to the mill owners: Beaton claimed that, should the mill go on strike, he would also see to it that the lumberjacks struck. This, to the lumber barons who ran the camp, was the emptiest of all possible threats. The local paper went so far as to describe Beaton's promise to organize a lumberjack strike as a "joke." Lumberjacks had never been amenable to the idea of unions before, lumber barons reasoned. Conventional wisdom was that they were unorganized and furthermore unable to organize. While a man might leave a job he did not like, he was extremely unlikely to take action as strong as a strike. It went against everything the lumberjack stood for.

But Beaton made good on his word: the day the mills went on strike, he organized flying committees to spread the word to the camps. With the strike on at the mills, the IWW had little choice but to support the action. The IWW local in Bemidji, 130 miles away, also agreed to send out flying committees into the woods, while the secretary promised the press that if necessary the central office of the IWW could mobilize twenty thousand members to reach the area.[3] The flying committees had clear orders: the men were to put together demands, including a ten dollar a month flat raise, and bring it to management. When demands were rejected, which was a foregone conclusion, they were to walk out on the first day of the new year.

Beaton's gamble worked. According to a reporter for the *International Socialist Review* who was embedded in the camps, the "result was that when a flying squad from Virginia, Minn, brought news to the northwoods camps that the sawmill men were on strike under the banner of the ONE BIG UNION, nearly four thousand

The Socialist Opera House in Virginia, Minnesota, where IWW officials Charles Jacobsen and Jack "Timber Beast" Beaton shared an office during the 1917 lumber strike. Courtesy of the Migration Institute of Finland.

lumberjacks came pell-mell out of woods as though driven by a forest fire."[4] While an IWW agitator may have had good reason to exaggerate the jacks' reaction to Beaton's orders, the facts stand: on the morning of January 1, 1917, men still left in the camps packed up their belongings, threw them over their shoulders, and walked out of the woods. They began in handfuls from the outer camps. As they walked the tracks their numbers grew. Handfuls turned into floods. By the end of the week, thousands of men had come out of the woods. Against the expectations of even the IWW, the Timber Beast had held his promise: the camps were on strike.

The crackdown on the strike was immediate and unforgiving. County police with help from state authorities issued and enforced a special order declaring all union members "undesirables" and "foreign agitators" and ordering them out of town at risk of arrest. Charles Jacobsen, a property owner, family man, and resident of Virginia for over two decades, was slightly more difficult. Labeling him a foreign agitator was nearly impossible given his standing in the community. Instead, he was arrested in his own office several months after the strike for loitering with "intent to do mischief." Many of the jacks fled Virginia for Duluth. Some holed up for some weeks in Bemidji. But more cracked and returned to work. By the end of the month, the camps were reopened. Beaton himself only appears once more in the historical record: standing for sentencing in Bemidji, four months after the strike, on spurious charges of manslaughter.

How do we make sense of this sudden explosion of activity after years of seeming quiet in the camps? Much of the historiography around lumberjacks has focused not on their resistance, but on their lack thereof. Agnes M. Larson's *White Pine Industry in Minnesota* mentions merely that "organized labor among loggers was uncommon. . . . The lumberjack grumbled and cursed, and occasionally there were strikes, but usually these were local affairs in no way tied up with unions." Her explanation for this was simply that "many of the laborers were farmers," and "with the return of the spring they were back on their own farms." But then in the next sentence she notes that the camps were made up of "transient labor [that] was not easily organized," and that "no red-blooded man in the forest would admit that he could not stand on his own feet."[5] Several others are equally quick to dismiss walkouts in lumber camps as individual grumbles.[6]

All that, however, rests on swallowing the myth of the contented lumberjack working in a family camp. That was certainly the image industry titans spun in the 1910s and 1920s.[7] And there are some reasonable causes for this assumption. For all that their pay may seem abysmal, lumber workers were—or at least could be—among the best paid laborers in their region. The 1890 Minnesota census concluded that loggers made a daily wage of $1.52—equal to, if not higher than, that of farm hands in the same period. But this wage was dependent on a central supposition that lumberjacks worked in a predictable and constant pattern. The Bureau of Labor calculated this wage on the assumption of full-time employment with winters spent in the camps and summers in the mills. But this was far from universal. Extensive research in contemporary newspapers, oral history records, and memoirs shows that lumberjacks were comprised far more of itinerant agricultural workers who might work in the mills, but also might work as "grassbacks" on farms, or might simply spend the summer looking for odd jobs.[8]

Moreover, the mere assumption that workers who were paid as well as farm hands (not, in and of itself, a particularly high standard) were happy is flawed. The equation of pay with happiness disregards the conditions under which the jacks labored, their standing in the community, and their lives outside the camps. Jacks had little to no opportunity for advancement. In a culture whose dominant discourses emphasized the vital importance of economic autonomy, the inability to become a "self-made man" was its own harsh condition. Socially isolated in towns, looked down on as the dregs of society, and deprived of the ability to advance, the lumberjacks were also forced to labor under appalling conditions. And it was conditions, more than anything else, that sparked unrest. For instance, when the 1917 strikes failed to spread to the Crookston Lumber camps near Bemidji, the *Bemidji Pioneer* confidently predicted that Crookston employees would not strike because the company provided "steel equipment in its housing, springs, good clean bedding and wholesome food for its employees." In several interviews the paper conducted with the local branch of the IWW, pay was not mentioned once, only the horrific conditions under which the jacks were forced to live.[9] Nor do we only have the words of socialist journalists or union organizers to conclude that the conditions in camp were far from romantic. State labor inspectors "regretted that [they] did not have the authority to order all the men out of the camp and burn the place to the ground."[10]

In light of the dangerous, infested working conditions and an economic situation that provided no hope of escape, the historical consensus that jacks did little to resist management and that when resistance did come it came from the outside seems curious. One of the most common explanations of the strikes was that the lumberjacks were essentially caught up in another industry's action and swayed by outside forces to act in ways that were out of character for them. At first glance, this argument, especially in 1916, seems to make an enormous amount of sense. That summer the Mesabi Iron Range had erupted in an at times bloody strike. Organized by the IWW and supported by local Finnish populations, the strike dragged on for three months, ending in September.[11]

The Mesabi strike doubtlessly contributed to the lumber strike. The Mesabi Range is contained, almost entirely, within the Northwoods, stretching from Grand Rapids to Babbitt, Minnesota. Moreover, there *was* Finnish influence on the strikes. Finns brought a long heritage of radical socialism with them from Finland to the Northwoods.[12] However, 1916 was twenty-five years into the period of Finnish immigration. The community centers and opera houses out of which Finnish radicalism operated were well established by 1916/17. As historian Gerald Ronning argues about iron range strikers, the attempt to link Finns to the strikes had more to do with industry bosses discrediting the strikers as "jackpine savages," racially inferior and irredeemably foreign, than it did with actual Finnish instigation of strike actions.[13] Surely the mere existence of Finnish radicals cannot, alone, explain why a workforce that had never struck before erupted that winter.[14]

By changing perspective, however, it becomes clear that there is no need look outside the camps, whether to Finns or to the IWW, for an explanation for the 1916/17 strike. If we take seriously the idea that walk-offs and itinerancy came not merely from laziness or the inherent shiftlessness of itinerant laborers, it is obvious that lumberjacks had a long history of resistance that satisfied their own

*The*
# INTERNATIONAL
# SOCIALIST REVIEW

FEBRUARY, 1917         PRICE TEN CENTS

The February 1917 issue of the *International Socialist Review* included coverage of the lumber strike in northern Minnesota. Courtesy of Marxists Internet Archive.

conceptions of independence as well as justice. This resistance consisted, primarily, of voting with their feet.

There is a long-standing assumption, repeated across both scholarly and popular literature, that regardless of their summer habits, once a jack hired on for a winter, they would stay where they were. Modern visitors to the Forest History Center in Grand Rapids, Minnesota—a faithful, fine-grained re-creation of lumberjack life—are told that men came two days' walk from town, and stayed from first snow until the summer breakup. There is a certain logic that underpins this assumption. To begin with, many camps were extremely difficult to access. They could be up to two days' walk from the nearest village. In the early days, before railroads, even the closest town might seem all but inaccessible during the winter. Moreover, some camps did create regulations that if a contract was not paid, the men who worked in that camp would not be paid either. This meant that the men would have to wait around until the end of the season, to see if they had cut as many logs as their camp was contracted to cut, before they would know if they themselves would be paid or would have worked all winter "for beans."

Mystifyingly this assumption that men worked all winter in one camp even showed up occasionally in the recollections of lumberjacks themselves. Wilfred Nevue, who wrote often about his experiences of lumber camp life and even dedicated himself to a study of their songs and ballads, averred that "lumberjacks did little shifting from one camp to another. The seasons were so short that the drifters could earn only meager money. Nearly all were illiterate, so there was scanty correspondence. In camps, or out, there was very, very, little associating. As a whole I conclude that I saw, and consorted with a good cross-section of lumberjacks of the old school in the logging years in Michigan."[15] Nevue, of course, seems to undermine his own certainty here, for if there was little associating, it is hard to understand how he consorted with so many fellow jacks. In a 1959 unpublished manuscript, Nevue further contradicted himself, claiming that lumberjacks "were floaters going from camp to camp and from one district to another."[16] Alton Van Camp is another lumberjack who remembered similarly that "a lot of those lumberjacks would come into camp in September and they would never leave that camp until April." But then moments later he notes that most men were "drifters."[17]

Two possible conclusions may be drawn from these contradictions. The first is that Nevue and Van Camp worked at camps that were exceptionally stable, but camp records show almost no camps to have kept the same crew for as long as Van Camp remembers after about the 1870s or early 1880s. The other is that these men are conflating their memories with popular understandings of lumber history by the time they were interviewed in the mid-twentieth century. The latter seems especially likely given that, in later years, stability became distinctly associated with the "good" kind of jack, and drifting with the "bad." The *Detroit Free Press* for instance noted in 1907 that "another great trouble with the men working in the woods at present is their migratory spirit. . . . In the old days the true 'lumberjack' went into the woods at the beginning of the season and he remained until the drive." Moreover, in addition to distinguishing between the type of men working today— immigrants and itinerants—and the "true" lumberjack, the *Free Press* makes the moral weight of staying in the woods explicit by explaining that "true" lumberjacks "eschewed the pleasures of towns all winter."[18]

Arthur J. Mulvey, timber cruiser, as an itinerant lumberjack in a studio photograph circa 1892. Photograph by Hugo Naumann. Courtesy of the Minnesota Historical Society.

This article is pure nostalgia; itinerancy had been widespread for at least three decades, perhaps longer. But given a choice between associating their habits with the troubling newer type of jack and the true lumberjack, its unsurprising that men like Van Camp and Nevue would choose the latter course. Nevue in particular seems to be drawing a line, if a very indistinct and constantly shifting line, to separate the "drifters" from a more respectable kind of jack. This distinction reflects later attempts to build lumberjacks up as a respectable American icon.[19]

Generations of historians have simply assumed that this mythology was, in fact, the case. Agnes M. Larson, author of what still stands as the most definitive study on logging in Minnesota, *The White Pine Industry in Minnesota*, notes merely of the period 1870–90 that "those were the days when men stayed upriver from November until the logging season was over."[20] Many amateur histories take this assumption further, relying on both nostalgia and one or two misleading pieces of evidence to conclude that all men, even in the later periods, stayed all winter at the camps. The assumption that feeds these mistakes is straightforward: camps were often far from town and difficult to access. In the perilously cold Northwoods winter, it seems only reasonable that a man would stay all winter. The piece of evidence most often relied on for this was the method of pay: for many camps, bills were only paid at the end of winter. In fact, if a camp did not make contract, sometimes the men's time-checks would be good for nothing. If men could not earn money as they went, but had to wait for spring to be paid, the logic goes, it only makes sense that they stayed in a single camp all winter.[21]

Going to the primary sources contradicts all of that. Lumberjacks were not, in fact, stable in employment during the winter any more than they were stable in their year-to-year homes over the summer. Rather, they drifted from camp to camp throughout the winter, despite the incredible physical obstacles in their way. The regulations that forced laborers to stay in one camp all winter in order to be paid were later innovations. They were instituted to address a problem, not to formalize an existing reality. In fact, many camp regulations and policies show that camps were aware that their workers were not particularly stable. Men were paid, throughout most of the region during its logging period, by day checks. These were pieces of paper that stated how long the jack in question had worked for the camps and at what rate. They could then be taken to local banks and exchanged for money. While being paid by the day was hardly unusual, this structure does show that it was not assumed that all men would spend the entire winter at camp, being paid for the season at the end. Camp log books also confirm the idea that lumberjacks were far from stable. But beyond anything, the memories and memoirs of lumberjacks themselves illustrate that itinerancy was a way of life for jacks, a way of life with profound implications for their ideals of masculinity and for the political ways in which they engaged with management.

In mid-November one year in the late 1890s, Miles Nelson set off by train from Sparta, Wisconsin, a small town about eighty miles northwest of Madison. He and a group of men he had met, all in search of jobs, took the train forty or so miles to Humbird, Wisconsin, a tiny railroad town that even in its heyday had only a clutch of buildings gathered around the depot. From Humbird, Nelson and eleven or so farm boys took off on foot for Neillsville, the county seat. It was only about eighteen miles as the crow flies, but twenty or more by foot. Ten miles or so into the journey, the small band of travelers met a man who was looking for workers. He was the owner of a camp about five miles off the main road, so Nelson and his boys followed him through the woods. They ate dinner at his camp and were told there would be work in the morning. But, come morning, the men decided they did not like the look of the camp—a storm had knocked most of the woods down, and the work was likely to be more clearing than cutting. Men who had done this kind of work before told their fellow jacks that "they would not stay there as it would be worse than working on the prairie in Minnesota." So the men voted with their feet—they left camp, walking the fifteen miles left to Neillsville that day.

The next day a few of the men headed north in the early dawn—most of the camps were another forty miles away, and they intended to make the trip on foot. By dark, they had made it to a camp in what is now Greenwood, Wisconsin, twenty miles north of Neillsville. The camp was not what they expected. It was late November, and logging should have begun, but the sleeping quarters were not yet finished, and actual cutting was weeks off. Nonetheless, they were a dozen miles from the nearest settlement, and they stayed the night. In the morning they surveyed the site and found the situation was worse than they had expected. But the camp needed an ox driver, and Nelson was experienced in driving teams. For three days he worked at this small camp, but by the third morning he had a complaint endemic to lumberjacks: the food was not up to scratch. On the third afternoon a horse cart from town came with provisions for the camp. Nelson explained that "the grub had got the best of [him]" and hopped on the cart as it left camp. The cart took him to a settler's home, where he spent the night before walking another six miles to a new camp. Here, Nelson and his fellow jacks "lived good," they "had venison every day—it was sure good." The work was acceptable, too. After over fifty miles of walking and three camps, he had found a place he was happy to stay.

Six weeks later, he moved on.[22]

Uncovering and understanding a lumberjack's itinerancy challenges two major strains in the historiography of the Midwest. The first is one that suggests that the towns and rural areas of the Midwest were fundamentally separated from the urban centers and had a history that was distinctively their own. This historiography suggests that what may have been true of the prairie towns was truer still of the Northwoods—they were fundamentally impenetrable, separated by the dark lines of pines from the rest of their states. The other, as we have seen, suggests that the strikes that eventually broke out in the lumber camps in the winter of 1916/17 were the result of outside meddling by the IWW and labor organizers. However, in examining the ways in which men circulated through the Upper Midwest in the 1870s through the 1920s two new themes emerge. The first is that the 1916 strike was not something new. Instead, I argue, it was a moment when a long-standing mode of resistance among lumberjacks emerged from the protective cover of the woods. The second is that the rural hinterlands were part of the urban industry, both in terms of the economies, and in terms of their cultures. Moreover, these hinterland villages were closely tied to one another through the human geography of itinerant workers. The bloodlines that tied villages to the cities and to one another were an endlessly circulating mass of itinerant workers.

Nelson's movements were not in the least unusual, even if they contradict most histories of the camps. All itinerant labor is to some extent "hidden."[23] Itinerants fall through the cracks of censuses. They exist outside familial structures that are easily tallied and understood by traditional methods of examining history. To a great extent, by the turn of the century, they had not been organized into unions, doubling their invisibility. But for lumberjacks, there was another factor that made their lives especially invisible: the forest. Itinerant farm laborers passed regularly through villages to obtain new work. Hobos came to be seen as a blight precisely *because* they were so visible to passersby. But lumberjacks walked camp to camp within the vast stretches of the Northwoods, where there were few settlers.

It took a rare event to expose these networks, or to show just how many itinerant men were wandering the woods. Among the grisliest demonstrations was in the autumn of 1894, when a series of firestorms swept through the communities surrounding Hinckley, Minnesota, creating, it was said, "a wall of fire three miles high." In the aftermath 415 bodies were recovered. Of the identifiable corpses, leaving aside those that were only fragments of bone and ash, 99 were unknown and unclaimed. The communities the fire ripped through were tiny, largely comprised of villages of under a hundred occupants. But almost a quarter of the dead were strangers. Moreover, the memorial of the fire prepared for the state makes clear from descriptions that the majority of these ninety-nine were doubtlessly lumberjacks, for who else would be alone, unidentified, and "age[d] about 30; wore blue mackinaw suit, heavy shoes."[24]

The workforce of the lumber industry did not begin as an itinerant group, and the methods of voting with their feet by walking from camp to camp were not widespread among jacks until the 1880s. In the very early days it appears that men, in fact, moved camp relatively rarely. The geography of early lumbering in the region made widespread itinerancy difficult in the early years. For the first few decades of lumbering, camps were not only small in scale, they were relatively small in number. To move every time you are dissatisfied requires the likelihood you'll find employment elsewhere. Above all, what was required was the certainty that, within a few days walk, there would be another camp and the high possibility of a job there.

The nature of the laborers and hiring practices in the earlier days of logging in the region also helped stabilize the workforce. Many of the first laborers in the Northwoods were long-standing lumberjacks who had come west from Pennsylvania or down from French Canada. These jacks were used to State of Maine camps, which operated with very small crews and usually only hired men already known to the proprietor. In fact, many of these camps were operated by families.[25] But even if a camp was not operated by a family, it seems that early foremen preferred to hire men they knew. Euclid J. Bourgeois recalled that when he and several friends arrived at a camp in the 1870s it was only when the boss "discovered [they] were all from the same neighborhood" that he decided they could stay on. In fact, Bourgeois recalled that, especially around the Panic of 1873, "you couldn't buy a job" and "death was required to create a vacancy."[26] The oral history record here seems to match that of logbooks. Agnes M. Larson found that in examining a logbook as late as 1881, the average number of days was very high indeed. Several loggers were paid for over one hundred days' work at a single camp.[27]

But by the turn of the century, at the height of logging, and in the decades that followed, this picture had changed drastically. It is not easy to get a clear cross-sample of camp pay since the books kept for the winter were largely destroyed. But some have found their way into business records in archives. A typical camp book from 1905 in the St. Croix valley shows that men were hired throughout the winter for different amounts of time. While there were some workers who worked the entire winter—three men worked over 140 days (and one of those was the clerk himself)—the majority did not. Some worked as little as two days. Altogether, averaging out the number of days for which men were paid, the typical worker at Camp #4 worked fifty-three days that winter.[28] The situation appeared to only deteriorate from there, to the point where fifty-three days started to look like steady

Seasonal travel occurred regularly between camps such as this one near Biwabik, Minnesota, circa 1892. The men carrying packs and snowshoes could be lumberjacks or part of a crew surveying the Mesabi Iron Range. Photograph by George A. Newton. Courtesy of Lake County Historical Society.

employment. In 1916, Frank Gillmor, an overseer, complained that the Virginia and Rainy Lake Company, which employed 1,924 workers at any moment, had, over the course of a season, settled up with 22,226 workers. This means that entire crews, for practical purposes, turned over every twenty-six days.[29] Even Euclid J. Bourgeois, who remembered deaths as the only cause of vacancy in the 1870s, took to tramping camp to camp in his later years.

What did this itinerancy look like, practically? We can only approximate by attempting to trace the paths of men who tramped camp to camp, following their own descriptions. Looking collectively at the relatively small number of oral histories that describe exact walking paths a few patterns emerge.

Their peripatetic wanderings brought these men to a wide region. It makes no sense to think of jacks within a single state. Men who walked across the Upper Peninsula would hardly hesitate on jumping a train into Wisconsin. They walked in overlapping stories across the three states. John Nelligan, for instance, logged up the Chippewa into Wisconsin but stayed primarily in Minnesota. He would have worked in Wisconsin with men who traveled to the Upper Peninsula for their next job. A lumberjack's walking range, when several stories are compared, appears to have been about one hundred miles.[30]

Oral histories and myths map out into interlocking circles across the Northwoods, with some men having only local fame, and other tales traveling hundreds of miles. The reputation of single famed jacks was often quite local. Figures like Hungry Pig Eye Kelly and Sam Christie (described, lovingly, by a biographer as "about the hardest man who escaped violent death more times than any in the early days of Itasca") show up repeatedly in WPA notes and articles about the area around Grand Rapids, Minnesota.

Other names, like Hungry Mike Sullivan, showed up both in Grand Rapids and as far away as Minneapolis, almost two hundred miles to the south.[31] Sometimes, too, specific stories will show up with different names attached to them. For instance, the tale of the cook who throws his cleaver at a greenhorn who unwittingly talked during mealtimes was told in Wisconsin and Minnesota, but whether that cook was named Pete or Kelly varied based on region.[32] The more abstract the story, the taller the tale, the further it traveled. The circulation of these stories, as much as the few clear records we have of the circulation of the men themselves, begins to paint a picture of the ties between rural and urban communities as well as the ties across state lines.

Songs and tall tales had the broadest circulation. A single song called variously the "Shanty Boys Alphabet," "The Lumberman's Alphabet," and "The Lumberjack's Alphabet" was popular in all three states. It's likely the song originated in French Canada and traveled, with Canadian loggers, across the region.[33] Other tales expose the cross-cultural connections between the Anishinaabe and Euro-American jacks. Take, for instance, the hodag. A fearsome, powerful beast with enormous teeth, he shot to fame in the 1880s and became nationally famous when Wisconsinite and former timber-cruiser Eugene Sheppard "caught" one in 1896 and displayed it at the Oneida County fair. Sheppard, the story goes, had little trouble catching a hodag, since he had invented it and had been flogging stories of the beast to newspapers for years. He claimed to have picked it up from stories told in camps, and local legend in his hometown of Rhinelander tells it that after Sheppard caught the hodag, the Smithsonian planned to send several scientists to investigate. That was the last straw for Sheppard, for apparently a man who would cheerfully fool his neighbors and take money off tourists drew the line at the Smithsonian.[34] The hodag's tale traveled across the span of the Northwoods and was mentioned as an already familiar figure in newspapers as far away as Bemidji, Minnesota—330 miles from Rhinelander—where he was hailed as an invention of jacks.[35]

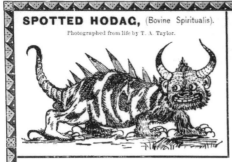

In 1896, the Centralia Lumber Company featured the complete history of the spotted hodag in a series of advertisements in the *Wood County Reporter*. The capture of the mythical beast was photographed the same year by A. J. Kingsbury of Antigo, Wisconsin. Courtesy of the Wisconsin Historical Society, WHS-36382.

But a little examination reveals a different, and far more complex, origin story. The hodag, as drawn by (and eventually created out of paper-mache by) Sheppard bears striking resemblance to the Anishinaabe Mishibizhiw, or underwater panther. Mishibizhiw is a king of underwater realms, often responsible for boating accidents and drowning, and has been part of Anishinaabe culture since the fourteenth century.[36] The two share a long spiny tail, horned head, and huge teeth and are both connected intimately to danger and mishaps, although the hodag's mischief is carried out mainly in the woods, not the water.[37] The origin of the crossover is easy to guess: Sheppard was a cruiser, the men employed to actually walk the land laid out in survey maps and find loggable stands of white pine. Cruisers traveled the woods using Anishinaabe footpaths, many of which were still in use by the Anishinaabe, and relied on Indigenous contacts to help them navigate the woods and find pine.[38]

The roots of lumberjack lore depict a camp and Northwoods culture far more permeable than later descriptions would lead historians to believe. And the distance and speed that these stories traveled from camp to camp indicates a broad circulation of that culture. The walking patterns of the men ensured that discrete pieces of culture—a mysterious beast or a particularly violent cook—entered both the lore of smaller towns, like Rhinelander (a town so small it did not even exist on the 1880 census), and Minneapolis.

Their culture was shaped by the environment in which they worked, an environment they, in turn, shaped by their work. So, choosing where they worked was paramount to their identity as lumberjacks. Much like the coal miners Thomas Andrews describes in *Killing for Coal*, jacks were bonded to one another by common workscapes—the landscapes of extractive work. Their familiarity with the woods, with their dangers and with the skills required to master them, fostered a common identity, for in the woods, as in the mines, the men were subject to the arbitrary cruelty of nature and dependent on their fellow workers' skill to protect them. That reliance created a bond between men, a trust based on their shared occupational knowledge—their shared identity as lumberjacks. It was not merely a matter of pride but a matter of safety that required them to distinguish themselves from the broader mass of itinerant agricultural workers.

While it is not easy to uncover the exact paths lumberjacks took, their reasons for walking out of camp are well established. As George Engberg established in his extensive studies of labor conditions in the industry, the most common problem to plague camp foremen was a shortage of men. The lumbering season was short, and to make contract all the wood had to be felled, scaled, and moved to the river's edge before the snow melted. Able-bodied men who appeared in camp never had trouble finding employment.[39] While their choice was limited, men could be somewhat picky about the work they took. Richard Louis Griffin remembered attempting to recruit men from a "snake room" (the rooms at bars where men could cheaply sleep) and, upon being told by the men that $5 a day for a river drive "taint enough," leaving "unable to hire a man," while the men themselves "rolled over and went to sleep."[40]

Andrews argued that in western coal mines, the "freedom of the miner resided not simply in his command over time and tools, but also in the power he exerted over the room or 'place' in which he worked."[41] For a logger, when that control was threatened, the answer was simple: he walked on.

When white jacks walked out of camps and into the deep woods, they often followed paths that had been established well before lumbering arrived in the woods: they walked on Anishinaabe footpaths. The Anishinaabe have long moved through the Northwoods, following seasonal changes to create a seasonal round that is part of the bimaadiziwin, or the pursuit of a good life.[42] Throughout the lumbering era, Anishinaabe jacks took to walking off work in ways that *looked* nearly identical to their white counterparts. In some ways, motivations were similar: both were rejecting work that did not suit them, and both were rejecting the capitalist imperative to accumulate wealth. The stark difference lay not in those choices, but in the relationship their actions had to wider communities. Lumberjack mobility flew in the face of contemporary white, middle-class, and even the majority of working-class mores. As a result, they were both shunned and feared by Northwoods settlers. The Anishinaabe, on the other hand, were not shamed, because their mobility was not a threat to their community; just the opposite, in fact: it was part of an effort to preserve culture and community against the relentless pressure to assimilate.

Anishinaabe harvests and seasonal labors are controlled by Chi Inaakonigewin, the natural laws that govern the relationships between humans and nonhumans. Chi Inaakonigewin recognizes all entities as separate beings in reciprocal relationships and understands the valuing of nature to be a notion of justice prior to any legal system; it is, instead, inherent to our identity as humans. This is even reflected in language: whereas the English language characterizes humans by gendered pronouns (he and she) and all other living and nonliving parts of nature by an object pronoun (it), Anishnaabemowin makes no such distinction. All beings are simply beings. Humans are just one kind of being in a reciprocal relationship of give and take, in which it is absolutely vital that you never take more than is necessary for survival. In this framework, seeing nature as a "resource" is nonsense: a resource is something that exists for us to use. Nature belongs to itself. Moreover, overharvesting for the sake of accumulating capital is similarly absurd, as it will lead, inevitably, to the degradation of nature and alter its life-giving capacity.[43] The problem is not just that capitalism is greedy, nor that it benefits the few. Chi Inaakonigewin leads not to a Marxist critique about just distribution of resources but rather to a simple assertion that capitalism is, at its core, irrational.[44]

White historians have long been blinded by our own assumptions of what "thriving" in an American economy might mean. Namely, it would mean to accumulate excess wealth, savings, and material goods. By this way of thinking, Indigenous Americans become a tragedy: a people reduced to dependence on the government, increasingly marginalized, and seemingly disappearing into the past. Lest it seem like this is an idea from a distant past, it's worth noting that a peer-reviewed journal article as recent as 2003 defined success by the metric of "Lumber Chief" David Shoppenagon choosing not to give in to "dependence" on the reservation, but instead performing the romantic stereotype of a "Noble Savage" for white eyes and dollars.[45] But this way of seeing Indigenous history puts no value on two things Anishinaabe people traditionally value highly: the autonomy of nature, and the preservation of culture and community.[46] Including lumbering as part of the seasonal round, using the cash to fund community needs, makes perfect sense here, as does stopping work once those needs are met. In that light, Shoppenagon may have succeeded in gaining capital, but at the sacrifice of community and culture. Alternately, those who immediately sold their allotments for cash before resuming the seasonal round on open land were, in fact, quite the opposite of dependent; they were maintaining cultural lifeways independent of the systems of capitalism the U.S. government was trying so fruitlessly to impose.

One of the great ironies of the lumbering era is that the very metric white authorities used to attempt to force Indigenous assimilation was the strongest possible tool in resisting it. As the U.S. government increasingly pushed the Native populations of Michigan, Wisconsin, and Minnesota onto reservations, they purposefully picked plots of land that were heavily timbered. The idea was that cutting the timber would clear the land for agriculture, and the cash generated by the sale of lumber would finance farming. Wage labor in the camps and the harvesting of timber would be steps on the way to the ultimate goal of a settled, agricultural society and a rejection of traditional lifeways.[47] At first, it even seemed to work. An Indian agent wrote approvingly in 1875 that of the men of the Red Cliff Band more than half were "engaged outside of the reserve in logging camps, cutting wood, and other civilized occupations."[48] But the Bureau of Indian Affairs was far from successful: by 1951, almost 40 percent of the white-owned cutover near Lake Superior had been turned to agricultural use; the reservations, on the other hand, had only small patches here and there, not enough to even register as statistically relevant.[49] The Dawes Act (1887) created allotments to force agriculture and a rearrangement of Anishinaabe lifestyles to match Euro-American, capitalist norms of individualism. But the Anishinaabe used one half of this logic against the other, by using the market economy to preserve their lifeways.[50]

Logging came at a key moment. After generations of fur trading, the arrival of white hunters, and the increasingly speedy destruction of forest habitat, the animal population of the Northwoods had decreased drastically. As early as the 1870s, Anishinaabe were having trouble finding enough meat to survive the winter part of the seasonal round, and many were forced to migrate further and further north to follow the dwindling wildlife.[51] Logging, then, could be a manner of surviving the winter while returning in the spring and summer to subsistence means of living.[52] In essence, logging helped bridge the gap for the Anishinaabe between finding ways of adapting to new reservations and being forced into fixed agricultural lifestyles.[53]

Resistance to capitalism was not uniform—it would be absurd to assume all of a diverse people adopted identical attitudes. But both the Anishinaabe and Menominee broadly resisted—and continue to resist—the integration into a capitalist market system. There were divides within the tribes. While Indian agents tended to characterize the difference between those who did and did not embrace capitalism as generational, based on the idea that elder generations rejected integration out of ignorance, that idea is patently absurd: through the fur trade, Anishinaabe and Menominee people had been engaged with capital markets for centuries.[54]

Indian commissioners characterized resistance to sales of land as a sign of a precapitalist, under-evolved savagery. In defending the lumbering on Anishinaabe land done under Mercer, Commissioner Binger Herman explained that "generally speaking, those full-bloods who have adopted the ways of civilization, and practically all of the half-breeds, are satisfied with the logging operations because they said all young men who would work earned $1 per day last winter." He then went on to describe "Indian councils," in which "young men, warmly dressed, with cropped hair and intelligent faces, took the floor and said they wished the camps to run; that they wanted work and had adopted the white man's way," while the only objections came from "old men, wearing blankets, carrying tomahawk pipe, and with long, matted hair [who] spoke with pride that they would never work for a white man."[55] Commissioners directly related their judgment of how "civilized" a man was to his ability to engage with the market: a "poor" Indian was one focused on the egalitarian division of subsistence-level harvests; a "shrewd" mixed-blood was one who was interested in accumulating individual wealth.[56]

If Indian commissioners framed their understanding of the Anishinaabe in racialized (and deeply racist) terms, Anishinaabe objectors were savvy in responding
in ways that spoke to their understanding of what, ultimately, the commissioners
wanted from them. In defending their right to communal property and the seasonal round, they couched their objections in the language of capitalism. In an
1898 letter to the commissioner of Indian affairs for Minnesota, Chief White Hair
explained that his anger was based on the fact that the forests the Office of Indian
Affairs was logging were "my own property," and that "we want our young men to
do this work and cultivate habits of industry in them." The commissioner's own report noted that only 30 percent of the labor on Anishinaabe land was carried out by
Native men, and Chief White Hair objected that the office was "having our timber
cut by the white men and half-breeds."

What White Hair objects to is not, in and of itself, the cutting of the community
resource, but the fact that the capital generated by that cut was leaving the community. He finished by saying that he "most positively object[ed] to the removing of our
timber from this reservation to some distant place." Instead, he wanted to "get some
benefit from it, not only by selling the timber, but it will give employment to *our*
young men and help supply *us* with the necessities of life" (emphasis mine). What is
clear here is that while Chief White Hair uses the capitalist language of industry and
property ownership, he in no way adopts the individualism behind it: the timber,
and the capital produced by its logging, are intended as communal resources.[57] His
lumping in of "half-breeds" with white men here is telling: half-breed often did not,
in fact, imply a specific ethnic makeup. The métis, whose mixed parentage was usually a result of the fur trade, were far more likely to engage in individualistic market
pursuits. Soon, the ethnicity came to stand in for the attitude: Anishinaabe regularly used terms like "half-breed" and "mixed blood" to refer to men and women
engaged in the market, regardless of actual ethnicity or lineage.[58]

Even the youngest, most market-oriented of the Anishinaabe were primarily focused on the shepherding of community resources. *The Tomahawk*, the newspaper
of the White Earth Reservation, was run from the village of White Earth, which historian Melissa Meyer has argued was where the most market-oriented of the White
Earth Anishinaabe clustered. And yet it, too, represented the woods as a community resource, and the capital generated by them to be the same. In 1903 it reported
that "a death recently occurred, (the relatives of the deceased being unable to pur-
chase coffin) no lumber being on hand for coffin purposes, the lumber had to be
borrowed from a distant neighbor who happened to have some. Such are the conditions on the reservation."[59] Lumber, here, is a free resource to be used when capital
is not available—a community resource.

In 1909, this Forest Service logging camp in Shawano County, Wisconsin, employed both Euro-American jacks and Menominee loggers. Photograph by E. A. Braniff, U.S. Forest Service Records, National Archives.

This pattern, at least in the White Earth newspaper, continued throughout the lumbering period. *The Tomahawk* published arguments throughout the 1910s and 1920s criticizing the mismanagement of Menominee resources by Indian agents as failing to protect the community, and protect the resources for future use. But, as a matter of fact, the Menominee were yet more successful than the Anishinaabe, managing to maintain control over both their lumber and finances. They were, moreover, deeply resistant to having white laborers in their camps, complaining that they seduced and raped Menominee women, and asking for police protection against them.[60]

And yet, one seemingly obvious contradiction remains: a tree is not wild rice or berries, and it does not regenerate within a year, or even many. But the difference between the two is a false dichotomy based on a short-term understanding of time. Anishinaabe ethics operate by the seven-generation rule: living men and women are responsible to the seven generations that came before them, and responsible for the seven that come after. When the future is not conceived of in years, or even decades, but in generations, the decision to use the forest to generate capital for the community makes sense. In seven generations they would, indeed, grow back. But the land, once lost, was lost for good. Keeping it in Anishinaabe hands was paramount.

The push and pull between Anishinaabe Chi Inaakonigewin and capitalist ideas of nature continues today. From 1976 to the early 2000s, the Sokaogon Chippewa battled Exxon's proposed mine at Crandon, partially by defining Manoomin (wild rice) as a culturally protected resource. In doing so they successfully argued that traditional lifeways (including wild rice harvesting) were still the center of Anishinaabe culture. In the late 1980s, Anishinaabe men attempting to reclaim treaty rights to fish walleye were attacked, instigating what were unofficially known as the "Walleye Wars," a pitched battle between local white populations and the Anishinaabe. While nominally a battle over the environmental protection of walleye, the racist undertones came to the surface almost immediately when one crowd of protesters began chanting, "Save a walleye . . . spear an Indian."[61] Further north, Anishinaabe in Ontario enacted a blockade in 2002/3 to stop logging on their lands and preserve hunting and fishing rights.[62] And it is still alive: one group of White Earth Ojibwe, for instance, are using their treaty rights to gather wild rice in order to sell that rice on and use the profit to buy back land lost in the allotment scandal known as the White Earth Tragedy.

Jacks, both Euro-American and Anishinaabe, walked out of camps for a dozen different reasons. For some it was about pay; for some it was because there was no need to work the whole winter. Moreover, as Nelson's memories of tramping through the woods reveal, men often left simply because the conditions were not what they expected. Low as the bar may seem, the jacks did expect certain standards. While men could not find their way up and out of the lumber system, nor could they save and invest in a different life, they could, within a limited framework, choose the conditions under which they would consent to work.

Their reasons might seem small-scale or trivial, or, in the minds of their employers, simply irrational. But it would be shortsighted to dismiss the kind of resistance that lumberjacks had been practicing for half a century before the strikes. The lumber barons themselves found it no small source of consternation. John Nelligan, who had himself been a lumberjack, was keenly conscious of the need to keep jacks around and made sure, when he came to own his own camps, that they "kept good order in the camps, furnished the best of board and paid the best of wages." As a result, "Some of [his] men worked continuously for [him] for twenty years."[63]

The Weyerhaeuser company in particular invested its time and energy in attempting to stanch the flood of labor away from their camps. J. P., Frederick's son, was convinced that "attractive, homelike assembly or social halls . . . could be powerful factors in overcoming the restless, roving, spirit now possessing many of our men." Moreover, he insisted that since labor unrest was higher if men were unmarried, there ought to be cheap portable houses provided for workers. Perhaps J. P. was right, but he would not have a chance to test his theory until the lumber industry had long since left the Northwoods. In Tacoma, Washington, Weyerhaeuser at last built the houses that were meant to stifle the roving ways of the Northwoods jacks.[64]

While the IWW was quick to take credit for the 1916 strike, and they surely helped execute it, attributing the jacks' strike to either Finns or communists, or both, misses a fundamental truth of the Northwoods lumber industry. A few months of underground organizers spreading One Big Union are hardly likely to have caused the sudden action of thousands of men. Nor is there good reason to believe that jacks were likely to respond to the careful organization of a distant authority. Moreover, if it was the call of union that took the jacks out of the woods, that can hardly explain their scattering to the wind soon after reaching Virginia, and returning to the camps with no concessions from management mere weeks after they left. But the call of Beaton—an itinerant man with a lumberjack's swagger and bravado, and a lumberjack's thirst for violence—tapped into their own endemic methods of resistance.

Over the final decades of the nineteenth century, in the years following the battle of Beef Slough, the lumber industry in the Northwoods underwent a massive transformation. Increased demand and changes in technology both inside the camps and in transportation led to unprecedented growth in logging. As corporate interests consolidated their power over the Northwoods, older, smaller, family-run camps were pushed out. Within the larger camps, men were separated by space and education to create increasingly rigid class stratification. Men who were once able to rise through the ranks to own their own camps were now shunted into a permanent working class. Lumber barons and their allies in the government and the press considered the lumber industry to be largely immune to the labor agitation that shook other industrial enterprises in the early twentieth century. Striking, they argued, was simply not in the lumberjack's *nature*. Newspapers in 1917, especially, wrote themselves in circles attempting to separate the strikers from the genial, egalitarian lumberjack that had already emerged as a modern folktale. The *Daily Virginian* of Virginia, Minnesota, covered the strike—a voluntary walkout of more than two thousand lumberjacks—with the headline "Armed Squads of IWW's Drive Lumberjacks Out of Camps."[65]

SMOKING HIM OUT.

A cartoon from the *Duluth News Tribune* in 1917 captures the response that many northern Minnesota towns had toward outside agitation from the IWW during the lumber strike. Courtesy of the Minnesota Historical Society.

It is true that jacks had long seen their independence from one another, in addition to their ability to walk out on a contract, as a valuable asset. It took the skilled organization of the Wobblies to convince them otherwise. But they hardly needed the Wobblies to explain to them that they lived and worked in nearly intolerable conditions under a system of labor that had little room for advancement. By 1917, and indeed by the turn of the century, logging camps were highly stratified sites of labor where authority and wealth were out of reach for most workers. Divided physical space as well as hiring and pay policies created a rigid class structure within camps and throughout the industry. In return, workers used what they considered to be a central tenet of their manhood and independence to bargain: the right to walk away.

Their itinerancy served a dual purpose. The networks of movement paradoxically created a mobile community among lumberjacks, tying together wandering workers into a cohesive laboring culture. Secondly, the lumberjacks used itinerancy as a method of resistance against their employers, walking out when conditions did not suit them. By striking en masse, lumberjacks were not using a new method of resistance but rather acting on several decades of tradition. While the jacks were itinerant, their actions and patterns of movement were far from random.

In the spring these men emerged from the woods. They came in packs with the melting of the snow, carrying their few possessions and their winter's check for the annual spree, before moving on to find work in sawmills or on farms. While some returned to family farms, most average jacks were unmarried "drifters," to quote one former logger.[66] During the spring breakup these itinerant men burst violently and loudly into the towns of the Upper Midwest. While some of these towns and villages, like Seney and Deer River, existed for the almost sole enjoyment of lumberjacks, others were more established cities, tied into the lifeways and labor practices of larger industrial centers.[67] Networks of itinerancy, cultural interchange, and labor practices that had been hidden by the forests poured out into the open with the melting snow.

# FIVE

# "SUCH PEOPLE MAY INVADE THE CITY"

## TRAMP SCARES AND SKID ROWS

The simplest plan probably, where one is not a member of the Humane Society, is to put a little strychnine or arsenic in the meat and other supplies furnished to him.

> —advice on caring for tramps, *Chicago Tribune*, July 12, 1887

"The town was more or less divided into the 'fine people' and the 'roughs.'"

> —reminiscences of Richard Hector Deadman

Toward the end of the nineteenth century, a new figure emerged on the American landscape as an object of concern, even of terror. He was a menace and a carrier of social disease—a product of what was broken in cities and in men, the dark underside of the Industrial Revolution. The French had named the disease that spurred him on: "fugue"—the rejection of place and a restless disposition to wander. It was the pathological form of what Americans had also begun to consider a disease, calling it "tramp fever" or the "tramp evil." Eventually and inevitably eugenicists classified him as having the inbred, lesser racial trait of "nomadism." The new order of Gilded Age America had created on its fringes a man for which society had no place: the tramp.

The problem felt particularly modern. For Gilded Age Americans the tramp scare was not merely a demographic phenomenon or cause for charitable concern, but an acute symptom of a cancer at the very foundations of society. Tramps represented a deterioration of moral certainty caused by an increasingly anonymous

111

The tramp scare of the late nineteenth century was typified in a cartoon in 1879 by James Albert Wales titled "I am the new constitution!" Courtesy of the Robert B. Honeyman Jr. Collection, Bancroft Library, University of California, Berkeley.

society. For Americans experiencing the breakneck pace of change in the second Industrial Revolution, tramps represented a rising wave of moral chaos unleashed by the Civil War and industrial society. It is true that during this period there was a marked increase in homelessness, a genuine symptom. But in a hypochondriac fervor Americans saw the tramp not just for what he was but also as a manifestation of something much larger, and much darker.

The reality was that while the Gilded Age caused a shift in the demographics of homelessness, the problem itself was not new. Transients, vagrants, seasonally employed men, and destitute families were not inventions of the late nineteenth century. Laws had existed from colonial times for "warding out" transients, keeping elements of unrest out of towns. For most of the colonial and antebellum periods, the problem was relatively small, and not the cause of great social commentary. Homeless people were understood to be—and in fact were—a mixed group. Immigrants, orphans, poor families, and unwed women made up an enormous proportion of transients. This was reflected in the gender-neutral language that referred to the wandering poor as "beggarly people." It was assumed that these men and women were still part of families, but merely in need of work. Men were not referred to as homeless, but masterless. But the language, gender composition, and size of the problem were all due to change drastically in the wake of the Civil War and the Panic of 1873.[1]

The war left huge numbers of men not merely unemployed, but cut free from their families and seemingly tethered to no one at all. The economic strain of the Panic increased the problem. Men lost factory work and took to the roads, tramping. Women still made up a significant proportion of the wandering poor, though the exact numbers are hard to estimate. But, unlike men who relied on municipal station houses, which kept thorough public records, for beds, women often fell upon private charitable organizations instead. With the dearth of records, it is hard to do much more than guess, but historians estimate women made up a little under one-fifth of the homeless during the Gilded Age.[2]

These numbers are hard to find for a reason: our knowledge about the Gilded Age tramping problem is hindered and obscured by the hysteria that problem caused—and that hysteria was in a large part *because* their numbers were unknowable. Across Europe and the United States, the late nineteenth century was a period of fevered counting, listing, and mapping. This was the era of censuses and poverty maps; while the former had been central to American democracy from the framing of the Constitution, they shot up in popularity in Canada and Britain as a means to better know the population. The more governments were able to know about their citizenry, the more they were able to transfer power from brute force to mobilizing consent in an increasingly controlled and regulated society.[3]

Gilded Age and Progressive Era Americans enthusiastically took up the banner of mapping, surveying, and turning populations into clearly legible statistics. The hope was that by doing so, they would be able to intervene more effectively to help uplift individual lives and create more orderly societies. But the process had an inverse effect, as well: the more Gilded Age Americans mapped and surveyed, the more they knew, and problems that had not previously been visible became sudden, dangerous forces. Moreover, some parts of urban life simply refused to be recorded in neat columns and categories. Transients could not be pinned down to an address, seasonal workers could not be described by their occupation, and wandering men refused to make themselves stable enough to submit to becoming statistics.[4] So while homelessness may not have been new, the tramp scare was. Suddenly, a single symptom became a monster embodying Americans' worst fears, the dark underbelly of the bright optimism of Gilded Age capitalism.

The fear of tramps obscured their reality. The extent of their growth is almost impossible to measure: not only were tramps left off any censuses or records, their numbers grew hand in hand with a popular terror, what historian Kenneth Kusmer has called an "antitramp hysteria," making it difficult to measure the gaps between the actual problem of homelessness and the cultural concern it spawned. As soon as the tramp had a name, as soon as Americans recognized him to be a problem, he was suddenly everywhere. As geographer Tim Cresswell argues in *The Tramp in America*, "the tramp was 'made up,' brought into being, by a body of knowledge it was claimed was actually *about* them."[5] Essentially, the more tramps were discussed and feared, the more visibly problematic they became. The fear of tramps made people notice tramps, and as soon as Americans saw them, they could not look away. Because while the physical fact of tramps may have been a result of war and financial crisis, the cultural understanding of them came to represent much, much more. The idea of the tramp came to fill a cultural role almost entirely separate from the reality of the tramp.

Vagrant men looked for work, rode the rails, begged for food, patronized saloons, and labored in a vast variety of industries. They were individuals: actual people with unique lives. But tramps, as a cultural creation, served an entirely different purpose: they defined the margins of society, and by doing so, they defined its core.

In 1910, activist and scholar Dr. Ben Reitman drew what he considered to be a conceptual map of the social geography of difference. The mainland was the Land of Respectability (a land not much appreciated by Reitman, who included the "peninsula of submerged hope" as part of it) surrounded by the Sea of Isolation, leading out into the Ocean of Despair. At the furthest borders of the map, connected by a small bridge to Criminal Island, was Vagrant Isle, with its cities of Hoboville, Trampie, Beggar, and Bumtown. It was even further from the mainland than the Poverty Islands or, indeed, Race Prejudice Isle. For Reitman, observing the American landscape in 1910, there was not any "other" more fundamentally different from the Land of Respectability than the hobo.[6] He was the outsider among outsiders: the definition of what did not, what *could* not, belong.

For middle-class Americans homelessness felt almost like a pointed attack on their dearest value: the moral certainty of the Victorian home. Through the early nineteenth century the idea of home, and home as synecdoche for the entirety of domestic life, took on increasing cultural importance. As Cresswell argues, settlement and the creation of a home become "surrounded by terms such as 'involvement' and 'commitment'—terms that insinuate transience and mobility to be morally ambiguous at best."[7] If a family at home was moral, countable, and stable, then hobos were just their opposite: vagabonds have no root in place. They are outside the moral framework of the home, signs of chaos and disorder.

In earlier generations the wandering poor had appealed to mainstream sensibilities, purposefully using their families as proof of their moral righteousness. When begging for work in the 1820s and 1830s, men petitioning the city of Baltimore pleaded, in part, on behalf of their families. One man's petition noted, for instance, a "helpless family entirely dependent on him for subsistence."[8] These pleas appealed strongly to one of the pillars of nineteenth-century middle-class manhood: supporting dependents.[9] Manhood hung on one's ability to keep and provide for families, servants, and other members of the household. These men may have been masterless, but they were hardly homeless. By emphasizing family, they appealed to their similarity to middle-class mores. Gilded Age tramps, on the other hand, looked utterly foreign.

Outside of home and family, men had no such ties to moral uprightness or community obligation. Tramps, then, were seen to embody a particularly modern, and particularly threatening, version of masculinity: one that had cut ties entirely with attempts at respectability. Unmoored from the anchor of home, tramps posed a particular threat to women and the sacred space of home. The fear of encountering a tramp at the door, a masculine presence in a feminine world, always came with the distinct threat of sexual violence. Posters, public safety campaigns, and even legal codes all make this abundantly clear.[10] In focusing on the home as a feminine space, however, historians have not gone far enough in understanding the threat that tramps posed to moral frameworks. While a strange man at the door surely posed a threat to the sanctity of a married woman's space, he also deeply threatened middle-class masculinity.

The tramp represented a masculinity that had parted ways with the most important institution not just for women, but for men. Domesticity was meant to temper masculinity, to instill it with honor and responsibility. Gilded Age manhood, especially for the middle classes, was a delicate balancing act. While men were increasingly invested in the physicality and aggression of manhood—pugilism, hunting, and bodybuilding were all on the rise as respectable pastimes—this aggression was not meant to be left unchecked. The home, the ties of domesticity, provided an important counterbalance. White men were meant to cultivate their raw masculinity, but they were also encouraged to learn to harness it and control its worst excesses. The responsibilities of the home provided both the carrot and the stick: a tranquil domestic life was the reward for protecting and investing in the home.

Even that most rough-and-tumble of arenas, the American West, was made safe only by the existence of domestic life. Americans had long lauded moving west as a natural way to ease class tensions, and that movement was idealized as specifically domestic. In John Gast's famous 1872 painting *American Progress*, it is single men who lead the movement west. But they are followed, hard on their heels, by settled farms and homesteads, wagon trains full of families, and quaint villages. The whole scene is lit and led by progress: Grecian, benign, white, and female. But the reality of the postwar West during the era of competitive capitalism was very different from the ideal. Extractive industries attracted thousands of men, and many came without families. And a man without the burden and blessing of a family had no incentive to reign himself in, no reason for restraint.

To contemporary observers, the connection was clear. One former logging camp cook—a married man himself—noted that he was so careful to let men who tended to fight go because "my goodness, they'd kill one another." He explained that it was all well and good in camps "where the farmers go up in the winter. That's different." Farmers had homes, wives, and responsibilities. But in his rural camp "there [are] very few of them that are married or have a home, they're just wandering. What you call a wandering Jew. Their place is . . . their home is where they hang their hat." Finally, he concluded, "Well, you've got to just be careful who you're dealing with, that's all."[11] Raw muscularity and rough masculinity was fine in a farmer. In a vagrant it was dangerous.

It was their wandering that made the homeless men into a source of moral panic in a way that the rough culture in which working-class men partook nationally was not. The tramp evil of the 1870s and later undermined the idea that men were held in check and balanced by families: it was mobility unmoored from civility; it was masculinity untempered by responsibility and domesticity. The "masterless men" who panicked colonial officials had become something much worse: homeless.

Popular magazines portrayed (and often still do portray) the homeless as a faceless threat, a group of interchangeable tramps. But from within, there was nothing homogeneous about vagrants. As multiple studies have shown, the vagrants of late nineteenth-century America were a heterogeneous mix of nationalities and backgrounds, from immigrants to native-born white-collar workers fallen from grace.[12] But more importantly to the men involved, vagrants and the homeless were divided into three fundamentally distinct groups: hobos, tramps, and bums. Bums were nonmobile and not seeking work. Tramps were mobile and used that mobility to avoid both work and the law. Hobos, on the other hand, were mobile, yes, but mobile in the pursuit of work, whatever work came to hand.

Hobos rode the rails to get to and from harvests, mills, and industrial sites. They followed the rhythms of the agricultural year. Perhaps most importantly, they were indispensable to the American economy. To hobos in particular, this distinction was fundamental. And to their own minds, lumberjacks were far from hobos. Their lives and community were defined not only around work, but also around the skills of their craft. They were a community of workers with a defined and deeply embedded culture. Yet their own definitions were not what carried the day.

From the outside, vagrants of all classes were painted with the same brush. For most Americans, there was no fundamental difference among the categories of vagrants, and the linguistics ran together. In 1884, *Century* magazine claimed the word "hobos" was in fact a nickname for tramp, not a fundamentally different kind of person. Moreover, to middle-class audiences the distinctions were a moot point, since men could easily slip from one category into another. As one contemporary commentator noted, distinctions among vagrants were useless since distinction "ignores the successive steps by which an ambitious worker may degenerate to the lowest derelict."[13] Vagrancy and homelessness were degenerate, dangerous, and highly contagious. When conceived of this way—from the outside in—the combination of unemployed tramps, urban homeless, and itinerant workers made the population of drifters in the Gilded Age seem impossibly large and deeply threatening. It is only through this lens that the deep antipathy Northwoods settlers had for lumberjacks becomes not only explicable, but nearly inevitable.

In the eyes of the residents of the Northwoods boomtowns, lumberjacks were a sickness, and all townspeople could do was hope to quarantine the infection. The itinerant workers of the Upper Midwest seemed to observers "like the flock of swallows that come in the springtime."[14] They were a natural phenomenon of the

W. A. Rogers, "Harvest hands on their way to the wheat fields of the northwest," published in *Harper's Weekly,* 1890. Courtesy of University of Michigan Library.

landscape, their appearance in town, and the appearance of the prostitutes who came to profit from them, a sure sign of "the coming of the spring." One North Dakota paper reported their "westward migration" to the plains "after a long winter's confinement to the logging camp of northern Minnesota." It went on to narrate the jacks as essentially unconscious beings, responding solely to nature when it warned that "the rain of today and warm sun of yesterday will stir their blood and they will be here for their annual stunt."[15]

But to many who reported on the jacks' appearance, they were less a weather phenomenon than a natural disaster. When the thaw came, men who had remained hidden in the woods all winter rushed into the cities in an uncontrollable tide.[16] A typical article, titled "Lumberjack Rush on Cities Begins," ran in the *Minneapolis Star* on April 3, 1906. The jacks were described as a seasonal occurrence, with "men are coming down from the woods for the spring." The article notes, with mild panic, that of the fifteen thousand men who worked the woods that winter, five thousand were likely to head for the Twin Cities, where "labor agencies have already begun to do a rushing business supplying them with new jobs." The jacks are then described to city-dwellers as an interesting, if foreign, animal with fascinating habits. "The average lumberjack," the paper tells the good people of Minneapolis, "knows little of the value of money. . . . It is simply something with which he can secure whatever his fancy desires." The horde is also curiously passive—the article declares that "the lumberjacks will be shipped to North Dakota, Wyoming, Oregon and Washington." The lumberjacks are presented, throughout, as a swarm of locusts set to descend upon the city, a pest and infestation that could not be stopped. At best, they would be deflected, at worst, endured.[17]

It is clear from these reports that lumberjacks seemed, to those who witnessed them from the perspective of urban order, something almost less than human. Indeed, historian Frank Higbie argues that this was true of nearly all migratory workers in the late nineteenth century. When comparing itinerants to other laborers, he argues, even organizers saw them not only as the bottom of the economic scale but as a "quasiracial other," who were marked with savagery.[18] They had nothing to restrain their worst impulse. Without a tether to home, they became a kind of beast. And lumberjacks were worse than most: if the point of statistics and maps were to make the invisible and chaotic orderly and legible, how much worse was it when the illegible, chaotic infestation emerged from unmapped forests, like the woods themselves inflicting their very worst pests on the towns.

The infestation, and anxious response to it, reached its height during the jack's annual rite of spring: the "spree." Sprees were infamous in Northwoods towns. Their tradition was noted in Minnesota as early as 1871, when Frank Johnson, a land scout, described a trip up the Crow Wing River. "This is the worst place I ever got into for drinking," he noted in his diary. "It is the first place the lumbermen can get any liquor after staying in the woods all winter and they all get on a spree. Lots of bed bugs."[19] Later, the spree became almost mythologized—a central characteristic of a good lumberjack was the ability to go on a truly destructive spree. The general outline of a spree shows up, again and again, in the memoirs of jacks. R. A. Brotherton's 1920s account of the early logging days of the Upper Peninsula lays out the typical format for townspeople remembering a spree:

All winter was spent in camp, saving his money as he had no opportunities to spend it, and when the spring break-up came he took his time check, sometimes amounting to several hundred dollars, and hiked to Escanaba, Menominee or Marquette for a good time.

He would proceed to make up for lost time, spending his money recklessly for booze, women and song, and would wake up from his spree either in jail or in an alley,

Lumber boomtowns like Eau Claire, pictured here circa 1870, were small enough that the arrival of lumberjacks in the spring was an annual event worthy of handwringing. Courtesy of the Chippewa Valley Museum.

his head aching, his clothes torn and his money gone. He would drift around for a short while and then go on the river drive or back to the woods to repeat the process.[20]

Sprees like this were widespread and considered a natural hazard to Northwoods life; like blizzards in the winter and prairie storms in the summer, the spree came with spring. Northwoods citizens recalled the sight of a hundred or more lumberjacks arriving in a small town. For some of the men, this would be one of the few days of the year they had money to spend. After a stop to cash their time checks, they would head directly to the saloon where they "became raucous and rough" and led the good people of town to "barricade their doors," since it was "not uncommon for them to engage in knifing and drinking sprees." John Nelligan recalled in his 1929 memoir that in Seney, he "could look out the window and see about five hundred drunks on main street." Luckily, they were at least considered to be

short-lived. After a Virginia, Minnesota, newspaper reported in 1912 that "the festive lumberjack again becomes an integral figure in Virginia. . . . Each comes with
a 'roll,' the result of their winter's saving," you can hear the relief with which they
conclude that "most of them will be ready to return to work, if they can find work,
within a fortnight."[21]

Nelligan's story is almost certainly an exaggeration, but the fear of lumberjacks,
and the assumption that they represented a sort of uncontrollable natural disaster,
was common. Hope Mineau, who grew up in southern Minnesota and eventually
married a retired jack, recalled the reaction of townspeople to the arrival of lumberjacks with the river drive:

> When the drive came down, why people stayed inside pretty much. . . . They were
> pretty rough, so when the drive was in, people stayed off the streets. If they saw a light
> and they were drinking they might shoot at it or something like that, but if folks stayed
> off the streets and left them alone, why those men wouldn't molest you.[22]

Mineau's sentiment that "if folks stayed off the streets and left them alone" they
would not be attacked is common. In her inelegant rationalization of the lumberjack's behavior, she betrays the insecurity inspired by the lumberjacks and their
seemingly uncontrollable behavior. At heart, it was the duty of every "civilized" person to stay out of their way. Their exuberance, violence, and likelihood to molest
passersby were seen as natural, immutable.

To those who lived among lumberjacks, their holding a town hostage once
a year was just the certain result of a winter spent in the woods. After months of
deprivation, those who watched the spree saw it as inevitable that lumberjacks
would overcompensate, regardless of any consequences. When Josephine Grattan's husband allowed their logs to be rafted to the mill under the supervision of
several jacks, both she and her husband felt it was only natural to fear that their
winter's work might be undone by alcohol. While the jacks supervising the logs
were "trusted men," there was "one danger. That is thirst." The men were already
having "a sort of fling celebrating [their] near completion of river work," and she
feared that after "men have been deprived of liquor so long, one drink will lead to
another, and soon they will be insensible." The logs, once safely guarded by trust-
worthy jacks, would become "an easy prey those who have plied [the lumberjacks]
with liquor."[23]

The men had nothing to control them and no moral framework in which to operate. Their behavior fundamentally threatened the respectability of Northwoods
towns. A minor newspaper report about a kerfuffle on a train in Port Huron,

Rowdy lumberjacks on the street in front of a saloon in Munising, Michigan, circa 1900. Courtesy of Superior View Photography.

Michigan, simply used the word "lumberjack" to describe any man of bad manners who failed to behave reasonably or respect ladies.[24] They were a hopeless case. The best that civilized townspeople could do was to create a district for the men and hope that they kept to it.

Cities and towns across the Northwoods joined in with other Gilded Age and Progressive Era attempts to quarantine these pests and ensure they did not infect the broader social body. Across American cities, this was just about the best they could do to control the problem of vice and sin, just as it was to control the epidemics that raged across American cities throughout the century and up to the 1918 Spanish Flu. Nineteenth-century Americans were still locked in fierce debates about the causes of diseases and contagions. In the middle of the century, vigorous mapping began to make legible where disease was spread, and it became the role of governments to take on the new role of enforcing "public health," isolating drains and wells that generated diseases, and quarantining populations who might spread it further. Once the source of a disease could be identified, the contagion was suddenly possible to treat and, moreover, necessary to treat to keep the rest of society healthy.

These ideas soon spread to "moral diseases" of vice, prostitution, drunkenness, and other "degenerate" activities. The leap was not necessarily as illogical as it may now seem if you encounter it from a Victorian mindset. Here, it is helpful to turn from the lumberjack to what was, in the minds of the respectable middle classes of the Northwoods, his constant companion: the prostitute. For, to observers, the two were inseparable: "It is not for drink alone this misspent money goes," wrote one eastern journalist in an 1893 article; "with the coming of spring, strange women whisk along the sidewalks of the lumbering towns with 'war-paint' on, ogling these giants of the woods, who, fresh from dingy winter camp and driving tent, are quick to lay their heads in the laps of these coarse carmined Delilahs, to be shorn."[25] Prostitutes here are just another symptom of the moral decay that lumberjacks brought in their wake when they infested a town.

Prostitution, for late nineteenth-century reformers, blurred the line between crime, contagion, and the actual human being who embodied both. Beginning with the British Contagious Diseases Acts, the clear solution to solving venereal disease seemed to be controlling its source: in this case, not the soldiers paying for sex but the prostitutes. The Contagious Diseases Acts of the 1860s set geographical boundaries to try to tie down the problem of prostitution: any women suspected of publicly selling sex within ten miles of military installations could be forced to be registered as a prostitute and tested every two weeks for venereal disease, with criminal punishment should they resist.[26] The prostitute, in this case, becomes the disease, the contagion to be controlled.[27]

But vice on the scale of the lumberjacks (and the prostitutes they frequented) could not simply be stamped out. These men were necessary workers, and late nineteenth-century ideals held that male sexuality needed a "safe" outlet if respectable women were to be spared. The very best towns could do was to attempt to corral the infestation and keep it somewhere where it could be controlled and avoided. The extent to which they failed gives a clear window onto the often enormous gap between the impossibly optimistic Victorian ideals of public sanitation and moral health and actual reality. The belief that men and women who failed to meet proper standards could be spotted by statisticians, diagnosed by medical and moral experts, and neatly tidied away by the legal system and emerging bands of social workers engaged in "public housekeeping" starts to seem either sweetly or menacingly naive when it is contrasted against the messy, intractable realities of urban and especially small-town life.

For while reformers, boosters, and memoirists insisted that their towns controlled contagions either by isolating them in big cities or, as will be discussed below, simply imagining them not to exist in small towns, the boundary was not nearly as resilient as they would have their audiences believe. Women in general, and prostitutes in particular, formed the most permeable boundary between the "nice" part of town and skid row, needed and despised in almost equal measure. Moreover, observers felt both more able and more obligated to interfere directly in the lives of prostitutes. Their gender opened prostitutes up to moralizing and beneficent projects that helped middle-class residents affirm their sense of moral civility. But at the same time, boomtowns were frontier towns—and as on the farther west frontier, women were in short supply. When pressed, boomtown residents relied on prostitutes to provide the "civilizing influence" necessary to a properly developed town. Examining the lives of Northwoods prostitutes makes clear just how little ideology and memory can resemble reality.

It is worth, first, stepping back to understand the threat of prostitution to middle-class ideals of respectability. As many historians have argued, for women in the American West, prostitution was often the best of a bad set of options, and one of the few ways for women to earn an independent living.[28] But to contemporary eyes, prostitutes represented one of two threats to the middle-class gender norms of the time. On the one hand they were victims of "white slavery," so-called innocent doves snatched from the bosom of their homes, reflecting the failure of the family and society to protect respectable, innocent, and universally white womanhood. On the other they were prostitutes by choice, fallen women who fundamentally failed to live up to the standards of respectability and earn the right of male protection. Middle-class reformers and politicians in the Northwoods took up both narratives when thinking about the "problem" represented by sex workers.

Contemporary sensationalism combined with Victorian ideals of chaste womanhood make it difficult to pinpoint the *actual* extent of prostitution in the Northwoods, and particularly impossible to correctly gauge the extent of forced prostitution. The line for nineteenth-century Americans between prostitution and white slavery was clear: one was the choice of a fallen woman, the other a crime against innocent girlhood. In fact, nineteenth-century Wisconsin law only made it a crime to entice a woman into prostitution if she had a "chaste character."[29] What this means in practice is that a spectrum of agency on the part of the women, as well as of abusive behavior and coercion on the part of her employers, was neatly divided into a binary. Behaviors in the middle—women forced to make the choice to enter prostitution, women who chose prostitution but were nonetheless coerced

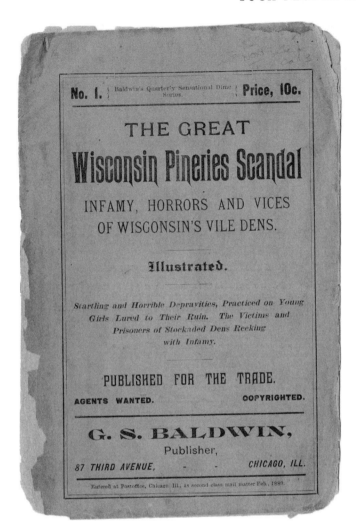

Vice dens of the Northwoods were revealed to the public in 1889 as part of a lurid profile published for Baldwin's Quarterly Sensational Dime Series titled *The Great Wisconsin Pineries Scandal*. Courtesy of Murphy Library, University of Wisconsin–La Crosse.

into hideous working conditions, women who led respectable lives off the back of money made in brothels—did not fit into this dichotomy and were left out of the dominant narrative. And in the Northwoods in particular, most prostitutes fell into that nebulous middle ground.

For female reformers, the prostitutes of the Northwoods fell almost universally on one side of the line: innocent victims who had been scandalously failed by their families and governments. "White slavery" was a preoccupation of the Gilded Age press. Scandalous, titillating, and helpfully linked to unwanted immigrants, it made for a perfect headline. Even the most respectable and prudish of progressive reformers could not object to the broad publication of salacious details if those details, at least in theory, served to save women from a fate worse than death. Courtrooms packed out for trials of sexual crimes, and stories of sexual scandals could dominate large urban papers as well as hometown journals for weeks. In a society increasingly preoccupied with a tightening of social mores and respectable silence around matters of sex and sexuality, white slavery scandals provided a sanctioned outlet for illicit conversations, a socially acceptable form of voyeurism.[30]

In the late 1880s, the eye of the press, and the approbation of the nation, fell on the Northwoods pineries. Starting in 1886, an alarming series of stories emerged from the woods. Julia Howden was promised respectable employment in the woods and found herself held in a fortified brothel, guarded by armed men. Minnie Pine was told she would work in a lumberjack hotel and was instead held down by two other women while forced to submit to sex with a stranger. More stories emerged across the late 1880s, sparking national public outcry.[31]

The progressive women and members of the Women's Christian Temperance Union (WCTU) responded with a flurry of articles and speeches painting an extraordinarily dark story of the lives of prostitutes in the Northwoods, speeches that just so happened to advance the public political lives of WCTU advocates. An article in a Kansas woman's rights newspaper reported a "large meeting" in the Detroit opera house to address the vice running rampant in lumber camps. This meeting took place in 1888, at the height of Michigan lumbering, and depicts an altogether disturbing image of the relationship between lumberjacks and prostitutes. Mrs. Obernauer, a WCTU leader, addressed the meeting on the subject of Northwoods prostitution, claiming that girls as young as fifteen were being tricked into lives of prostitution in the woods. Young women seeking employment in the Northwoods would follow seemingly reputable employment agents only to find themselves "taken to a deserted cabin and retained as close prisoners for the vilest purposes," where they were "forced to submit to terrible indignities." Other lurid tales included girls who had hung on to the branches of trees in the dead of winter to save themselves from dogs that were set on them by their captors. Mrs. Obernauer readily admitted that she had "been charged with over-stating the facts," but defended her claims as true.[32]

The work of Dr. Kate Bushnell lends some credence to Obernauer's claims. Bushnell, sneered at by the press as boyish, ungainly, and unattractive, devoted several years of her life to exposing what she saw as the great moral failure of her time: rampant white slavery in the Northwoods. Bushnell spent much of the mid-1880s in the Northwoods, exploring and exposing "dens of sin" in Wisconsin. She described finding "innocent girls entrapped by villains, their clothes exchanged for indecent costumes, escape made impossible, from six or eight to seventy-five imprisoned in each house, guarded in one known case by bull-dogs." Several reports confirm girls as young as thirteen "subjected to dreadful treatment, until a physical wreck." Overall, she found between thirty and sixty saloons in the Northwoods, all of which depended on lumberjacks for their primary trade.[33]

On the other side of the coin, local officials found little evidence to corroborate these stories. While prostitution was certainly common enough, white slavery as it was reported in the press baffled district attorneys in Wisconsin and Michigan. The governor of Michigan defended his district attorney's failure to prosecute white slavers by pointing out that the only evidence the public had of white slavery in the first place was that "respectable residents have told you these things are true."[34] Meanwhile, the governor of Wisconsin sent a private detective, James Fielding, to the Northwoods. Fielding reported that the guard dogs were petted by the women, that no one was required to stay, and that the only rule prostitutes were required to abide by was enforced sobriety.[35] Finally, a report to the Wisconsin State Legislature on "the White Slave Traffic and Kindred Subjects" in 1913 concludes that while prostitution was widespread in the state, little or none of it fell under the strictest definition of "white slavery" as defined by women being held behind bars.[36]

All this evidence, however, adds up to very little. In fact, once you filter out the interpretation and sensationalism, it becomes clear that there is very little difference in the *facts* of Bushnell's and Fielding's reports. The question of whether it was a horrific injustice in need of immediate legal action or an acceptable, if slightly unsavory, state of affairs stemmed not from a difference in evidence, but from a difference in attitude. Bushnell's account and outrage are based on an understanding of the women involved in Northwoods prostitution as victims, plain and simple. Her report does not linger on the character of the women, but rather on their treatment.

Fielding, the governors, the legislatures, and much of the press, however, saw things differently. White slavery stories succeeded because they traded in Victorian ideals of white womanhood. When it was "white slavery," the victims, readers were assured, were entirely innocent. They had left home seeking respectable employment and were forced into sex slavery against their will.[37] As early as 1889, the *Ashland Weekly News*, a Northwoods paper, complained that Dr. Bushnell was unfairly singling them out for critique. The paper happily admitted that there was "a bad state of affairs in northern Wisconsin in the line of dives and houses of bad repute . . . [that] are undoubtedly about as bad as they can be." But the paper pointed out that this was not remarkable, grumbling that "she could get more material in any [large city] in one day's walk than she could find in a month in northern Wisconsin." Bushnell's work was "sensational" and "emotional." This was not, the author insisted, really a problem at all.[38]

When Fielding reported that the sex workers in the woods were there by choice, he implied that they immediately rescinded their right to the legal protection to which an innocent girl would be entitled. The prostitutes, he insisted were "street walkers or taken from the dens or lowest houses of ill fame in Chicago. . . . There was never a girl but that was an old timer." To his eyes these women, having made this choice, were being treated as well as they could possibly expect. He noted that "a girl that comes here is treated well and if not [it is] her own fault. If she don't be-have she is driven away."[39] Given that lumberjacks later jokingly reported stories of dragging women out of brothels by their hair when asked to, it seems likely that even if women were there by choice, that does not mean they were "treated well."

It was under this legal framework, one that insisted that women be of "chaste character" to deserve the protections of the law, that governors, district attorneys, and local law enforcement tacitly sanctioned prostitution regardless of the treat-ment of women. In Minneapolis, efforts to close the houses of prostitution in the infamous First Avenue district were, in the words of the Minneapolis Vice Com-mission report of 1911, "in the nature of an abatement of a local nuisance than a crusade against vice on universal moral grounds."[40] The report noted that simply segregating prostitution into a vice district had "until very recently . . . been the un-challenged policy." Prostitutes in Minneapolis would report to the court monthly, plead guilty, and pay a nominal fine. As late as 1901, there was a move to lower the fine from $100 to $50, to make it less onerous to the prostitutes, whom the city con-sidered to be providing an unsavory, but necessary, service. The complaint of those districts that wished to remove brothels was not one of protecting the prostitutes, but rather that "it was difficult for the most respectable women to appear even in the street-cars near this district at night, without being subjected to insult by row-dies and men half intoxicated."[41] That the women who chose to be prostitutes might be treated poorly by the same men was not a matter for concern.

The same 1913 report to the Wisconsin legislature that found no evidence what-soever of white slavery reported something very different when that specific title was dropped. When the definition of coercion was widened from the kidnapping of girls to include "every instance where restraint is placed upon the free action of women and girls, through intimidation, debt, or pure lack of personal responsibil-ity," then there were dozens of instances.[42] The Minnesota commission likewise concluded that while they had "been unable to secure any evidence of the existence of an organized system" of white slavery, nor of more than "one or two" instances of forced detention, those figures did "not have reference to the quite common practice of exercising duress on inmates . . . by keeping them in debt."[43] These in-stances, however, were simply not considered to be worth the legislature's time

A PINERY DEN DANCE HALL IN FULL BLAST.

An illustration from *The Great Wisconsin Pineries Scandal* (1889) shows women carousing with lumberjacks in the pinery dens of the Northwoods. Courtesy of Murphy Library, University of Wisconsin–La Crosse.

or energy. When Bushnell, surrounded by scores of women from the WCTU, gave a rousing hour-long speech to the Wisconsin legislature, the response was polite attention and precisely no legislative action. To their minds, there simply was not much to be done, and these women—unlike true victims of white slavery—were not necessarily worth the effort. The vast forests protected the crime they hid, and the governor of Wisconsin groused that "many earnest, well-meaning people actually believe that if I just wave the executive wand over those vast, interminable forests of our Northern border, and mutter incantations, the den-keepers will be punished."[44] They were lost to sin, and lost to the woods. It was only when they crept back into cities that they, like the jacks they accompanied, became an issue for civic concern.

The very geography of the Northwoods' major cities betrays the extent to which the residents feared and despised lumberjacks as tramps to be quarantined along with the prostitutes whose services they purchased. City planners and legal authorities attempted to geographically and culturally isolate lumberjacks from more respectable elements of the cities, making literal the social geography of Ben Reitman. In the Gateway district in Minneapolis or the Cribs in Duluth, cities purposefully created an area in which transients could pass through without disturbing the more genteel elements of the town. Like shantytowns before them, these transient districts were built not only to house but to control their residents. By grouping the poor together and isolating them, middle-class Americans created an emotional distance from which they could judge the morality of the men housed in such squalid conditions. As Lisa Goff argues, "denigration of shanty dwellers sometimes tipped over from labeling them as foreign to describing them as inhuman."[45] The poor were already seen as a contagious threat that was difficult to contain when housed. When mobile, they were yet that much more unpredictable, that much more in need of control.

In larger towns, lumberjack areas were physically set aside from the more respectable parts of the city. There is, perhaps, more than a little hypocrisy in this. The larger cities of the Northwoods region were fed almost entirely, at least in the early days, by the lumber industry. While they were more likely to be made of brick and mortar than board and lathe, they were nonetheless the products of the Northwoods, and of lumberjacks. Secondary industries were directly tied to the primary task of cutting and milling wood. Shipbuilding took hold in Marquette, foundries produced the iron and steel products needed for milling, and agricultural markets thrived on the custom not only of the camps in winter but also of the large influx of men in the spring and summer. General merchants sprang up across the Northwoods, providing supplies to contractors and foremen in the fall, and new clothing and boots to lumberjacks in the spring. Lumber barons brought demand for ostentatious hotels. By the end of the lumber era these cities were no longer necessarily conceived of as lumber towns: saw-milling centers like Marquette, Saginaw, Alpena, and Bay City in Michigan, Eau Claire in Wisconsin, and Grand Rapids, Cloquet, and Stillwater in Minnesota created mixed economies able to survive the end of the industry. Duluth, perhaps the greatest success story of the lumber era, kept growing at its end. A city that had grown from fourteen families in 1869 to more than twenty-eight thousand people in 1890 simply turned its able harbor to shipping copper and iron. Some, like Minneapolis, moved on to other milling enterprises—what had been a wood city easily became a flour center—and yet have trundled on either as milling centers for second-growth wood or moved on to become mining towns.[46] Their geographies, however, betray their initial growth off the back of lumber.

The men who provided the labor that spurred all this growth were separated out, and towns attempted to make them as invisible as possible. While the towns happily defined themselves as lumber towns and lumber cities, it would not be until well into the twentieth century that Northwoods communities would laud the

A row of saloons lines the boardwalk along St. Louis Avenue in Duluth, Minnesota, circa 1875. Skid row districts were deliberately set apart from the more prosperous areas of town. Photograph by B. F. Childs. Courtesy of the Minnesota Historical Society.

lumberjack himself. In the era of the lumber boom, he was confined, with other vagrants, to an area where his morals and behaviors could not be infectious. At the same time, since vagrant laborers were huge sources of income, cities did not want to ban them. Instead, municipalities created quarters where police winked at, or even protected, certain vices.[47] This served the purpose of keeping jacks in town, but away from townspeople.[48]

The areas housing jacks became famous, or rather infamous, for the concentration of brothels, taverns, and hotels that filled them. In Muskegon, it was the Sawdust Flats, an area of "unspeakable whoredom and violence," in East Saginaw it was White Row, the Catacombs in Bay City, the Cribs in Duluth, and, with the greatest forthright economy of language, Dirtyville in Alpena. The use of the term "skid row" to refer to the worst part of town comes from the name for the ice roads on which the jacks skidded logs to the river, and referred to the area inhabited by

When a new paddy wagon arrived in Duluth, Minnesota, in 1909, the *Duluth Evening Herald* quipped, "What other city in the state can offer a lumberjack a free automobile ride as a grand climax to the customary spree?" Photograph by Hugh McKenzie. Courtesy of the Jim Dan Hill Library, University of Wisconsin–Superior.

lumberjacks.[49] These areas were seen as necessary evils to be tolerated by the better citizens of town. You can almost hear the Republican mayor-elect of Duluth in 1900 hold his nose as he admitted that "if we must have saloons, and the law allows them, let us try to make them as unobjectionable as possible." His best answer was to concede that "by common consent [they] are allowed to exist within certain bounds and under certain restrictions." He declared of gambling, prostitution, and carousing: "One thing I do know, and it is that there is no occasion or excuse for its existence in the residence part of Duluth." But of those who practiced these pastimes he could only admit that "such people may invade the city."[50]

To render them invisible, Duluth constructed an elaborate legal framework that allowed "sporting houses" to continue to operate within a constrained geography.

Separated out, they were less threat than local color. Frederick Jackson Turner, growing up in the Northwoods town of Portage, Wisconsin, barely took note of the lumberjacks, except to describe the colorful event when their rafts of logs appeared in the spring. Otherwise, they hardly show up in his own work. They were separate enough that in Marquette in the early 1900s a ladies' organization hosted an afternoon lecture to teach the middle classes some of the colorful language of the lumberjacks—surely something that would hardly be necessary if the two groups interacted with any regularity. Towns seem to have managed to keep this psychological separation despite the truly enormous numbers of men involved. During the 1880s some fifteen thousand men traveled annually to the cities along the Saginaw River in Michigan alone.[51]

The problem was more complicated for the smaller lumber towns. Places like Seney, Michigan, Hurley, Wisconsin, and Deer River, Minnesota, were dependent not just on the lumber industry, but on the trade of lumberjacks themselves. They were small centers near large tracts of woods that existed, almost in their entirety, to cater to jacks as they came off winters in the woods. More notorious than their larger counterparts, it was these little towns that became the stuff of legends. When F. Scott Fitzgerald wanted to invent an ideally ambiguous, mysterious past for Jay Gatsby, he made him come from Little Girl Bay, right outside Hurley.[52] None other than Ernest Hemingway decided that Seney was the ideal setting of rough-and-tumble masculinity for his "Big Two-Hearted River." Many of these towns died out to nearly nothing when the lumber industry moved on. Deer River, which once claimed twelve saloons, now has only a scattering of commercial storefronts, one café, and the Wagon Wheel bar. Seney experienced an even larger decline. The city that was once known as a capitol of sin is now a small crossroads, barely marked on the map. One café, two gas stations, and a small historical museum make up the heart of what once was "Incredible Seney."

In these small towns, the ideological drive to separate the contagion of vice was as strong as it was in the larger cities. J. C. Ryan recalled, growing up in a small town in the Minnesota Northwoods, that his mother warned him not to go near "certain houses" on the edge of town, because "little boys were not welcome" and "bad women lived there."[53] In places like Seney and Deer River, there was almost nowhere that was distant from the "bad" part, yet in his loving history of Deer River's early days John Zeterstrom mentions neither jacks nor their lodgings until halfway through his manuscript. Even then he only mentions them briefly. Clearly, for a man who grew up in the village, lumberjacks were an inevitable part of town life, but not—at least in the minds of its more well-heeled residents—an integral part of the town's character.

By the first decade of the twentieth century, Seney, once the busiest lumber town in Michigan's Upper Peninsula, was a mere ghost of its former self. Courtesy of Bentley Historical Library, University of Michigan.

Residents of these small towns, both in the height of the timber boom and in the years after, would insist that the reputation was unearned and unjustified, ignoring or denying the presence of moral contagions if they could not contain them. One journalist, in 1885, described Seney as having, and here we must forgive the author's faulty math, "altogether 21 houses in the village divided as follows: saloons, eight; hotels with bar, three; hotels without bar, one; music hall, one; drug store, one; dwelling houses, four; and one altogether unnecessary house of ill-fame, which comprises the twenty-one."[54] Later, Wilfred Nevue, in a hysterical defense of the lifestyles and morals of lumberjacks, insisted that Marquette County was home to only three short-lived houses of prostitution in the late 1890s, and men who frequented them were ostracized in the community.[55]

However, the historical record gives lie to these attempts to erase prostitution, violence, and vice from the landscape. Marquette County is right next to Seney. While the journalist insisted that the "house of ill-fame" was unnecessary, and Nevue claimed that they fell to ruins, it is not hard to find evidence to the contrary. Seney's historical society maintains photographs of the hotels on main street that clearly show prostitutes leaning over the upper balcony of at least two hotels, as well as one clearly marked brothel.[56] Deer River, Minnesota, a town with an equally dissolute reputation, had only seven schoolchildren in 1890, but twelve saloons and four hotels lined up on Whiskey Row. Meanwhile, a report on prostitution in Wisconsin described a "town of twenty five houses [in which] eleven were saloons and two dens of infamy," as well as "another town of four or five hundred inhabitants [which] contain[ed] four dens of infamy, each having from two to five inmates."[57] And it's worth noting that while vice commission reports found no white slavery, none of the legislative commissions in either Wisconsin or Michigan bothered to deny that there were prostitutes plying their trade in the Northwoods.

In the sparsely populated Northwoods towns, the actual lives of prostitutes showed how far the ironclad dichotomy of respectable versus fallen womanhood was from reality. Take the women leaning over the brothel balcony in Seney, for instance. Victorian morality and the fear of social contagion would lead a casual reader to assume they were ostracized from the "better" parts of town. And yet among the few photographs that remain of Seney in its lumbering heyday, one captures a group of women formally arranged for a portrait. They are a ladies' music group, a small sign of civic society in a rough town of three hundred. And yet, looking at another photo of women leaning over the balconies of the hotels where they worked as prostitutes, some faces look familiar: at least two of the band members were also prostitutes. With few women present in a town like Seney, it seems that the most civilized of pastimes could not afford to leave out prostitutes. In Muskegon, Michigan, town authorities went so far as to incorporate local prostitutes into their Independence Day celebrations in 1887. The city's prostitutes hosted a dance on a large pavilion built in the center of town for the occasion. In one Wisconsin town, the year after a brothel was burned down and its inhabitants run out of town, the Business Men's Association reached out to invite them back.[58] With few other women present, prostitutes took up the labor of "respectable" women as public civic figures engrained in the town's culture.

It is easy to see, here, that the isolation sketched into urban landscapes, and the warnings to stay away from the wrong houses, were more theoretical than real. In some places they were clearly effective, for instance in isolating Anishinaabe men and women in town. White concerns about the Anishinaabe often paralleled those of their concerns about jacks: they were uncountable since their location was never static and resistant to capitalism and its attendant social mores.[59] To this, a potent dose of racism was added. The Anishinaabe, too, were purposefully isolated in towns. An 1881 Mackinac Indian Agency report found that in the relatively small town of Marquette, Michigan (just over 4,500 in 1880), there was a community of

"Whiskey Row" in downtown Deer River, Minnesota, 1906. Courtesy of the Minnesota Historical Society.

about seventy Anishinaabe living in town. Yet they were so isolated that "few of the best acquainted residents of the city were aware that so many dwelt in their midst."[60]

This purposeful isolation, both by geographically constructing districts dedicated to the lumbermen and by writing them out of cities' central identities, lumped the jacks into a class with hobos. In the Northwoods (as around the country) hobos provided fundamental labor to keep the economy afloat. But this labor is not just underrepresented in our histories, it was also nearly invisible even at the time. Work at below living wages, the kind of menial, temporary, unskilled labor that could not support a family, fundamentally undermined the narrative of American prosperity built on the back of stable domestic families.

In the Gilded Age as now the increasing prosperity of the wealthy cannot be separated from the poor: rather than two separate stories of rising wealth and devastating poverty they are, as historian Seth Rockman puts it, "flip sides of the same coin," since "prosperity came to Americans who could best assemble, deploy and exploit the physical labor of others."[61] There is no such thing as American progress without the backs of laborers, laborers who were often left out of the story.

What is true of urban laborers is doubly true of vagrant workers. Their homelessness not only fundamentally threatened the narrative of material progress but defied the notion of home as a powerful organizational tool.[62] They undermined the moral strictures of domesticity. They were the necessary creations of capitalism—large-scale farming and industrial labor could not happen without a highly mobile workforce—but they also were visible signs of how disorienting industrial capitalism was. As historian Frank Higbie described it, "The paradox presented by seasonal laboring men was that they were at once strangers and familiars, homeless and linked to communities, marginalized socially and central to the extractive economy. Both their labor and degradation were pillars of American society."[63]

But of course lumberjacks did not conceive of themselves merely as tramps. In the woods they developed a distinctive culture, one that carried over into the boomtowns in summer. And while from the outside they may have appeared like a flock of swallows or a storm to be borne out while huddled behind locked doors, the spree and their lives in town take a different shape when seen through the eyes not of the horrified residents of the Northwoods towns but of the lumberjacks themselves.

# SIX

# FIVE HUNDRED DRUNKS IN THE STREET

## SNAKE ROOMS, SPREES, AND SALOONS

We've a camp stack to spend at the long winter's end,
And they're waiting to see us come down;
They are cracking up ice and they're raising the price
Of every damned thing in the town.
When the camp stacks are gone, and we'll see the gray dawn
And the fiddles are playing no more
When the pleasure has passed and we're busted at last
With a head that is hellishly sore
With no sighing or sobs we'll go looking for jobs
And thank the good Lord we're alive
For there's work and there's fun and white water to run
Down the Boardman along with the drive.

—"Winter Desires" from *Songs of the Michigan Lumberjacks*

The violence of lumber boomtowns reached the levels of legendary cow-towns. Men stood on corners challenging one another to fights, brawls broke out in the street, and police stalked the borders of vice districts. From the outside it looked like pure chaos, a moral contagion, and something to walk past quickly while holding your nose. Which is why we should not be looking at it from the outside. To understand lumberjacks' culture, we need to compare them neither to the middle-class observers nor to the family-oriented, "manly" trade unionists, whose stories populate much of our labor history. Instead, we need to see lumberjacks on their own terms.

When lumberjacks came into town, they entered as working-class vagrants into a world in which the identity, especially the gendered identity, of working-class men was far from clear-cut. Much of the study of working-class culture, up until the 1990s, was concerned with the culture and life ways of craft laborers. Their appeal to manly ideals—emphasizing respectability, domesticity, and skill—served to bolster the craft union movement.[1] But studying this group *alone* leaves out any comprehensive understanding of unskilled labor. Over the 1980s and 1990s a new historiography emerged detailing the "rough" culture of unskilled laborers that celebrated violence, drinking, cursing, and hypermasculinity. In the wake of these two historiographies, a third, compelling argument has emerged: what characterized the lives of most working men in the late nineteenth century was, in fact, neither of these, but rather the tension between them. As anthropologist Mark Walker concluded, "The contrast between rough and respectable masculinities was an ideal, not a reality. Most men experienced expectations of masculinity not as choices, but as tensions."[2]

And yet we still know very little about these men, and particularly little about their ideals of manhood. Historians tend to study what we can see—the stories that documents tell us. Craftsmen in their unions left us a rich store of documents. There were union newspapers and meeting minutes, bills for union dances; there are manifestos, and there are pamphlets. Many craftsmen themselves were literate and politically involved, meaning we have speeches and letters and for some men full archives of their personal papers. Itinerant workers and the urban poor had little of this. Often illiterate, rural itinerants did not even have a geographical base from which they could organize. Their alienation is so complete that it is nearly impossible to view them as anything but the beaten down, exploited residents of Reitman's Vagrants Isle, abandoned at the very edge of desolation. As a result, they enter our histories only as the flotsam of capitalist expansion, nameless victims tossed about by ruthless extractive industries.

And of course, there is some small truth to this: the lives of itinerant workers were unquestionably formed by alienation, shaped by capitalism, and the rhythms of their lives followed the cycles of extractive industry. But seeing them this way, as a lesser class of craftsmen fallen victim to the tides of history, loses a rich culture and ignores the ways in which these men shaped their own lives by making their own choices. Because for many that's exactly what tramping was—a choice.

While it is true that the rapid changes in capitalism in the late nineteenth century altered the power of workers with startling speed and finality, it is also true that for many who took to the rails or walking, there was nonetheless a choice involved.[3] As much as cities worked to section off rough elements from the more genteel parts of society by restricting districts of brothels, saloons, and flop houses to a small area, hobos and tramps purposefully sectioned themselves off from the control of the law and the rules of industrial respectability. On the edges of cities across the west, transients built "jungles," tent cities that were often positioned just far enough from town to be outside the prying eyes of the law.

To understand their culture, we need to look at them from *their* point of view. One of the earliest historians of rough working-class masculinity, Peter Way, warned in the 1990s against valorizing working-class struggle and class identity. He argued that giving too much agency to workers loses sight of the context in which they operated. Because of their exploitation, he argued, historians would do well to remember that "their culture (or, more accurately, cultures) reflected their alienation as much as it did a sense of community." The experience of unskilled workers, according to Way, "remained similar from industry to industry and over time," and portrayed a story not of "vibrant oppositional culture" but rather of "persisting powerlessness and social dislocation," because "it was impossible for them to build a stable community and institutional base from which to parry the thrust of history."[4]

And yes, certainly we must remember that when we write about working-class men, whose stories were rarely recorded, we do well to remember that these cultures came, in part, from a sense of alienation. There is a reason that the histories of so many of the very poorest and most destitute are yet to be written. They have existed as the alienated underclass, not even included in most labor history, which has relied on the much richer sources and clearer ideology of craftsmen. But it is possible to tell their stories, even from the scant sources we have, while still understanding their culture as something they did on purpose, not just a reaction to their bosses. After all, stories that present unskilled workers as the hapless victims of capitalism have been given more than enough attention already.

If we only see these men as victims, we miss their lives entirely. We frame our histories in the same way Gilded Age Americans formed their morality: if a man is not part of a home, if he is not attached to a family, then it must be because he was unable to have those things, too poor and too hard up to form a decent life. But that's not how itinerants saw their own lives. Whether it was for a few years or for a lifetime, tramping was a choice. To understand the ideas of masculinity and the ideals of community embraced by the very poorest laborers, we must attempt to see things their way. We must attempt to change the standards by which both masculinity and community are defined. For in assuming that vagrancy meant lack of community, and roughness meant a failure in manliness, historians—just as the lumberjacks' contemporaries—can fail to see the actual contours of their lives.[5]

Rather it is easiest to return to the image of men's understanding of their masculinity being arranged along a series of vectors—not a switch that turned on and off, but rather a series of dials tuned to different levels. Class, geography, age, skill, and

Men gather outside the offices of the Itasca Lumber Company in Deer River, Minnesota, circa 1910. By foot and train, lumberjacks descended on Northwoods lumber towns each spring for their annual spree. Courtesy of the Itasca County Historical Society.

race could all play a part in how far along the scale of, say, respectable to rough, any one man went. Studies of railroad construction workers, whose lives in many ways paralleled those of lumberjacks, demonstrate that the extent to which workers were likely to adhere to temperance rules correlated closely with their skill level.[6] Those of a higher skill, regardless of pay, tended to conform more strictly to the codes of temperance demanded of union members.

What is most vital of all is to understand that not all working-class behavior occurred in direct reaction to middle-class standards. It is not that lumberjacks "failed" to live respectable lives. In seeing the spree and rough masculinity as reactions to the culture of respectability, historians can fall into the trap of seeing behavior entirely through the eyes of the sources, most of which were written by middle-class men. But if one measures masculinity not on that scale, but on, for instance, the scale of camaraderie to selfishness, it becomes clear that lumberjacks were not so much failing one standard as succeeding at another.[7]

It was these different standards that made all hobos, including lumberjacks, completely inscrutable to the middle-class reformers determined to save them. In his history of hobos, Frank Higbie recounts the story of a man who, after two months working harvesting ice outside Chicago, ran into a charity worker who had helped him find employment earlier. The worker told her he was no longer looking for work. Not because he had found work, nor because he had inherited a steady income. Rather, he had worked two months and now he had enough money for the moment. When pressed, the worker told her, "I've *got money* . . . I don't need to work any more."[8] The charity worker was dumbfounded. His attitude, to her mind, made no sense. Work was something one had, something one needed—like a home. But to a lumberjack, who walked off jobs when he did not like the work and blew his stake as quickly as possible in the summer, this attitude toward work would have been familiar.

In order to understand the way lumberjacks functioned outside of the camps, we have to discard the standards of middle-class respectability entirely and instead try to understand their values on their own merits. To do so, we need to follow these transient workers out of the camps and into their other most stable community and natural summer home: the taverns that crowded the streets of the lumber towns.

It was in the run-down corners of town, crowded with brothels and saloons, that the lumberjacks enacted their most public annual ritual: the spree. For the jacks themselves, however, the spree went beyond a natural side effect of freedom after a long winter: it was a central pillar of their culture. Jacks looked forward to sprees all year. Fitzmaurice remembered that there were "men in camp so mean and penurious that they would pull threads out of an old coffee sack to mend their worn out socks. Half-sole a sock with a kit and a kit with a sock. Go to their work poorly clad, and suffer the worst pains and penalties the woods could inflict . . . and all to have a big stake in the spring."

For Fitzmaurice, who only spent part of one winter as a "shanty boy" and made his living as a journalist (and eventual temperance crusader), this was insanity. Here were men who could save their money and partake in the struggle for financial success. They emerged annually from the woods with enough money to begin to save toward education or land—enough money to buy into middle-class ideals of self-improvement, to make themselves, in historian Antony Rotundo's terms, "marketplace men." Instead, these men let "the hard earned dollars roll away, till in ten days or two weeks at the farthest, all the boy's money is gone. . . . His new coat is torn down the back, and sick in body and soul."[9]

An original window display of one of the progressive stores in Duluth. A typical lumberjack with his worn-out mackinaw and his pack rack returns from the woods and is transformed into a stylish city chap. Photo by Maher; taken at midnight.

Perhaps hoping to lure in as a would-be customer a passing logger in town on a spree, a window display advertises "The Spring Transformation of the Lumberjack" at Columbia Fine Clothing in Duluth, Minnesota, circa 1908. Courtesy of the St. Louis County Historical Society, Archives and Special Collections, University of Minnesota Duluth.

Lumberjacks did not see the spree as insanity. Instead, they saw it as a central moment of very publicly asserting their identity as working men, indulging in intemperance, violence, and excess as demonstrations of their own brand of manhood—a manhood that did not invest in market capitalism and instead invested, very heavily, in the ideals of camaraderie, masculinity, and risk.

Many of the proofs of manhood and belonging that lumberjacks engaged in were banned in camp. Fighting, drinking, and women were all strictly off-limits while in the woods. But come the spring break-up, shanty boys had a chance to prove their membership in the "red sash brigade" of real lumberjacks; it was in the sprees and the junk hotels of the lumber boomtowns that lumberjacks found their community. The very spaces middle-class observers abhorred welcomed jacks home. They remember these spaces with nostalgia and warmth. In his memoir of his logging days, E. H. Pelton warmly remembers that in Perham the jacks had "a big boarding house on the river by the sawmill," where they would have dances on Saturday nights. These hotels had a reputation almost as bad as that of the brothels, and Pelton recalled that when the jacks had "blown their stakes," they resorted to stealing kegs from the local brewery. Pelton, like many jacks, was fond of these memories.[10] Later, as reformers attempted to "fix up" the skid rows of the North-woods cities, they found men unwilling to leave. One man, resettled from a narrow bunk in Minneapolis's Gateway district to a bright, larger space outside the city, returned after just a few months. He asked his case worker to move him back home.[11]

The heart of the spree, and the heart of the boomtown lumberjack community, was the saloon. In the Northwoods boomtowns, saloons sprouted like weeds. Bars lined the streets in Whiskey Row, the central street of Grand Rapids, Michigan. Twelve saloons sprang up in tiny Deer River, Minnesota. In Muskegon, Michigan, Sawdust Flats, "six solid blocks of establishments catering to the amoral lumber-jacks," appeared in the 1870s. Some towns became famous for vice—John Emmett Nelligan recalled that in Florence, Wisconsin, in the 1880s, "every other house was a saloon, or a house of prostitution, or a gambling hall, and usually all three were under one roof." Most famous of all was Seney, Michigan—a town of only a few hundred permanent residents said to have between eight and eighteen sa-loons. As a contemporary newspaper remarked, "the saloon is the real Mecca of the lumberjack."[12]

The saloon was the in-town equivalent of camps—an almost entirely homosocial world. Women entering saloons as customers was a rare enough occurrence that it often led to social disturbance. Miles Nelson, a jack who worked the Minnesota camps in the late 1890s, remembered as a famous tale the story of a lady from Grand Rapids who, on a trip to Duluth, "stepped into a saloon in the bowery for a beer" and immediately found herself unwelcome. The bartender told her to leave, and when she asked a cop whether or not this saloon was a place of public business, the cop "grabbed her arm and said 'not for you, so get out or I will run you in.'"[13] Those few women who worked in the saloons were either the daughters of the own-ers (whom jacks recalled to be apparently universally astonishingly beautiful and sexually completely unavailable)[14] or prostitutes. Neither were remembered as making the space even a modicum more feminine.

The men who frequented these saloons, especially those of native-born stock who had come from the cities of the East and Midwest, would have been familiar with the saloon as a center of working-class social life. As the locus of work shifted in the nineteenth century from the workshop to the factory, the drinking that had been an integral part of the workday moved to its own locus: the saloon. The saloon was essentially a working-class space—warmth and shelter were provided, as were toilets, food, and drink. In the words of historian Jon Kingsdale, saloons were so central to the nineteenth-century laborer that they "came into contact with almost

Alcohol was strictly forbidden in camp, so during the springtime rush on the lumber towns of the Northwoods lumberjacks frequently congregated with miners and dock workers in saloons like this one in Duluth, Minnesota, circa 1907. Courtesy of the St. Louis County Historical Society, Archives and Special Collections, University of Minnesota Duluth.

all aspects of his life."[15] For lumberjacks, they were meeting spaces, hotels, employment offices, and ad hoc banks where jacks could often cash their winter's pay—or at the very least turn it quickly into alcohol. In the spring it served as a meeting place for jacks who had worked at separate camps for the winter, and in the fall it often became the de facto hiring office for camps in the region.

Within the male, working-class space of the saloon, men crafted a gender ideal that did not trade in the capitalist imperatives and moral uprightness of middle-class morality. In many ways, it was, in fact, an outright rejection of middle-class mores, albeit a not particularly articulate one. By spending all their money in saloons, and refusing the culture of capital accumulation, working-class men in saloons stepped away from the capitalist organization of the family.[16]

Yet, while it clearly did not fit within the standards of the middle class, it is a mistake to see the homosocial world of saloon-going as solely a rejection. It was not a reactionary ideal built around rebelling against middle-class control. Rather, it was the deep embrace of an entirely different ideal, one that laborers found sorely lacking in the lumbermen who made their homes as far as possible from the camps they owned: camaraderie.

In the world of union labor, camaraderie has long been recognized as the basis for organization. Men in unions organized themselves into brotherhoods, a theme seen throughout the trade union movement. These brotherhoods were incredibly strong—indeed, some historians have argued stronger than fealty to one's own family. But in the tavern as well as in the camps, it is clear that it did not require a craft union for lumberjacks to style themselves upon what historian Ava Baron has termed the "egalitarian and exclusionary" lines of brotherhood.[17] It was to create this sense of community that, for instance, the IWW encouraged the creation of "jungles" where hobos would live together: by creating space, they created community; not a community based on the home, but based on an entirely different network, with saloons as a central component.[18]

In saloons lumberjacks found a brotherhood that was nothing like that of the fraternal orders of their superiors.[19] Here there were no women's auxiliaries to promote the domestic interests of families, nor invocations to moral uplift. The lumberjacks promoted brotherhood, both in its egalitarian aspects of camaraderie and its exclusionary bouts of demonstrative violence in the saloons. Between camps, saloons, and junk hotels they created a network of spaces where they were guaranteed to encounter brethren. The memoirs and stories of lumberjacks are filled with coincidental meetings, drinking buddies, and friends helping friends home to the hotel at the end of a spree. Instead of carefully saving, money was spent not only on personal excess, but on the treating of others. As Jack London concluded after an extended session in a saloon: "Money no longer counted. It was comradeship that counted."[20]

This comradeship, especially in lumber towns, closely mirrored the conditions of living in a lumber camp. Even the living arrangements in saloons closely re-created those of camps. If anything, the men were more tightly packed with fewer comforts. While there were, especially in the larger and more established towns, decent and even comfortable accommodations, most jacks seemed to think them a waste of money. Instead, many ended up sleeping in "snake" or "flop" rooms— rooms at the back of lumberjack hotels that had neither beds nor even mattresses. The men simply slept where they lay. Richard Griffin, an ex-lumber company employee, remembered visiting a snake room on a recruiting trip. He and the labor recruiter walked into "a large room at the back of the bar room where broken lumberjacks usually slept on the floor, using mackinaws, boots and rubbers for pillows." There they found "sixty or more men laying on the floor in all positions."[21]

The Bridge Street House boarding house, located in an area of Muskegon, Michigan, known as Sawdust Flats, circa 1860. The boarding house included a saloon that was frequented by loggers staying in town. Photograph from the collection of the Lakeshore Museum Center.

These conditions were no better, if not worse, than those in a camp, and fostered the same conditions of bodily intimacy—only here without the strictures against women, drink, and fighting.

Since the whoring and fighting that were banned in camp rarely came before the drinking that spurred them on in town, it was alcohol and its intemperate consumption that proved the first test of a lumberjack's masculinity in town. Excessive drink was a sign of physical endurance—a proof of the rugged strength so prized in the woods. As a contemporary put it, "If a man don't drink here he is not considered anybody."[22] Tales of lumberjack drinking border on the improbable, and many were surely exaggerated. But what is without a doubt is that drinking in the summer in the saloons was part of what made a man both a real man and a real lumberjack. Any man could work a winter in the woods, but the hard drinking in the saloons is what made him a part of the brotherhood. When gathering notes

In its lumbering heyday, Seney, Michigan, was home to as many as eighteen saloons as well as three brothels housed in boarding houses and hotels like the Grondin, pictured here circa 1890. Courtesy of Superior View Photography.

in Grand Rapids, Minnesota, from former lumberjacks, WPA workers in the early 1930s noted that lumberjacks described themselves as "a strong, rough bunch . . . who worked hard in the woods and who drunk hard at the bar." Elsewhere the same writer wrote:

> A man had to have certain strong, vigorous characteristics or he could not survive. These times made vigorous men. Trees were to be cut, timber hauled and floated down the river. On every hand were activities which made for physical strength and courage, great endurance and ability. The drinking of that day was not so much from a desire to become intoxicated as . . . an expression of the man's nature.[23]

Lumberjacks out on the town in caulked boots and Mackinaw coats pose for a photograph in the studio of G. A. Werner in Marquette, Michigan, circa 1900. Courtesy of Superior View Photography.

For lumberjacks, putting away a massive amount of liquor was, primarily, a sign of one's indisputable manhood.

Yet, in descriptions of these feats of drinking, one thing appears again and again: the social, brotherly aspect of the lumberjacks' use of alcohol. Ceylon Lincoln, who grew up around, and eventually worked in, the camps in the 1870s remembered that "they would urged [sic] everyone they meet to have a social drink with them, it seemed that every man you met was full, and before you was aware you would be full yourself." In fact, the ritual of drinking together was strong enough that there was a standing tradition in Northwoods saloons: if a jack could not afford a drink himself, he could claim to be sick. And if a jack was sick, you bought him a drink.[24] To middle-class observers, this seemed a failing both of temperance and of financial management, but as one ex-jack put it, "The one great fault of these bluff working men is that they spend their own money in ways not wise. But are there not 'gentlemen' who spend, instead of their own money, that of other people, in ways not more wise?"[25] It may not have been approved of by middle-class commentators, and it certainly did not aid in forming stable families, but for lumberjacks spending freely in saloons to build camaraderie was a wise investment.

While drinking and partaking fully in the culture of camaraderie was the standard for admission to the brotherhood of lumberjacks—often nicknamed the "red sash brigade" for the cloth tied around their waists—it also led to a simmering culture of gory violence in the lumber towns. Jeremy W. Kilar's careful demographic studies have concluded that lumber town violence, condoned by the authorities, was just as high if not higher than in the western cow towns. Fortified with whiskey and freed from the bans of camp, men proved strength through hand-to-hand combat.

"Lumberjacks," explained one former woods worker, "fought with fists, teeth and feet. . . . It was accepted by lumber-jacks as quite the proper thing and a necessary activity so that the husky he-men could find some outlet for their pent-up energy." The description of fighting as an outlet for energy skips handily past the incredible damage that could be inflicted in lumberjack "dustups." But at the same time, it demonstrates a pattern that quickly emerges from examining fight stories: apart from some retributive justice, most fights were fought to prove individual merit and gain acceptance among peers. Much like in camps, violence was to enforce social boundaries, not inflict harm.[26]

While most dustups were described as just that, some battles were genuinely, sickeningly violent. Rex J. Dye remembered "seeing one lumberjack stomp his caulked boots across the face of another man he had down on the floor. The face of the man who was stomped resembled fresh and bloody hamburger." Similarly, John Nelligan's memoirs are filled with tales of men who, "made boastfully brave by drink," fell into bloody "rough and tumble lumberjack fight[s]."[27]

Examining the more brutal battles closely, two reasons emerge for violence to spill over from demonstrating strength to inflicting harm. The first was to do with personal grudges: a man ended up stabbed after a theft or another beat to a pulp for slipping out on a bar tab, for instance. While Nelligan claimed to not fully understand why he had been "licked" in a fight, he did note that he had pushed several of the Anishinaabe men who worked for his assailant over a dam earlier that week.[28]

But the bulk of these violent conflicts were far more like the violence in camps. They were in the name of social order, preserving the ethnic hierarchies of camp

Arriving in Honor, Michigan, on their annual spree, loggers stand with teams of horses and sleds in front of the pool room of the Brundage House, circa 1905. Courtesy of Superior View Photography.

in town. C. C. Kelly remembered in his memoirs when speaking of Canadians and Mainers that "those from one loved not those from the other. . . . Hence, there were many fights. No natural weapons barred, one round to finish, which was when one was unconscious, dead, or had squealed."[29] Less romantically, newspapers reported without comment fights ending in death over ethnic differences. "In a saloon fight between Poles and lumberjacks," the *Times Herald* of Port Huron, Michigan, reported, "Walter Dumbrowski's jaw was broken in three places and his head crushed. He died." A lumberjack in the same fight was stabbed in five places and killed. It merited a minor news item just below a long section on judges' salaries on page 2. Another news item from 1911 notes that "a huge Austrian" was charged with clubbing to death two men in a fight with "other lumberjacks." There is little explanation given for the violence save the fact that he was a lumberjack and Austrian. That was, apparently, reason enough.[30]

These fatal or near-fatal encounters were not the majority of fights though. Most fights were short-lived, and mundane enough that a bored and disillusioned Frank A. Johnson, a lumber company clerk, noted in his diary as a full explanation of the fortnight from May 14 to 28, 1871, "Every day the same thing over, more drinking and fighting."[31] These endlessly repeating fights did not serve the purpose of restoring justice or of establishing an ethnic superiority, but rather of proving one's worth as a member of the lumberjack brotherhood. By fighting and roughhousing, lumberjacks paid one of the prices of entry into the "egalitarian and exclusionary" brotherhood.

Some men outdid themselves on this front, and out of these fights grew some legends, known city-, state-, or region-wide for their fighting skills. Stories from across the region feature Silver Jack, Joe Fournier, T. C. Cunion, Con Culhane, and Sam Christie. Cunion makes a particularly colorful story, given that his well-known tendency was to stand on street corners, chewing a piece of raw cow's liver, bellowing "I am T. C. Cunion, the man-eater from Peterborough, Ontario," as he challenged men to fights.[32] Joe Fournier became famous as being almost unkillable, as did Sam Christie, although WPA researchers found three completely different and contradictory explanations of his death. Men they interviewed could not agree on whether Christie was shot in the chest by Pig Eye Kelly, the mild-mannered bartender, bludgeoned to death by Steve Hicks, the small but wily lumberjack, or slashed across the throat by Kelly the Cook, the hot-headed camp cook. That, within decades of his death, the stories of him could have spread enough to change into three such different versions speaks to the level of fame he achieved during his fighting days.

But for most men fights did not lead to individual glory so much as acceptance. There is a story about Con Connaught, an Upper Peninsula logger, who would force any man who came to find work in his camp to fight him. When one young man managed to fully beat Con, he gave him the plum job of straw boss. Fighting was a way of proving that you were a "real" lumberjack, and summers were marked by "friendly" fights where ten or twenty jacks might enter in a brawl before all leaving as friends. Tale after tale ended with a line like this one from John Ira Bellaire: "Usually when it was over they walked together friends to the nearest saloon to buy one another drinks." Fighting in no way undermined camaraderie. Rather, it reaffirmed it. In his memoirs from the turn of the century, William Warren Bartlett describes lumberjacks, within the same breath, as "ready to fight" and "fine fellows, good hearted and open handed." The two were merely, for Bartlett, affirmations of one another.[33]

Jacks walked a particularly narrow line between respectable manhood and rough masculinity when it came to their attitudes toward women. Both contemporary

A QUESTION OF TITLE

An illustration from *Harper's Monthly* in 1861 captures a rowdy scene in an industrial boomtown. From "A Peep at Washoe" by J. Ross Browne. Courtesy of the Bancroft Library, University of California, Berkeley.

reports and memoirs emphasize the lumberjack's respect for women and his innate chivalry. In 1900, a reporter for the *Atlantic* claimed that "as at sea and on the plains, the open air breathes a spirit of chivalry. Suppose a man affronts a waitress: twenty defenders leap to their feet."[34] Josephine Grattan, the wife of a foreman on Michigan's Hemlock River in the winter of 1884–85, recorded an entire winter in camp in her diary. It is clear that, again and again, her position as foreman's wife entitled her to special care and respect from the men who worked for her husband. When she gave birth in camp, the jacks spared nothing in taking care of her every need, even going so far as to offer to "hurry down river, grab a doctor, kidnap him if necessary, and . . . carry him all the way up to us."[35] This idea of the rough but courteous lumberjack was reflected across dozens of accounts. But this courtesy only extended to certain women.

Femininity was delicate, and to the Victorian mind required the careful protection of a man. While perhaps needed as musicians or hostesses, prostitutes rarely earned that protection. Many of the stories of prostitutes that survive are jovially told anecdotes of women like "Big Delia, who weighed 225 pounds and chewed a package of tobacco a day" and portray prostitutes as "sturdy women" who "fought like men."[36]

John Nelligan's memoirs clearly reflect the moral lines he drew between those who did and did not deserve respect and protection. Nelligan recalled in 1929 that "no man could offend, insult, or molest a woman on the street, no man could even speak lightly of a woman of *good reputation* without suffering swift and violent justice at the hands of his fellows."[37] Two stories from his time as "walking boss"—or the head of several camps within a single region—makes the delineation between worthy and unworthy clear. In Nelligan's first anecdote, he recounts coming into one of his camps near dusk and finding "a woman sitting there crying with a six weeks old baby in her arms." The woman told him that she had come to see her husband. He had left her living with her aunt, but after a quarrel, she had left. Nelligan "had the cook get her a warm lunch and told the chore boy to build a fire in the office where [he] installed her. She had walked six miles through soft snow and she was soaked to the knees. . . . It was really a wonder that she ever arrived at the camp."[38] Here a respectable married woman arrived in camp and not only was extended the basic courtesy of a free meal, at that time universal in Northwoods camps, but was afforded extra care. Nelligan clearly considered her not only worthy of protection but in dire need of it.

Only a few pages later, Nelligan recounts a very different tale. He brings up, as a humorous anecdote, the story of Maude, "a woman of wide but not worthy reputation." Like the first woman, Maude appeared, unannounced, at his camp. Also like the first woman, she came on foot, through the snow. When Maude appeared, she insisted on seeing a Frenchman whom she described as her husband. Nelligan refused her entry to the camp. Assuming she was drunk, he turned her back out into the Michigan winter to walk herself back to town.[39] Regardless of status, camp etiquette required that any man who appeared was given food and shelter at least for a night. Far from being afforded the careful concern and protection Nelligan extended to the first visitor, Maude could not access even the basic aid of a warm meal.

Nelligan's lines between respectable and not, between a worthy and unworthy reputation, only extended so far as refusing comfort and shelter to one woman while protecting another. While there are few records depicting the lives of Northwoods prostitutes, it is clear that for many, their "not worthy" reputations left them not only without the protection of chivalry, but also open to the threat of violence. Descriptions of both the Sawdust Flats in Muskegon and the Cribs in Duluth mention the presence of police. The police were not there to control the trade of the prostitutes working in these districts, but rather to be on hand "in case of an unwanted visitor."[40] The need for police protection is only a small glimpse into the violence many prostitutes must have experienced. Other sources draw the outline of a much darker and more dangerous existence.

"Gay Days in the Woods," a local history story written in the 1940s for the *Milwaukee Journal*, is colored by memory and myth: the entire piece seeks to conjure a time of rough and tumble fun. In this spirit of lighthearted tall tales the author writes about the Seney railroad depot. The depot had, in its very early days, been rarely used outside the timbering months. As a result, a group of prostitutes had taken up residence and opened for business within the depot's storehouse. An enterprising railroad employee, the author of "Gay Days in the Woods" tells us, "hunted up a brawny individual named Pig-Foot MacDonald and offered him $100 if he would rid the warehouse of its feminine occupants." Already it seems unlikely that a man would be offered three months' winter wages for a single day's work, so perhaps it's no surprise that "Pig-Foot needed no urgin." With several of his "fellow roughnecks" he went about clearing the warehouse: "he slugged the men, dragged the cursing women around the floor by their hair, ripped down the fixtures, broke the doors and left happily with sacks of bottled liquor." This anecdote ends with the author telling us that "the station agent paid the $100 as agreed and Pig-Foot accepted it, although he said he felt it was hardly right to take money for an afternoon of pure fun."[41] The story is obviously embellished—the $100 paycheck alone establishes that. But it offers a fleeting glimpse of the attitudes lumberjacks who "would never molest a woman" held toward prostitutes.

Yet in hundreds of oral histories, memoirs, diaries, and letters, the lumberjacks rarely mention prostitutes as anything but another gay adornment of town life in the summers. There is only one exception: John Nelligan, as ever giving a vague reference with no full explanation, remembers that in Florence, Wisconsin, "the white slave trade throve . . . and more than one of the girls had a dissipated bully living off the wages of her sin, ever ready to beat her up if she didn't hand over every dollar she earned."[42] Otherwise these girls are merely decorations.

The stories of "white slavers" taking advantage of innocent girls who did not speak a word of English bear striking resemblance to some of the perhaps less repugnant tales of life in the woods. In Josephine Grattan's diary from the winter of 1884–85 she often discusses mail-order brides, especially those who came for her Finnish workers. But while these stories are often told as sweet tales of domestic bliss, at least once a lumberjack's enthusiasm for a new bride spilled over into violence. She tells the tale of one man who went to meet his friend's bride at a station forty miles from camp, during the winter. As Grattan tells it, this man was so overwhelmed by enthusiasm that he failed to heed the description given to him and

The railroad depot at Seney, Michigan, seen here in 1912, was reportedly used as a brothel during the lumbertown's heyday. Photograph by Charles Hansel. Courtesy of Bentley Historical Library, University of Michigan.

seized, instead, the most beautiful of the handful of women on the platform. Not speaking Finnish, he could not communicate to her what his intentions were. He traveled with her for three days in silence, at times carrying her, to bring her to camp. Shortly before reaching camp the authorities caught up with him, switched out the brides, and set the story straight. Set within the confines of marriage, Grattan tells this story as a charming anecdote.[43] From the perspective of a new immigrant with no English, it would be difficult to tell the difference between this and the "white slavery" Obernaur decries.

There is ample evidence of lumberjacks subjecting women to beatings, coercion, and extravagant violence. In their convenient amnesia, lumberjacks left this out of their recollections. When they claimed they were respectful to all women, they meant all the women who were *deserving* of respect. The gap between their memories and their actions points to the way in which frontier conditions pushed at the boundaries of ideological categories, and showed the relative weakness of those categories. As historian Ruth Rosen points out, "the Victorian policy of quiet toleration suggests underlying attitudes towards prostitution that were quite different from the public expressions of condemnation."[44] What was true of the urban centers went double for the Northwoods. There, on the edge of the world, hard rules made no sense.

When the lumberjacks walked out the woods, proud members of the red sash brigade, they saw themselves as members of a brotherhood. The winter's work, enduring violence and risk and participating in the network of itinerancy, gave a man access to the community. But his behavior in summer is what cemented it. While part-time jacks might return to farms, "real" lumberjacks did not return to a home community on the prairie, but rather to a network of sites where they were welcomed and could affirm their identity as lumberjacks and as men. As Alton Van Camp remembered, "the average lumberjack was just a drifter. A lot of them wasn't even married—most of them wasn't." Instead of a respectable man tied down to a domestic marriage, the true lumberjack was, according to one former logger, "a hard drinking, very profane, improvident, careless of dress, happy-go-lucky person, yet with it all, kind hearted . . . and never bashful about using his fists. . . . He was a woodsman born and a woodsman he lived and died."[45]

From the bird's-eye view of middle-class observers, these men were hobos, and part of the tramp scare. Town planners and citizens purposefully isolated the lumberjacks, creating "crime districts" where they could be quarantined from the respectable elements of town. And, indeed, their culture, soaked in whiskey, simmering with violence, and predicated on the abuse of prostitutes, was not a safe or particularly savory one. But it was also not unanchored.

Within these districts a culture flourished that understood place differently. Where they were seen as "homeless," and thus threatening to community control and domestic influence, they had a community, and a network of places that were their own. Ted Grossardt in his article "Harvest(ing) Hoboes," argues that the great success of the IWW was to create community where there was none. They turned an "informal reaction to spatial exclusion" into a "formalized spatial strategy in its own right." As a result, they offered hobos "a conceptual map of themselves as members of, and participants in, an alternate system of sites and connections."[46]

In the Northwoods, this community happened much earlier. The saloons, junk hotels, and brothels of the Northwoods boomtowns gave lumberjacks a space that was their own, in which they were guaranteed to meet with their brethren. It was a space that valued camaraderie highly and fiscal responsibility not at all. Above all, perhaps, it was a space that was aggressively male. As Jack London wrote of western saloons, so it was also true of the Northwoods that, at least in the minds of the men who inhabited them, "in the saloons life was different. Men talked with great voices, laughed great laughs, and there was an atmosphere of greatness."[47]

Throughout, both those within and those outside of the skid rows were finding ways to understand the massive migrations of single unmarried men. In writings and rewritings, middle-class residents of the boomtowns tried to find a way to make sense of lumberjacks and the other "unsavory" elements of their Northwoods towns. The men who flocked to these saloons, too, were trying to create a lasting meaning. As working-class men, they defined their manhood in the tension between roughness and respectability—the sprees on the one hand, nostalgic memoirs on the other. A true jack could inhabit both.

Boomtowns made their own rules and created systems that were malleable, but systems nonetheless. When the governor of Wisconsin complained that respectable citizens wanted him to "wave the executive wand over those vast, interminable forests of our Northern border, and mutter incantations,"[48] he was acknowledging a frustrating truth to urban reformers: the woods were out of reach of the regulatory influences of the states. As itinerants whose business was necessary but presence was detested, they were sequestered in vice districts, out of reach of the social mores that grew up in urban centers.

But this would not be how they were remembered. Even during the height of lumbering, a different story emerged: one of a chivalrous man of the woods, at one with nature, conquering the wilderness, and clearing it for civilization. As the industry moved west, abandoning the Northwoods to a deep economic depression, these myths took on a life of their own. Lumberjacks, Northwoods residents, industry titans, and a group that seemed almost entirely unrelated—elite journalists and writers of eastern urban centers—began a pitched contest to define how the lumberjack would be remembered.

PART III

# IN MEMORY

Sheridan, too, spurred Nelligan to try to remember matters which would prove interesting to the reader. Paul Bunyan tales are a case in point. Apparently Nelligan, despite his diversified experience in the woods of New Brunswick, Maine, Pennsylvania, Michigan and Wisconsin, had hardly so much as heard of the redoubtable Paul or of his blue ox, Babe. . . . At the good last Sheridan was forced to take a few items out of a book; for Bunyan stories belonged in the chapter on camp recreation!

 —Editor's introduction to John Nelligan's *Life of a Lumberman*, 1929

When Highway 34 becomes East Broadway, just before you get to the Akeley post office if you're headed west, you'll see him. He's kneeling down at the entrance to Memorial Park, just beside the plaque dedicated to veterans. If tourists are in town, there will be one, two, maybe three kids sitting in his giant hand. In Bemidji he's next to the lake, right across the street from Morell's Chippewa Trading Post, next to the chamber of commerce. In Brainerd he's sitting, waving, twelve feet high and glossy, among the picnic tables scattered at the edge of an empty parking lot. In Paul Bunyan Land he's twenty-five feet tall and animatronic, frightening children when he greets them by name. And he's just before the big drop on the log flume ride in the Mall of America. Altogether there are five Paul Bunyans in Minnesota, three in Wisconsin, and two in Michigan.[1] There is Paul Bunyan Telephone and Paul Bunyan's Cook Shanty, Paul Bunyan State Trail and Paul Bunyan's Animal

A giant talking Paul Bunyan greets children at the Paul Bunyan Center in Brainerd, Minnesota, circa 1950. Courtesy of Minnesota Historical Society.

Land. Dotted across the Northwoods and threaded through maps, Paul Bunyan has been written, thoroughly, into the very landscape of the Northwoods.

Paul Bunyan is just the beginning. Grand Rapids, Minnesota, celebrates Tall Timber Days annually, while Mackinaw City, Michigan, has its Jack Pine Lumberjack Shows. In Big Bay, Michigan, you can drink at the Lumberjack Tavern, or you can watch the Lumberjack World Championships hosted in Hayward, Wisconsin. You can visit the Lumberman's Monument in Michigan, the Lumberjack Steam Train and Forestry Museum in Wisconsin, or the Forest History Center in Minnesota. The men who were once shunted to the edge of town, considered at best romantic outsiders and at worst dangerous miscreants, now form the backbone of Northwoods identity.

Understanding this shift, from outsiders to heroes, requires widening our lens beyond the Northwoods, and beyond the Midwest. The invention of the heroic lumberjack was part of a national project of redefining white masculinity. Faced with the disorienting and manufactured world of the modern city, increasingly competing for jobs and authority with racial minorities, immigrants, and women, they valorized the heroes of the frontier: cowboys and explorers, adventurers and, increasingly, lumberjacks. But the lumberjack they wrote about and reenacted was created not to celebrate the real men who worked the Northwoods, but to fulfill a deep cultural need. They were images built to suit the specific needs of the urban middle classes, corporations, and industrial tycoons. Eventually, they were adopted by their homeland, promoted by local tourism bureaus and boosters to rebrand the cutover as "Vacationland" and the "Great North Woods." The lumberjack as hero was stripped of his class and, therefore, of his resistance. He had camaraderie without drink, violence, or saloons. He labored without complaint. He worked with nature, rather than against it.

The honest, good-natured, gentlemanly lumberjack that came down to modern Americans through cartoons, advertisements, nostalgic novels, and Monty Python sketches bears only a superficial resemblance to the men who gave limbs and sometimes lives to their labor in the Northwoods. But as the scars on the land healed and second-growth trees came to tower over the lakes and rivers of the Northwoods, that cheerful, ersatz image survived.

The lumberjack, a true "gentleman of the woods," stands with tankard in hand in an image that anticipates the heroic likeness of Paul Bunyan. Artist J. E. Baker; published circa 1873. Courtesy of Library of Congress.

An early appeal to conservation, this lithograph by Joseph Keppler from 1883 depicts a female figure labeled "Public Spirit" warning two lumberjacks of the dangers of deforestation. Courtesy of Library of Congress.

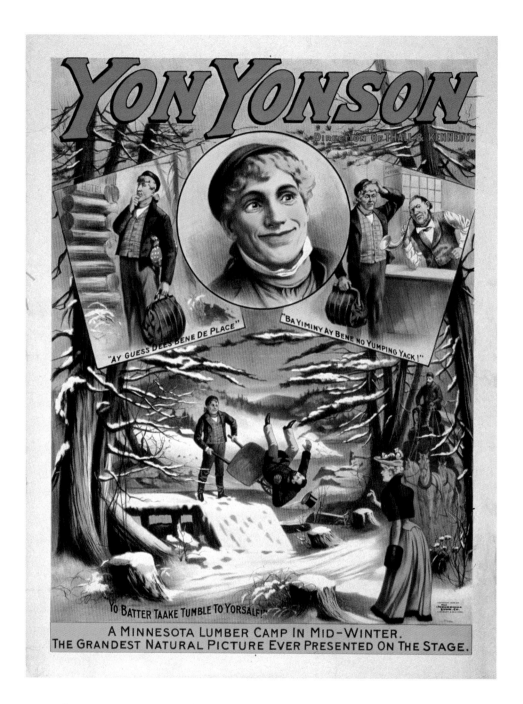

Poster for an 1899 presentation of *Yon Yonson,* a Scandinavian dialect stage comedy by Gus Heege and W. D. Coxey. Swedes and Norwegians were often the butt of jokes and were considered irreparably un-American, or, as Yankee jack Horace Glenn put it, "disgusting, dirty lousy reprobates." Courtesy of Library of Congress.

## Fosston Mackinaws.

The "Fosston Mackinaw" is the product of a system of manufacturing, that is as nearly ideal as money and brains can devise.

As practically all of the material that goes into the mackinaws is made under our own supervision it is a better guarantee, that the high standard of quality will be maintained, than were the woolens manufactured by other and different mills.

Every mackinaw is a work of art and so far as the quality of wool, the beauty of the color and weave, the style, fit, general appearance and workmanship are concerned, it is unquestionably without an equal.

Every stage of the garment is closely watched from the time the wool is inspected at the mill until the finished jacket is ready for shipment.

The wool Mackinaw coat, seen here in an advertisement for the F. A. Patrick Company of Duluth from 1909, was essential to the lumberjack's limited wardrobe. Courtesy of Duluth Public Library.

*Paul Bunyan's Pictorial Map of the United States* depicting some of his deeds and exploits, drawn in 1935 by Ray DeWitt Handy, a cartoonist for the *Duluth News Tribune*. Courtesy of the Osher Map Library and Smith Center for Cartographic Education.

*Paul Bunyan's Playground in Northern Minnesota,* an illustrated map produced in 1936 by the Paul Bunyan Playground Association. Courtesy of the David Rumsey Map Collection, David Rumsey Map Center, Stanford Libraries.

This promotional booklet published in the 1930s by the Braun Lumber Company of Detroit features artwork by Oliver Kemp. Although it later faded from lumberjack imagery, the red sash was so central to nineteenth-century lumberjacks that they sometimes referred to themselves as "the red sash brigade."

Amid a flurry of amusement park rides, tourists crowd around the shrine of Paul Bunyan in Brainerd, Minnesota, 1956. Courtesy of Steve Fasnacht.

*Early Logging at Koochiching Falls,* a mural created by Lucia Wiley in 1937 for the post office of International Falls, Minnesota. Photograph by Tom Parker.

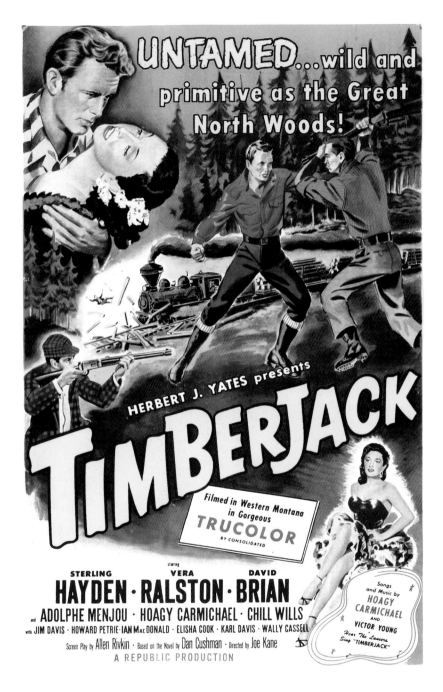

The brawling lumberjack takes center stage in *Timberjack,* a film from 1955 starring Sterling Hayden. The film's poster directly links his rugged masculinity to the "untamed" wilderness. Courtesy of Everett Collection, Inc. / Alamy Stock Photo.

In the late 1940s, three thousand square miles of the Brainerd lakes region in central Minnesota were rebranded as Paul Bunyan Vacationland with pictorial maps and brochures.

Art Weinke's Paul Bunyan Lookout along Route 23, in Spruce, Michigan, one of several roadside attractions throughout the Northwoods celebrating the massive lumberjack. Photograph by John Margolies. Courtesy of Library of Congress.

Paul Bunyan's Cook Shanty welcomes hungry visitors to Wisconsin Dells with lumberjack-sized meals. Photograph by John Margolies. Courtesy of Library of Congress.

Paul Bunyan's likeness was used by Western Air Lines on this poster luring would-be tourists to the Land of 10,000 Lakes, circa 1950s. Courtesy of Delta Air Lines Corporate Archives.

The image of the lumberjack as a symbol of rugged manhood lives on into the twenty-first century. In 2013 the Duluth Trading Company wished customers "a manly Christmas" in a series of animated advertisements for its Free Swingin' Flannel.

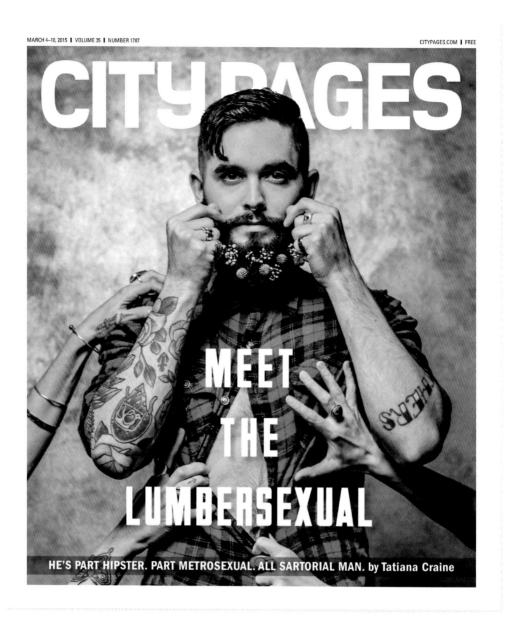

MARCH 4–10, 2015 | VOLUME 35 | NUMBER 1787

CITYPAGES.COM | FREE

# CITY PAGES

## MEET THE LUMBERSEXUAL

**HE'S PART HIPSTER. PART METROSEXUAL. ALL SARTORIAL MAN.** by Tatiana Craine

In 2015, the cover of *City Pages,* an alternative weekly newspaper of Minneapolis and St. Paul, announced the arrival of the lumbersexual: "Part Hipster. Part Metrosexual. All Sartorial Man."

# THE ONLY AMERICAN HERO

## REINVENTING THE LUMBERJACK

Above on every side rose great, many-windowed buildings; on the street the cars and carriages thronged, and jostling crowds dashed headlong among the vehicles. After a time he turned down a street that seemed to him a pandemonium filled with madmen. It went to his head like wine, and hardly left him the presence of mind to sustain a quiet exterior. . . . He grew hungry with longing for the dirty but familiar cabins of the camp, and staggered along with eyes half closed, conjuring visions of the warm interiors, the leaping fires, the groups of laughing men seen dimly through clouds of tobacco smoke.

—Elia W. Peattie, *A Michigan Man*

He has been called America's only genuine folk hero. His statue adorns car dealerships and theme parks, national forests and small-town main streets. But the Paul Bunyan we know—the Paul Bunyan who decorated pavilions at the World's Fair and spawned operas and poems and symphonies—is largely an invention of the early twentieth century. He rarely appeared in print before the 1910s, and in early stories he is a cruel, demanding boss, nothing like the Paul that America came to know and love. That lovable Paul, by all accounts, was likely first born in the mind of William B. Laughead, an advertiser for the Red River Lumber Company who had, as a younger man, worked in the Minnesota woods as a lumberjack. In 1914, he published a small pamphlet of Paul Bunyan stories as advertising. These stories were relatively well received and soon led to other branding products and a comic. Soon after, other authors began to print tales of the giant jack.

163

William Laughead, with his cheerful, pipe-smoking Paul Bunyan in the background, circa 1920s. Courtesy of the Paul Bunyan Collection, University of Minnesota Libraries.

By mere decades after his birth, Paul was well established. Critics who disliked Benjamin Britten and W. H. Auden's operetta *Paul Bunyan,* which premiered in New York in 1941, complained that Auden and Britten had failed to "penetrate far into the sturdy Americanism of this legend," taking for granted that that legend was genuine. That same year, the *San Francisco Chronicle* described Paul as "probably our best known and most authentic folk character free of European or Indian origins." His purity was sung forth again and again; not only was he the "most authentic" hero, as the *St. Paul Pioneer Press* insisted in 1938, he also occupied "an authentic niche in Americana, [since] his worship is untrained by commercialism." He had starred in ballets, poems, and orchestral pieces. John Henry, who was likely if not certainly an actual man, has been, disappointingly, inevitably, described as the "Paul Bunyan of the Negroes."[1]

To point out that Paul was manufactured is not to discredit his importance. The invention of Paul Bunyan, and moreover the invention of his type, should not be discounted simply because the medium of his birth was advertising and the commercial press. And yet, for decades, this is precisely what happened. Folklorists throughout the first half of the twentieth century were fixated on the medium as much as the message. Folklore learned through a book or over the radio was not "real" and only spoke of the death of the folk at the hands of mass media. Richard Dorson's careful studies of lumberjack folklore in the 1950s focused exclusively on the medium through which his subjects learned their folklore. He coined the term "fakelore" to encompass stories that had the "raw data" of folklore falsified by "invention, selection, fabrication and similar refining processes."[2] Determined to find the genuine culture of real Americana, hoping to present to the public a folk culture worth embracing, Dorson was dogged by the widespread fondness for a corporate cartoon.

Of all folk heroes, Dorson was particularly furious at Bunyan's persistent and irritating existence. He was not a great hero being popularized, but a "perversion" of pure folk culture. Dorson stated as fact that "because the average American thinks that Paul is his country's leading folk hero does not of course make Bunyan a folk hero." In fact, he spent a great deal of his time trying to debunk Paul and heaped disdain upon the Americans who ate up Bunyan stories. He argued, fundamentally, that Paul Bunyan's fame was an attempt to dupe Americans in the name of capitalism. He was the definition of "fakelore."[3] He was famous because he "represent[ed] a syndicated colossus useful for promotional stunts and feature copy." Dorson snidely concluded that "were he more truly folkloric, he would be less newsworthy."[4]

But folklorists' (and subsequently historians') focus on Paul Bunyan is to miss the forest for one, admittedly startlingly large, tree. The point is not just that Paul is "fakelore." It's that, as they are publicly remembered and celebrated, *all* lumberjacks are. After all, none of this is about Paul alone. Great as he is, Paul can only stand as part of a richer background of stories and characters. Paul Bunyan stands in as a synecdoche for the popular memory and understanding of lumberjacks and logging culture in general. Ask a child to draw Paul Bunyan or a lumberjack and, except for a possible blue ox, the drawings will be the same. The Brawny paper towel man is not technically Paul Bunyan, but without the trees behind him for scale it would be hard to tell. Contemporaries, too, often saw Bunyan as a larger-than-life representation of a type. A review of *Logging Town: The Story of Grand Rapids*, noted that "each lumberjack . . . however humble or obscure he may have been seems to have led a strutting, strenuous existence on a scale almost as gigantic as that of the great god Paul."[5] So far, this is where the majority of the scholarship on the memory of lumberjacks has stopped. They were real enough as men, but Bunyan was a fake invented to sell lumber and used since to sell a great many other things.

These conclusions raise more questions than they answer. Fake or not, what is it that made him such an instant sensation? To become a quintessential American hero in three decades flat is perhaps even more impressive if he is fake. Why is the popular image of lumberjacks—kind, big-hearted naturalists—so different from the understanding their contemporaries had of them within the Northwoods? How did men whose job it was to destroy the wilderness come to be associated with the wild itself? And, most bafflingly, why did the people whose land was destroyed by the lumber industry take, with such fierce enthusiasm, to the memorializing and valorizing of lumberjacks?

For decades historians have been investigating the history of memory. Moving beyond concerns like Dorson's about whether something is what *really* happened, historians investigate what people *think* happened. After all, most people act as much, if not more, on what they think the past was than on the basis of actual events. As Adam Domby has proved in relation to the lost cause of the Confederacy, it's not merely that Americans conveniently forgot some facts about the Civil War; rather, some determined to save their reputations simply lied, and embedded those lies in the historical narrative.[6]

In understanding how Americans nationally, and Northwoods residents in particular, came to embrace the memory of lumberjacks, we must untangle a thick knot of distortions, corporate deception, and commercial advertising. Because the story of lumberjacks is not one of spontaneous tales told by a fire, but rather of the purposeful marshaling of cultural memory to recover from the devastating aftereffects of extractive, industrial capitalism. And as with any story that is sold aggressively, the best way to understand why it was sold is to trace whose interests

The title page of *The Marvelous Exploits of Paul Bunyan* (1922), William Laughead's illustrated collection of tall tales featuring the famous lumberjack. Courtesy of the Paul Bunyan Collection, University of Minnesota Libraries.

it served. And so, to explain the meteoric rise of America's great fake folk hero, we first turn far from the lumber camps of the Northwoods to the great urban centers of Gilded Age America.

The romantic vision of lumberjacks as hardworking, honest, gruffly masculine, and, above all, authentic was first produced for consumption not within the lumber towns, but by outside audiences, largely in cosmopolitan cities. Well-respected eastern magazines sent correspondents to the woods for local color pieces. These articles valorized the men of the woods in terms that were geared specifically to appeal to the late nineteenth-century urbanite.

Two stories in particular, "Life in a Logging Camp," from *Scribner's Magazine* in 1893, and "Notes on a Michigan Lumber Town," which appeared in the *Atlantic Monthly* in 1900, illustrate the central themes of the emerging romantic vision of lumberjacks in the 1890s. Both articles were written to eastern audiences, both by well-educated Massachusetts men.[7] The lumberjacks, in both articles, are honest, fun, simpleminded, and outstandingly physically strong.

In Rollin Lynde Hartt's article for the *Atlantic Monthly*, the men pass the time after dinner fighting and playing games and singing with admirable ardor. They express themselves cleanly and clearly; they wear their sweethearts' photographs as badges. They are not ashamed of their emotions, but neither are they overcome by them—one part sentiment balanced by one part strength. They are extremely skilled: both authors linger over long descriptions of their exploits rolling logs and pulling them through the woods. But the lumberjack's knowledge comes not from extensive training or eastern schools, but from his own natural abilities. As Arthur Hill describes it in *Scribner's,* "On the side of what is called book-learning they are not educated. It has been a life habit with them to inspect and observe rather than read the observations of others."[8]

For both Hill and Lynde Hartt, part of the strength and ardor of the lumberjacks comes from their total freedom from the strictures of manly duty. In fact, for both authors, the lumberjacks seem to combine all the bodily strength of an ideal man with the joyful exuberance of a boy. For Hill, lumberjacks are free of responsibilities, boy-like, and jovial: they are "improvident, good natured fellows." But this boyish boisterousness is seen less as a vice than as a piece of bright-eyed innocence. The tone of the article is admiring of their lack of restraint and refinement. Even their reckless drinking and financial self-ruin is looked on with a charitable eye and explained away by their larger-than-life masculinity. Hill claims only that a lumberjack is "inclined to all the small vices which, from the ardor of his nature, become in him large ones." Even when amplified by their "ardor," their vices are, at heart, small. They are men, for Hill, entirely free of the trappings of modern urban fashions, since, "Like boys, they are not schooled to restraint of feelings nor jaded with sensational fads."[9]

Lynde Hartt lingers lovingly on this same trait: the boyishness of the men. He describes them going to breakfast by saying, "Talking, they joke; joking, they romp." In town, he respects their gruff, straightforward manner because "it speaks of youth and ardor and strong life." Describing their songs, Lynde Hartt notes that "in quite this boyish spirit the errant chevalier sang for this love, when knighthood was in flower."[10]

Knighthood seems an apt metaphor for what fascinated Lynde Hartt and Hill. Both authors focus on the sense of camaraderie and brotherhood the lumberjacks shared. Hill recounts a touching scene oft repeated in camps to demonstrate that "the shanty boy is by nature sympathetic and free-hearted." He tells of what happens when

> a falling limb mashes some poor fellow's shoulder. The ready cant-hook fails to catch and stop the rolling log, and there is a crunched leg, or perhaps a maimed and lifeless body. . . . Then you see how pitch-stained hands can be gentle, and rough hearts generous. To send the injured comrade to hospital and provide him care, or to the coffin and send his saddened home the ones who life so suddenly ended, the boys raise a fund, each and all giving freely. And to their honor let it be here said that in those primal traits of manhood—courage, generosity, and honesty—these men are equal to any.

Lynde Hartt, too, dwelled on the generosity of men toward each other, describing meals in taverns where men "unpack their inmost souls, disembosoming themselves gratuitously of half their family history." What is striking here is that the generosity and the brotherhood that Hill and Lynde Hartt admire are both based around emotional expression. It is the lumberjacks' willingness to be forthright, honest, affectionate, and loyal that takes their urbanite observers by surprise.[11]

But the strongest link between the articles is their deep sense of longing. Hill's article ends with the shanty boys packing off to town: "the drive ended, the peavies stacked, the last meal eaten . . . the shanty boy starts with sturdy stride and merry heart for town." Hill then pulls away from the boys he has spent the article admiring as they dive into the taverns, away from him. The shanty boy strides, "his footing always sure . . . [over] familiar door-sills, and humble floors," and there "amidst meets and greetings [Hill left] the shanty boy, wishing him all the good he deserves, and who is there that deserves more?" The deep desire to stay with them and the melancholy at his forced separation are palpable. But it is not only space and class that separate Hill from the lumberjacks. Toward the end of the piece there is a growing understanding that time, too, is separating Hill from the "real" lumberjacks. He notes that it has been "a few years since every river driver wore a long, red sash, and they were known as the Red Sash Brigade." These true men of the lumber frontier are a dying species. Lynde Hartt, too, displays a mournful yearning for a disappearing world. He closes his article by lamenting that "little is left of the elder order. The whole land is rapidly being lumbered out. . . . Only the northern peninsula lumbers as once Alpena lumbered. The camps move farther away each year."[12]

This yearning for an authentic America on the part of both writers was the symptom of a growing interest in the "authentic" and search for "reality" in the late nineteenth century. An interest in reality did not require, to the nineteenth-century mind, actual reality. Rather, Gilded Age Americans were interested in something that represented the "truth" about a place, idea, or group of people. Increasingly aesthetics were founded around the *appearance* of reality. Photographers would go to great trouble to create scenes that were real, but impossible to capture on film, using careful trickery to create snowstorms without snow, or night scenes in the studio. Among the most prominent critics of the period, it was more important that things *seem* real than that they were—for the "truth" that was being conveyed by art was not literal truth, but a broader and, to the Gilded-Age mind, more profound truth.

Late nineteenth-century middle-class Americans fully expected this kind of "truth" from representation. To modern eyes, for instance, the fact that Jacob Riis manipulated the subjects of *How the Other Half Lives* undercuts their documentary truth. The subjects may indeed have been poor street children, but his choice to ask them to pose as though they were sleeping or sit in a particular spot seems thoroughly disingenuous. But to late nineteenth-century eyes there was nothing in the least duplicitous about this practice. His photos represented the entire category of "the urban poor." That each one was staged, that his subjects were often mugging for the camera, in no way undercut what was seen as an honest and forthright portrayal of type. The closer the photograph fit to the "truth" of urban poverty, no matter how much posing was required to get there, the more honest it was.[13]

This understanding of what was "true" or "real" can be seen carrying over to other forms of popular entertainment. Perhaps the most famous entertainer of his day was known, even at the time, to be possibly something of a fraud. But across American cities, in European courts, and on the fringes of the Columbian Exposition, Buffalo Bill advertised himself as the real deal. Posters declare "authentic characters" and "real scenes," even though careful research shows much of what he portrayed could not have happened. Moreover, it hardly mattered—even if it had been real once, the re-creation of it, inside a ring in Chicago, a mile from Chinese villages and faux Roman courts of honor, near the plasterboard buildings that made up the dazzling White City of the 1893 Columbian Exposition, Buffalo Bill's Wild West Show could hardly be "real." What Buffalo Bill's popularity reflected was a hunger not for literal truth, but for an honest reproduction of "truth." And that, from his insistence that he was a terrible actor to his touring with dozens of Dakota, was what Buffalo Bill provided. In fact, in the eyes of many visitors to the Columbian Exposition, it was the Wild West, not the White City, that was the real American exposition.[14]

# SCRIBNER'S MONTHLY.

VOL. XV.   DECEMBER, 1877.   NO. 2.

THE WOODEN AGE.

THE FIRST STROKE.

*Scribner's Monthly* declared the 1870s "The Wooden Age" in its December 1877 issue. The issue was one of several published throughout the later nineteenth century that popularized the lumberjack's image for middle-class readers.

This insistence on authenticity was by necessity part of a binary. There can be no deep longing for the authentic without a conviction that the reality around us, the world in which we live every day, is somehow inauthentic. The scrambling search for reality was a result of a growing sense that lives in modern cities were disturbingly unreal. The unrealities of modern life were myriad. Cities were jumbled and crowded, technology was growing apace, changing the shape of life at a dazzling pace, and the growth of modern capitalism was beginning to give birth to the outward-focused man, a man who put on a face of respectability for the crowd, but whose real personality could not be known.[15] This man even had his dark counterpart: the confidence man. Confidence men, later known as con men, were impossible without the technologies and growing cities of nineteenth-century America. Men and women traveled the country and poured into cities and had to be accepted at their word, since no reputation could follow them all those miles. Erik Larson's *Devil in the White City*, detailing the case of a grizzly killer during the Columbian Exposition, showcases the uncanny ability of modern life in the Gilded Age to hide reality: dazzling buildings could be pasteboard; charming men could be murderers.[16]

The language of authenticity seeped into everyday life at the turn of the century. As cheaply reproduced art and mass-produced goods became widely available, they spawned what literary critic Miles Orvell has called the "late nineteenth-century culture of imitation." In response to the widespread availability of copies, art forms—from literature to the increasingly powerful medium of advertising—focused on authenticity. One of the earliest slogans for Coca-Cola in the 1890s, long before "the real thing," was "Get the genuine."[17] It is hardly a surprise, in this context, that a great American folk hero would first gain notoriety as an advertisement. Advertising is, by its very nature, part of the modern culture of imitation. It is the printed form of the confidence man, a stranger arriving in town and fooling innocents out of their money by his straightforward demeanor. Emphasizing the authentic, "genuine" nature of your product, tying it to the frontier and to the folk, was an attempt to create a genuine message that would give substance to a disingenuous medium.

As large-scale corporate capitalism transformed the way men and women worked, it also fundamentally disrupted the source of their identity. Work had long formed a backbone of identity across class divides, but industrial labor was different from everything that had come before. Increasingly Americans no longer felt their labor constituted, or even reflected, their identity. While you may have come from generations of masons, you were unlikely to have come from generations of office clerks or assembly-line workers. From the working classes through the middle and upper middle classes, work was no longer necessarily hereditary, nor did it dictate your social position. Moreover, there was less and less pride in this labor, and it often required a great deal of subservience to men for whom you may not have had any inherent respect. Anthropologist Charles Lindholm argues that this feeling of subservience led to a growing distaste for role-playing in the late nineteenth century. While a strong, middle-class puritanical streak in parts of Europe and the United States had long disliked the artifice of aristocracy, Lindholm argued that, because of industrial work, that dislike extended to "a generalized contempt for role-playing." As a result, those things that were the opposite of role-playing, specifically "spontaneous emotional expressivity and overturning of all forms of pretense," were increasingly prized.[18] Ironically, the attempt to find real authenticity often led to a new form of role-playing: city folk attempting to imitate what they saw as the unfettered simplicity of rural ways.

These notions of what was "real" and what was "fake" merged gender and class. Americans set up authenticity, the stronghold of the "folk," against the frippery and femininity of the wealthy with their fussy clothes, frilly furniture, and heaving dinner tables. In the world of literature, American Realism gave a pointed critique to the excessive refinement of urban modernity. Inherent in American Realism was a rejection of the inflexibility and "unreality" of the aristocracy. In Henry James's *The Bostonians*, Basil Ransom declares that "the whole generation is womanized. . . . The masculine tone is passing out of the world; it's a feminine, a nervous, hysterical, chattering, canting age, an age of hollow phrases and false delicacy and exaggerated solicitude and coded sensibilities."[19] Reality was plain, forceful, and masculine; urban life was soft, fussy, and feminine.

Realist authors sought to portray the "common man" and "real" problems, often in direct contrast to the "unreal" lives of the wealthy and elite. In the common man's rough culture portrayed on the page, realists saw a more virtuous and truer America. In Arthur Hill's description of logging for *Scribner's*, he argues:

> It is from the gallery always that virtue triumphant is heartily cheered, be it ever so awkward, and from box and parquette that vice, if artistic and "natural" gets kid-glove applause. And so with these shanty songs, the rules of music and of metre are as nothing to the sentiment they carry, and the voice of the singer to please must come not from an educated thorax but from the heart. Honest love, and words which tell of toil and trials and adventure, make the chief burden of their song verses.[20]

The effeminacy and artifice of "kid-glove applause," with all its celebration of artistic expression, could not match the "triumphant," hearty, masculine virtues of the folk. These parallels of virtue with simple masculinity and vice with artificial femininity were made manifest in the Gilded Age fascination with the male body.

Accounts of lumberjacks and lumber camps began from early days to linger over the strength and musculature of the men, carefully describing their physicality. Papers sang the praises of, as an Ohio newsman put it, "big, brawny, deep chested, square shouldered men, with muscles of steel."[21] This fascination with male musculature was widespread: the famed and admired bodybuilder Eugene Sandow, when asked why he transformed himself into a pillar of towering strength, responded always with a story. When he was ten, he claimed, he had visited Rome with his father. Marveling at ancient statues, he asked his father why modern men did not look like that. His father explained that trains had made men weak. They were modern marvels of technology and inventions, but they were too modern—they took the work out of life. If the brain had triumphed over the body, then the body had become enervated and impotent in the process.[22]

Whether it be a nearly naked Sandow on display or, for instance, former lumberjack and writer John Nelligan's description of lumberjacks as "strong and wild in both body and spirit, with the careless masculine beauty of men who live free lives in the open air. They seemed the finest specimens of manhood [he] had ever seen," admiring the bodies of well-muscled men was not outwardly indicative of anything except a deep interest in the origins and future of white manhood.[23] Before modern conceptions of homosexuality crystallized in the early twentieth century, this kind of language, homoerotic though it may have been, did not indicate that the speaker was sexually pursuing men. Admiring the physique of other men did not, or at least not necessarily, come with any overtones of sexuality. White, male bodies were admired and discussed as works of art, as tools of conquest, and as specimens of superiority.[24]

But while admiration of a male body was not considered to be indicative of the speaker's sexual inclinations, the longing of middle-class men to escape to a world of homosocial masculinity was nonetheless freighted with sexual anxieties. Small gay enclaves had an increasing presence in coastal cities at the turn of the century. While men have had sex with men as long as recorded history, it was only at the close of the nineteenth century that what had been, to middle-class eyes, an act (sodomy) became an identity (fairies). Increasingly, urbanites began to believe they could assume a man's sexual activities based on his appearance. In *Political Manhood*, his study of New York politics at the turn of the century, Kevin P. Murphy explores the convincing connections between the image of prissy, effeminate "mugwump" reformers with the emerging and increasingly salient image of homosexuals. Reformers who took up "unmanly" causes like temperance would find themselves painted with the title of "political hermaphrodite"—the same terminology medical experts were using to classify "sex inverts." That this could be seen as a political attack demonstrates one thing very clearly: men—men who wanted to be taken seriously *as* men—did not want to be associated with these stereotypes.

Therefore, while the men who wrote about lumberjacks clearly longed for their hypermasculinized and homosocial world, they took care to clarify what kind of men it was they sought to be around. Describing the muscular strength of the bodies and the hard work of which they were capable, they separated themselves from men who might be classified as in any way effeminate or "hermaphroditic."[25] Homosexuality was aligned not with the admiration, even the highly sexually charged admiration, of the male body, but with the artifice and vice of effeminate men.

An employee of the Red River Lumber Company poses in William Laughead's studio as a muscular figure study for Laughead's book *The Marvelous Exploits of Paul Bunyan* (1922). Courtesy of the Paul Bunyan Collection, University of Minnesota Libraries.

The timing of these cultural changes is hardly a coincidence. All of them—the break between modern effeminacy and folk masculinity, the deep longing for authenticity, and the soaring increase in interest in folk culture—happened just as the western frontier "closed." Americans had understood the frontier, the West, as the wellspring of their democracy. From Jefferson onward the boundless land of the West was the guarantee of an equal republic. As long as there was open land, there was a bulwark against the development of aristocracy, and all the threats to a democratic republic that an established aristocracy brought. That this was all a construct, that the land was not empty and that it in no way guaranteed democracy, was irrelevant: the idea had a powerful allure. And so its end, fictional or not, was devastating.

In 1890 the census declared the frontier was officially closed. The source of renewal and democracy Americans had long counted on had disappeared. In 1893, at the Columbian Exposition in Chicago, Frederick Jackson Turner delivered his famed "The Significance of the Frontier in American History." Historians have long been unable to resist the perfect symbol this supplied: Turner providing a meaning for American history at the very fair thrown to exhibit the great success story that was the first four centuries of European colonization. And it was no coincidence that Turner gave his address so near to the arena where Buffalo Bill reenacted thrilling battles nightly. As Turner was declaring the frontier over, Buffalo Bill was giving Americans a new way to keep it in their lives: through the use of folklore, of myth.

A poster from 1899 advertised Buffalo Bill as "a living monument of historical and educational magnificence . . . not a 'show' in any sense of the word." The poster insisted the performers would "repeat the heroic parts they have played in actual life upon the plains."[26] The stories were neither tales nor false narratives, but authentic experiences in which the viewers themselves could participate. Elaborately painted backdrops drew on the already famed paintings of western landscapes produced by American romantics. Viewers found in the Wild West shows a symbolic representation of "real" America, an America with a common heritage and common mission, in which they could enmesh their own lives and find meaning. They owned this landscape—even if they had never seen it in person—and their character came from it. All Americans needed to do was tell themselves, again and again, the story of what the cowboy was, and what he meant.

The cowboy, as Buffalo Bill and others have portrayed him, is a creation not of what is, nor even of what is past, but of what *should* be. It is nostalgia as a road map, created to, in the words of Jennifer Moskowitz, "appeal to disparate—and would-be warring—cultural factions and economic classes."[27] Buffalo Bill and his show, as well as the dime novels, ballads, advertisements, and, eventually, movies that depicted the Wild West, operated in what anthropologist and mythologist Bronislaw

Malinowski called a "social charter" function of mythology. The social charter theory sees myths as a way for a society to lay out its rules and values, articulate its aspirations, and mediate its conflicts. They are not simply foundational myths that tell us our history, but are instead road maps to our future. By this understanding, Arthurian legend was powerful not so much as a prehistory of the English monarchs but as an example to solve a problem: in the fifteenth century, there was a growing resentment of the aristocracy as entitled, lazy rulers. The Knights of the Round Table with their chivalric code both gave knights a good example to which to aspire and justified their existence to a restive public. This is the way that cowboys work in American culture: it is not that we came from cowboys, nor from any of the frontiersmen; rather, cowboys and ranchers, Daniel Boone and Buffalo Bill, serve as crystallizations of cultural values and examples to which to aspire.

The West, especially the heroic Wild West of Buffalo Bill, was not a story of where we came from, but an explanation of how Americans could continue to thrive if they followed his example. The myth of the West provided a script for modern Americans at the turn of the century that gave an alternative to the disaster of the closing of the frontier. That script, in the words of historian David Hamilton Murdoch, said: "There. In that place and that time, it was the way it should be. Now it is gone forever. But all is not lost. We carry within us its spirit, so it will continue to flourish if we let it. Now all we have to do is go on retelling the story to keep us on the right track."[28]

And Americans did. They retold the stories again and again, so that the myth of the West built on itself. The more it was repeated, the more the myth became the thing that was real, and the "reality" behind it became unimportant. The extent to which something was perceived as "authentically" western was directly correspondent to the extent to which it was *stereotypically* western. The myth acted as an endless loop, in which to be accepted as really western, one had to perform a kind of western drag. If a cowboy's body appeared to be not up to the task, then the assumption was not that the audience was wrong about the West, but that that was not a real cowboy.[29] Like with Jacob Riis's photographs, what was important was not that images, reenactments, and stories be true in the documentary sense. It was instead that his photographs, like cowboy shows, captured an essential truth and translated it to their audience.[30]

This was the cultural context of a growing literature on lumberjacks. Authors prominently and purposefully placed the lumberjack and the cowboy side by side as embodiments of America's heroic frontier past. By the late 1920s the comparison between the two was ubiquitous. John Nelligan's 1929 memoir of his lumbering days did all it could to eulogize and glorify the lumberjack as "an unsung pioneer,

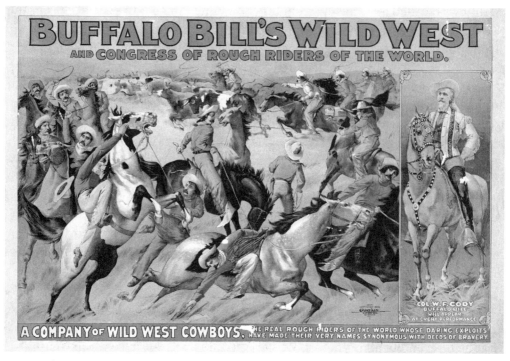

A poster from 1899 advertises the "daring exploits" of the "real rough riders of the world" in Buffalo Bill's Wild West shows. Courtesy of Library of Congress.

the hero of a passing epic drama, a gentleman and—more than a gentleman—a man!" In describing the Northwoods, he regularly drew parallels to the western frontier, describing the lumber regions of the lake states as "as tough and turbulent a frontier as this country has ever known." But it was in the closing of his memoir, which along with Stewart Holbrook's *Holy Old Mackinaw* is the single most cited source for historians and enthusiasts covering midwestern lumberjack life, that he made the comparison to cowboys explicit. He told his readers that the lumberjacks were "hard-living, hard-drinking, hard-fighting, blasphemous pioneers who have gone the way of our other typically American pioneers, the frontiersmen and the cowboys, and are now nothing more than a tradition." A decade later the WPA writers who recorded the history of Grand Rapids, Minnesota, echoed Nelligan, calling lumberjacks "as typically American as the cowboy, and fully as colorful."[31]

Reading and consuming this culture proved a powerful antidote to an increasing sense of dislocation. In the twentieth century, the immediacy of mass media meant that these images, memories, and ideas came to be part of individual memories and identities. While most Americans had never been to the Wild West or cut down a tree in the great woods, they nonetheless felt those memories and stories to be central to their identity—what historian Alison Landsberg called "prosthetic memories": experiences that may not be our own, but whose memory we use as though they were.[32]

But for many, it was not enough. An increasing number of Americans began to try to put themselves into the narrative itself. Modern anthropologists who study authenticity argue that the best method to restore authenticity is to tie oneself, through "perfect simulation," to a past narrative. As ethnographer J. Dwight Hanes explained it, this attempt to relive or revive a past is "an expression of the belief that an essentialized form of authenticity correlates to past forms of landscape and behavior."[33] We can see this in the explosion of modern interest in reenactment: putting on the clothes and going through the motions ties the reenacted more closely to their own past, giving them a sense of place, meaning, and narrative otherwise missing. By miming a narrative, we become part of it.

Today, it is adults going through the motions. But 130 years ago, the transformative power of mimicry was most apparent in the growing interest in childhood reform. In the late nineteenth century, the concern over the state of white American manhood quickly spread as an attempt to ensure that the next generation would grow up stronger than their fathers. Central to these reforms were the ideas of G. Stanley Hall, a reformer who promoted "recapitulation," a process through which boys would evolve through stages of savagery to civilization, thus ensuring that they would build up the necessary strength and nerve-force in their "savage" childhoods to withstand the strains of modern life.[34]

Some reformers took these ideas to heart in a quite literal way. Ernest Thompson Seton, a follower of Hall's, founded the Woodcraft Indians. His group brought boys up through "nature study," in which they would be close to the healthful benefits of the wild. His methods, however, went further, including mimicry of the "noble savages" as a way to access savage boyhood. His pupils would dress in mock-Indian garb, sleep in teepees, and participate in pseudo-Indian rituals. Even those men who did not follow Hall's ideas still incorporated similar mimicry into their educational programs. Daniel Beard, who dismissed Seton as insufficiently American (partially because of his respect for Native Americans) and had no interest in recapitulation, founded the Sons of Daniel Boone. In his group boys would access their inner strength not by imitating savagery, but by modeling themselves on the great pioneers of the American West.[35]

Dime novels marketed to younger boys and boys' adventure stories gave youths a version of manhood worth looking up to and mimicking, and protected boys against an adulthood that reformers like Hall saw as "strewn with wreckage of body, mind, and morals."[36] While the ideal was obviously experienced in the outdoors, the proper reading material could provide a bulwark against overcivilization. Boys' adventure novels balanced savagery with manly restraint to point to a way in which young men could have real emotions and authentic experiences, while embodying the responsibility and restraint expected of a Gilded Age man. In the dozens of novels churned out from 1890 to the early twentieth century documenting the life of Buffalo Bill, for instance, many told tales of the way in which he embodied the virtues of an ideal man. By the age of eleven he was, armed with guns, capable of protecting his mother and sisters from Confederate soldiers. In one particularly effective story, he is forced to kill his beloved horse to save his friends. With a single tear trickling down his manly cheek, the fourteen-year-old William Cody squeezes the trigger and goes on to save the day.[37] While the cowboy formed the most vital backbone of dime novel heroes, the genre quickly spread to include lumberjacks.

Lumberjack books lauded the same virtues as those that featured cowboys, because in similar ways, the fictional lumberjack represented what Peter Hobbs called "untainted/untamed manhood."[38] They both exist outside of civilization, where their true (white) manhood can shine unconstrained by the effeminacy of modern society. A typical genre piece, *The Golden Boys with the Lumberjacks* from 1916, shows our two young heroes visiting a lumber camp owned by their father and setting up for the night under false pretenses as drifters. As the men come in from their day's work in the woods, the boys notice that they are "hard as nails." Among them is a bully, a French-Canadian who fights at the tiniest instigation and speaks in an exaggerated, comic accent. But the boys are American boys, well trained in outdoor exercise and manly sports. Again and again, the Golden Boy, Bob, finds himself able to defeat the Canadian because "to [Bob's] joy he quickly discovered that the man knew nothing of scientific wrestling." Where the Canadian has brawn, the American has brains to go with his muscles. Bob goes on to ensure, once the bully is roundly defeated, that he has ice and a beefsteak for his face, adding generosity to his list of idealized traits. As the story progresses, Bob and his brother are in turns brave and brilliant, eventually saving their father's camp and being accepted as part of the lumberjack fraternity.[39]

Other boys' adventure novels followed the same general outline, all focusing on the importance of imitating the heroic manhood of the lumberjacks. In 1910, Stewart E. White, a Michigander who wrote several novels for adults about the Northwoods, published *The Adventures of Bobby Orde*. The very first chapter has young Bobby, a mere ten years old, learning to log roll in the company of Jimmy Powers. Jimmy is friendly, good-natured, highly skilled, and incredibly strong. Bobby is an anxious, effeminate boy, terrified that his mother will find out he has

Ernest Thompson Seton with a group of the Woodcraft Indians at his Wyndygoul estate in Cos Cob, Connecticut, circa 1903. Courtesy of the Ernest Thompson Seton fonds / Library and Archives Canada / PA-187508.

been disobeying her rules, and afraid that falling in the river on a warm spring day will give him a cold. By the end of the second chapter, he is closing his prayers by asking God to "make Bobby grow up a big man like Jimmy Powers." These stories taught clear lessons to boys about what they were meant to strive for as they grew into manhood: the lumberjack heroes are even-handed and good-natured, powerful and adventurous.[40]

For many, the mimicry continued past childhood. Anthropologist Frank Hamilton Cushing took his escape from modernity to the somewhat ridiculous extent of refashioning his New York apartment to resemble a Zuni kiva and dressing only in Zuni garb. Others took a somewhat less dramatic approach. The late nineteenth century saw a proliferation of interest in "simpler" pre- or antimodern cultures.

Books about cowboys and frontiersmen exploded in popularity, feeding the impulse of wealthy men and women who looked to escape to the country, where people were real.

Urbanization had far-reaching consequences for late nineteenth-century Americans, but for the wealthy one of the most penetrating was a new realization that their friends and neighbors might not be who they thought they were. But worse yet, they might not know themselves. As historian T. J. Jackson Lears argues, in the late nineteenth century the center began to fall out and the idea of false, or multiple, identities grew increasingly troubling. For the snake oil salesman and confidence man of the antebellum and early postwar era there was a self—a fundamentally rotten core. He might trick others but at heart he knew who he was. For the Gilded Age, middle-class, white American it was no longer clear that the "self" was as solid as had been believed. As *The Atlantic* noted in 1886, "this whole matter of the individual identity—the I-ness of the I—is thick with difficult questions."[41]

Modern urbanites thus increasingly sought ways to connect with their most "authentic" selves. Their search was to find a simpler, historically earlier, and more primitive version of themselves to offset the dislocation and overwork of modern city life. For those with the ability to, this often meant an escape into the actual country. As the same *Atlantic* writer noted, there were "lives that do go on with apparently unbroken coherence—tranquil, native or village lives," and some attempted to imitate those lives when they had the time and space to do so.[42]

Others were forced to make do with the closest thing they could find: namely, the escapist contact with nature and primitive manhood they received through consulting the folklore that described the heroic manhood of the West. As Grace Hale writes of another historical moment, the 1950s and 1960s, when white, middle-class urbanites found themselves feeling that they were living in a manufactured, inauthentic society: "encounters with outsiders enabled some middle-class whites to cut themselves free of their own social origin and histories and in identifying with these others to imaginatively regain what they understood as previously lost values and feelings."[43]

The short stories, novels, and magazine reports about lumberjacks published for an eastern audience emphasized the authentic, emotionally raw, unpretentious, and vigorous nature of the lumberjack, explicitly tying his good health and good nature to the nature in which he toiled. His primitive surroundings—the rough bunkhouses, downtrodden hotels, and pristine forests—played a part in creating a more primitive, virile, authentic, and honest version of white manhood.

For Gilded Age Americans, that virile manhood was, by definition, a product of place. It grew out of man struggling with nature. The best example of this is Elia

Peattie's 1905 story "A Michigan Man." Written by a woman who lived in a log cabin on what she called the "frontier" (well, Omaha), it emphasized the tie between the surroundings of the lumberjack and his mental, moral, and physical well-being. Within the woods, both man and nature exist within a premodern framework untouched by industrialization. The story opens in a forest whose stillness is "as awful and as holy as a cathedral." Here we find the lumberjack at peace among nature's "expression of solemnity and solitude." Her language emphasizes the woods' position as pure, untouched, silent, and sanctified. Just as the trees themselves do not interact with modernity, neither do the lumberjacks within them. Our hero, Luther Dallas, can fell a tree so swiftly that "the resounding footsteps of Progress driven on so mercilessly in this mad age could not reach his fastness." He is so removed from the modern world that "it did not concern him that men were thinking, investigating, inventing. His sense responded only to the sonorous music of the woods."[44]

After he is injured by a tree, Luther wanders to Chicago, hoping to find his long-lost sister, convinced that any man "unless he were 'shiftless'" could not want for a job. But from the moment he steps off the train Luther is thrown into a chaotic modern world that threatens to kill him. He is greeted at the station by "the whistles and bells [that] kept up a ceaseless clangor." The streets were filled with "such an illumination as he had never dreamed of," and the sidewalk "seemed to him a pandemonium filled with madmen." The noise, the lights, and the rushing people "went to his head like wine." Within five minutes of arriving in Chicago, Luther, the great woodsman, was overwhelmed, and "the distressing experience that comes to almost every one at some time of life, of losing all identity in the universal humanity, was becoming his."

Luther was experiencing the tolls of modernity—the confusion, the disjointed identity, the sense of unreality—all at once. He saw, too, the way the city was killing other men, observing the "gaunt, scrawny, transplanted specimens that met his eye" with despair. Mad with hunger, impoverished, and weak, Luther is eventually arrested for attempting to chop down a telephone pole. That night, in jail, he dies, hearing the night-winds through the forest in his dreams, imagining "there would be hoarfrost on the trees in the morning."[45]

This vision of lumberjacks as embodiments of man's strong connection with nature, and of the heroism and manly perseverance to which that connection led, proved enormously popular to elite audiences. They rebuilt the lumberjack as a hero, not a pest, and found a new, wealthier audience for lumberjack stories. And, in time, they came to serve a secondary purpose: the attempted rehabilitation of the lumber industry's reputation in the very region it had destroyed.

# EIGHT

# PAPERING OVER A WASTELAND

## CREATING A CORPORATE MYTH

In the short years from his first appearance in the press to his stature as America's only "authentic" folk hero, Paul Bunyan underwent a sea change. Before 1914, Paul Bunyan's name was relatively unknown outside Wisconsin, though within the pineries of northern Wisconsin he may have been quite well known. A Kentucky jack named M. M. Gambill who spent a winter in the Northwoods reported to his home paper in Louisa, Kentucky, in 1910 that "his exploits are related in every . . . logging camp in northern Wisconsin," and that "the men in traveling from camp to camp—for the lumberjack is a rover—swapped these yarns."[1]

Where he was known, he was on a more human scale—eight feet tall, not twenty—and known primarily as a cruel boss, a swindler, and an abuser of the working man.[2] Gambill recalled that he was told Bunyan was "eight feet tall and weighed 300 lbs" and "had a voice like a bull roaring." While hardly small, this is not the soaring giant whose footsteps made lakes. Moreover, Paul Bunyan was a first-class jerk, who "ruled with an iron hand over the 2,000 men under him." His yelling was so loud "the noise broke the branches off trees," and it made it so that "every man in his employ jumped when he spoke."[3]

But by 1920 Paul Bunyan had transformed entirely. Stories of his generosity and good nature followed along with his enormous size. The tone of 1920s Paul Bunyan stories, much like later tales up to the present day, focused on the fun and games, hijinks, and impossible feats of strength of Paul and the men in his camp. Paul, the foreman, and Johnny Inkslinger, the camp clerk, were close to the men and participated in their games and their labor. As a foreman of his camp Paul was never removed from his men in any way—never seen without an ax in his hand. The overall impression is of a cozy family that happens to labor on the side. But this Paul, the Paul America came to know and love, was a corporate invention.

To understand why Paul was remade—and the entire mythic lumberjack along-side him—we must return to the world of industrial capitalism and environmental degradation. By the early teens, the timber stocks of the Northwoods were quickly dwindling, and a growing conservation movement fueled by Gifford Pinchot and supported by Teddy Roosevelt was turning the tide of opinion toward measured, more sustainable timbering.[4] For the lumber firms that had flourished in the Northwoods, these developments proved to be a series of stumbling blocks. While large companies moved on to logging in the Pacific Northwest, they still held thousands of acres of clear or nearly clear-cut land. When their first attempt to sell the cutover as farmland failed, they turned to a new stream of income: they instead moved to sell the land as a prime tourist destination, a pristine woodland untouched by modernity and industry.

But of course, this, too, came with a catch: these were the very companies who had entirely reshaped that land with aggressive industrial extraction. In trying to square this circle, lumber companies turned to an unexpected mascot. They reinvented the lumberjack's image from dissolute wage worker in a massive industrial system to a folksy, premodern woodsman in a small-scale industry that had barely touched the wilderness.

By the 1910s the land that had once been so thick with trees that "seventy mills in seventy years" could not exhaust it was nearly clear cut.[5] Some stands remained—those on privately owned land, some on reservations, and a few that were too far from rivers or railroads to be easily logged. In Minnesota, only one large stand of virgin white pine was left: a forty-acre lot that had been accidentally surveyed, in 1892, as a lake. Today it's a state park, where visitors go to marvel at the trunks three grown men cannot wrap their arms around, and stare up at the crowns of white pine towering ten or more stories over their heads. It is one of the few glimpses anyone after the 1920s can have of what the Northwoods once were. By then the northern stretches of Wisconsin were barren, and the Upper Peninsula of Michigan had turned to mining, its stores of white pine stripped.

When Julie Anderson arrived in Michigan in the early twentieth century, she described a land in which "only stumps remained where once virgin pine had stood."[6] By 1913, Walter Benjamin described traveling through the Minnesotan Northwoods only to "see the blackened stumps and ruined camps, mute witness that a once great industry will soon exist only in memory."[7] In 1917, an eight-year-old Don Benson arrived in northern Minnesota with his family. Looking across the land, he "could see a man standing here anywhere [since] there wasn't a thing here taller than a man right here." The whole land was charred. What had once been rich

By the time this photograph was taken in 1912, wildfires and extensive logging left a slash-and-burn landscape of scattered stumps across much of Wisconsin, Minnesota, and Michigan's Upper Peninsula. Photograph by C. W. Ward, U.S. Forest Service Records, National Archives.

forest land was "just bare . . . just burned slick." Benson remembered picking blueberries and putting his lunch pail under a four-foot bushwillow for shade. It was the tallest tree in sight.[8]

The land left behind, covered in stumps and the detritus left by the industry, was in many areas of a terribly poor quality for farming. Even where the farming was good, the industry's legacy still left homesteaders open to enormous risks. Firestorms ripped across the Northwoods from the late nineteenth century through to the 1920s. Some were truly enormous, destroying hundreds of communities. The Cloquet Firestorm of 1918 may have taken as many as five hundred lives and left over ten thousand as homeless refugees.[9] The firestorms in Wisconsin in 1871 remain the deadliest in American history, claiming the lives of anywhere from 1,500 to 2,500 people.

Even the economic boom brought on by the industry faded away quickly. When the industry moved on there were few if any jobs for those who had worked in it. Very few areas managed the transition smoothly: those that were rich in other natural resources transitioned to different extractive industries; larger cities like Saginaw and Muskegon had formed mixed economies that, while primarily dependent on lumber, had other industries to fall back on; some regions, like parts of the Minnesota Northwoods, had passable farmland under the rotting logs and dried brush of the cutover. But for many areas stripped by the lumber industry, there was nowhere to turn.

For the corporations who owned this land, the drying up of timber resources posed several problems. As corporations like Weyerhaeuser and Red River Lumber shifted their attention to the Pacific Northwest, they were left with vast tracts of stumpland. The land beneath the woods was not the idealized farmland settlers had hoped for when they began to settle the upper plains in the 1850s. Instead, what was left was largely sandy land, not particularly good for any form of agriculture other than forestry. Yet the companies that owned it needed to unload their now essentially valueless land.

Trying to make a little more money while offloading land, colonization companies sprang up in the 1910s selling the sandy, poor farmland to new settlers. Some of the companies were owned outright by lumber companies; others consisted largely of smaller contractors who had bought land from the lumber companies and resold it for a profit.

None of these companies were under any great illusions as to the quality of the land they had to sell. The key was to, in the words of folklorist (and lumber company skeptic) Asher Treat, unload "these worthless and tax encumbered wastes" as quickly as possible, even if that meant "many poor immigrants parted with a lifetime's savings, only to find themselves stranded in a god-forsaken wilderness where they faced the choice of starving to death or making the land support them."[10] Treat wrote in 1939, when northern Wisconsin agriculture had failed so comprehensively as to make it one of the poorest regions in the nation. But there's evidence to suggest that lumber companies were aware of the land's shortcomings much earlier—in fact, from the very beginning.

Correspondence between colonization companies and the timber companies make clear that speed was the key contingency. They were willing to bend easily on price, just so long as they could unload the land quickly. In 1916 a Mr. Fermin, the head of the Logged Off Land Department of Weyerhaeuser Timber Company, wrote to the American Immigration Company for help. Frederick Weyerhaeuser had made his name in the Northwoods, but the company's attachment was to timber,

*Clover-Land Magazine,* published by the Clover-Land League of Municipalities, advertised the bountiful riches of the Michigan cutover in 1916. Courtesy of Marquette County History Museum / J. M. Longyear Research Library.

not to land or to settlers. While they had managed to sell "quite a little land" of their own accord, J. P. Weyerhaeuser, one of Frederick's sons, had suggested Fermin turn to the AIC—a syndicate of his father's company—for advice in selling off the rest. Fermin is straightforward about the company's goals: they were "endeavoring to speed up the sale" of cutover land. As an afterthought he noted that "as a general thing," the lands were "rather rough and . . . probably better adapted for grazing purposes than they are for any kind of agricultural industry."[11]

Once they took possession of lands from the lumber companies, colonization companies divided their lots into two main categories: lake frontages, and the wide tracts of stumplands that separated them. The lake fronts were sold to appeal to a burgeoning tourist market, with promises that "nothing seems to have been overlooked to render it attractive to the lover of outdoor life."[12] The stumpage, on the other hand, was sold unscrupulously and quickly. Local papers and midwestern farm papers like the *Farmer's Dispatch, Wisconsin Agriculturist,* and *Hoard's Dairyman* advertised "good eighties . . . partially improved" at "low prices" with "easy terms."[13]

The largest buyers for this kind of land were not farmers but other land agents. These agents were well aware of the value of the land they were buying. The operator of a telephone company hoping to make a quick buck wrote to the American Immigration Company plainly asking for a "tract of cut over timber land that you can sell cheap and on very easy terms." Others were less discriminate still, M. W. Balfour, a "Dealer in Good Farm Lands," by his own description, wrote asking simply to "get in touch with some one or some company who own a large tract of cut-over lands in either Wisconsin or Minnesota, who wish to dispose of the land at a reasonable price and on good terms."[14]

To turn a profit, these agents stripped what few resources still existed before selling the land on. Homeseeker's Land Company sold on to a North Dakota land agent whose contracts, for instance, reserved the rights to any trees of more than eight inches in diameter for five years, as well as the exclusive use of any waterways that could help bear the lumber to market. Not only would the farmer be unable to till the land the trees occupied, he would not even be able to sell the trees for his own profit.[15]

When buyers were allowed to access the wood on their land, colonization companies purposefully misled them about the timber's value. Removing leftover stumpage without expensive equipment was backbreaking work, and while companies like the American Immigration Company assured buyers that "the salvage in timber from land clearing if properly handled, has become an item of considerable profit," that work was slow, and the lumber companies themselves had left behind hardly anything of value. In addition to stumps, they left poplars and other soft woods, which fetched very little at market. In fact, an executive from American Immigration Company wrote to F. E. Weyerhaeuser, another son of the timber magnate and investor in the company, that they had at that point possession of almost half a million acres of cutover lands with "no timber of any value except for fuel."[16]

Clearing that land of the leftover timber meant farmers could not cultivate crops for at least a year. An American Immigration Company pamphlet admitted to buyers that "land covered with stumps, brush and trees, is the most serious drawback . . . in a word, is the only objection raised by the homeseeker," but goes on to assure prospective buyers that "it is not as formidable as at first it appears." Should the new settler find money tight as he spent his first year breaking land, the pamphlet assured him that any "man of poor means" could find work those first winters

Stump clearing in the Wisconsin cutover, circa 1920. Photograph by Melvin E. Diemer. Courtesy of the Wisconsin Historical Society, WHS-1915.

in plentiful logging camps.[17] But of course, the land was only available because the logging camps had long since left.

The new farmer, therefore, found himself in a jam. Clearing land came, in the early twentieth century, to thirty dollars an acre, more than the cost of the land.[18] First years of farming required heavy investment of capital, so while companies could offer "easy terms," what was more necessary still was a line of credit. But that credit was not forthcoming. The U.S. Department of Agriculture baldly reported in 1931 that "few banks or commercial mortgage companies" would provide loans, and even the colonization companies had stopped financing their own projects by then.[19]

Perhaps, then, it's little wonder that most companies ignored the presence of stumps altogether. The American Colonization Company's letterhead featured a field of wheat and a prosperous dairy farm without a tree in sight, despite the fact that their lands in northwestern Wisconsin were almost entirely cutover. Others insisted to European immigrants unfamiliar with the land that "sandy soil is not necessarily poor soil," and "who intends to buy land can get work right away. . . . Anybody can get work which will please him."[20]

Part of the problem was that the cutover clearly lacked some of the romance and promise of the West. Americans and new immigrants alike were ready, even eager, to move to the fertile lands of the far West. As C. B. Hanson, a land agent from North Dakota, wrote to the American Immigration Company, "Western lands find a ready market always. But they cost more money, and if I can buy twice as much good land in Wisconsin and in Montana that is what we will do." However, he seemed to have doubts that that was possible, or that, indeed, the American Immigration Company was presenting itself honestly. Mr. Hanson closed his letter begging to know "about the conditions as they now are," as he himself had not been to Wisconsin in a quarter century and "always thought Northern Wis was compound of sand and swamp."[21]

One solution was to sell to mostly foreigners. Revenue books from the American Immigration Company, the Homeseeker's Land Company, and the American Colonization Company show that many of their advertisements were placed in ethnic newspapers in Chicago and other major centers where the newly arrived might not know of the Northwoods as a land of sand and swamp.

The other solution was to appeal to an ideal, to attach their lands to the promise of a prosperous future and hope that the romance carried buyers away. They sold farming as an ideal, manly alternative to the caprices of the market. A pamphlet advertising land in the Cutover region of Wisconsin (the origin of the region's common name comes, of course, from the remnants of the lumber industry) told settlers that "the lack of permanent and regular employment, and the low wages now being paid, are causing many laboring men . . . to turn their attention countryward . . . away from the influence of strikes and lockouts, and where he is not dependent for his daily bread upon the caprices of any boss; where, in fact, he can be a free man in the full sense of the term."[22] As industrial capitalism grew and wealth was consolidated in the hands of a small few, the ideal of the self-sufficient farmer grew in appeal.

But the truth was that in the end, farming was never going to be the solution, a fact that became clear by the end of the 1910s. The disastrous results of seventy years of intensive logging were beginning to show in earnest by the 1920s. Poor land burned again and again. Men and women had watched their futures go up in flames. Some regions managed to survive or even thrive by pivoting: the Iron Range in Minnesota and the Upper Peninsula of Michigan were on rich mineral deposits. Both turned to another kind of extraction, and Duluth roared on as a major port, exporting iron from Minnesota's rich Iron Range as well as the last of the timber

Lumber tourism came early to Michigan. In 1906, Ephraim Shay's short-lived Harbor Springs Railway was primarily a log-hauling operation but also carried vacationing summer tourists for a fare of twenty-five cents. Courtesy of Library of Congress.

from its forests well into the twentieth century. But others fared less well. In central Wisconsin, there was little to replace logging, and the land was more degraded than elsewhere. Crops failed regularly, and the region came to be a center of tax delinquency and land abandonment. Just south of it, by 1934, a dust bowl—smaller than its famous southern neighbor, but still devastating—ruined some of the few farmers who were hanging on. It is no surprise that when the Great Depression hit Wisconsin the cutover, which housed just one-sixth of the state's population, sucked up one-third of its relief money.[23]

As it became increasingly clear that agriculture would not be a viable future for much of the cutover, colonization companies pivoted to tourism. The Upper Peninsula Development Bureau, which had been created to sell the cutover as farmland, was already earmarking three thousand dollars of its budget for tourism. Others followed suit: the American Immigration Company was selling "Recreational Land in large tracts with lake and river frontage in Sawyer and Bayfield Counties, Wisconsin, at reasonable prices" as early as 1916, advertising this new tourist haven in papers as far away as the *Omaha World-Herald*. By 1931, they were no longer selling farmland at all, but instead advertising "highly desirable lakefront" as "wild and partly improved" to buyers in Chicago and Kansas, noting their "lake and trout stream: good fishing: ideal location." Of course, their land was not, in fact, "wild," and "partly improved" mostly spoke to existing roads leftover from timbering days.[24]

Selling this land as pristine wilderness ideal for a retreat from the strains of modern life (especially when it was arms of the very companies who logged it that were doing the selling) seems, at first glance, so glaringly hypocritical, to say nothing of false, that it's hard to believe it was successful. And yet, it was.

At the heart of it was the need to rehabilitate the image of the industry, and to do that, there needed to be a wholesale makeover of its most visible aspect: the thousands of lumberjacks who worked in the camps. Starting in the early 1910s, lumber companies began to market the lumberjack in ways that directly contradicted his existing reputation in the Northwoods and appealed to the growing middle-class veneration for nature and muscled, masculine, "authentic" men.

The version of the lumberjack promoted by the major logging concerns came with three distinct but important elements: the first was that the clearing of the land was part of a heroic national project of expansion; secondly they portrayed the industry, even at its very height, as a small-scale, family operation; and finally that there had once been a great race of men, a race of giants—the original lumberjacks—but that those men had been wiped out by the introduction of cheap eastern European labor in the early twentieth century. Together, these three claims created a powerful, effective narrative, one that trapped the lumberjack in a romantic past and distanced the industry from the repercussions of extractive industry.

The first important aspect of this corporate myth was that the land that was left behind—the Cutover in Wisconsin, the Iron Range in Minnesota, and the impoverished tracts of the Upper Peninsula—were in fact cleared as part of a great project of national and moral improvement. In a 1956 oral history interview, George W. Dulany, a former lumber baron, the son of a wealthy tobacco planter and member of the Concatenated Order of the Hoo-Hoo, argued that the lumber industry had provided a vital role in laying the foundations for a fruitful future for the Midwest. When the interviewer indicated that the industry might have hurt the land, Dulany complained, "we have heard people say that the timber people, lumber people, of the Upper Mississippi River Valley slaughtered and wasted the natural resources.

We who know about it resent that statement, because we didn't slaughter it; we used it." He went on to argue that without the timber barons, the vast timberlands, "would have died, rotted, been eaten by bugs or destroyed by fire. There was so much timber in those days that no one could enter into reforestation because there was a surplus of timber." Finally, he concluded that there had been "no other way" to continue the process of American expansion; "they had to clear timber land to make farm land."[25]

The claim was compelling: for centuries Euro-Americans had understood the clearing of the wilderness to make way for civilization as a fundamental premise of their nation. Moreover, this very idea had been invoked in the early days of lumbering in the Northwoods to justify illegal encroachment on Anishinaabe land and rampant theft. Men who cleared land they had not yet bought justified their actions under the guise of, ultimately, serving the public good.[26] But the claim was also obviously false: even had those motives been honest (and it seems unlikely that profit was not at least *one* of the primary motives of the lumber industry), the results had clearly been disastrous.

The second theme was a persistent tendency to make the industry into something small-scale, even folksy. In the good old days of the industry, those who ran it insisted, the foremen took care of the men as their own brothers. E. O. Olund, the owner of the Olund Employment Service in Duluth, Minnesota, complained that men's dissatisfaction with camps from the 1920s onward came from the unions that "perpetrated a false idealism." As a result, the men are "discouraged" for, now that they have white sheets and their own homes, spring beds and wages enough for good bottled cooking gas, they no longer felt at home. In the old days, before labor reforms, the men "knew they would be taken care of." They could arrive at a camp and it was "a 'home' to the jacks, despite the bad conditions. There was plenty of food. . . . If he was sick, or under the weather and unable to keep up his end of the work for a few days, it didn't matter."[27] There is some truth here. Men were often fed when they arrived on site, and older men could find work as bull cooks. But there are conditions that Olund skates over. He told his interviewer, for instance, that if men showed up without clothes they would be outfitted. He does not mention that that outfitting might cost half a month's wages, or that many men left camp having spent almost all their earnings over the winter at the company store.

Portraying the industry as a cozy family both erased the class conflict within the camps and, as a direct result, made any antagonism seem entirely unreasonable. In the 1915 novella *The Boy and the Man*, Seward D. Allen, an upper-middle-class writer and lawyer friendly to the lumber barons, depicted labor agitators as troublemakers and unreasonable dissidents in a serene family environment. In the second

A jack buys a shirt from a clerk in the "van," a supply store run in connection with the Simpson Lumber Camp at the Pine Island area near Big Falls, Minnesota, circa 1900. Photograph by H. A. Bliler, U.S. Forest Service Records, National Archives.

chapter of the book, our hero, a lawyer lost in the woods, stumbles into a camp. While he pretends to sleep an argument breaks out among the men. One man, Bill, had fallen earlier that day and says he is surprised he did not lose his head, since "a man that's fool enough to risk his life for two and a half a day on property that's as much his and anyone's, don't have much of a head anyway." Bill goes on to complain that "the men that risk their lives in getting this timber get next to nothing out of it. The government, our government, that you and me elect, just hand it over to the lumbermen to get to be millionaires on, so they and their idle families can swell around and look down on us."

Up to this point, Bill's argument follows the common complaint that the barons were robbing the region of its land and wealth to make their own fortunes. But the chapter quickly turns its focus away from Bill to Joel Meeker, the gentle old man who owns the camp and sleeps in the bunk with the men. The other men turn to Mr. Meeker and laugh, saying "you're just a common, everyday millionaire in disguise, beguilin' us of our patrimony and our toil! I'm shocked, lightly shocked, Mr.

Meeker!" Bill tries to save himself claiming that among owners is "where labor finds its worst enemy . . . in the boss, the middle man, who's always turning his back on his own class to make himself solid with the employing class." But the men are having none of it. Their ringleader points out that Meeker is "on the job himself" and claims Bill's central problem is that he is "so afraid [he'll] have to do a bit more than [he has] to." When Bill tries to respond, it is clear to the watching lawyer that "the sympathy of the men was evidently not with him."[28] This little scene reinforces the idea that in the cozy, family-run world of the lumber camp, unrest is unnatural. The men love their boss—he is one of them. The language of unionism and class warfare are comical in such a serene setting. They can only have come from an outside agitator intent on sowing discord.

This disdain for the complaints of working men was reinforced by a persistent emphasis on the ability of lumberjacks, should they put effort into it, to raise themselves from laborers to owners. Throughout the 1880s and 1890s, as the divide between lumberjacks and the lumber camp owners grew increasingly stark, editorialists damning "lazy" lumberjacks claimed that it was not difficult to rise through the ranks. Near the turn of the century the *Princeton Union* of Princeton, Minnesota, complained that the editors of the Deer River *Democrat* had failed—in an article caricaturing lumberjacks—to consider the "men who were once lumber jacks . . . that are holding prominent and responsible positions in our legislative halls, [and] our churches and colleges." Never mind that these few men could hardly claim to characterize the thousands who worked in the woods.[29]

Fictional accounts also echoed the idea that all the great owners had come from a beginning as lowly workers. A slim 1922 novel called, quite simply, *Timber* has its protagonist, a wealthy lumber baron, telling his son that "the start I got . . . was standin' to my waist in the Saginaw, with th' river gone made with ice an' logs. . . . Come next fall he took my savings and what they bought give me my chance to buy pine of my own—Pine!" In this story as others of its ilk, the great baron longs for his days of simple, healthful work among the "boys." He finishes his fine speech by telling his son that he would "give it all, every dollar, every cent; give my credit to the last dime to be back there again with an' ice-cold river huggin' my legs an' a peavy in my hand."[30]

The image of working men moving up through the ranks, of bosses who come from among their men and sit side by side with them on the deacon's seat telling stories in the smoky evenings before moving on to great fortunes and positions of power is lovely and poetic. But it's also fiction. The "men of great prominence" rarely if ever came from the working stock of jacks. The wealthy, powerful, and prominent were often "lumbermen," but not "lumberjacks." They were more likely to be owners than jacks, to belong to the Masons than to sleep in a snake room on skid row. The men who managed to move up began almost entirely in positions of some power. They were foremen, owners, cooks, and clerks, as opposed to jacks. There were of course exceptions. There were some, like Andrew Glenn, who worked to pay for college, and others who spent their summer becoming literate. As Arthur Hill noted in an 1893 article for *Scribner's*, there were lumberjacks who had "families, for whom they faithfully toil and slave. Others are steady, thrifty young men who have bought, and out of their earnings are paying for, a piece of land, or perhaps are supporting a good old mother, or paying off the mortgage on the home farm."

But Hill is clear about one thing: these are not the "typical" lumberjacks. Those who considered themselves real lumberjacks felt separate from these men. The typical jack "works only fitfully in the summer . . . going back to the woods in the early fall." In fact, as C. E. Blakeman, a Michigan jack, remembered, those who went back to their farms were "always despised . . . by the *real* [emphasis added] woodsmen who followed camp work the year around."[31] For those who had worked their winters and summers in the woods, it was clear that work in the camps was not a road to the "prominent and responsible positions." Rather, they formed a brotherhood precisely because of their social isolation from those halls of power. The transformation of the cultural perception of woods work from an endless roundabout of fruitless labor into a heroic struggle toward the betterment of the country and self is clear in the remarkable transformation of America's most famous lumberjack from the 1880s to the 1920s.

The final theme in the corporate myth was one that would become perhaps the most familiar, and in many ways most destructive, of all: that there had been, in their heyday, a race of great men, of giants, who were wiped out by the influx of cheap northern and eastern European labor and a "lesser" kind of jack. The earlier kind of jack was strong and honest. He worked hard and saved money to try to seek a better life for himself and his family. In the words of former foreman George Dulany, he "went back to work from daylight to dark; . . . that was typical of the hard-working serious type of fellow." Newer jacks on the other hand were profligate, prone to "drink and wild living." As soon as they got paid, they would "insist they had to go out to Duluth . . . and spend all their money in riotous living." Dulany, as with many of his contemporaries, set these two types of men in direct opposition to one another. There were the "strong, powerful men" determined to do good by their families, and the others, the men you "couldn't get . . . to stay on the job . . .

floaters." Or in the words of Walter F. Benjamin, a former foreman surveying the field of workers in 1912, "the average 'lumberjack' of today is but a miserable apology for his predecessor."[32]

According to these ideas it was not conditions, not even the IWW, but lumberjacks themselves that were weakening the morale that had long existed under older models. The older jacks seemed to be cut of tougher stuff, not only in masculine strength, but in a moral respect for the old order. In 1907 the *Detroit Free Press* lamented, "conditions now are not what they were in years gone by." Once upon a time, the paper complained, "the men who worked in the camps were born lumbermen," as opposed to the newer kind of jack. Back when "real" lumberjacks worked in the woods, "the boss had no trouble with them if he was satisfied with a faithful performance of the duties of the camp." This language echoes that of those who mythologized the small, family-run lumber camp. Good men respected good bosses who could, in turn, rely on their men. But now those days were over, and the contractor "must employ wholly inexperienced laborers, most of whom are foreigners." The native-born woodsmen were born with the work in their skin. They were natural lumberjacks. But even though many Scandinavian laborers were intimately familiar with woods work, there was a pervasive conviction that, as the *Free Press* put it, "almost double the number of those men is required to do an amount of work equal to that performed by real 'lumberjacks' in former years."[33]

In explaining what made the "lesser" jacks so damaging, industry leaders and middle-class memoirists settled on two salient features: they came later, and they came from parts of the world—eastern Europe and Finland—that Americans found suspect. Chronologically, they came last. An unpublished 1936 article in the archives of the *Grand Rapids Herald* gave a quick and clear rundown of the differences between a "real" jack and his later incarnations. C. C. Kelly, a local resident, told the paper that "in reverse English of excellence came the lumberjack. Best, better, good, indifferent—he came in successive waves, so to speak, and the best came first." While once upon a time jacks had been strong, now they were weak, listless, troublesome, and terrible workers.[34]

But Kelly goes on to highlight what was to many contemporaries the most important defining characteristic of newer, weaker lumberjacks: their ethnicity. He argues that the earliest of jacks were "tough enough to eat Harveyized Steel," and that "pillows, latrines and such-like effeminacies to him were unknown." His wages were low, and his life difficult, but he was "the best man and the damnedest fool." This robust manhood was, for Kelly, strictly tied to his ethnicity. Kelly told the paper that "this best lumberjack as a rule came from Maine or Canada," and that "white man he was always."[35] His days were over and the best had left when a

As the popular press began lamenting the demise of "authentic" lumberjacks in the 1930s, WPA photographers began documenting the vanishing logging life in towns like Margie, Minnesota. Photograph by Russell Lee. Courtesy of Library of Congress.

"heavy inflow of foreign labor, mostly Scandinavian," came to the woods. Others agreed with Kelly. In 1906 the *Detroit Free Press* complained, "except during recent years the lumberjack was not the riffraff of foreign countries that is now being dumped on American shores, but was largely of the old Yankee stock."[36] The ability to pick "true" lumberjacks apart from "foreign riffraff" became a fundamental component of an understanding of who lumberjacks were and were not, which allowed the lumbermen and newspapers who supported them to remember a heroic jack at the expense of his modern, itinerant, and, at times, unionized brethren.

Newer, "weaker," foreign laborers came to bear the brunt of the blame for problems that had been endemic to the labor system in the lumber industry for decades. When strikes broke out in 1916, both owners and many newspapers blamed the introduction of "foreign elements" for the breakdown of labor relations. But while the 1916 strike was, indeed, partially orchestrated out of the Finnish Socialist Opera in Virginia, Minnesota, and did have support and help from the IWW, it did not introduce a fundamentally new element of resistance. Rather, the IWW and Charles Jacobsen built on existing tensions and methods of resistance that jacks had used for decades. The greatest instigator of the strike, Jack Beaton, was nothing if not the "old" kind of lumberjack. Nonetheless, newspapers hundreds of miles away in Wisconsin recorded the strike as an "attempted invasion" by the IWW.[37]

Great lumber organizations seemed to be unable to recognize that resistance might be coming from within, even when it appeared to be staring them in the face. While the Weyerhaeuser Corporation, the largest of the lumber giants, eventually pioneered creating housing for their lumberers, forming social halls and separate shacks in which jacks might settle down in a domestic manner, their peers strongly disagreed with this method. Hunt Taylor, a fellow lumberman, wrote to Rudolph Weyerhaeuser in 1919 that if he were in Weyerhaeuser's position he would "get ahold of some good Temperance Finn" to write pamphlets. Taylor assumed that the problems of IWW agitation and foreign influence were one and the same. He advised Weyerhaeuser to "off-set the propaganda" of the Finns. The problem was not terrible work conditions nor low pay but rather that the owners had not maintained "a press bureau from the beginning, to set off a lot of their arguments." What the lumberjacks fundamentally needed, according to Taylor, was someone to "preach American citizenship in all its value and loyalty to the American flag to a greater extent than we have." By Hunt Taylor's understanding the fundamental problems with the industry's labor force were new, not decades old. They were the way in which new, weak, unmanly laborers had undermined the patriotic citizenship and corporate loyalty of the "good" jacks.[38]

It was in selling this set of ideas that Paul Bunyan came to take center stage. A close look at the changing nature of Paul Bunyan stories, as they appeared scattered in the press, traces the shift from folk hero of wageworkers in a large-scale industry to smiling corporate mascot.

No story shows this shift better than that of the Round River Drive. The "Round River Drive" first appeared in print in the *Oscoda Press* of Oscoda, Michigan, in 1906. In the story, Paul attempts to trick his men out of their due pay by forcing them to drive the same logs around and around a river. Paul, driving his men to distraction without any promise of success, reflects not a hero, but a worker's nightmare come to life. Twenty years later, when this story appeared in collections of tales, it was re-worked as a tale of charming buffoonery, in which Paul was no wiser than his men to the fact that the drive they were going on was taking them in circles.

In the first, older version, the story works to express frustration and solidarity. The joke here is not that the boss is a buffoon. Instead, he is relentlessly cruel; this story comes from the same world of laborers who called employment offices slave markets. It reflects the fundamental belief that underpinned so many men's choice to abandon one camp or another after a few weeks' work: that bosses would try to take advantage, and it was the laborer's job to watch out for himself and not get caught endlessly toiling in fruitless labor. This is the story you might imagine from a lumberjack who complained, as one jack told a reporter, that he might defend "highway robbery . . . compared with the slavery of a lumber camp."[39] The second, commercialized version portrays an entirely different understanding of the rela-tionship between laborers and management. All its biting cruelty and bitterness is gone, and everything is all in good fun. The boss now, gregarious and foolish, is just part of the gang.

In other stories from the early period, Paul is constantly tricking and ruining his men. In one, a French worker falls in the water. Two new lumberjacks jump in to save him, only to be met with censure by Paul, for whom "in case of accident or mishap, tools and equipment were to be saved first." Another has Paul, upon realiz-ing he does not have the money to pay his workers, running through camp shouting that "they had been cutting government pine and were all to be arrested," where-upon all his men fled and Paul "cleared his camp without paying his men a cent for their labor." In the few records of Bunyan stories before he was famous, the con-stant refrain is of a man who "ruled with an iron hand," a man for whom "every man in his employ jumped."[40]

In 1914, a young clerk for the Red River Lumber Company named William Laug-head conceived of an advertising scheme for his company. He would sew together the odds and ends of stories he knew from his own time working in the camps and create a booklet, at first in a limited run, of lumberjack tales. These stories would humanize the giant lumber industry. The Paul of Laughead and other professional writers' imaginations was friendly, kind to his men, and involved in good-natured japes. He had the rough constitution of a thoroughly masculine American hero with the gentlemanly demeanor and generous big heart of a manly reformer.[41] And he was a nearly immediate success. He served as the industry's figurehead, a sign that the lumber industry, unlike oil or steel, was made up not of giant corporations but of small, romantic camps filled with strong, jovial, and fundamentally classless white men.

The Lumberman's Monument, conceived in the late 1920s by promoter W. B. Mershon as a memorial to the loggers of Michigan. Courtesy of Midland County Historical Society.

In the late 1920s, Michigan's lumbermen banded together to promote this image of jacks with an enormous project: the Lumberman's Monument in Oscoda Township, Michigan. The enormous statue—each of the three men it depicts are over nine feet tall—was meant to rehabilitate the image of lumbermen. In the words of the project's central promoter, William B. Mershon, "The old time Michigan Lumbermen are deserving of recognition . . . for they had pretty poor picking and were looked upon more as forest destroyers than they were public benefactors." Mershon was a timber baron, one of the wealthy men who made their fortunes in the woods. He had been central to a reforesting project that brought wealthy timbermen to the Au Sable River to plant Norway pine saplings in the cutover in order to address the aesthetic concerns of the cutover and promote new, scientific forestry.

Pleased with the success of this first commemorative foray, he set out on the far larger project of building a monument in the second-growth forest. The statue consisted of three men: At the center was a landlooker, whom Mershon intended to be the "'boss': he is the lumberman whom [they were] commemorating," flanked by his two employees. The lumberman was to be "of a higher type" than the others, while the riverman and lumberjack would be "of the type of a regular old time French Canadian—jovial and smiling." Mershon regularly insisted that what he was commemorating was "the old type" of lumberman, and it is telling that his enormous brass fantasy was funded by the leading lumber families of Michigan, along with the Kiwanis Club and the Northeast Michigan Tourist Association.[42]

Over time, portrayals like those of a friendly Paul and cheerful jack came to dominate the memory of the lumber camps. But this process was not a given: it was one thing to have corporate advertisers and lumber barons endorsing a public memory of the camps as homey, preindustrial sites of honest labor. Had this image only existed in coastal magazines and advertising campaigns, it may have faded away. Or perhaps it would have come to be seen as the happy housewife of 1950s advertisements: a fantasy on the part of advertisers so over-the-top as to cross over, by a couple decades later, into kitsch.

For the lumberjack to gain the lasting impact he has had, for the image of the hardworking, cheerful jack to survive as long as it has, something else had to happen. The lumberjack in the Northwoods had to come to be embraced every bit as much as the cowboy in the West. He had to be adopted by his homeland.

# NINE

# THE PASSING OF THE PINES

## BUYING AND SELLING LEGENDS

The Michigan State Conservation Commission has recently made
provisions to restore a number of abandoned lumber camps, in
order that tourists may have a real idea of how the lumberjacks
lived. . . . The camps will be located in at least 385 different sites
over the State.

—*Washington Post,* April 23, 1938

There is a wave of interest in Paul Bunyan of late. . . . The Paul
Bunyan and lumberjack festivals at Brainerd, Bemidji, Stillwater,
Bayfield, Washburn, and Manistee and the birling tournament at
Escanaba have much to do with this revival of interest. A number
of lumbering towns are erecting mammoth Paul Bunyan statues,
while museums of lumbering relics have been established at the
Wisconsin state Capitol in Madison, Rhinelander, and Eau Claire.

—*Escanaba Daily Press,* May 26, 1938

For "fakelore" to be folklore, for the line between memory and myth to be fully
obscured, the stories of lumberjacks and of Paul Bunyan himself had to move outside the realm of eastern magazines and lumber barons. They had to seep into the
broader culture and be claimed even by those who knew lumberjacks firsthand, regardless of the contempt they may have had for the jacks or the devastation caused
by the timber industry. Those whose houses were lost in the firestorms of the early

twentieth century, who wrote of jacks as vagrants or criminals, or who built entire districts to isolate jacks within the city had to reclaim them as beloved heroes. And they did: in September 2016 the *New York Times* ran a piece on Paul Bunyan in Minnesota, claiming that "it is no exaggeration to say that many Minnesotans still hold a certain gargantuan lumberjack in reverence."[1] And it is not only Paul. Statues litter the lake states honoring lumberjacks; towns and businesses celebrate them. Perhaps the greatest puzzle of all is how the very people who were most damaged by the industry—the settlers of the impoverished, fire-ridden cutover—came to have such astonishing reverence for the lumber industry and, above and beyond that, for the lumberjack himself.

By the 1920s, towns across Minnesota, Wisconsin, and Michigan had stopped remembering lumberjacks and begun memorializing them.[2] When Stillwater, Minnesota, introduced its first Lumberjack Days in 1934, there was no hint of the lumberjack as tramp, lout, or hobo. The violence, drinking, and prostitution of the era were wiped clean, and instead festivals "revived the spirit of the era when Stillwater was a roaring town."[3] These festivals spread across the region. Similar affairs, with parades of floats, lumber kings, and "Indian princesses" were established across the lake states. Some, like Tall Timber Days in Grand Rapids, Minnesota, continue to the present day. They were undoubtedly community affairs, put on with great pride. In *The Passing of the Pines*, a dramatic pageant performed as part of the Muskegon centenary festival, the entire history of Michigan was traced through the single story of pine. Over nine hundred local citizens participated in the pageant, casting themselves as actors in a history that centered on the great deeds of lumberjacks.[4]

The key reversal at work for those who lived on the land destroyed by seventy years was a careful reconstruction of the lumberjack not as a destroyer of the forests but as a creation of them. Lumberjacks were reimagined, and reremembered as premodern and preindustrial. Logging trains, tractors, tree farms, and all the equipment of lumbering in the 1920s and 1930s were removed from a nostalgic vision, and what was left was the lumberjack as naturalist. His presence in the woods was portrayed as "natural" and, in multiple ways, paralleled with a fictionalized version of the Anishinaabe. So as the region turned increasingly to tourism as a source of revenue the memory of the lumberjack was solidified not as an industrial worker, nor even as a worker at all, but instead as a part of the landscape.

The environment made the move from lumber centers to resort cities an obvious step. Lumber mills had to be on rivers, near or in the woods, in the pine-heavy landscape that was (and is) dotted with picturesque lakes. The industry's needs, then,

Tom's Logging Camp between Duluth and Two Harbors on Minnesota's north shore of Lake Superior, circa 1958. Photograph by L. Perry Gallagher Jr. Courtesy of the St. Louis County Historical Society, Archives and Special Collections, University of Minnesota Duluth.

demanded proximity to landscapes that also offered fishing, boating, and camping. And so, in the ravaged landscape left by logging, tourism was a uniquely appealing prospect for new income—so long as the ravages could be hidden.

Residents took up this new industry with enthusiasm. Unlike the far West, where federal agencies created much of the tourist infrastructure, much of the impetus for Northwoods tourism came from state, county, and city sources.[5] Local residents exerted control over the image of the Northwoods. Unemployed laborers, put out of work by the end of extractive industries, found jobs as guides and hosts. Eventually Anishinaabe fishers and hunters, denied treaty rights to hunt and fish until the 1990s, turned their hands to guiding as well. For locals, the second growth of forests that gradually formed over the scarred land provided, in the words of historian Aaron Shapiro, "a new cash crop." This transformation was underway as early as the 1920s. As a result of their efforts, their landscape—once seen as a bank of natural resources—came to be "experienced as a place of leisure instead of labor, a retreat from urban life rather than an economic storehouse of timber, iron, and copper."[6]

Yet the woods and rivers that made alluring vacation spots were exactly the landscapes the logging industry had decimated. The trees that tourists might want to spend long afternoons under had been chopped down. Fires had ripped through the landscape. Especially in the Upper Peninsula of Michigan and on the Iron Range of Minnesota, the devastation of logging had been compounded with massive mining damage. Canoes glided over the sunk logs that litter the bottom of the Northwoods rivers.

Nonetheless, as early as the 1920s, tourism pamphlets were already beginning to rebrand the Northwoods as "virgin" wilderness, untouched by industry. These pamphlets practiced a kind of erasure: a 1921 pamphlet put out by the *Minneapolis Journal* told readers they could "follow the trail to lonelier spots, there to enjoy Nature in virgin woods and lakes."[7] It bears repeating here that by this point there was only *one* virgin stand of white pine in the entire state. And it was just under forty acres.

Were it merely a cynical attempt by Minneapolis-based agents at branding the barely sprouted second growth as virgin woods, it may well have failed. But by the 1930s it became increasingly clear that the people of the Northwoods, the settlers of the towns that had once done all they could to physically segregate jacks from the respectable main streets, had fully embraced the romantic notion of the jack. Citizens associations, tourist boards, resort owners, and booster clubs had to find a way to square the opposing images of pristine landscapes and heavy industry. Reimagining the lumberjack as a preindustrial naturalist far removed from extractive industrial capitalism allowed them to do just this.

In 1918, the newly formed Ten Thousand Lakes of Minnesota Association invited visitors to "The Nation's Summer Playground" where motorists could visit "primeval forests" and "breathe deeply of the fragrant tonic breezes of Minnesota's piney wood." Courtesy of the Borchert Map Library, University of Minnesota.

Two festivals in particular, one in Muskegon, Michigan, and another in Stillwater, Minnesota, illustrate how the residents of former lumber towns came to embrace the lumberjack, and which image in particular they chose to promote. Stillwater was among the first towns to embrace lumberjacks not as degenerates, or laborers, but as heroes. Starting in 1934, the town gambled heavily on the nostalgia that the "old time" lumberjack would inspire, merely thirty years after the real-life ones stopped walking the mill town's streets.[8] That spring, John J. Sullivan, former lumberjack, now warden of the local jail and head of the fair committee, promised spectators at St. Paul Saints' games and listeners of radio stations in Minneapolis and Madison that they would, if they cared to come to Stillwater, see an authentic replica of old days. Modern shops would be "made over into gay ninety stores and saloons," and the citizens themselves would participate by transforming themselves into "red shirted, heavy booted, tobacco chewing lumberjacks, and laughing, very much dressed and bustled ladies."

Sullivan encouraged visitors to get into the spirit of things, explaining that "white collars and up-to-the-minute styles will be a strange sight . . . so if you aren't able to get the clothes such as worn by jacks . . . wear any of your old clothes." With the help of the public, Warden Sullivan hoped they would once again make Stillwater "the rendezvous and home of lumberjacks, those colorful and industrious fellows were the backbone of this territory." He went on to give the now familiar description of a "typical" jack, the kind of jack they were there to celebrate: "They were a familiar and gay sight with their bright-colored shirts, shag-pants, and heavy boots, and in spite of their rough and ready attitude toward life, they were real gentlemen and a good-natured, kind-hearted lot."[9]

Among a grab bag of other, at best tenuously related civic events ("a talking picture depicting operations and facilities of the Federal Barge Lines," the showing of their local show horse the Shiek of Hedjaz, bicycle parades, businessmen's a capella choirs, and an unsettling array of clowns), the festival focused on celebrating a very specific, nostalgic image of Stillwater's lumberjack days. Everything possible was billed as "old-time"—old-time camp, old-time hoedown, old-time orchestra, and old-time caller. Entertainment focused on log rolling, bateau racing, and other "river sports." Music was provided by the Lumberjack Glee Club, and there were shanty-song sing-a-longs.

Over the years, Lumberjack Days developed a more self-conscious narrative. By the third program, the festival began with the ceremonial "arrival at Stillwater of lumberjacks and immigrants on steamboat." These distinguished guests were then met by the city's mayor in a horse-drawn carriage. By their fourth year, the Stillwater committee was building a full lumber camp in the center of town, where they encouraged old-timers to register as authentic jacks and then "flop in a good old fashioned straw bunk" and wile away the afternoon where "everything has been done to make you feel right at home." With this, tourists could make the collapsing of time between past and present easier still: come to Stillwater, and you could meet the disappearing genus of the Authentic American Lumberjack.

As the festival grew in popularity this narrative became more elaborate but kept its basic shape. The steamboat came to include "an old time train, Indians, lumberjacks and immigrants," and by the fourth year it was the governor, not the mayor, who met its arrival. By its sixth year, in 1939, organizers boasted that it was "nationally advertised . . . good clean entertainment." Town boosters used the festival as an excuse to create new tourist attractions, dedicating monuments to the Sioux, the Chippewa, the first pioneers, and the lumberjacks—all in the first six summers.[10]

But none of this was just the idea of the tourist bureau. It was not only a few businessmen who participated, but the entire community. In a letter circulated to cities throughout the Midwest in 1939, the chairman of the festival committee advertised that "the color to this celebration is that all, in the entire community, don our lumberjack, pioneer, or gay nineties clothes." The organizers gave prizes annually to

*Left to right:* Minneapolis mayor Thomas E. Latimer, Stillwater mayor Fred Merrill, state senator Karl Neumeier, and Minnesota governor Floyd B. Olson greet festivalgoers at Lumberjack Days in Stillwater, 1935. Courtesy of Hennepin County Library.

those dressed in "typical" clothes. The very word "typical" assumes that everyone present, the participants and the judges, knows what a lumberjack ought to look like. For those who did not have the correct attire, the committee recommended they "come to Stillwater wearing a flannel shirt."[11]

Photographs of the early years of the festival attest to the community interest in typical, that is to say stereotypical, attire and a complete lack of interest in authenticity. Groups of men and women stand in front of stores or gather around men participating in flapjack-eating contests. The men are well-scrubbed and clean, in work pants and flannel shirts with suspenders and flat caps. Except for the exquisite condition of their clothes and tidy appearance, they look much like photographs of jacks in the summer from the 1880s. The women standing next to them, however, form a comic contrast. Done up with huge bustles and no corsets, with fancy feathered bonnets, strings of pearls, and carefully set ringlets of hair, they look like extras from a production of *Hello, Dolly!* Equal attention (and prizes) went to the Gilded Age belles as to the rough-and-tumble workmen. They were not interested in actually representing the past. Instead, in the spirit of good fun, both men and women dressed themselves as cartoonish versions of the past, and as idealized forms of manhood and womanhood that had been left behind. The lumberjack and the bustled elegant lady were both symbols of a faded, nostalgic past.[12]

Local boosters were following what were already becoming well-worn paths in the tourist industry. The postbellum South had already long-embraced nostalgia as a way to sell their region and draw in tourists. Charleston remade itself as a dream of antebellum, *Gone with the Wind*–style glory in the early twentieth century. The far West, too, was working to sell Americans on dude ranches and cowboy camps where they could reenact past pleasures. In doing so, and in promoting tourism with catchy slogans and arresting visuals, they helped remake American memory, creating a clean, sanitized past that could be easily, and pleasurably, visited.[13]

A few years later, the nostalgic reremembering of the lumber past and the commercial image of the lumberjack came together at the centennial celebration of Muskegon, Michigan. The Muskegon festival, in scope and in hype, made earlier fairs look like amateur county fairs. Newspapers across the region published a relentless stream of stories and advertisements in the lead-up: "Largest Cow to Be Exhibited at Muskegon Fete!" "Percy Grainger Leads Famous Band at Muskegon," "Girards Will Birl in 2 Weeks at Festival."[14] They even sent a car turned into a covered wagon on a tour of southern Michigan, with a fiddler and dulcimer player performing live in the back.[15] The covered wagon, which had little to do with Michigan's own history, was a nice touch. It tied the Lumberjack Festival to the pioneers as just another part of the American frontier spirit.

The combination of forces breathing life into the lumberjack legend were laid bare at the fair: the Lumberjack Festival was backed by 130 local civic organizations, as well as city, county, state, and even federal governments. And well they might all jump on board: the city reported expecting over half a million visitors.[16] Moreover, they made the most of the visiting press to show off their city. Editors from the *Eau Claire Leader-Telegram* wrote that after a special train bearing newspaper editors was met by a caravan of automobiles, they were taken on "a motor tour of $3,000,000 of harbor developments," as well as beaches and parks, the art gallery ("one of the finest small art galleries in America"), golf courses, yacht clubs, and tennis courts. The whole thing was meant to show the visiting editors how "in the cavalcade of a century . . . the Michigan community has grown to be a famed resort center and a thriving metropolis of diversified industry and culture." After their visit to the fair, a special Pullman car whisked editors away "farther north in

Five ex-lumberjacks dressed in festive checkered overalls at Lumberjack Days in Stillwater, Minnesota, 1935. Courtesy of the Minnesota Historical Society.

Michigan's famous resort country." It all sounds rather glamorous and expensive, but the publicity was certainly worth it.[17]

The boosters of the Muskegon Citizens Centennial Association made clear that the role of Muskegon as a lumber city and its current status as a resort town were one and the same. The official program noted that the festival celebrated a number of anniversaries—150 years since the organization of the Northwest Territory, 100 years since Michigan's statehood, and several others—before finishing with the most important point, that 1937 was the "50th anniversary of the days when Muskegon was 'Lumber Queen of the World.'" While the organization of the territory and other major landmarks earned their own line of text, celebrated as separate achievements, Muskegon's status as "Lumber Queen" was combined effortlessly, in a single sentence, with Muskegon's status today as "a famed resort center." For the organizers it was out of the city's reputation as the "Lumber Queen" that its current resort status grew.

The grounds of the festival were divided into three areas. Visitors entered by foot through stockade gates and were greeted by a large open area centered on an enormous, multistory statue of Paul Bunyan. To his back stretched the heart of the festival. A series of exposition buildings dedicated to agriculture, communications, electricity, and both Michigan and Muskegon history lined a broad path ending at a large auditorium, the "Centennial Nightclub," and a grill. Running at an angle back from Paul's left hip, the midway was filled with rides and concessions, a rebuilt No-ah's ark, a monkey circus (which, after some research, appears to be exactly what it sounds like), and a stage that hosted various acts including clog dancers, fiddling contests, and addresses by the governor, mayor, and other dignitaries.

But across the railroad tracks, separated from both the rides and attractions of the midway and the educational exhibitions of the exhibition path, there was another large, less-organized section. This enormous field represented the untamed past. It had no roads running through it and hosted fewer exhibits. On one end were a trout stream and a small waterfall run by the state's Conservation Department. Scattered across the field there were pony rides and bears and a fire tower, but there were only three major exhibits listed: an Indian Village, a Wild West Show, and the Saw Mill and Lumber Camp. This was the world of the natural and the mythical. Indians, cowboys, and lumberjacks were placed by trout streams, waterfalls, and bears—all museums to America's natural past. If cowboys represented, as Murdoch argued, the past as a place where "it was the way it should be," then lumberjacks did, too.[18] By placing lumberjacks side by side with cowboys, these writers, as well as the organizers of the centenary, were making sure they would be viewed in the same light as cowboys: heroic and iconic figures of a recent, yet nonetheless mythic, past.

As much a part of "nature" as the Indian village, as much a part of folklore as cowboys, lumberjacks were set apart both as the living past and as representatives of powerful national myth. By the 1920s, as Philip Deloria argues in *Playing Indian*, Indians had come to represent "authenticity" to a variety of Americans. They were understood by mainstream culture as "reflections of a primitive stage of cultural existence outside modernity."[19] Ethnographic films, popular in early cinema, had by this point introduced Americans to what scholar Bill Nichols calls "Typofications": reenactments removed from time and context that did not refer to any specific people or action, but rather stood in for a generalized understanding of Native Americans as a single, homogeneous other who were trapped in a primitive stage of development. In travel and ethnographic films, these fictionalized representations came to be synonymous with the American West.[20] This understanding then presents the three exhibits side by side—the Wild West, the Indian Village, and the Lumberjack Camp—as three different depictions of an antimodern heroic past.[21]

A statue of Paul Bunyan made from recycled car parts looms over spectators at the Muskegon Centennial and Lumberjack Festival in July 1937. Next to him a man posed in fictionalized Indian garb poses as another memento of the region's mythologized past. Photograph from the collection of the Lakeshore Museum Center.

Of course, the Lumber Camp and Saw Mill were not the only place lumberjacks featured in the Centennial and Lumberjack Festival. There was also, for two straight weeks, a five-times-daily lumberjack show featuring champion logrollers and pole-shimmers. There was the huge, or as the organizers advertised it, "mammoth" *Passing of the Pines* historical pageant, and there was the statue of Paul himself. The enormous statue of Paul, the heart of the festival, signaled to visitors the importance of the lumberjack in all his forms to the region. He greeted visitors, and four nights of the festival ended with live music and dancing around his feet. The other three linked together the past and present of jacks.[22]

Lumberjack shows and lumberjack games served as a living reminder of the old ways of doing things in camps. By the 1930s those who competed in lumberjack games were no longer demonstrating skills needed to butcher wood—instead they were reliving the nostalgic past. Originally, lumberjack games had grown out of the activities in camp. Logrolling appeared in the late nineteenth-century Midwest, followed by tree-climbing and topping contests in the Pacific Northwest. Birling, the sport that in modern parlance is known as logrolling, had been around long

Logrolling during the Muskegon Centennial and Lumberjack Festival, July 17, 1937. Photograph from the collection of the Lakeshore Museum Center.

enough that by 1901 an Oregon jack could claim that he had, at a Labor Day contest in Wisconsin, seen "the best log birling . . . in fifty years of following the timber." The games spread quickly, and by the 1930s and 1940s were a cornerstone of county and civic gatherings.[23]

But almost all the skills involved were rendered obsolete by the chainsaw and the logging train. Men no longer drove logs down rivers, and so no longer needed to balance them. Since the mid-twentieth century, logging has rarely used the spar poles that required men to shimmy fifty or more feet into the air. A few modern skills, like chainsaw carving, made their way into shows but have always remained a side affair to the main spectacle of men shimmying up fifty-foot poles, throwing axes, sawing for speed, and rolling logs.[24] This was the performance of skill as proof of an authentic connection with the woods, and with the values they represented. As with dressing as cowboys and spending time on a dude ranch or participating in rodeos, the mimesis of reenacting lumberjack rituals allowed Americans a way to relive their frontier past, to keep the virtues of rugged individualism alive. It is no coincidence that the first enactment of what would become the Calgary Stampede was in 1896, and the very first Cheyenne Frontier Days were sponsored not by cowboys, but by the local paper and the Union Pacific Railroad in 1897—right as *Scribner's* and *The Atlantic* were publishing gushing articles about the rugged lumberjack.[25]

*The Passing of the Pines* served to tie together the past and present of the region under a single, heroic tale of forestry. While the title of the pageant seems tragic, it was misleading. The story wove together 150 years of white settlement from the early frontier settlers to the present, through the age of lumbering, as a romantic saga. Instead of ending with a landscape ravaged by industry, the pageant ended on the renewed life of the town as a "modern port city and metropolis of diversified economy." In the words of historian Daniel J. Rypma it "linked the romantic labor of the lumberjack with the industrial labor of the 1930s worker," glorifying both in the process.[26] When combined with the nostalgic Lumber Camp near the Indian Village, the pageant helped freeze lumberjacks in memory as romantic (in the mildly misleading words of festival promoters, "glamorous") vestiges of the past. The city had moved on to industrial labor but used lumberjacks as a way of promoting its forest setting and increasing its appeal as a resort city. The lumberjacks had not destroyed nature; they *were* nature. And their continued presence, even in mythic form, allowed Muskegon's citizens to demonstrate that as much the city had modernized, some things would never change.

Americans enthusiastically embraced the cultural memory crafted by these festivals.[27] By 1933, papers as far from the Northwoods as North Carolina were carrying pictures of champions of lumberjack games and proclaiming the Edenville, Michigan, Lumberjack Festival "the greatest of its kind," with "over 20,000 visitors."[28] Towns across the Northwoods took up the practice of memorializing the woods and their workers through the 1920s and 1930s. While enthusiasm for this kind of public festival waned over time, several continue today. Stillwater only had its final Lumberjack Days in 2015, and Grand Rapids still celebrates Tall Timber Days every August. Lumberjack games and sports have stayed a popular cornerstone of these festivals—but so has the memory of loggers, frozen in time, as a living, romantic past.

Moreover, festivals were only one branch of a growing industry of nostalgia production. As the Northwoods recovered from the economic devastation left behind by the lumber industry, all three states turned increasingly toward tourism as a generator of revenue. To those who have grown up in and around the Upper Midwest, nothing is quite as deeply tied to summer as a cabin on a lake. Camps for young boys and girls popped up across the region (two of the oldest, Camp

Logging museums like this one sponsored by the American Legion in Rhinelander, Wisconsin, sprang up throughout the Northwoods in the 1930s. Photograph by J. O. Grove, U.S. Forest Service Records, National Archives.

Mishawaka and Camp Kamaji for Girls, still run today), and small, family-oriented resorts opened on hundreds of lakes, boasting fishing and adventure in an untouched northern wilderness.

It is not an inevitable outcome that a beautiful place will generate tourism—it is an active decision on the part of those who promote destinations and tourist sites.[29] In the 1920s and 1930s, boosters for sites across the United States began to promote themselves to the burgeoning tourist population by linking themselves to national narratives.[30] Sites along the Oregon Trail grew in popularity, as did dude ranches. The newly founded tourism organizations of the Northwoods traded on natural beauty, but also on collective memory—a nostalgic longing for a simple past and an unsullied landscape. The growing use of the lumberjack as a symbol for tourists encapsulated this project.

Nature tourism had existed in the United States almost as long as the country had, but from the eighteenth century into the middle of the nineteenth, it was a pastime only of a small elite. Starting in the years after the Civil War, however, it took on a new importance to middle-class Americans. The push toward nature sprang from an interest in what contemporaries called muscular Christianity, namely the idea that if the body is the house of the spirit, it needs to be a robust home. Preachers encouraged their flocks to engage in struggle with the wilderness, in the kinds of heroic actions of true pioneers. But for most of their flock, pioneering was out of the question; the wilderness around Boston and New York hardly needed to be tamed. However, on a vacation, there was opportunity for simplicity, for struggle, even for heroism, if the holiday were sufficiently rustic.[31] While seeking amusement at a billiards hall might be morally questionable, recreation was, according to an 1851 description, "something which recruits, restores, and prepares the man for better service." Nature tourism was no amusement; it was honorable and worthwhile recreation. By the end of the nineteenth century, middle-class Americans had come to see a vacation as not a privilege but a necessity for their spiritual and physical health.[32]

Throughout the nineteenth century, this health tourism had focused mostly on East Coast resorts. Beginning with fashionable watering holes and beach resorts in the late eighteenth century, nature tourism barely spread west of the Adirondacks until the last quarter of the century. For those who went west, it was the astounding scenery of the far West that appealed most. Group camps appeared in the Grand Canyon, and in the 1880s wealthy tourists increasingly found their way to Yellowstone.[33]

Michigan, Minnesota, and Wisconsin soon came to see the potential of tourism as a source of revenue, especially as the attempt to sell the cutover to farmers began to falter around the First World War. As early as the 1880s, Mackinaw Island became a fashionable destination for wealthy industrialists from Chicago, Minneapolis, Detroit, and Cleveland. With its grand hotel, strict dress codes, and elegant manners, Mackinaw imitated the elite spa towns of the East Coast. But Mackinaw would prove an outlier.

The real future of Northwoods tourism would lie not in elite visitors to rarefied hotels, but in the mass expansion of tourism to the middle- and working-class citizens of midwestern cities. From the very beginning, Northwoods organizations advertised themselves as a place where those who could only afford a week or a few days away might find peace, fresh water, and pine-scented air.[34]

But there are contradictions inherent in the combination of tourism and conservation. Early advocates of tourism argued that tourists did not run down the resources of the states, and it's clear the state governments agreed: tourism and recreation management were placed within conservation departments in all three states. But tourism also meant massive infrastructure: it meant the Forest Service building access to cabins, it meant hotels, and it required highways. It meant an influx of consumers who saw the land as a packaged object for their pleasure, and limiting or outlawing older uses of the land by regulating farming, hunting, and

Tourist bureaus used the legend of Hiawatha frequently in the 1920s and 1930s to evoke a fictitious paradise of unspoiled nature in the Northwoods. Courtesy of Bentley Historical Library, University of Michigan.

fishing rights, forcing Anishinaabe and Menominee hunters and fishers to try to gain a foothold in the tourist market. Paradoxically, to create "nature," state and private actors had to carefully orchestrate the building in the real world of an imagined Northwoods.[35] But its artifice did not take away from its appeal. As Elizabeth Outka argues was the case with re-created quaint English villages that popped up in turn-of-the-century Britain, this mythical Northwoods was "better than the original, for these new hybrids were accessible, controllable and—in their ability to unite seemingly antithetical desires—tantalizingly modern."[36]

The Minnesota Scenic Highway Association advertised the land as both remote and accessible, setting up a dichotomy between modern and prehistoric that would continue to characterize Northwoods tourism for decades. Tourism would both provide a means of development for the area and necessitate the conservation of its natural resources and rural character. In fact, Northwoods organizers in the early twentieth century attempted to advertise it as not only a pure, natural landscape, but specifically a primitive one.[37] Across all three Northwoods states, for instance, localities evoked *The Song of Hiawatha* as a way of connecting their landscapes with a national narrative, and specifically with a narrative of "primitivism." This turn toward the imitation of Native Americans was part of the escapist fantasy of tourism:

as cities grew increasingly complex and confounding, Americans sought to find a simpler time away from these pressures.[38] Tourism in the Northwoods fused two contradictory impulses, allowing people to buy access to an escape from commercial life. By advertising productions of *The Song of Hiawatha* next to hotels, train schedules, and highway maps, Northwoods promoters insisted that the primitive past did not mean sacrificing modern conveniences. Here were the real, virgin Northwoods, a true escape to our natural history, and all within a convenient drive of your self-catering cabin.

A 1957 pamphlet advertising vacations in "Paul Bunyanland"—otherwise known as central Minnesota—touted the area as "truly wilderness with all the conveniences of modern times." This juxtaposition shows up time and again. Brochures mention the Mayo Clinic beside the Boundary Waters, or suggest, as Paul Bunyan, Vacationland! did, that visitors may wish to incorporate in a single drive the "headquarters of the Manganese mining of the state" and "numerous lakes and resorts . . . beauty beyond compare."[39] A 1959 pamphlet, meanwhile, noted with pride that among the "famous lakes and forests . . . industrial plants are common sight in small communities as well as the three largest cities."[40]

By investing in a tourist industry that advertised a scenic, untouched landscape, the states, businesses, and local boosters committed themselves to creating just such a landscape out of the stumps and dead and down logs of the cutover. But if what tourists were buying was an untouched landscape, a scenic getaway to nature, then what of the extractive industry that preceded it? How could virgin woods be reconciled with the lumbering past? The symbol of the cheerful, premodern lumberjack cemented the lumbering industry in the past, as a romantic prelude to modern vacationland.

In bringing the camps back to life, towns, roadside attractions, and festivals tried to cash in on an increasingly large market of heritage tourism. Disenchanted with all that seemed fake, shallow, and manufactured about modern urban life, Americans started turning to heritage tourism in the late nineteenth century. But what was originally the purview of the few elite who had the time and money to travel exploded in popularity as the nation's tourist infrastructure and access to cars grew in the first half of the twentieth century. Heritage tourists set out to discover what it was that made America great: "See America First" campaigns, National Parks advertising, and the mushrooming growth of tourism to the West and South all emphasized that it was only by traveling the nation that Americans could have authentic encounters with their own past, and learn what it was that made them unique.[41] In the midcentury, growing nationalism and focus on patriotism made seeking out the American past not merely pleasurable, but noble, too.

Tourists visited several logging sites in northeastern Minnesota by automobile on the state university's "Seeing Minnesota First" tour in 1914. The guides included the Cloquet and Two Harbors Commercial Clubs. Courtesy of the University Archives, University of Minnesota Library.

Yet, for all their veneer of authentic heritage, lumberjack festivals and roadside attractions were not really encounters with history. Instead, they were part of what Katrina M. Phillips calls "salvage tourism." Salvage tourism, like the salvaged pieces of a historic home, is made up not of things preserved in their original setting and intent, but instead bits and pieces of historic content, taken out of context and rearranged to create a narrative and new meaning. Phillips's study of Indian pageants—historical epics presenting something vaguely related to, but not in any real way representative of, Native American history—demonstrates how salvage tourism stuck Indigenous history permanently in the past, as part of the necessary prehistory that made American identity unique. Shows did not present Native Americans as modern people still living in the country, but instead as a piece of the past that had to be saved before it disappeared forever. Performed alongside Wild West shows, Indian pageants gave Americans a chance to discover their own ethnography and history—accuracy be damned.[42]

Americans consumed lumberjack sites in much the same way: as a story about what it meant to be American. And in fact, much like Indian pageants whose narratives were based on Indigenous history being a necessary stage of the past, one that had to make way for civilization, lumberjack sites managed to erase the violence of history and create a soothing, uplifting narrative. By celebrating the lumberjack as naturalist, boosters drew attention away not only from industrialization, but from colonialism. The Gilded Age ideal of the progress from savagery to civilization allowed Americans to understand the dispossession of Native Americans not as an act of aggression, but as an inevitable tragedy. Valorizing the men who "tamed" the West similarly decentralized dispossession. As Cynthia Culver Prescott argues of the proliferation of statues of triumphal pioneers, "emphasizing pioneers' success in dominating wild lands rather than wild peoples" meant frontiersmen could be conquerors without having to worry about the fate of the conquered.[43] The past here is not a full, nor a representational one, but it is a *useful* one. It is a past that reinforced the values of the festivalgoers and left their consciences untroubled.[44]

While tourist brochures from the early 1920s for "Vacation Land" emphasized only the Native American heritage of the region, across the 1930s lumberjacks began to creep in as part of the natural, and primitive, history of the Northwoods landscape. "The Heart of Lake Land," a pamphlet that dates from the late 1920s or early 1930s, opens with two photographs facing each other. One is of a birchbark canoe on a placid lake, and the other is of a dozen or so lumberjacks perched on top of an enormous pile of logs. The only other picture in the pamphlet is of an Ojibwe man, with the caption "A 'Blanket' Indian." All these images attempt to conjure a romantic image of a simple past and rely on a cultural memory that sees both the "blanket Indian" and the group of lumberjacks as part of the same narrative. Here the distinction of lumbering from the "natural" history of the state has already disappeared, and the Northwoods are advertised as a secret, pristine region, ready to be discovered. Tourists are told that "only a few brief years ago the entire northern Minnesota region was unknown except to the lumbermen and to the Ojibwas."[45] The two were two sides of the same coin, the two natural and noble inhabitants of the great "unknown" Northwoods.

A thick pamphlet advertising *Carefree Days in Itasca County, Minn: The County of a Thousand Lakes*, describes Itasca County as a place where "men were men (loggers incidentally) and the tales run as high, wide and handsome as any of the biggest logger himself." Stories of jacks and the Anishinaabe share the page, and both are tied to the natural landscape. The pamphlet describes various natural features like Pokegama Lake, Jack the Horse Lake, and Lake Otenagen, telling the story behind each name. In these stories Ojibwe maidens and tough lumberjacks are side by side

Bemidji's iconic statues of Paul Bunyan and Babe the Blue Ox were the stars of the 1937 Bemidji Winter Carnival. Courtesy of the Minnesota Historical Society.

as semimythical progenitors of modern Minnesota.[46] Some tourist brochures went so far as to include Native Americans, lumberjacks, *and* Vikings in the same images advertising a "land of legend, adventure and beauty."[47]

As tourism became a truly mass industry in the 1940s, lumberjacks proliferated throughout the promotional literature. The symbol of the lumberjack came to represent the odd dichotomy between modern industry and primitive nature that epitomized the appeal of the Northwoods vacation. From the beginning of the efforts toward mass tourism, pamphlets engaged in the same kind of erasure of the legacy of the extractive industry's past that festivals celebrated.

By the 1950s the nostalgic connection between lumberjacks and the wild was set, and tourism companies no longer cared to concern themselves with the labor these men had done. Pamphlets advertised "virgin stands of Norway and White pine," with enticing pictures of rugged lakes, while cartoonish maps served to visually define the meaning of the region. A 1959 edition of *Buick Magazine* advised motorists to take a seven-day road trip in Minnesota, marking their map with only three figures: a cartoon of a young Indian girl, Paul Bunyan, and Babe the Blue Ox. These figures together with graphic designs of lakes and trees represented all that Minnesota had to offer the enterprising motor-tourist.[48]

Throughout the 1940s and 1950s Paul Bunyan, in particular, became a symbol for tourism bureaus. Paul's status as a mythic hero reinforced the association of the lumber industry not with industry, but with forests. But more than this, Paul himself squared a circle: he allowed the simultaneous representation of industry and nature, with no acknowledgement that one might have come at the sacrifice of the other. Kitsch images of Paul and other generic lumberjacks fishing, logrolling, and camping adorned countless brochures put out by car and gas companies, local tourism boards, and business associations.

But one of the curious things about Paul was that while he was forever wielding an ax, he seemed to leave the actual forests untouched. There appeared to be no cognitive dissonance inherent in a cartoon of industry representing the untouched wild. In the 1930s several resorts, tourist organizations, and county tourist bureaus banded together to create Paul Bunyan's Playground Association. Together they put out pamphlets advertising the "north central section of Minnesota" as the home of "America's only legendary hero." The association touted a natural landscape as well as "famous historic pageants . . . with their casts of native Indians and woodsmen."[49]

The lumberjack came to serve a double purpose in the public image of the Northwoods as it was presented to tourists. The first was to tie the tourist sites themselves to a national, romantic narrative embodied by the primitive jack: the conquering of

Here's Your Story of

PAUL BUNYAN

Come

TO BEMIDJI IN THE LAND OF FRIENDLY LAKES

from

BEMIDJI MINNESOTA

Paul Bunyan's Headquarters

Where

PAUL BUNYAN SIZE FISH ARE APLENTY

Many Northwoods towns claim Paul Bunyan as their own, including Bemidji, Minnesota, whose local chamber of commerce capitalized on the enormity of the Bunyan legend in the 1950s with a series of historical pamphlets.

the West by hardworking men, the "winning" of land from Native Americans, and the expansion of the nation in the nineteenth century. But it also had a secondary purpose. In the lumberjack, Northwoods advertisers found a way to solve—or at least appear to solve—a seemingly intractable problem with nature tourism. How could a state develop economically and build the modern amenities tourists craved without endangering the conservation of the very nature they came to see?

The narrative presented by tourist sites, festivals, posters, and even road maps are only effective stories, however, if there's an audience willing to buy them. Americans were not, and continue not to be, interested in *all* their heritage. Just an hour east of the successful Forest History Center in Grand Rapids, and west of Tom's Historic Logging Camp and Trading Post in Duluth, is the cautionary tale of history no one was interested in buying: Ironworld. The tourist site outside Hibbing, Minnesota, was a desperate plea on the part of Iron Range boosters to turn their declining mining industry into tourist gold in the 1970s. Yet despite regular transfusions of state money and a series of expansions, Ironworld has never managed to make a financial success. While the taconite mining of the Mesabi Range could also claim to have built America, just as the timber industry did, their narrative held little of the hope, or curated natural beauty, of the Northwoods. Mining could not be disappeared into the past, and the land scarred by it (even when filled in, as the mine outside Ironworld is, with an enormous artificial lake) cannot market itself as a virgin wilderness and escape from the modern world.[50] That said, it has not stopped them from trying. Joseph Whitson's analysis of the narratives told at three industrial mining sites in northeastern Minnesota argues that all three combine to do the same thing lumber histories do: portray white settlement and extractive industry as natural, erasing Indigenous history and the violence of settler colonialism in the process.[51]

In consuming the historical sites of the Northwoods, whether at Historyland, a re-created logging camp, a festival, or one of dozens of statues and monuments that sprouted across the Northwoods, tourists shaped their understanding of history.[52] Going to see a place to learn about it is never quite as straightforward as it seems. While visiting a plantation museum, one does not actually step into the past. Instead, we are guided through a particular version of the past. Tourists are told what matters, and what does not. Certain features of the landscape or historic site are emphasized; others are downplayed or simply not marked on the maps. Roadside attractions like Historyland purported to give tourists an ability to have an authentic, local experience. Its reenactors and time-trapped buildings had an immediate emotional appeal that a book or dry museum never could, presenting what historian Alison Landberg describes as "the fantasy that one might actually have unmediated access to the past by looking at or touching 'authentic' objects."[53]

More curiously still, the version of the past presented at festivals was so convincing as to become its own, more authoritative, history. The re-creations of the logging camps, the display of "authentic" logging era materials, and even the statues of Bunyan created physical evidence of an imagined past that, in places, stayed long beyond the festival. These new creations became the watermarks by which the "authenticity" of new logging displays were judged. As the century wore on, the re-enactments that began as part of festivals became permanent, most prominently at Historyland, a historical theme park meant to replicate both an authentic logging camp and a "real" Indian village. Both were presented as unchanging and timeless, a past through which visitors could, with satisfaction, judge their progress. Like with Westerns and Buffalo Bill's Wild West, logging museums and history attractions like Wisconsin's Historyland were deemed accurate in proportion to how well they reflected the stereotype of lumberjacks.[54] Joseph Feinberg argues that authenticity is judged by the relationship between appearance and essence.[55] But if we only know—or think we know—what the essence of something is based on the sites of salvage tourism we have consumed, the myth becomes self-reinforcing.[56]

The symbol of the lumberjack allowed for a peaceful coexistence of industry and nature. He could simultaneously symbolize the violent conquering of the landscape by industry and its quaint, primitive past. The lumberjack as he was conceived of in the cultural memory of the twentieth century became something more than a woodcutter: he was a woodsman. Thus, stripped of his destructive power, tourism associations could use lumberjacks as a way of acknowledging an industrial past without disturbing the carefully crafted and packaged image of virgin wilderness. In iterations from the 1920s through to millennial hipsters in plaid shirts, the lumberjack as he was conceived of, celebrated, and used in the Northwoods has come to symbolize a balance between man and nature. He makes his living through the woods, he lives his life among the trees, but all the bite is gone from his ax.

In the space of less than a generation, the lumber industry had gone from the destroyers of the Northwoods to a part of their natural history. The woods, almost entirely second growth, were lauded as unknown and untouched: a pristine wilderness that grew on top of industrial-scale logging and bands of semiemployed hobos.[57] The romantic image of the lumberjack—heroically individualistic, deeply connected to nature, manly and frozen in a time before machines—became the public memory of an enormous, corporate effort that cut down all but a few of the two-hundred-foot pines that once grew as far as the eye could see.

In 1965, visitors to Historyland in Hayward, Wisconsin, could take part in an all-inclusive Northwoods experience, complete with a logging camp, Indian village, and river cruises aboard the *Namakagon Queen* paddleboat. Courtesy of the Wisconsin Historical Society.

Writing the history of her tiny community at the edge of the Northwoods in the late 1960s, Manita L. Kromer romanticized the "jackpine savages" who settled her town. She described her pamphlet as a tribute to the way simple people could live good lives, and how "beautiful the simple way of life can be in contrast to the frantic, frustrating pace of today." She wrote about kind, honest men who lived together "harmoniously and comparatively free of discord." Yet even Kromer, in the midst of her misty-eyed recollections of idealized community life, had to admit that the logging of the Northwoods had been both "an epic and a tragedy."[58]

This was the conflict at the heart of the Northwoods: that which had brought prosperity had left poverty; that which had made the region famous had left it ravaged. For those left to tell the story, the mythic lumberjack became at least a partial bandage. He made the destruction of the woods natural, muscular, and masculine. Rather than remembering the era of lumber barons as a time when enormous corporate entities stripped the region bare of resources, it was instead a time when honest, simple, romantic men emerged from the woods, building the great American cities with their axes.

The myth of the heroic jack did not survive because it was any truer than that of the degenerate jack. Both were layered on top of the lives of actual jacks to serve the interests of multiple groups. For those who stripped the land, the folksy memory of heroic jacks served to obscure a history of environmental degradation and labor strife; for metropolitan, middle-class Americans, he stood as a symbol of heroic white manhood in the face of ever-increasing challenges from immigrants, racial minorities, and women; and for those left behind, those who had to eke out a living from the land, he made a proud past that made sense of the epic, and the tragedy, that had swept through their lives, leaving in its wake generations of lumberjacks' children and acres of stumps and ashes.

# THE STORIES WE STILL BUY

"It is strange how attitudes change over the years," wrote Georgia Arndt in *Lumberjack's Daughter,* thinking back on her days growing up in the camps. "I realize now that many of the things I wrote about in these memoirs are things I wanted to forget, not only forget, in fact, I wanted to hide. What I wanted to hide, now I want to publish for all the world to read. Perhaps some will benefit from my experiences in ways I can't imagine."[1]

Arndt grew up in the Northwoods, a region shaped by the lumber industry that tore through on a rampage. By the time she was born in the twentieth century, most of the giant pines that had once dominated the landscape were gone. The industry ate up and spat out the land, leaving a territory scarred by fires and poverty, but building Chicago, Minneapolis, St. Louis, and Detroit in the process. When she was a young woman, the Civilian Conservation Corps had begun the long work of making a barren cutover back into a placid, picturesque wilderness. By the time my parents first came to the Northwoods in the 1950s, it already seemed untouched, and when I went to camp in the 1990s, less than a century after the height of the industry, we sang without irony about "waters so pure and fresh, untouched by human flesh."

The land itself is changing again, and quickly. New studies place Minnesota as one of the fastest-warming states in the country, and the nature of the second-growth forests is shifting as increasing numbers of warmer-weather deciduous species make their homes among the pines.[2]

The iconic statue of Paul Bunyan in Bemidji, Minnesota, 1939. Photograph by John Vachon. Courtesy of Library of Congress.

But, for now, the myth holds: in nearby Grand Rapids, we take houseguests to visit the Forest History Center, where interpreters in costume guide visitors through a 1900 camp, letting them blow the dinner horn and saw a log themselves. At my brother's wedding on Deer Lake, they hired a one-man-band who offered them a short list of possible costumes: Santa Claus, soldier, Finnish immigrant, lumberjack. At my own wedding, fifty miles away near Bemidji, guests who wandered downtown passed two statues: one of Paul and Babe, standing near the lake, and facing them, outside Morell's Chippewa Trading Post, an old Muffler Man statue made over into a buff, shirtless Native American, his arm raised toward Paul. The two are still twinned together, wrapped up in an imagined, nostalgic past. Both myths, the stereotypical Indian of the distant past and the friendly giant whose footsteps became the great lakes, are as fictional as one another.

The myth of the lumberjack rests on an inherent tension between conservation and industry that is barely contained—a tension that exploded into the foreground in the 1980s in Oregon where environmentalists pitted themselves defiantly against lumberjacks, vilifying loggers as the destroyers of nature. Local loggers responded in kind: frustrated with the lack of empathy for the jobs that would be lost through conservation, they tore down the idea of logger-as-naturalist, popularizing the once-ubiquitous Oregon bumper sticker, "Are you an environmentalist, or do you work for a living?"

Yet, despite this, the idea of lumberjacks as men of the woods, free from the feminizing constraints of civilization and at one with nature, has proved remarkably resilient. This study ends in the 1950s, but the myth has endured long beyond that, gathering new associations as it goes. Timbersports promotional materials feature hypermasculine men wielding chainsaws in tank tops and the tagline "the original extreme sport," fusing modern technology onto the hyperbolic masculinity of jacks. Urban ax-throwing bars walk the line between glorifying the lumberjack and reveling in the kitsch of plaid shirts and backwoods decor. In Brooklyn, artisan shops sell hipsters pine-scented beard oil. And while I cannot get my husband to use such a thing as beard oil, he did, from our old apartment in Boston, take up whittling. The Duluth Trading Company runs TV ads of a cartoon lumberjack getting his armpit licked by a moose to promote their brand that, in partnership with STIHL chainsaws, has a line of "dress like a lumberjack" clothes. A few years ago, a friend sent a YouTube profile of Smoke and Flame, an artisanal firewood maker. It wasn't until I noticed that it was uploaded by CBC's satirical *This Is That* show that I could be *sure* the leather-aproned, heavily bearded firewood maker was an actor. It can be hard to tell since it's *actually* possible to buy a three hundred dollar artisanal ax.[3]

In 1954, Wilfred Nevue started a campaign to save the lumberjack. Not the actual laborers: Nevue, a retired lumberjack, lived in the Upper Peninsula of Michigan, an area that had not seen major lumber operations for decades. But he was determined to save their memory. In Nevue's opinion, the good name of hardworking lumberjacks had been hijacked by a sensationalist press. "The rotten reputation that was smeared on the lumberjacks," he wrote in the Marquette *Mining Journal*, "seeped through the dirt of those who would show off and also capitalize on their salacious stories."[4]

His long, outraged article in the *Mining Journal* proposed to set the record straight. He wrote that his article, presumably in contrast to those he was so opposed to, included "information from research in records and also many questionnaires filled out by genuine old-timers who adhere to the truth and abhor distortions and glamorizing." It was a full-throated defense of lumberjacks as honest, quiet, hardworking men who never stepped on the wrong side of the law. "This writer never heard of a lumberjack being arrested in camp for misconduct there or out," he insisted; "he never saw one real drunk in town nor one who became unruly." He wrote that lewd songs were frowned upon in camps, that never was a lumberjack charged with felony. They never swore; toward alcohol, they were puritanical; toward women, they were perfect saints. "No men in any occupation," he insisted, "were more observing of the pure morals and sacredness of womanhood and of generally decent behavior." In Marquette County, he vowed, there was only ever one house of prostitution. It "maintained three madams, and it lasted about three years in the late nineties. . . . Those women starved out. This writer recalls distinctly that if a young man of Champion availed himself of the house he was ostracized in the community, and that attitude prevailed in other towns."[5]

Much of Nevue's screed cannot be proven either way. His memory of his experience in the camps cannot be checked. But where there are discernible facts, Nevue is universally wrong. There is no record as to whether or not prostitution thrived in Marquette. But in Schoolcraft County, just next door, a single town of a thousand housed three brothels—and based on photographs, no one in them seemed to be starving. In other places Nevue saves the reader fact-checking by contradicting himself. Logging was done by "men who lived in the communities," but huge numbers of lumberjacks "were drifters." He "never saw [a lumberjack] real drunk in town," but because they didn't drink in camp, they went on "binges" when they left. These inaccuracies are telling. Nevue was clearly out to prove something regardless of evidence: something he felt was very important.

Nor was Nevue alone. From Lansing, Lewis Beeson, the executive secretary of the Michigan Historical Commission, vociferously agreed: "There is no question,"

Benson wrote to Nevue, "but that the sordid and vicious part of the lumberjack life and the old lumberjack period has been magnified out of all proportion to the point where, to most people, the term 'lumberjack' is a synonym for all this evil." Bruce G. Bell, chief forester of the Northern Paper Mills, joined with Benson in his support. "I agree with you that the lumberjack has been exaggerated," Bell wrote. "Most of them were sober, working men."[6]

What had men like Bell, Benson, and Nevue so worked up were stories like "Gay Days in the Woods"—a local history piece that ran in the *Milwaukee Journal* in 1947. In it, an anonymous author, claiming to be a retired lumberjack, wrote a much more colorful account of life in the Northwoods. "The loggers," he explained, "had three enthusiasms—liquor, women and fighting. Enterprising residents of the near-by town saw to it that they were supplied with the first two items, and the 'jacks themselves took care of the third."[7] He went on to tell stories of famous loggers, like "T.C. Cunnion, the man-eater from Peterborough, Ontario" who would chew raw liver while shouting this title to the streets. T. C., according to "Gay Days" ended his life by fighting bulldogs with only his teeth. He also wrote of Muskegon's Sawdust Flats—the city's red-light district—and Old Lou, a madam said to have been a proficient blasphemer in eight languages.

"Gay Days in the Woods" certainly makes better reading than pursed-lipped defenses of the honor and integrity of lumberjacks, and it was only one of hundreds of similar articles that appeared in newspapers both in the Northwoods region and across the country from the 1870s onward. These articles told the tale of rough-and-tumble men—lumberjacks who were "all man and half wildcat." They were "hard-living, hard-drinking, hard-fighting, blasphemous pioneers," well known to visit the "carmined Delilahs" of the lumber boomtowns.[8]

But can either tale—lumberjacks as upright gentlemen or notorious scoundrels—be trusted?

The story of the lumberjacks and their memory challenges the myths on which a region, and in many ways the nation, hinges: that the men who conquered the West were simple heroes, unfettered by capitalism; that the people who inhabited that land have simply disappeared into the mists of time; that roughness and violence are simply the nature of men; and that tramps, itinerants, and other plagues of society are drains, rather than the fundamental basis, of our economy. One history cannot do that, but I still remember the first time I learned about Black cowboys. It struck me in that moment that all my memories, not the ones I formed myself but the ones we share, the ones I made watching TV and movies, reading novels, and visiting kitschy tourist attractions, might be wrong.

# ACKNOWLEDGMENTS

This book began as a ten-page summer essay, researched at the Forest History Center in Grand Rapids, Minnesota, in August 2007. That there is almost nothing in it that is recognizable from that first fascination with lumberjacks almost twenty years ago is thanks to the hard work, support, and help of a small army of friends, mentors, and colleagues. I cannot begin to thank them all, but I would like at the very least to give it a shot.

Teaching for the past decade has allowed me to finally see from the other side all the unending and difficult work that went into teaching me. Those teachers—particularly Jim Johnk, Nancy Fiedelman, Neil Tonken, John Elko, Ed Crow, and Brian Garman—made me passionate and curious, and helped me fall in love with writing. At Middlebury College and Oxford University I was fortunate to benefit from the wisdom and guidance of Paul Monod, Perry Gauci, Rob Saunders, and Susan Brigden. At the University of Virginia Peter Onuf shaped the kind of questions I have learned to ask and the rigor with which I've asked them. Joseph Kett, Max Edelson, Gary Gallagher, Brian Balogh, Sarah Milov, and Christian McMillen offered me the advice, critique, and direction that helped me learn what kind of history I want to do and modeled for me what kind of teacher I want to be. Molly Angevine, Jenni Via, Kathleen Miller, and Ella Wood put up with more than was reasonable from me and were always gracious and kind in doing so. Thank you to the Buckner W. Clay Endowment for the first summer of my research. I'm equally grateful to the pie restaurants of Durham.

My work at the University of Virginia and the original dissertation that served as the basis of this book are primarily attributable to the extraordinary intellectual and personal generosity of two remarkable women. Cori Field has been a better mentor than I could have hoped for. Whoever made the TA assignments in the fall of 2010 gave me one of the greatest strokes of luck I have ever had. For her encouragement of every ambition, her willingness to read drafts, her generous life advice, and for teaching me to teach, I am deeply grateful. But above all, my thanks go to my advisor, Elizabeth Varon, who once reminded me when I was upset about a round of critiques that the great thing about edits is that someone does all the work and, in the end, you are the one who looks better for it. Her endless patience and guidance, her thoughtful critiques, her encouragement, and her ideas made this project what it is and always made me look the better for it.

Research for this book took me to every corner of the Northwoods and all across the lake states. But during nearly a year of research, I stayed in hotels a grand total of nineteen nights. I can never hope to repay the generosity of old friends and perfect strangers who opened their doors. Hall Crowther and Lee Smith, Kat Steiner and Jeff Noreen, the Minnemans, Elizabeth Kohl, Frank and Elizabeth Hoadley, Myra Palmero and Jimmy Smith, Leslie and John Carothers, and Stevie Smith all welcomed me, despite my being a complete stranger to some. The Midwest has proved, time and again, to be nicer even than its reputation. Similarly, long chunks of this book were written in the guest rooms of others, and my particular gratitude must always go to Meg and Mark Parker-Young when in D.C. and Martin Tunstall and David Bellwood in London for continuing to make my deeply implausible style of living not just possible but impossibly joyful.

Most of the surprisingly long work of turning this from a dissertation to a book was completed during nearly eight years in Boston while working as a preceptor in expository writing at Harvard University. I would not have been able to do so, and to learn so much as a person and teacher, without the tireless enthusiasm and support of Thomas Jehn and Karen Heath, as well as the bottomless patience of Becky Skolnik. Nontenured labor in academia is the underrecognized spine of the modern university. While the continued exploitation of that labor threatens the entire system, it was a joy and a relief to find myself in a particularly well protected, encouraging pocket. I loved entering 1 Bow Street, and my colleagues and students made me an inarguably better writer and scholar.

Thank you to the staff and librarians of a number of wonderful institutions for helping me find what I needed and, more often than not, discover things I would never have thought of on my own. In North Carolina, thank you to the staff of the Forest History Society and Steve Anderson in particular for their warm welcome. In Wisconsin, the Wisconsin Historical Society staff and resources are unmatched, and thank you to the staff of the University of Wisconsin Eau Claire archives for leading me to colonization records. The Bentley Library in Ann Arbor; the Minnesota Historical Society in St. Paul; Michigan Technological University, Finlandia

University, Seney Historical Society, and Marquette Regional History Center in the Upper Peninsula; Forest History Center and Itasca County Historical Society in Grand Rapids, Minnesota; and the Beltrami County Historical Society in Bemidji were all invaluable.

At the University of Minnesota Press I must grovelingly, gushingly thank the passionate, brilliant Kristian Tvedten for finding my project and making it come to life. I have never felt so clearly that someone got what I was trying to do as I always have in my conversations with him, and his deep understanding of the stories embedded in images were the making of this book. The design team made an object so lovely that I whooped out loud when I saw the cover, and the publicity team convinced me some people might even read it. I also want to thank Deborah A. Oosterhouse for her painstaking, brilliant copyediting, and Rhys Davies for making what were essentially footnoted word-clouds into legible, beautiful maps, and Thomas Veccihio for creating a thorough index in record time.

Finally, I give my thanks to those who kept me on track, held my hand, listened to me jabber on, and read passages of this project for most of a decade. There are too many to name, but a few deserve special thanks. In Charlottesville, Evan McCormick, Jim Ambuske, John Terry, Sarah and Cody, Ryan Bibler, Chris Cornelius, and especially Tom Butcher made the best of colleagues and the dearest of friends whose advice and friendship kept me somehow, improbably, from dropping out of grad school. Dana Mueller, Sarah Fort, and Morgan Snell made living in that mountain town a joy. In London, I have had the sort of clever, gregarious, generous urban family people make sitcoms about, and I am deeply grateful to them all: Rose, for tolerating my Trouble; Alfie, for always inspiring me to be curious about the past; Claire, with apologies for the kettle incident; and Sophie, Tom, Gordon, Jenny, Clara, Austen, Lissy, Martin, and David for making every trip to London a trip home. In Boston, Margaret Willison, Laura Koenig, Kip Richardson, Miranda Popkey, and Henry and Christy Lichtblau kept me sane and (very) occasionally even kept me on track. Without Topper Teal and Anne Nou I would have been unrooted and helplessly lonely: they made Boston home, and I benefited from the advantage of countless dinners with a writer much better than I. Here and there and everywhere, Nick Rego, Ruth Steinhardt, Kiana Scott, Ashely Clark, Meg Young, Charlotte Graham, Kate Gage, Sophie Purgavie, Kaki Albriton, Kate Thorman, and Amadea Britton commented on drafts and listened to endless woes. Elliot B. Quick believed in me always in life, and his memory serves as a constant reminder of the importance of loving your friends as family while you can and of taking beauty and joy seriously.

My deepest gratitude goes to my family. My grandmother always believed in me more than I believe in myself. I miss her every day, and if I can be half as smart, adventurous, and ambitious as she thought I was I will have done well. Thank you for loving your wild girl. My many uncles and loving aunts have been a source of constant support and inspiration. Nicholas Brown kept me in check, read thoughtfully, and gave me all the benefit of his tremendous talent. Teal Brown Zimring encouraged me endlessly and has always loved me fiercely; her belief that I'm brilliant balanced my belief that I'm an imposter. Šara Stranovsky and Mark Zimring have made remarkable in-laws and did more than their fair share of telling me I was smart enough, good enough, and, God dammit, people like me. I have been lucky to find in-laws as loving and enthusiastic as Chuck and Ellen Feuer, Jared and Heather Feuer, and Hannah and Mike Levenberg, all of whom immediately supported me. Ilsa, Ronan, Jude, Ayla, Jax, Zoë, Huckleberry, and Odysseus make the future bright.

Above all, two people created me, raised me, supported me, believed in me, encouraged me, fed me, clothed me, housed me, traveled with me, taught me to think, and loved me no matter what, even when I was furious with them. They are the smartest, kindest, fiercest, often funniest, and certainly most loving people in my life. Without them I would, doubtlessly, have long ago given up. Alison Teal and Sam Brown are the best parents, and the best role models, I could dream of.

Finally, thanks to my Ethan, the greatest gift of the pandemic and a better partner and friend than I knew was possible. Through moves and career shifts, travel and IVF, you have made me stronger, happier, and a little more in love with life each and every day. I was in your living room for only the second time (with Ernest honking out his kennel cough) when I first learned this book would be published. We were engaged by the time I finalized the manuscript. I am so thrilled that when I finally hold a copy, it will be in our home.

Oh! And Ernest: you're a good boy.

# NOTES

## INTRODUCTION

1 The Northwoods are the forests that covered the northern expanses of three lake states: Michigan, Wisconsin, and Minnesota. The most exact definition of the Northwoods is as USDA Forest Service Ecoregion 212, or the Laurentian Mixed Forest Province. USDA Forest Service, "Ecoregions of the United States," https://www.fs.usda.gov/land/pubs /ecoregions/ecoregions.html, "212 Laurentian Mixed Forest Province," https://www .fs.usda.gov/land/ecosysmgmt/colorimagemap/images/212.html.

2 There are dozens of terms that refer to men who cut down trees for a living. In the late nineteenth century, the most common were "shanty boys" and "loggers," though "lumberjack" was gaining popularity. "Lumbermen," on the other hand, referred almost exclusively to the class of men who owned and operated camps. To avoid confusion, I use "lumberjack" or "jack" throughout to refer to the workers, and "lumbermen" or "lumber barons" to refer to owners.

3 Scott Magelssen, "Remapping American-ness: Heritage Production and the Staging of the Native American and the African American as Other in 'Historyland,'" *National Identities* 4, no. 2 (2002): 161–78.

4 "Logging History" and "Logging Camp," Tom's Logging Camp, https://www.tomslogging camp.com, accessed June 23, 2020.

5 Thomas R. Cox, *The Lumberman's Frontier* (Corvallis: Oregon State University Press, 2010), 149. Cox's is by far the most thorough of the modern histories of the lumber industry, but there are also excellent regional studies. Each of the three lake states has its

own standard-bearer, but the best is certainly Agnes M. Larson's *The White Pine Industry in Minnesota* (Minneapolis: University of Minnesota Press, 1949), which fared well enough to be reprinted in 2007. For Michigan, see Barbara Benson, *Logs and Lumber: The Development of the Lumber Industry in Michigan's Lower Peninsula, 1837–1870* (Mount Pleasant: Clarke Historical Library, Central Michigan University, 1989); and for Wisconsin, see R. F. Fries, *Empire in Pine, the Story of Lumbering in Wisconsin, 1830–1900* (Ellison Bay, Wisc.: William Caxton, 1989). For a significantly more succinct overview of the process, see "The Wealth of Nature: Lumber," in William Cronon, *Nature's Metropolis: Chicago and the Great West* (New York: W. W. Norton, 1992).

6  For more, see "The Wealth of Nature: Lumber," in Cronon, *Nature's Metropolis*.

7  Peg Meier, ed., *Bring Warm Clothes: Letters and Photos from Minnesota's Past* (Minneapolis: Minneapolis Tribune, 1981) 7.

8  Richard Louis Griffin, "Forests and Logging in the Vicinity of Hibbing, Minn." (unpublished manuscript, 1930), Richard Louis Griffin Papers, P1169-2, Minnesota Historical Society, St. Paul, Minnesota.

9  Manita L. Kromer, "Thorpe, 1968" (unpublished manuscript, n.d.), P655, Minnesota Historical Society, St. Paul, Minnesota.

10  The loggers of the Northwoods, though diverse in national origins, were perhaps the whitest of any of the major lumbering workforces in the nineteenth or twentieth centuries. While there were Native Americans working in the camps, there was little other racial diversity. This helped cement the lumberjack myth in the Northwoods, as opposed to the South where a huge portion of the workforce was African American, or the West where up to 80 percent of the loggers were Chinese. For more on the demographics of lumberjacks in other American regions, see Sue Fawn Chung, *Chinese in the Woods: Logging and Lumbering in the American West* (Urbana: University of Illinois Press, 2015); and William P. Jones, *The Tribe of Black Ulysses: African American Lumber Workers in the Jim Crow South* (Urbana: University of Illinois Press, 2005).

11  William Bartlert, "The Lumbering Story" (unpublished manuscript, n.d.), William W. Bartlett Papers, Wisconsin Historical Society, Eau Claire Area Research Center, Eau Claire, Wisconsin.

12  Frederick W. Kohlmeyer, "Northern Pine Lumbermen: A Study in Origins and Migrations," *Journal of Economic History* 16, no. 4 (December 1956): 529–35.

13  Kohlmeyer, "Northern Pine Lumbermen." For more, see Robert F. Fries, "The Mississippi River Logging Company and the Struggle for Free Navigation of Logs, 1865–1900," *Mississippi Valley Historical Review* 35, no. 3 (December 1948): 429–48; and Cox, *The Lumberman's Frontier*, 171–86.

14  Jesse H. Ames, "Reminiscences, 1955," 12, Wisconsin Historical Society, Madison, Wisconsin.

15 In an unfortunate, if not unusual, irony the lowest paid workers also faced some of the greatest dangers. Because sleds could carry weights well over a ton, riding ahead of them carried significant risk. Were a runner to catch on something in the ruts—something the road monkey had not yet got to—they were directly in the path of the sled's load of logs.

16 For more on the relationship between cultural memory and power, see particularly Michel-Rolph Trouillot, *Silencing the Past: Power and the Production of History* (Boston: Beacon, 1995); Margaret MacMillan, *The Uses and Abuses of History* (Toronto: Viking, 2008); Sarah Farmer, *Martyred Village: Commemorating the 1944 Massacre at Oradour-sur-Glane* (Berkeley: University of California Press, 1999); Danielle Drozdzewski, Sarah De Nardi, and Emma Waterton, "The Significance of Memory in the Present," in *Memory, Place, and Identity: Commemoration and Remembrance of War and Conflict*, ed. Sarah De Nardi and Emma Waterton (London: Routledge, 2016), 1–16; Alan Rice, "Creating Memorials, Building Identities: The Politics of Memory in the Black Atlantic," in *The Public History Reader*, ed. Hilda Kean and Paul Martin (London: Routledge, 2013), 323–41; Laurent Dubois, "Haunting Delgrès" in *Contested Histories in Public Space: Memory, Race, and Nation*, ed. Daniel Walkowitz and Lisa Maya Knauer (Durham, N.C.: Duke University Press, 2009), 311–28; Viet Thanh Nguyen, *Nothing Ever Dies: Vietnam and the Memory of War* (Cambridge, Mass.: Harvard University Press, 2017); Guy Beiner, *Forgetful Remembrance: Social Forgetting and Vernacular Historiography of a Rebellion in Ulster* (Oxford: Oxford University Press, 2018).

17 For more on the ways in which cinema and other modern technologies create a more intimate, emotional bond between modern spectators and the past than that of earlier generations, see Alison Landsberg, *Prosthetic Memory: The Transformation of American Remembrance in the Age of Mass Culture* (New York: Columbia University Press, 2005) and *Engaging the Past: Mass Culture and the Production of Historical Knowledge* (New York: Columbia University Press, 2015); Marita Sturken, *Tourists of History: Memory, Kitsch, and Consumerism from Oklahoma City to Ground Zero* (Durham, N.C.: Duke University Press, 2007); Karen L. Cox, *Dreaming of Dixie: How the South Was Created in American Popular Culture* (Chapel Hill: University of North Carolina Press, 2013); Gary Cross, *Consumed Nostalgia: Memory in the Age of Fast Capitalism* (New York: Columbia University Press, 2015).

18 Nguyen, *Nothing Ever Dies*, 15.

19 Cross, *Consumed Nostalgia*, 8.

20 Scott Magelssen, "Introduction," in Patricia Ybarra et al., *Enacting History* (Birmingham: University of Alabama Press, 2011), 8.

21 For more on the idea of multidirectional and contradictory memory, see the brilliant introduction of Michael Rothberg's *Multidirectional Memory: Remembering the Holocaust in the Age of Decolonization* (Palo Alto: Stanford University Press, 2009).

22  For more, see Jacqueline M. Moore, "'Them's Fighting Words': Violence, Masculinity, and the Texas Cowboy in the Late Nineteenth Century," *Journal of the Gilded Age and Progressive Era* 13, no. 1 (January 2014): 28–55; David Hamilton Murdoch, *The American West: The Invention of a Myth* (Reno: University of Nevada Press, 2001).

23  In examining lumberjacks as workers, this book joins a growing history of capitalism. While surveys of this developing field are mushrooming too quickly to count, these are some excellent overviews of the promises and critiques of the new history of capitalism: Quinn Slobodian, "New Histories of Capitalism: A Comment," *Australian Historical Studies* 50, no. 4 (2019): 522–26; Maxine Berg, "Commodity Frontiers: Concepts and History," *Journal of Global History* 16, no. 3 (November 2021): 451–55; Fred Burrill, "Redeveloping Underdevelopment: An Agenda for New Histories of Capitalism in the Maritimes," *Acadiensis: Journal of the History of the Atlantic Region* 48, no. 2 (Autumn 2019): 179–89; Nan Enstad, "The 'Sonorous Summons' of the New History of Capitalism, Or, What Are We Talking about When We Talk about Economy," *Modern American History* 2, no. 1 (March 2019): 83–95; Bryan D. Palmer, "'Mind Forg'd Manacles' and Recent Pathways to 'New' Labor Histories," *International Review of Social History* 62 (2017): 279–303; Younsoo Bae, "Rethinking the Concept of Capitalism: A Historian's Perspective," *Social History* 45, no. 1 (2020): 1–25; Hannah Forsyth and Sophie Loy-Wilson, "Introduction: Political Implications of the New History of Capitalism," *Labour History: A Journal of Labour and Social History*, no. 121 (November 2021): 1–7; Julie McIntyre "Nature, Labour, and Agriculture: Towards Common Ground in New Histories of Capitalism," *Labour History*, no. 121 (November 2021): 73–98; and Michael A. Peters and David Neilson, "New Histories of Capitalism: From Delineation to Critique," *Educational Philosophy and Theory* 51, no. 13 (2019): 1399–1407.

   In joining this field, I am cautious for a few reasons. Partially it is the sudden ubiquity in the culture at large of critiques of capitalism that have, by making the word "capitalism" mean nearly anything, also led it to meaning almost nothing. But I am also cautious lest the quick rise of the field, and dismissive swagger of some of its practitioners, makes the use of capitalism as a framework appear to be being trendy for the trend's sake. In fact, one of the field's irritants (to those who are irritated) is the new history of capitalism's constant claim of novelty. Historians have long been engaged in the work of chronicling capitalism as a force. As far back as 1981 economic historian David Montgomery said that what he was trying to "get at" was the "history of capitalism." "Once Upon a Shop Floor: An Interview with David Montgomery," *Radical History Review* 23 (1980), 47. For more on the swagger of those who claim novelty I cannot recommend enough Nan Enstad's truly delightful takedown in "The 'Sonorous Summons' of the New History of Capitalism."

While capitalism is an enormous subject, I specifically speak of capitalism using Youngsoo Bae's definition: capitalism is a set of power structures in which political and economic power are separated from one another, and in which traditional restraints are removed from individuals seeking to attain money. But I would add to his definition this: capitalism's system of power (or as Bae also calls it, a "civilization") gives such primacy to economic power that it seeks to organize both people and resources—the land itself—in order to maximize profit. Bae, "Rethinking the Concept of Capitalism." Here I am also, to some extent begrudgingly, indebted to Marx's formulation of capital exploiting people and soil. I begrudge it only because the handwringing over whether or not any particular analysis is or is not Marxist takes up space that might well be used more productively.

24  Palmer, "'Mind Forg'd Manacles,'" 289. The call for local histories is most explicitly made by Maxine Berg in "Commodity Frontiers," 451–55.

25  Part of the problem is capitalism is everywhere, and so hard to study without reinforcing the idea that it is the only possible system. It is, in some ways, the same problem as writing an entire book (like this one) studying white men. My hope is to, by examining them, make us consider white men and capitalism as merely categories of analysis—the way we might have histories of Indigenous economies or of Black women. For too long, we have thought of those as "other" histories and white men as the normal. In thinking about the "normal" as a category like any other, I hope to, in part, answer the call of Hannah Forsyth and Sophie Loy-Wilson who asked, "How might historians centre capitalism in our histories, without also naturalising it? How do we think about alternatives to capitalist economies through history and as the global economy changes?" Forsyth and Loy-Wilson, "Introduction," 2.

26  Palmer, "'Mind Forg'd Manacles,'" 301.

27  For a fabulous, detailed analysis of the cruiser's work, see Craig William Kinnear, "Cruising for Pinelands: Knowledge Work in the Wisconsin Lumber Industry, 1870–1900," *Environmental History* 21, no. 1 (January 2016): 76–99.

28  Here the cutover bears striking resemblance to the dust bowls of the United States and Australia in the 1930s—I'm indebted for this analysis to Julie McIntyre's "Nature, Labour, and Agriculture."

29  For a more complete comparative overview of the lumbering practices in the United States, see Cox, *The Lumberman's Frontier*, 149.

30  Michael Edmonds, *Out of the Northwoods: The Many Lives of Paul Bunyan* (Madison: Wisconsin Historical Society Press, 2009).

31  For more on the trouble with defining the Midwest, see Hervé Varenne, *Americans Together: Structured Diversity in a Midwestern Town* (New York: Teacher's College Press,

1977); James R. Shortridge, *The Middle West: Its Meaning in American Culture* (Lawrence: University of Kansas Press, 1989); Andrew R. L. Cayton and Susan E. Gray, "The Story of the Midwest: An Introduction," in *The American Midwest: Essays on Regional History*, ed. Andrew R. L. Cayton and Susan E. Gray (Bloomington: Indiana University Press, 2001), 1–26; Jon K. Lauck, *The Lost Region: Toward a Revival of Midwestern History* (Iowa City: University of Iowa Press, 2013); Mark Vinz, "Our Midwests," *Studies in Midwestern History* 1, no. 3 (April 2015): 25–29; Mark Vinz, "Writing with a Chip on Your Shoulder: Some Notes on Regionalism," *Studies in Midwestern History* 2, no. 3 (February 2016): 33–37.

32  Hayes quoted in Cayton and Gray, "The Story of the Midwest," 10. For more on Beecher and evangelicals in the West, see Willa Hammitt Brown, "If the Great Battle Is to be Fought in the Valley of the Mississippi: Lyman Beecher, Theodore Weld and the Fate of the West, 1830–1834" (master's thesis, University of Virginia, 2010).

33  Jon Gjerde's *The Minds of the West: Patterns of Ethnocultural Evolution in the Rural Middle West, 1830–1917* (Chapel Hill: University of North Carolina Press, 1997) argues that it was the very vastness of space on the Midwestern plains that caused foreign-born immigrants to cluster together by ethnicity.

34  In examining the culture of lumberjacks through their geography and labor, I am deeply indebted to generations of environmental historians who have been at the forefront of uncovering the connections between laborers and the vast spaces they traverse and shape. See especially Donald Worster, *The Dust Bowl* (Oxford: Oxford University Press, 1979); Richard White, *The Organic Machine* (New York: Hill and Wang, 1995); Thomas Andrews, *Killing for Coal* (Cambridge, Mass.: Harvard University Press, 2010); Erik Loomis, *Empire of Timber*: Labor Unions and the Pacific Northwest Forests (Cambridge: Cambridge University Press, 2017); and especially Cronon, *Nature's Metropolis*.

35  "The Sexual Enslavement of Woman," *Fair Play* (Valley Falls, Kansas), November 23, 1888. For more on the infinitely fascinating and tragically understudied pirate king and his Strangite followers, see Karl W. Detzler, *Pirate of the Pine Lands* (Indianapolis: Bobbs-Merrill, 1929); Mark Strang, *The Diary of James J. Strang: Deciphered, Transcribed, Introduced and Annotated* (East Lansing: Michigan State University Press, 1961).

36  Euclid J. Bourgeois, "Reminiscences" (manuscript, n.d.), SC 2215, Wisconsin Historical Society, Madison, Wisconsin.

37  Arthur Hill, "Life in a Logging Camp," *Scribner's Magazine*, June 1893, 700; Interview of Alton Van Camp and John Boyd by Dennis East and Joe Smith, Wisconsin Historical Society, John Boyd Papers, Tape 370A, Wisconsin Historical Society, Madison, Wisconsin.

38  Bourgeois, "Reminiscences."

39  Minnesota Bureau of Labor Statistics, *Second Biennial Report, 1899–1900*, Great Western Printing Co., 1901.

40  John Sirotiak interviewed by John Esse, September 10, 1975, Grand Rapids, Minnesota.

41  Abraham Johnson Papers, P1538, Minnesota Historical Society, St. Paul, Minnesota.

42  John Emmett Nelligan, *The Life of a Lumberman* (n.p., 1929), 19. While few oral histories and memoirs mention working in sawmills, the labor fit perfectly with the seasonal round of the jacks. The Minnesota Bureau of Labor Statistics assumed, in compiling its 1899–1900 data on lumberjacks, that they worked in sawmills all summer, since "neither the mill work nor logging work alone represents the full years work." Minnesota Bureau of Labor Statistics, *Second Biennial Report, 1899–1900.*

43  Nelligan, *The Life of a Lumberman*, 27. *The Life of a Lumberman* was later reprinted as *White Pine Empire: Life of a Lumberman* (St. Cloud, Minn.: White Star Press, 1969). While the 1969 version is far more easily available, several portions were excluded. All quotes in this book are from the 1929 original.

44  Henry Belting, "Reminiscences" (manuscript, n.d.), 15, SC 213, Wisconsin Historical Society, Madison, Wisconsin.

45  For more on invented traditions, folk culture, and nationalism, see Eric Hobsbawm and Terence Ranger, eds, *The Invention of Tradition* (Cambridge: Cambridge University Press, 1983); MacMillan, *The Uses and Abuses of History*; Alan Gordon, *Time Travel: Tourism and the Rise of the Living History Museum in Mid-Twentieth-Century Canada* (Vancouver: UBC Press, 2016). For the specific importance of invented tradition within the emerging American state, see Michael D. Hattem, *Past and Prologue: Politics and Memory in the American Revolution* (New Haven, Conn.: Yale University Press, 2020).

46  Christine Ravela, "On the Weird Nostalgia of Whiteness: Poor Whites, White Death, and Black Suffering," *American Studies* 59, no. 1 (2020): 30–37.

47  While 1890 was by no means the end of the frontier period, by nearly any definition, the census report had a curiously strong cultural influence, perhaps best seen in Frederick Jackson Turner's flat declaration that it was a "brief official statement," which marked the "closing of a great historic movement." The reality hardly mattered—in the imagination of easterners, the moment for the heroic settlement of the West had passed. Frederick Jackson Turner, "The Significance of the Frontier in American History," address to the American Historical Association, in *The Frontier in American History* (New York: Henry Holt, 1920), 1.

A NOTE ON SOURCES

1  Interview of Alton Van Camp and John Boyd by Dennis East and Joe Smith.

2  Both of these memoirs went through heavy rounds of editing. Nelligan's book in particular is in many ways a better source for the way myth was introduced than for the actual lives of lumberjacks. The main editor convinced Nelligan that although Nelligan

had never heard of Paul Bunyan, they should include Bunyan stories in the memoir. Nelligan, *The Life of a Lumberman*, 5; Stewart H. Holbrook, *Holy Old Mackinaw* (New York: Macmillan, 1938).

## PART I. IN THE WOODS

1 Sophronius Stocking Landt, "Autobiography" (unpublished manuscript, 1925), Minnesota Historical Society, St. Paul, Minnesota.

## ONE. BULL COOKS AND WALKING BOSSES

1 E. N. Saunders, "Reminiscences," Proal and Saunders Family Papers, Minnesota Historical Society, St. Paul, Minnesota.

2 Bart Foss to mother, October 14, 1918, Bart Foss Papers, Minnesota Historical Society, St. Paul, Minnesota.

3 For more on the fires, see Robert W. Wells, *Peshtigo Fire* (New York: Prentice Hall, 1968); Francis M. Carroll and Franklin R. Raiter, *The Fires of Autumn: The Cloquet-Moose Lake Disaster of 1918* (St. Paul: Minnesota Historical Society Press, 1990); Daniel Brown, *Under a Flaming Sky: The Great Hinckley Firestorm of 1894* (New York: Lyons Press, 2016); William Lutz and Denise Gess, *Firestorm at Peshtigo: A Town, Its People, and the Deadliest Fire in American History* (New York: Henry Holt, 2002); and Stephen Pyne, *Fire in America: A Cultural History of Wildland and Rural Fire* (Seattle: University of Washington Press, 1997), 199–219. The absence of these fires from both academic literature and popular memory is curious, even if cultural amnesia about Peshtigo can be easily explained by the much greater attention paid to the simultaneous fire in Chicago.

4 Donald Worster's *Dust Bowl* (1979), in addition to being one of first true environmental histories, was the first to link the Dust Bowl to the exact same causes as the market crash of 1929, arguing that it was not a separate environmental disaster that compounded the depression, but part and parcel of the same financial crisis.

5 William Wilkinson, *Memorials of the Minnesota Forest Fires in the Year 1894* (Minneapolis: Norman E. Wilkinson, 1895), 36.

6 William H. Ellis, *Pick-Ups and a Horse: From the Region 'Round about the AuSable River* (n.p.: Mary Jane Hennigar, 1975), 7.

7 Nelligan, *The Life of a Lumberman*, 29.

8 "Among the Loggers," *Harper's Weekly*, June 29, 1889.

9 Cox, *The Lumberman's Frontier*, 201.

10 *St. Paul Pioneer Press*, October 17, 1901.

11 Bruno Vinette, "Early Lumbering on the Chippewa" (unpublished manuscript, n.d.), William W. Bartlett Papers, Wisconsin Historical Society, Eau Claire Area Research Center, Eau Claire, Wisconsin; "Cooke's Diary, Written in 1868 Tells of Logging War,"

*Eau Claire (Wisc.) Leader*, April 10, 1918. For more on Beef Slough, see Fries, "Mississippi River Logging Company and the Struggle for Free Navigation of Logs"; Cox, *The Lumberman's Frontier*, 171–86; Larson, *The White Pine Industry in Minnesota*; "Strategy of a Lumber King," *The Timberman*, April 20, 1889, 7.

12  Benson, *Logs and Lumber*, 81–82.

13  For more on Anishinaabe and Menominee lumbering, see chapter 3.

14  "Those Days of Yore," *Princeton (Minn.) Union*, February 18, 1897.

15  In fact, decolonial theorists argue that the very idea of "wilderness" is inherently both capitalist and colonialist. The idea is, essentially, that the mere idea of there *being* a wilderness is premised on the idea that humans exist separate from nature: there is land we control, and land we are yet to control and capitalize. North American Indigenous ideas of land do not engage in this separation. Cynthia Morinville and Nicole Van Lier, "On Nature, Degradation, and Life Making in Late Capitalism," *Capitalism Nature Socialism* 32, no. 4 (2021): 43–61. For more on the implications of capitalist ideas of nature, see chapter 5 of this book.

16  For more on land theft, see Cox, *The Lumberman's Frontier* and Melissa L. Meyer, *The White Earth Tragedy: Ethnicity and Dispossession at a Minnesota Anishinaabe Reservation, 1889–1920* (Lincoln: University of Nebraska Press, 1994).

17  Laura Eleanor McLeod, "Hungry Spirits: Anishinaabe Resistance and Revitalization" (PhD diss., University of Minnesota, 2014).

18  The preceding information comes from a series of articles in the *Minneapolis Journal*: "Mercer is Aroused" (March 19, 1901); "Call on the Governor" (April 3, 1901); "Light on Indian Timber Cutting" (April 23, 1901); "Indians Will Arm" (May 8, 1901); "Settling for Timber Poaching" (June 5, 1901); "Log Rescale to Continue" (June 8, 1901); "Reds Get Their Money" (October 28, 1901); "On Mercer's Trial" (October 28, 1903); "Stripped of Green Timber" (May 7, 1904).

19  "Mercer's Dilemma" *The Tomahawk* (White Earth, Minnesota), May 12, 1904; and "Carlisle's New Principal," *The Tomahawk* (White Earth, Minnesota), August 18, 1904.

20  David Beck, *The Struggle for Self-Determination: History of the Menominee Indians since 1854* (Lincoln: University of Nebraska Press, 2005), 46–62; and Ronald L. Trosper, "Indigenous Influence on Forest Management on the Menominee Indian Reservation," *Forest Ecology and Management* 249 (September 2007): 134–39.

21  "The Wrongs of the Menominee Indians," *The Tomahawk* (White Earth, Minnesota), February 22, 1917.

22  "A Proposition," *The Tomahawk* (White Earth, Minnesota), December 4, 1903.

23  Benson, *Logs and Lumber*, 18, xiii–xiv.

24  Bourgeois, "Reminiscences."

25  Hill, "Life in a Logging Camp," 711.

26  The idea of merit as a measure of success over luck or birth has a long history in the United States, where Joseph Kett argues it was "among the founding principles" of the republic. In the late nineteenth century, however, merit was caught up in the craze for scientific standards and made into a testable quantity with intelligence tests. In the Gilded Age, then, merit became a physical reality that could be used, as inherited wealth could, to advance in the world, with the end result that "the more merit one acquired before exiting school the farther one would advance in life." Joseph Kett, *Merit: The History of a Founding Ideal from the American Revolution to the Twenty-First Century* (Ithaca, N.Y.: Cornell University Press, 2013), 263, 182. For more on the cultural power of the self-made man in Gilded Age America, see Thomas Winter, *Making Men, Making Class: The YMCA and Workingmen, 1877–1920* (Chicago: University of Chicago Press, 2002); Jeffrey Louis Decker, *Made in America* (Minneapolis: University of Minnesota Press, 1997); James Catano, *Ragged Dicks: Masculinity, Steel, and the Rhetoric of the Self-Made Man* (Carbondale: Southern Illinois University Press, 2001); and Richard Weiss, *The American Myth of Success: From Horatio Alger to Norman Vincent Peale* (New York: Basic Books, 1969).

27  Adam Tomczik, "'He-Men Could Talk to He-Men in He-Men Language': Lumberjack Work Culture in Maine and Minnesota, 1840–1940," *Historian* 69, no. 4 (Winter 2007), 700.

28  For more on western expansion and the increased demand for timber resources, see Cronon, *Nature's Metropolis*; Cox, *The Lumberman's Frontier*; and Kevin Connor Brown, "'The Great Nomad': Work, Environment, and Space in the Lumber Industry of Minnesota and Louisiana from the 1870s to the 1930s" (PhD diss., Carnegie Mellon University, 2010).

29  Cox, *The Lumberman's Frontier*, 175–90.

30  John Esse interview with Carl Bruno, Cloquet, Minnesota, September 30, 1975, Forest History Oral History Project, OH 142.1, Minnesota Historical Society, St. Paul, Minnesota. Esse also remembered a story in which, when Shaw visited a camp, he saw a jack who was riding a log with a pike pole fall into the river. Shaw apparently ordered, without humor, that the men should "never mind that fellow, save that pike pole." For more on the geographical development of separate neighborhoods in the booming towns of the lumber frontier, see Jeremy W. Kilar, *Michigan's Lumbertowns: Lumbermen and Laborers in Saginaw, Bay City and Muskegon, 1870–1905* (Detroit: Wayne State University Press, 1990); and Elizabeth Faue, *Community of Suffering and Struggle: Women, Men and the Labor Movement in Minneapolis 1915–1945* (Chapel Hill: University of North Carolina Press, 1991). For more on the wealthy origins of late nineteenth-century lumbermen, see Ruth Birgitta Bordin, "A Michigan Lumbering Family," *Business History Review* 34, no. 1 (Spring 1960): 65–76.

31  "Milwaukee Is Deitz Crazy," *Eau Claire (Wisc.) Leader*, October 11, 1911. Myra Dietz, the daughter who was shot, recovered well and, off the back of the fame and public

sympathy the case brought her, went on to "accept one of the number of offers made to appear on the vaudeville stage." "News" *Eau Claire (Wisc.) Leader*, October 21, 1911.

32 Bradley J. Gills, "Navigating the Landscape of Assimilation: The Anishinaabeg, the Lumber Industry, and the Failure of Federal Indian Policy in Michigan," *Michigan Historical Review* 34, no. 2 (Fall 2008): 57–74.

33 John Esse interview with Carl Bruno, Minnesota Historical Society, St. Paul, Minnesota.

34 Jason Lee Newton, "Forging Titans: The Rise of Industrial Capitalism in the Northern Forest, 1850–1950" (PhD diss., Syracuse University, 2017), 794.

35 C. E. Blakeman, *Report of a Truant* (Grand Rapids, Mich.: self-pub., 1928), 11.

36 Blakeman, *Report of a Truant*, 23.

37 Nelligan, *The Life of a Lumberman*, 55.

38 Horace Glenn to family, n.d., Andrew Glenn and Family Papers, Minnesota Historical Society, St. Paul, Minnesota.

39 Horace Glenn to Andrew Glenn, January 6, 1901, Andrew Glenn and Family Papers, Minnesota History Society, St. Paul, Minnesota.

40 Florence Tripp and Garnet Tripp, *Life in a Lumber Camp: Articles from Alpena News, 1914* (Alpena, Mich.: Montgomery County Tribune, 1990), 13.

41 Tripp and Tripp, *Life in a Lumber Camp*, 12.

42 Horace Glenn to Andrew Glen, February 24, 1901, Andrew Glenn and Family Papers, Minnesota Historical Society, St. Paul, Minnesota.

43 Martin Kuarala, "Memoirs" (unpublished manuscript, Winter 1990), 3, Michigan Technological University Archives, Houghton, Michigan.

44 Rollin Lynde Hartt, "Notes on a Michigan Lumber Town," *Atlantic Monthly*, January 1900, 100–110.

45 This source merits a little by way of explanation. The *Alpena News* correspondent gives readers some reason to doubt his word about the camps: Firstly, he is anonymous, so there is no way to be certain he was, in fact, a lumberjack. More importantly, the columns appeared in 1914, twenty years after the period he is describing, as the mythic lumberjack was just beginning to be implanted into the national consciousness. Additionally, his writing is peppered with a disdain for the ignorance and habits of his fellow lumberjacks, as well as an ostentatious vocabulary that hints at a more educated, if not necessarily middle-class, viewpoint.

Yet, there are also good reasons to trust that he was a jack in the Wisconsin camps, as he claims. To begin with, he echoes the common tropes of most lumberjack-correspondents who wrote local color and local history pieces for Northwoods newspapers in the early twentieth century. Like his compatriots, for instance, he rails against the frail, modern middle classes and claims that "the man who never had a taste of lumber camp life, as lumber camps were conducted in this region of Thunder Bay in the early history of Alpena, has something to learn about 'hard work,' and will never know how much he has missed." This language so directly echoes that of other jacks quoted in this book as to indicate that he clearly held a shared set of ideals and vernacular. It is also clear from his letters that he must have, in fact, worked for at least one if not several winters in the Alpena camps. He displays an intimate knowledge of the working of the industry, methods of lumbering, and life within the camps.

46  Jon Lewis to Charles E. Brown, March 30, 1941, Box 5, Folder 1, Charles E. Brown Papers, Wisconsin Historical Society, Madison, Wisconsin.

47  Tripp and Tripp, *Life in a Lumber Camp*, 8–10.

48  Notably, only these two observers—one avowedly middle-class, the other possibly the same—attribute this separation to habits or refinement. All other descriptions of camps account for the separate living quarters as being necessitated by the later working hours of foremen and scalers who often stayed up into the night keeping accounts.

49  For more, see Winter, *Making Men, Making Class*.

50  W. H. Laird, as quoted in Larson, *The White Pine Industry in Minnesota,* 217; "The Evangelist of the Lumber Woods," *Northern Tribune* (Cheboygan, Michigan), February 24, 1883.

51  In order to imagine just *how* unpleasant, see Eric Loomis's evocative description of the nearly identical logging camps in the early Pacific Northwest in *Empire of Timber*, 18–24.

52  Harrison George, "Hitting the Trail in the Lumber Camps," *International Socialist Review* 17, no. 8 (February 1917): 455–57. For more evocative descriptions of the conditions in camp, see Nelligan, *White Pine Empire* and Holbrook, *Holy Old Mackinaw*.

53  C. C. Kelly, "An Observer in the Woods" (unpublished manuscript, 1934), Itasca County Historical Society, Grand Rapids, Minnesota.

54  Tripp and Tripp, *Life in a Lumber Camp*, 7.

55  Tripp and Tripp, *Life in a Lumber Camp*, 8.

56  Benson, *Logs and Lumber*, 78–79.

57  Hill, "Life in a Logging Camp," 700; Interview of Alton Van Camp and John Boyd by Dennis East and Joe Smith. Cooking was also the only possible role for women in camps. In early camps especially, the foreman's wife might act as cook, or his daughters as cookees. Nelligan, *The Life of a Lumberman*; Tripp and Tripp, *Life in a Lumber Camp*; Margaret Turner Wise, "Reminiscences" (unpublished manuscript, n.d.), Margaret Turner Wise Papers, Bentley Historical Library, Ann Arbor, Michigan; R. A. Brotherton, "Early Logging Days" (unpublished manuscript, n.d.), Marquette County Historical Society, Marquette, Michigan.

58  Horace Glenn to parents, March 10, 1901, Andrew Glenn Papers, Minnesota Historical Society, St. Paul, Minnesota.

59  While it is true that rural midwesterners settled in ethnically homogeneous enclaves, cultural isolation is nonetheless overemphasized in the historiography. Much of midwestern historiography has tended to separate the urban from the rural. Jon Gjerde's

wonderful *The Minds of the West* sets the template for midwestern rural cultural patterns: in vast spaces, ethnic groups clumped together and avoided interaction. But in separating urban from rural, these studies fail to take note of itinerant workers. This book joins a growing body of work, most notably Frank Higbie's *Indispensable Outcasts* (Urbana: University of Illinois Press, 2003), that addresses this gap.

## TWO. "HIS FLESH HUNG IN TATTERS AND STRINGS"

1  *Motley Register* (Little Falls, Minnesota), December 10, 1880.

2  While the Minnesota Bureau of Labor reports are extremely incomplete—with much of the types of data that were included in one report left out of the next year's—it is possible to glean an approximate idea of the scale of workplace injury and death in the woods. In 1887, for instance, the bureau reported 332 deaths out of between 10,000 and 15,000 workers. In 1900, while the exact number of deaths was not reported, the statistics show a higher rate of injury than any profession except railroad workers—and this after years of safety improvements in camps. Minnesota Bureau of Labor, *Biennial Report*, 1887 and 1900, Minnesota Historical Society, St. Paul, Minnesota. For more on the vast scale of industrial death, and what one British newspaper noted was America's "unenviable reputation of being the most backward of civilized nations" on the issue of worker safety in the late nineteenth century, see Michael K. Rosenow, *Death and Dying in the Working Class, 1865–1920* (Champaign: University of Illinois Press, 2015), 8.

3  WPA notes, Grand Rapids File, Minnesota Historical Society, St. Paul, Minnesota. For more on the selling of hospital tickets, see Nelligan, *The Life of a Lumberman*; John W. Fitzmaurice, *The Shanty Boy OR Life in a Lumber Camp: Being Pictures of the Pine Woods* (Ann Arbor: Historical Society of Michigan, Berrien Springs, Mich.: Hardscrabble Books, 1979); Hill, "Life in a Logging Camp."

Actual tickets reveal a fascinating insight into the likely injuries a jack might sustain. J. J. Synnott, a traveling salesman, sold tickets to Dr. Ravn's Hospital in Merrill, Wisconsin, which admitted men for "wounds, injuries or sickness hereafter received or contracted and which shall disable him from the performance of manual labor," but precluded "insanity, chronic and contagious diseases." All of that seems normal enough for a workman's ticket, but there are two curious clauses. While women were banned from camps and the ticket was nominally for injuries sustained by working, they did allow for the treatment of venereal disease. Oddest of all, in a nod to the filth of camps, if men found no other way to use the tickets they could exchange them at the hospital for "free Baths, including Turkish, Russian, Plunge and Shower." Ticket to Dr. Ravn's Hospital, J. J. Synnott Papers, 1896–1916, Wisconsin Historical Society, Madison, Wisconsin. For more descriptions of lumbering work and its dangers, see Larson, *The White Pine Industry in Minnesota* and Edmonds, *Out of the Northwoods*.

4  Frank A. Johnson Papers, Folder P2217, Minnesota Historical Society, St. Paul, Minnesota.

5 Nelligan, *The Life of a Lumberman*, 138. For more firsthand descriptions of the drive, see Fitzmaurice, *The Shanty Boy*; Holbrook, *Holy Old Mackinaw*; and "On the Log Drive," *Northland Bethany Record* (Bethany, Minnesota), January 1, 1903. For more on the danger of log jams, see Richard Cornell, "Knights of the Spike-Soled Shoe," *Wisconsin Magazine of History* 89, no. 4 (Summer 2006): 36–48.

6 Of course, as in camp, deaths were not limited only to the most obvious causes. Even if a man did not slip under the crushing pile of logs, there were many ways for things to go awry. For instance, the *New York Times* reported in 1888 that a "party of log drivers . . . attempted to thaw some dynamite over a cook stove in their shanty. The result was a terrible explosion," which killed three men. "Three Men Killed," *New York Times*, April 24, 1888.

7 Hill, "Life in a Logging Camp," 702.

8 Josephine Raimesbothom Grattan, "Dear Little Diary," 3 (unpublished manuscript, n.d., transcribed 2009), Josephine Raimesbothom Grattan Papers, Bentley Historical Library, Ann Arbor, Michigan. While foremen were reasonably concerned about not losing their workforce, legally they had little obligation to protect them. The law protected employers against suit when they had taken reasonable precautions and when the worker was assumed to be aware he had chosen to work in dangerous conditions. J. L. Rosenberger, *The Law for Lumbermen: A Digest of Decisions of Courts of Last Resort on Matters of Interest to Lumbermen* (Chicago: American Lumberman, 1902).

9 "Shanty boy" was a much older name for lumberjacks than "loggers" and was used at least as far back as Maine. It referred to the temporary shacks, or shanties, they lived in during the winter. But the word itself was weighted, both by those who were lumberjacks and those who were not. As Lisa Goff argues in *Shantytown, USA: Forgotten Landscapes of the Working Poor* (Cambridge, Mass.: Harvard University Press, 2016), shanties, shantytowns, and the people who inhabited them were seen by urban Americans as early as the 1830s as "obstacles to urban development, and indeed, to civilization itself" (56), but loggers proudly embraced the pejorative, seeing it as a sign of their rough-and-ready nature.

10 Earl Clifton Beck, *Songs of the Michigan Lumberjacks* (Ann Arbor: University of Michigan Press, 1941), 50; "Gerry's Rocks," Charles E. Brown Papers, Box 5, Folder 1, Wisconsin Historical Society, Madison, Wisconsin.

11 Beck, *Songs of the Michigan Lumberjacks*, 52.

12 Histories of working-class masculinities, in particular the bodily turn of recent years, have been incredibly instructive and fundamental to my analysis. See, in particular, Steven Maynard, "Rough Work and Rugged Men: The Social Construction of Masculinity in Working-Class History," *Labour/Le Travail* 23 (Spring 1989): 159–69; Ava Baron, "Masculinity, the Embodied Male Worker, and the Historian's Gaze," *International Labor and Working-Class History*, no. 69 (Spring 2006): 143–60; and Edward Slavishak, *Bodies*

*of Work: Civic Display and Labor in Industrial Pittsburgh* (Durham, N.C.: Duke University Press, 2008).

13 Beck, *Songs of the Michigan Lumberjacks,* 139.

14 Quoted in Cox, *The Lumberman's Frontier,* 127.

15 The change in American attitudes toward the wilderness, from a place of threat and expulsion to a place of respite and peace, began as early as Thomas Jefferson, and by the time Henry David Thoreau declared that "in Wildness is the preservation of the World," the idea had gained strong currency in the East. However, the attitude of westerners seems to have been more ambivalent—not least, one would suspect, because they had the arduous task of actually wrestling with the wilderness. For more on changing attitudes toward the wilderness, see Bryan McDonald, "Considering the Nature of Wilderness: Reflections on Roderick Nash's *Wilderness and the American Mind,*" *Organization & Environment* 14, no. 2 (June 2001): 188–201; Philip J. Deloria, *Playing Indian* (New Haven, Conn.: Yale University Press, 1998); William Cronon, "The Trouble with Wilderness; or, Getting Back to the Wrong Nature," *Environmental History* 1, no. 1 (January 1996): 7–28; and, of course, Roderick Nash's classic *Wilderness and the American Mind* (New Haven, Conn.: Yale University Press, 1968).

16 Quoted in Cox, *The Lumberman's Frontier,* 128.

17 For more on the boundaries of the lumberjack community and the transfer of songs, see chapter 3.

18 The hodag has the intriguing distinction of being the only one of these critters whose origins can be precisely traced. He was created by Eugene Sheppard, a long-time timber cruiser and lumberjack and eventual owner of a small rustic resort near Rhinelander, Wisconsin, and seems to have been based on the Anishinaabe water-panther Mishibizhiw. Luke Sylvester Kearney, *The Hodag and Other Tales of the Logging Camps* (Madison: Democratic Printing Company, 1928); Willis C. Ward, "Reminiscences of Michigan's Logging Days," *Michigan History Magazine* 20, no. 3 (Autumn 1936): 305; Interview with Layton Shepherd, Layton Shepherd Papers, SC 1004, Wisconsin Historical Society, Madison, Wisconsin.

19 Ward, "Reminiscences of Michigan's Logging Days," 305.

20 For more on their behavior in saloons, see part II. For more on risk and luck, see Jackson Lears, *Something for Nothing* (New York: Viking, 2003); E. F. Parsons, "Risky Business: The Uncertain Boundaries of Manhood in the Midwestern Saloon," *Journal of Social History* 34, no. 2 (Winter 2000): 283–307; and Gunther Peck, "Manly Gambles: The Politics of Risk on the Comstock Lode, 1860–1880," *Journal of Social History* 26, no. 4 (Summer 1993): 701–23.

21 I use the language of risk and luck here nearly interchangeably, since the notable difference between the two is the ability to control risk (while luck is out of our hands.) But when there were relatively few options for avoiding risk, that control seems less

notable. I see the attitude of jacks here to be distinct from the attitude Christopher Herbert identifies among men in gold mines a few decades earlier. Herbert argues that by focusing on the ability to rationally engage in risk, prospectors made their gamble acceptable to eastern standards of restrained manliness. Lumberjacks, on the other hand, were not from the middle classes and had no pretensions of conforming to their ideals. Their different language around risk, more than the nature of the work (which in both mines and camps required hard manual labor away form the comforts of home), makes clear the different class position of lumberjacks from gold miners. Christopher Herbert, *Gold Rush Manliness: Race and Gender on the Pacific Slope* (Seattle: University of Washington Press, 2018), 109–35.

22  Much of the work on Gilded Age men still follows on the foundational work by E. Anthony Rotundo in *American Manhood* (New York: Basic Books, 1993), but other scholars have given a variety of names to these two archetypes: in *Manhood in America* (New York: Oxford University Press, 2013), Michael Kimmel, for instance, refers to the "marketplace man," while Amy Greenberg, among a wide variety of manhoods, offers the "restrained man" and the "martial man" as the two most dominant types in *Manifest Manhood and the Antebellum American Empire* (Cambridge: Cambridge University Press, 2005). In *The Gentlemen and the Roughs* (New York: New York University Press, 2010), Lorien Foote rightly calls into question the entire practice of naming "types" when historians are well aware that men constructed their manhood from a variety of models. However true this may be, it can be helpful for situating scholarship to be able to see the broad strokes of types, even if they were far from rigid and men picked from more than one. While the names differ and new, more nuanced studies have picked apart these types, Rotundo's formulation still proves useful in laying out the dominance of self-control as a central tenet of hegemonic masculinity.

23  One indication of the overwhelming importance of mastery to the middle-class man was the fact that saloon keepers could be sued for having taken a man's mastery of himself away by overserving him. E. Anthony Rotundo, "Learning about Manhood: Gender Ideals and the Middle-Class Family in Nineteenth-Century America," in *Manliness and Morality: Middle-Class Masculinity in Britain and America, 1800–1940*, ed. James Anthony Mangan (Manchester: Manchester University Press, 1987), 39; E. F. Parsons, *Manhood Lost: Fallen Drunkards and Redeeming Women in the Nineteenth-Century United States* (Baltimore: Johns Hopkins University Press, 2003). For more modern work on middle-class manhoods at the end of the nineteenth century, see Greenberg, *Manifest Manhood and the Antebellum American Empire*; Brian P. Luskey, *On the Make: Clerks and the Quest for Capital in Nineteenth Century America* (New York: New York University Press, 2010); and Foote, *The Gentlemen and the Roughs*.

24  The aggressive masculinity promoted to men and boys in Victorian cities seems to sit at odds with the ethic of restraint. Gail Bederman's argument in *Manliness and Civilization*

(Chicago: University of Chicago Press, 1995) helps bridge the gap. Bederman argues that young boys were taught to firm up their masculinity as a kind of moral bulwark. Their masculine strength would help them in the spiritual realm of battling sin.

25  For more, see Foote, *The Gentlemen and the Roughs*, 41–66.

26  Carol Srole, *Transcribing Class and Gender: Masculinity and Femininity in Nineteenth-Century Courts and Offices* (Ann Arbor: University of Michigan Press, 2010), 5.

27  Arwen P. Mohun, *Risk: Negotiating Safety in American Society* (Baltimore: Johns Hopkins University Press, 2013), 120–60.

28  Lears, *Something for Nothing*, 24.

29  In their embrace of physical risk, lumberjacks were outside the norms of middle-class manhood. But they weren't as far away from more mainstream norms as it might seem. While physical risk was neither required nor encouraged, men in the late nineteenth century were increasingly expected to take up their roles as specifically capitalist citizens. As a result, historian Jonathan Levy argues, Americans embraced a "vision of freedom that linked the liberal ideal of self-ownership to the personal assumption of risk." Jonathan Levy, *Freaks of Fortune: The Emerging World of Capitalism and Risk in America* (Cambridge, Mass.: Harvard University Press, 2012), 5.

30  Beck, *Songs of the Michigan Lumberjacks*, 8.

31  Jacqueline Moore, *Cow Boys and Cattle Men: Class and Masculinities on the Texas Frontier, 1865–1900* (New York: New York University Press, 2010), 68.

32  Beck, *Songs of the Michigan Lumberjacks*, 163.

THREE. ON GREENHORNS AND WHITE MEN

1  My gratitude to John Beltman for walking me through the sketch, which I had not seen in several years. If you find yourself in northern Minnesota, I cannot recommend a visit to the Forest History Society highly enough. John Beltman, email to the author, June 23, 2022.

2  John Zitur, Greg Scherer, and Mark Scherer, *In Their Own Words: Lumberjacks and Their Stories*, vol. 4, *Murder and Mayhem* (Brooklyn Park, Minn.: Scherer Brothers Lumber Company, 1985).

3  Francis S. Flynn to family, January 17, 1876, Francis S. Flynn Papers, Manuscripts and Notebooks, P2349, Minnesota Historical Society, St. Paul, Minnesota.

4  For a detailed discussion of class within the camps, and the separation of foremen and scalers from the crew, see chapter 2.

5  Here I am, of course, indebted to the work of bell hooks, Kimberlé Crenshaw, and all who followed after in creating intersectional feminist analyses. bell hooks, *Ain't I a Woman* (Boston: South End Press, 1981); Kimberlé Crenshaw, "Mapping the Margins: Intersectionality, Identity Politics, and Violence against Women of Color," *Stanford Law Review* 43, no. 6 (1991): 1241–99.

6 Gail Bederman, "Manhood at Harvard: William James and Others (Review)," *Journal of American History* 84, no. 2 (September 1997): 680–81; Bruce Dorsey, "A Man's World: Revisiting Histories of Men and Gender," *Reviews in American History* 40, no. 3 (September 2012): 452–58. For a more in-depth critique of the absence of gendered power from American histories of men, see Toby L. Ditz, "The New Men's History and the Peculiar Absence of Gendered Power: Some Remedies from Early American Gender History," *Gender & History* 16, no. 1 (April 2004): 1–35; and Joanne Meyerowitz, "A History of 'Gender,'" *American Historical Review* 113, no. 5 (December 2008): 1346–56.

7 See for instance Richard Stott's *Jolly Fellows: Male Milieus in Nineteenth-Century America* (Baltimore: Johns Hopkins University Press, 2009). While Stott gives an outstanding overview of the activities—fighting, drinking, and joking—of men within all-male spaces across the nineteenth century, he does little to consider the motivations for taking part in these activities in the first place. Instead, he seems to consider the masculinity of these activities to be inherent in the male body, and therefore examines only how and why they were curtailed by the changing roles of men, the emergence of a hegemonic middle-class masculinity that emphasized restraint as well as increasingly feminized public spaces. This method assumes that within the male-only spaces of "jolly fellows" shared masculinity was a given, threatened only by feminizing influences on the outside.

8 Among the many histories that take a more comprehensive view toward gendering homosocial worlds, I am particularly grateful for Susan Lee Johnson's *Roaring Camp: The Social World of the California Gold Rush* (New York: W. W. Norton, 2000); Lorien Foote's *The Gentlemen and the Roughs*; Martha Santos's *Cleansing Honor with Blood: Masculinity, Violence and Power in the Backlands of Northeast Brazil, 1845–1889* (Stanford, Calif.: Stanford University Press, 2012); and Christopher Herbert's *Gold Rush Manliness*.

9 Jacqueline M. Moore recently found a similar phenomenon among cowboys: as the prairies became increasingly settled, the extralegal violence that had once been celebrated became increasingly distasteful to the cowboys' neighbors. But to cowboys themselves, Moore argues, violence was a way of regulating social behaviors and hierarchies. Moore, "'Them's Fighting Words.'"

10 Nancy Cott had a prescient suspicion that "if the boundary between private and public does become more elusive when men are studied as gendered subjects that may focus needed attention on it," which has proven true—recent histories have thoughtfully questioned the stark separation of private and public. Nancy Cott, "On Men's History and Women's History," in *Meanings for Manhood: Constructions of Masculinity in Victorian America*, ed. Mark C. Carnes and Clyde Griffen (Chicago: University of Chicago Press 1990), 209. This is where this study, by necessity, diverges from the straightforward consideration of lumberjacks as working-class men. As Lou Martin recently pointed out, for most working-class men, ideals of manhood "included earning a 'family wage' to

support a wife and children." It was the desire for that wage and stability that required them to keep up a "manly bearing" toward employers, and only use violence as a last resort. Here, as elsewhere, the itinerancy of lumberjacks undermines the ability to group them with working-class men as a whole. Lou Martin, "'So Nobly Struggling for Their Manhood': Masculinity and Violence among Steelworkers in the Wheeling District, 1880–1910," *Labor History* 60, no. 5 (2019): 430.

11 For more on recruitment methods, see Larson, *The White Pine Industry in Minnesota*.

12 Santos, *Cleansing Honor with Blood*, 4.

13 For a convincing argument that this was, in fact, the way in which middle-class men measured their value, see Luskey, *On the Make*.

14 Nancy Quam-Wickham, "Rereading Man's Conquest of Nature: Skills, Myths and the Historical Construction of Masculinity in Western Extractive Industries," *Men and Masculinities* 2, no. 2 (October 1999): 131–51.

15 Foundational to this discussion were Anne Phillips and Barbara Taylor, "Sex and Skill: Notes Towards a Feminist Economics," *Feminist Review*, no. 6 (1980): 79–88; and Jane Gaskell, "Conceptions of Skill and the Work of Women: Some Historical and Political Issues," *Atlantis* 8, no. 2 (Spring 1983): 11–27. For applications of this idea to single-sex workplaces, see Maynard, "Rough Work and Rugged Men"; Johnson, *Roaring Camp*; Quam-Wickham, "Rereading Man's Conquest of Nature"; Steve Meyer, "Rough Manhood: The Aggressive and Confrontational Shop Culture of U.S. Auto Workers during World War II," *Journal of Social History* 36, no. 1 (Autumn 2002): 125–47; Herbert, *Gold Rush Manliness*; and particularly Stephen Meyer, *Manhood on the Line: Working Class Masculinities in the American Heartland* (Champaign: University of Illinois Press, 2016).

16 "The Evangelist of the Lumber Woods," *Northern Tribune* (Cheboygan, Michigan), February 24, 1883.

17 For more on pictures of champion loads, see John Vincent Jezierski, *Enterprising Images: The Goodridge Brothers, African American Photographers, 1847–1922* (Detroit: Wayne State University Press, 2000), 190–200. The Minnesota and Wisconsin Historical Societies both keep excellent galleries of images online.

18 Nelligan, *The Life of a Lumberman*, 124–26; Bruno Vinette and W. W. Bartlett, "Early Logging on the Chippewa" (unpublished manuscript, n.d.), Bartlett Papers, 977.75, Wisconsin Historical Society, Madison, Wisconsin. For more, see John Zitur, Greg Scherer, and Mark Scherer, *In Their Own Words: Lumberjacks and Their Stories*, vol. 2, *In the Camps* (Brooklyn Park, Minn.: Scherer Brothers Lumber Company, 1985).

19 Bruce Harding, interview with Leonard Costley, International Falls, Minnesota, August 3, 1957, Forest History Society Interviews, Box P2385, Minnesota Historical Society, St. Paul, Minnesota.

20 Zitur, Scherer, and Scherer, *In Their Own Words*, vol. 2.

21  Helen M. White, interview with Margaret Orr O'Neill (Mrs. Charles O'Neill), St. Croix Falls, October 1, 1955, Forest History Society Interviews, P 2385, Minnesota Historical Society, St. Paul, Minnesota, 9.

22  For more, see Ella Johansson, "Beautiful Men, Fine Women and Good Work People: Gender and Skill in Northern Sweden 1850–1950," in *Among Men, Moulding Masculinities*, vol. 1, ed. Ed Søren Ervø and Thomas Jonhansson (New York: Routledge, 2003), 66–80.

23  Bourgeois, "Reminiscences," and F. D. Haddock, "The Woods Crew," *Eau Claire (Wisc.) Leader*, April 27, 1925.

24  Zitur, Scherer, and Scherer, *In Their Own Words*, vol. 4.

25  For excellent overviews of the cultural development of the Northwoods to the late nineteenth century, see Biloine Whiting Young, *River of Conflict, River of Dreams: Three Hundred Years on the Upper Mississippi* (St. Paul, Minn.: Pogo Press, 2004); Jay Gitlin, *The Bourgeois Frontier* (New Haven: Yale University Press, 2010); Mary Lethert Wingerd, *North Country: The Making of Minnesota* (Minneapolis: University of Minnesota Press, 2010). For more on the Menominee, see Thomas Davis, *Sustaining the Forest, the People and the Spirit* (Albany: State University of New York Press, 2000); and Beck, *The Struggle for Self-Determination*. For more on Anishinaabe history, see Erik M. Redix, *The Murder of Joe White: Ojibwe Leadership and Colonialism in Wisconsin* (East Lansing: Michigan State University Press, 2014); and Chantal Norrgard, *Seasons of Change: Labor, Treaty Rights and Ojibwe Nationhood* (Chapel Hill: University of North Carolina Press, 2014).

26  Paul Buffalo quoted in Norrgard, *Seasons of Change*, 106.

27  Horace Glenn to parents, March 10, 1901, Andrew Glenn and Family Papers, 1842–1919, Minnesota Historical Society, St. Paul, Minnesota.

28  Frederika Bremer, *The Homes of the New World; Impressions of America*, vol. 2, trans. Mary Howitt (New York: Harper & Brothers, 1854), 56.

29  Gerald Ronning, "Jackpine Savages: Discourses of Conquest in the 1916 Mesabi Iron Range Strike," *Labor History* 44, no. 3 (2003): 359–82. For more on European migrations to the Northwoods, see Jon Gjerde's classic *The Minds of the West* as well as *From Peasants to Farmers: The Migration from Balestrand, Norway to the Upper Middle West* (Cambridge: Cambridge University Press, 1985). More recently, see Edward Watts's *An American Colony: Regionalism and the Roots of Midwestern Culture* (Athens: Ohio University Press, 2002); Philip J. Anderson and Dag Blanck, eds., *Norwegians and Swedes in the United States* (St. Paul: Minnesota Historical Society Press, 2012); as well as the excellent People of Minnesota series from the Minnesota Historical Society Press in St. Paul: Jon Gjerde, *Norwegians in Minnesota* (2002); Kathleen Neils Conzen, *Germans in Minnesota* (2003); Anne Gillespie Lewis, *Swedes in Minnesota* (2004); and Arnold R. Alanen, *Finns in Minnesota* (2012).

30  Matthew Frye Jacobsen, *Whiteness of a Different Color: European Immigrants and the Alchemy of Race* (Cambridge, Mass.: Harvard University Press, 1999), 69.

31  Gjerde, *The Minds of the West*; Jon Gjerde, "'Here in America There Is Neither King Nor Tyrant': European Encounters with Race, 'Freedom,' and Their European Pasts," *Journal of the Early Republic* 19, no. 4 (Winter 1999): 673–90; and Jon Gjerde, "The Effect of Community on Migration: Three Minnesota Townships 1885–1905," *Journal of Historical Geography* 5, no. 4 (October 1979): 403–22.

32  The obsession with these seemingly small ethnic differences is hard to overstate. Gift shops across the region sell "Lena and Ole" joke books that catalog the endless stupidity of a Scandinavian couple and their friends—the most recent, *Ole and Sven's Bucket List*, was published in 2013. However, the simplest method of demonstrating it is walking into Wisconsin's popular Norske Nook restaurant and mentioning, as I once did, that you are a Swede by descent. You will not be allowed pie.

33  Horace Glenn to parents, March 10, 1901, Andrew Glenn and Family Papers, 1842–1919, Minnesota Historical Society, St. Paul, Minnesota.

34  Francis Lunden Manuscript, Minnesota Historical Society, St. Paul, Minnesota; Kuarala, "Memoirs"; Kromer, "Thorpe, 1968."

35  Franz Rickaby, *Ballads and Songs of the Shanty-Boy* (Cambridge, Mass.: Harvard University Press, 1926), xxi; Richard Dorson, "Personal Histories," *Western Folklore* 7, no. 1 (January 1948), 28.

36  Horace Glenn to Andrew Glen, February 24, 1901, Andrew Glenn and Family Papers, 1842–1919, Minnesota Historical Society, St. Paul, Minnesota.

37  Interview of Alton Van Camp and John Boyd by Dennis East and Joe Smith; Interview of Jhalmer Berg by Rober Wheeler, Buyck, Minnesota, May 30, 1977, Oral History Collection, Minnesota Historical Society, St. Paul, Minnesota.

38  Grace Hale, *Making Whiteness* (New York: Pantheon Books, 1998).

39  Moreover, much of this irritation comes from the idea that what began as part of a radical cultural Marxism seems to have been watered down beyond recognition. Roderick A. Ferguson argued that "whiteness has yet to demand the one thing required of genuine self-criticism—redistribution." Roderick A. Ferguson, "The Distributions of Whiteness," *American Quarterly* 66, no. 4 (December 2014): 1101. What Ferguson reflects are the roots of whiteness as a historical category in Marxist thinking. In a somewhat cantankerous overview of the field, John Munro, "Roots of 'Whiteness,'" *Labour/Le Travail* 54 (Fall 2004): 175–92, wrote that, in the eyes of many, whiteness had become meaningless. Citing a study on *Star Trek* among others, he reflects a growing grumbling about whiteness being divorced from Marxist roots and losing its rigor. Peter Kolchin is in many ways as hesitant as Munro, but not out of an irritation that whiteness has abandoned Marxism. Kolchin's critique, instead, boils down essentially to the idea that while whiteness is useful, its usefulness has distinct limits. Once historians use whiteness to explain too much, Kolchin argues, they are prone to exaggerating it into a vast, almost ahistorical force whose precise meaning is impossible to pin down.

As a result, Marxist historians have largely moved on from examining the category of whiteness: David Roediger, whose seminal *Wages of Whiteness* (London: Verso Books, 1992) established the importance of the category in nineteenth-century history, has since moved toward more modern and more overtly political commentary on labor and unions. But abandonment of Marxist analysis hardly undermines the purpose of whiteness studies. There is radical potential in understanding from where inequality comes. In *Making Whiteness*, Grace Hale writes that "if we understand the past as always having been only white and black, what will be the catalyst that makes the future different? The epiphany that erases the bloody divisions?" It seems to me that there is no reason this cannot be true even if whiteness is looked at outside a consideration of Marxist economics.

For more on the history of the field, and the history of infighting over the purpose of the field, see Eric Arnesen, "Whiteness and the Historian's Imagination," *International Labor and Working-Class History*, no. 60 (Fall 2001): 3–32; and especially Peter Kolchin, "Whiteness Studies: The New History of Race in America," *Journal of American History* 89, no. 1 (June 2002): 154–73.

40  Goldstein also argues that it is "white Americans' anxious attempts to obscure the fissures that divided them internally" that reveals "just how tenuous the notion of a stable, monolithic whiteness has been in American life." While that logic might at first seem a little tortured, it is, after all, no different than Foucault's claims about sexuality and does as much, if not more, to undo damaging historical myths. The invention of a stable white past as the basis for future action is surely more relevant in the post-Trump era than ever before. Eric L. Goldstein, *The Price of Whiteness: Jews, Race, and American Identity* (Princeton, N.J.: Princeton University Press, 2006), 3.

41  Goldstein, *The Price of Whiteness* and Jacobsen, *Whiteness of a Different Color*, 6. For more on ethnicity, the unstable definition of "race," and attempts to gain entry to the category of "white," see Noel Ignatiev, *How the Irish Became White* (New York: Routledge, 2009); and Gjerde, "'Here In America There Is Neither King nor Tyrant.'"

42  Kolchin, "Whiteness Studies," 165.

43  Norrgard, *Seasons of Change*, 86–88. There's an interesting parallel here with the historical memory of lumberjacks themselves. As I argue in chapter 5, the mythical lumberjack was constructed as being a part of the forest: while he destroyed it, he was also only naturally at home in the woods. This is especially apparent in the short stories of Elia Peattie, in which jacks, once removed from the woods and replanted in cities, quickly deteriorate and die. This made sense in a middle-class view where lumberjacks were part of the wild frontier, a lost past that could not be resurrected any more easily than the pines could be regrown. Elia W. Peattie, "A Michigan Man," in Peattie, *A Mountain Woman* (Chicago: Way and Williams, 1896; Project Guttenberg, 2007), http://www.gutenberg.org/ebooks/23176.

44  For more, see chapter 4.

45  This pattern of behaviors and contingent definition of skill as dependent on race bears striking resemblance to the racial hierarchies Geoff Mann found in northern California pineries where African Americans worked in the late nineteenth century. See Geoff Mann, "Race, Skill, and Section in Northern California," *Politics & Society* 30, no. 3 (2002): 465–96.

46  Robert F. Berkhofer Jr., *The White Man's Indian: Images of the American Indian from Columbus to the Present* (New York: Alfred A. Knopf, 1978), 30.

47  Ter Ellingson, *The Myth of the Noble Savage* (Berkeley: University of California Press, 2001), 196.

48  Bederman, *Manliness and Civilization*, 218–25.

49  J. C. Nott, quoted in Berkhofer, *The White Man's Indian*, 30.

50  Jill Doerfler, "An Anishinaabe Tribalography: Investigating and Interweaving Conceptions of Identity during the 1910s on the White Earth Reservation," *American Indian Quarterly* 33, no. 3 (Summer 2009): 295–324.

51  Deloria, *Playing Indian* and Bederman, *Manliness and Civilization*.

52  Paul Buffalo quoted in Norrgard, *Seasons of Change*, 106. Norrgard argues that Buffalo was remembering incorrectly or was, at the very least, an anomaly. She asserts that there was terrible discrimination against the Anishinaabe in the woods, but uses as evidence merely the fact that the camps themselves were violent. While I have found many examples of violence against the Anishinaabe at the hands of lumberjacks *outside* the camps in town, I have found no evidence that there was violence or an unwillingness to work together *within* camps. The best evidence I can find for this, as detailed below, is that Indians and Finns were often asked to work together in the lowest-paying and most dangerous positions.

53  Interview of Alton Van Camp and John Boyd by Dennis East and Joe Smith.

54  Norrgard, *Seasons of Change*, 101.

55  Norrgard, *Seasons of Change*, 106.

56  Roland Martin, "The Life of a Lumber Camp Cook: An Interview with Edward Francis" (1953, transcribed, annotated, and appended by Kerri L. Ferstl and Rosemarie Brod, 2009), Wisconsin Historical Society, Madison, Wisconsin.

57  Norrgard, *Seasons of Change*, 98. See also Gills, "Navigating the Landscape of Assimilation," 58–60.

58  Nelligan, *The Life of a Lumberman*, 60.

59  C. H. Cooke quoted in Mark Wyman, *The Wisconsin Frontier* (Bloomington: Indiana University Press, 1998), 272.

60  Millard L. Gieske and Steven J. Keillor, *Norwegian Yankee: Knute Nelson and the Failure of American Politics, 1860–1923* (Northfield, Minn.: Norwegian-American Historical Society, 1995), 346. This crossing over of types in which newer immigrants were constructed

as being evolutionarily closer to the Anishinaabe came back with fierce aggression in 1916 when the immigrant laborers of the Northwoods finally went on strike. For more, see Ronning, "Jackpine Savages."

### PART II. IN TOWN

1 I am deeply indebted to the theoretical framework of Christine M. DeLucia's *Memory Lands: King Philip's War and the Place of Violence in the Northeast* (New Haven, Conn.: Yale University Press, 2018). Her work roots memory, something that can seem abstract, to place, bridging the gaps between environmental history and the study of cultural memory.

### FOUR. THAT RESTLESS, ROVING SPIRIT

1 The 1917 strikes came the same winter as massive labor uprisings in the camps of the Pacific Northwest organized by the IWW. While the language and fervor of those strikes surely informed the Minnesota strike, the IWW itself did not believe the Minnesota jacks ready for (or even capable of) striking. For more on the Pacific Northwest strikes, see Loomis, *Empire of Timber*.

2 John E. Haynes, "Revolt of the 'Timber Beasts': IWW Lumber Strike in Minnesota," *Minnesota History* 42, no. 5 (Spring 1971): 165.

3 *Bemidji (Minn.) Daily Pioneer*, January 3, 1917.

4 George, "Hitting the Trail in the Lumber Camps," 455.

5 Larson, *The White Pine Industry in Minnesota*, 370. Barbara Benson in *Logs and Lumber* comes to the same conclusion with equal speed as Larson. Thomas R. Cox, in *The Lumberman's Frontier*, doesn't even mention strikes or resistance during the period of lumbering's "full flower" in the Northwoods, nor does Robert F. Fries in *Empire in Pine*, nor Randall E. Rohe in "Evolution of the Great Lakes Logging Camp, 1830–1930," *Journal of Forest History* 30, no. 1 (January 1986): 17–28.

6 George B. Engberg, "Collective Bargaining in the Lumber Industry of the Upper Great Lake States," *Agricultural History* 24, no. 4 (October 1950): 205–11; and "Lumber and Labor in the Lake States," *Minnesota History* 36, no. 5 (March 1959): 153–66; and Haynes, "Revolt of the 'Timber Beasts,'" 162–74. I do not include in this the work of Jeremy Kilar, whose excellent "Community and Authority Response to the Saginaw Valley Lumber Strike of 1885," *Journal of Forest History* 20, no. 2 (April 1976): 67–79; *Michigan's Lumbertowns*; and "The Lumbertowns: A Socioeconomic History of Michigan's Leading Lumber Centers: Saginaw, Bay City and Muskegon, 1870–1905" (PhD diss., University of Michigan, 1987) deal entirely with strikes in the sawmills, not the camps themselves.

7 For more on the publicity campaign enacted in response to the strikes, see chapter 5.

8 For more on the off-season habits and lives of lumberjacks, see chapter 6.

9 *Bemidji (Minn.) Daily Pioneer*, January 2, 1917.

10 Minnesota Department of Labor and Industries, *Fourteenth Biennial Report*, 1914, Minnestoa Historical Society, St. Paul, Minnesota. Erik Loomis, using Rob Nixon's idea of "slow violence," demonstrates that for workers in the Pacific Northwest these conditions were the central motivation for organizing. Loomis, *Empire in Timber*, 1–30; Rob Nixon, *Slow Violence and the Environmentalism of the Poor* (Cambridge, Mass.: Harvard University Press, 2011). It is noteworthy that the acute violence of dangerous conditions in the woods were less demoralizing, ultimately, than the day-in, day-out degradation of poor living conditions, food, and medical care.

11 For more on the Mesabi Iron Range strike, see Robert M. Eleff, "The 1916 Minnesota Miners' Strike against U.S. Steel," *Minnesota History* 51, no. 2 (Summer 1988): 63–74; Neil Betten, "Riot, Revolution, Repression in the Iron Range Strike of 1916," *Minnesota History* 41, no. 2 (Summer 1968): 82–93; and Higbie, *Indispensable Outcasts*.

12 For more on the influence of Finnish radicalism on midwestern politics, see Richard M. Valelly, *Radicalism in the States: The Minnesota Farmer-Labor Party and the American Political Economy* (Chicago: University of Chicago Press, 1989); and Paul A. Lubotina, "Conflict and Community Building: The Dichotomy of Immigrant Life on Minnesota's Mesabi Iron Range, 1893–1930" (PhD diss., Saint Louis University, 2006).

13 Ronning, "Jackpine Savages."

14 The truth is that while some lumber historians note the Mesabi strike and many mention the 1917 strike, very little attention has been paid to the strikes in the last thirty years. The strike histories that were written in the 1950s and 1960s, with the exception of Engberg's study, were looking for resistance that looked like labor unionism. If there was no union, there was no strike. Those walk-offs that happened spontaneously were relegated to "grumbles" and not taken seriously by historians. Moreover, the vast majority of work on the Northwoods lumber industry has been focused not on lumberjacks but on either the more stable, and therefore more easily studied, mill hands or on the lumbermen (the owners and managers). Engberg, "Collective Bargaining in the Lumber Industry," and "Lumber and Labor in the Lake States"; and Haynes, "Revolt of the 'Timber Beasts,'" 162–74.

15 Wilfred Nevue, "Lumberjack Ballads and Stories: An Evaluation" (unpublished manuscript, n.d.), Wilfred Nevue Papers, Bentley Historical Library, Ann Arbor, Michigan.

16 Wilfred Nevue, "Logging in the Huron Mountains" (unpublished manuscript, 1959), Wilfred Nevue Papers, Bentley Historical Library, Ann Arbor, Michigan.

17 Van Camp, "Reminiscences."

18 "Palmy Days Are Over," *Detroit Free Press*, January 14, 1907.

19 Nevue is particularly likely to have purposefully blurred the lines, since he was also, through the 1940s and 1950s, a great booster for the respectable history of lumbering.

His bizarrely full-throated defense of the reputation of Seney, Michigan, for instance, steps beyond merely massaging the truth into fully lying about the town. In an article titled "'Incredible' Lumberjack Stories Debunked by Veteran of the Camps," tellingly published in a newspaper owned by lumber manufacturers, Nevue insisted that Seney provided all or most of the labor for the four to eight camps in its vicinity, and only a "few lumberjacks drifted in." Seney, in the years in which he was insisting it provided more than 400 able-bodied laborers, had a total population of 254, 74 of them women. Wilfred Nevue, "'Incredible' Lumberjack Stories Debunked by Veteran of Camps," *Mining Journal* (Marquette, Michigan), February 13, 1954; "Logging in the Huron Mountains"; and "Lumberjack Ballads and Stories"; Interview of Alton Van Camp and John Boyd by Dennis East and Joe Smith.

20  Larson, *The White Pine Industry in Minnesota*, 181.

21  This assumption appears, among other places, in Robert B. Porter, "Northwoods Pioneers: A Collection of Twelve Actual Interviews with Pioneers Living between Northome and Deer River, Minnesota" (unpublished manuscript, n.d.), Minnesota Historical Society, St. Paul, Minnesota; John Zetterstrom, "The Story of a Logging Town" (unpublished manuscript, n.d.), Minnesota Historical Society, St. Paul, Minnesota.

22  Miles Nelson, "Reminisces," Miles Nelson Papers, Minnesota Historical Society, St. Paul, Minnesota.

23  For a history of midwestern itinerant labor, there is no better source than Frank Higbie's *Indispensable Outcasts* as well as his "Rural Work, Household Subsistence and the North American Working Class: A View from the Midwest," *International Labor and Working-Class History*, no. 65 (Spring 2004): 50–76.

24  Wilkinson, *Memorials of the Minnesota Forest Fires*, 125.

25  For more on early State of Maine camps, see Larson, *The White Pine Industry in Minnesota*; Cox, *The Lumberman's Frontier*; and Ward, "Reminiscences of Michigan's Logging Days."

26  Bourgeois, "Reminiscences."

27  Larson, *The White Pine Industry in Minnesota*, 183–84.

28  "Log Book, 1905," Camp #4 (Cable, Wis.) Records, 1908, Wisconsin Historical Society, Eau Claire Area Research Center, Eau Claire, Wisconsin. This is one of several such books kept by the Wisconsin and Minnesota State Historical Societies. Most were kept only to note debts at the store and did not include days worked.

29  Frank Gillmor, "Annual report notebook, 1910–1928," Frank Gillmor Papers, P2334, Minnesota Historical Society, St. Paul, Minnesota.

30  Nelligan, *The Life of a Lumberman*; Bourgeois, "Reminiscences"; Henry McCann, "Veteran of Logging Days Writes of Vivid Experiences" (unpublished manuscript, 1938), Wisconsin Historical Society, Madison, Wisconsin; Blakeman, *Report of a Truant*; Rex J. Dye, *Lumber Camp Life in Michigan* (Hicksville, N.Y.: Exposition Press, 1975); Nelson,

"Reminiscences"; Martin, "The Life of a Lumber Camp Cook"; Robert J. Baird, "Reminiscences," SC 2420, Wisconsin Historical Society, Madison, Wisconsin; John Henry Goddard, Diary, M77-538, Wisconsin Historical Society, Madison, Wisconsin; "Pioneer Recollections" (radio transcripts), WPA Files, Wisconsin Historical Society, Madison, Wisconsin; E. O. Olund interviewed by Frederick Kohlmeyer, Olund Employment Service, Duluth, Minnesota, May 10, 1956, Fredrick W. Kohlmeyer Research Files, Minnesota Historical Society, St. Paul, Minnesota; and "Notes on Lumbering Days in Northwest Wisconsin and in Tennessee Communicated to Charles E. Brown by Mr. Dan E. Thomas of Shell Lake, Wis., Oct. 1912," Box 5, Folder 1, Charles E. Brown Papers, Wisconsin Historical Society, Madison, Wisconsin.

31  "WPA Notes," WPA Files, Minnesota Historical Society, St. Paul, Minnesota; *Minneapolis Star Journal* quoted in the *Ottawa Journal*, January 26, 1943. For more on the extensive use of nicknames in camps, see Interview of Jim Knight by John Esse, September 22, 1975, Oral History Collection, Minnesota Historical Society, St. Paul, Minnesota.

32  Interview of Alton Van Camp and John Boyd by Dennis East and Joe Smith; Martin, "The Life of a Lumber Camp Cook."

33  *Bemidji (Minn.) Daily Pioneer*, March 16, 1914. Lynde Hartt, "Notes on a Michigan Lumber Town"; Beck, *Songs of the Michigan Lumberjacks*.

34  Kearney, *The Hodag and Other Tales of the Logging Camps*; Ward, "Reminiscences of Michigan's Logging Days," 305; Interview with Layton Shepherd, Layton Shepherd Papers, SC 1004, Wisconsin Historical Society, Madison, Wisconsin.

35  Interview with Layton Shepherd, Layton Shepherd Papers, Wisconsin Historical Society; William T. Cox, *Fearsome Creatures of the Lumberwoods, with a Few Desert and Mountain Beasts* (Washington, D.C.: Judd & Detweiler, 1910), 35. For a particularly heated debate over the nature of the hodag in Minnesota, see the *Bemidji (Minn.) Daily Pioneer*, June 7, 1900, July 19, 1900, and January 24, 1901; *Virginia (Minn.) Enterprise*, January 20, 1905.

36  This represents the earliest pictograph of Mishibizhiw (whose name is variously spelled Misshipeshu, Mishi-bizheu, and Mishibijiw and translated as everything from underwater panther to great lynx), but oral representations of him might have originated much earlier. Meghan C. Howey, "Other-Than-Human Persons, Mishipishu, and Danger in the Late Woodland Inland Waterway Landscape of Northern Michigan," *American Antiquity* 85, no. 2 (2020): 347–66; for more, see also Damara Zawadzka, "Rock Art and Animism in the Canadian Shield," *Journal of Archaeology, Consciousness, and Culture* 12, no. 2 (2019): 79–94. My deep thanks to Chantal Norrgard for drawing my attention to the Anishinaabe roots of the hodag during her panel at the Organization of American Historians in 2022.

37  The hodag's tales followed a course parallel to Paul Bunyan: early stories of him were about something fearsome and threatening, but by 1896 the Brown Brother's Lumber

Co. was running a promotion in which any order would come with a booklet of stories about this now largely comic beast who strained like an ox to carry heavy loads of logs. H. H. Ryan, *The Wide World Magazine* 35 (April 1915): 83–85; "Advertisement 16," *The Timberman*, February 1, 1896, 42.

38   Kinnear, "Cruising for Pinelands."

39   Engberg, "Lumber and Labor in the Lake States."

40   Griffin, "Forests and Logging in the Vicinity of Hibbing, Minn."

41   Andrews, *Killing for Coal*, 168.

42   For more on the seasonal round, see Norrgard, *Seasons of Change*; Bradley J. Gills, "Navigating the Landscape of Assimilation: The Anishinaabeg, the Lumber Industry, and the Failure of Federal Indian Policy in Michigan," *Michigan Historical Review* 34, no. 2 (Fall 2008): 57–74; as well as the detailed personal history of Jean M. O'Brien, brilliantly analyzed in "Memory and Mobility: Grandma's Mahnomen, White Earth," *Ethnohistory* 64, no. 3 (2017): 345–77, where O'Brien explicitly ties her Anishinaabe side of the family's mobility to her grandmother's "non-Indian father's sense of adventure or wanderlust . . . [in which] they continued a longer tradition of movement in her family." This chapter will focus primarily on Anishinaabe relations with the timber industry; for excellent overviews of the Menominee experience, see Brian C. Hosmer, *American Indians in the Marketplace: Persistence and Innovation among the Menominees and Metlakoatlans* (Lawrence: University Press of Kansas, 1999); Brian Hosmer, "Reflections on Indian Cultural 'Brokers': Regional Oshkosh, Mitchell Oshkenaniew, and the Politics of Menominee Lumbering," *Ethnohistory* 44, no. 3 (Summer 1997): 493–509; Beck, *The Struggle for Self-Determination*; and David L. Mausel, Anthony Waupochik Jr., and Marshall Pecore, "Menominee Forestry: Past, Present and Future," *Journal of Forestry* 115, no. 5 (2017): 366–69. For similar patterns in the Pacific Northwest, see Vera Parham, "'These Indians Are Apparently Well to Do': The Myth of Capitalism and Native American Labor," *International Review of Social History* 57 (2012): 447–70.

43   Sâkihitowin Awāsis, "Gwaabaw: Applying Anishnaabe Harvesting Protocols to Energy Governance," *Canadian Geographer* 65, no. 1 (2021): 8–23. There's a parallel here with O'Connor's idea of the "second contradiction of capitalism" in which, as the process of capitalism speeds up, the cheap nature required to produce it diminishes—eventually the system cannot sustain itself. James O'Connor, *Natural Causes: Essays in Ecological Marxism* (New York: Guildford, 1998). The Anishinaabe understanding of harvesting, in which leader plants are left alone and harvesters are careful not to *over*harvest, is one of the many aspects of Anishinaabe environmental practice that exists not as "pre" capitalism, but simply outside the entire capitalist framework of understanding.

44   Morinville and Van Lier, "On Nature, Degradation, and Life Making in Late Capitalism."

45  Robert M. Hendershot, "The Legacy of an Ojibwe 'Lumber Chief': David Shoppenagon," *Michigan Historical Review* 29, no. 2 (Fall 2003): 41–68; for more on the evolution of this mindset in historical studies and the academic literature, see Alexandra Harmon, Colleen O'Neill, and Paul C. Rosier, "Interwoven Economic Histories: American Indians in a Capitalist America," *Journal of American History* 98, no. 3 (December 2011): 700–711; and the introductory portion of Chantal Norrgard, "From Berries to Orchards: Tracing the History of Berrying and Economic Transformation among the Lake Superior Ojibwe," *American Indian Quarterly* 33, no. 1 (Winter 2009): 33–61; and Jason Edwards Black, *American Indians and the Rhetoric of Removal and Allotment* (Oxford: University of Mississippi Press, 2015).

46  There is increasing research to show that those who resist by maintaining culture are more resilient. Psychologists argue that identification with, and pride in, tribal affiliation has a strong mitigating effect on the mental health crises caused by historical loss. Charlee N. Brisette et al., "Associations of Historical Loss, Resilience, and Coping with Loss-related Emotional Symptoms in the Anishinaabe," *American Journal of Health Behavior* 44, no. 2 (March 2020): 244–51.

47  Michelle M. Steen-Adams, Nancy Langston, and David J. Mladenoff, "White Pine in the Northern Forests and Ecological and Management History of White Pine on the Bad River Reservation of Wisconsin," *Environmental History* 12, no. 3 (July 2007): 621.

48  Annual Report of the Commissioner of Indian Affairs, 1875 quoted in Norrgard, *Seasons of Change*, 98.

49  Michelle M. Steen-Adams et al., "Influence of Biophysical Factors and Differences in Ojibwe Reservation versus Euro-American Social Histories on Forest Landscape Change in Northern Wisconsin, USA," *Landscape Ecology* 26 (2011): 1171–72.

50  Norrgard, *Seasons of Change* and "From Berries to Orchards"; and Hosmer, *American Indians in the Marketplace*. For more on the changes the Dawes Act wrought both on Euro-American conceptions of Native peoples and on decolonial rhetoric, see Black, *American Indians and the Rhetoric of Removal and Allotment*, 81–102; and Frederick E. Hoxie, *Talking Back to Civilization: Indian Voices from the Progressive Era* (New York: St. Martin's, 2001).

51  Hendershot, "The Legacy of an Ojibwe 'Lumber Chief.'"

52  Higbie, *Indispensable Outcasts*, 110.

53  There are many excellent histories of the use of lumber and lumbering as a method of resisting assimilationist pressures. I am particularly indebted to Chantal Norrgard for both *Seasons of Change* and "From Berries to Orchards"; Hosmer, *American Indians in the Marketplace*; Brian Hosmer, Colleen O'Neill, and Donald Fixico, *Native Pathways: American Indian Culture and Economic Development in the Twentieth Century* (Boulder: University Press of Colorado, 2004); and Parham, "'These Indians Are Apparently Well to Do.'"

54 McLeod, "Hungry Spirits"; for more on the history of communal resources, see Thomas Peacock and Marlene Wisuri, *Ojibwe Waasa Inaabidaa—We Look in All Directions* (Afton, Minn.: Afton Historical Society Press, 2002).

55 Binger Herman, "Report of the Commissioner of the General Land Office Regarding the Ceded Chippewa Indian Lands," January 10, 1899, Minnesota Historical Society, St. Paul, Minnesota.

56 Melissa L. Meyer, "Signatures and Thumbprints: Ethnicity among the White Earth Anishinaabeg, 1889–1020," *Social Science History* 14, no. 3 (1990): 320.

57 "Minutes of a Council Held at Leach Lake, January 7, 1898, by the Pillager Indians," in "Report of the Commissioner of the General Land Office Regarding the Ceded Chippewa Indian Lands," January 10, 1899, Minnesota Historical Society, St. Paul, Minnesota.

58 Meyer, "Signatures and Thumbprints." White Cloud specifically noted that while he had heard "Indians and mixed bloods do purposefully start fires just to get a chance to log" (when green, or living, timber was restricted, it was still legal to log dead-and-down or burned wood), he immediately differentiates the two groups by saying that each time there is such a fire "my people come and tell me," but that no fire has been started by "my people." There are fires, he is admitting, but they are all the fault of mixed bloods, whom he does not see as "his." White Cloud and Mash Ege Shig, "Letter to Hon Binger Herman," August 2, 1898, in *Correspondence Relating to Timber on the Chippewa Indian Reservations*, Document 70, Senate Records of the 55th Congress, 3rd Session, 1899.

59 "Note," *The Tomahawk* (White Earth, Minnesota), December 4, 1903.

60 Beck, *The Struggle for Self-Determination*, 46–62; Trosper, "Indigenous Influence on Forest Management"; and Hosmer, "Reflections on Indian Cultural 'Brokers,'" 503.

61 For an excellent overview of the Walleye Wars, as well as a subsequent action killing hundreds of cormorants that were (nominally, at least) threatening walleye populations, see Harold A. Perkins, "Capital, Subsistence, and Lakeside Violence: Walleye Wars and the Killing of Cormorants in the North Woods," *Human Geography* 3, no. 1 (March 2010): 89–107.

62 Anna J. Willow, *Strong Hearts, Native Lands: The Cultural and Political Landscape of Anishinaabe Anti-Clearcutting Activism* (Albany: State University of New York Press, 2012).

63 Nelligan, *The Life of a Lumberman*, 114.

64 Letter from J. P. Weyerhaeuser to F. Weyerhaeuser, Frederick W. Kohlmeyer, Lumber industry labor history research files, 1903–1956, P2068, Minnesota Historical Society, St. Paul, Minnesota.

65 William G. Rector, "Lumber Barons in Revolt," *Minnesota History* 31, no. 1 (March 1950): 33–39.

66 Interview of Alton Van Camp and John Boyd by Dennis East and Joe Smith.

67 Tracing the extent to which a town might be said to be a true lumber boomtown is difficult. Two factors help corroborate the accuracy of oral histories that remember these towns as lumberjack centers with little permanent business. Seney, according to the 1900 census, had a population of just 255, less than a third of whom were women. Yet photographs from nearly the same year show three hotels, at least two of which appear to be brothels, and several saloons. Oral histories claim that up to ten thousand men poured into Seney at the end of seasons. Even allowing for exaggeration, the town must have grown, minimally, ten times each April. While there are no photographs of turn-of-the-century Deer River, the census records point to a similar scene. The town had a population of just 502 in 1900, only a quarter of them women.

## FIVE. "SUCH PEOPLE MAY INVADE THE CITY"

1 For early American homelessness, see Kenneth Kusmer, *Down and Out, on the Road: The Homeless in American History* (Oxford: Oxford University Press, 2002); and Ruth Wallis Herndon, *Unwelcome Americans: Living on the Margin in Early New England* (Philadelphia: University of Pennsylvania Press, 2001). Most scholarship on hobos in American history focuses on the late nineteenth century including Roger A. Bruns, *Knights of the Road: A Hobo History* (Methuen: New York, 1980); Higbie, *Indispensable Outcasts*; Tim Cresswell, *The Tramp in America* (London: Reaktion Books, 2001); Todd Depastino, *Citizen Hobo: How a Century of Homelessness Shaped America* (Chicago: University of Chicago Press, 2003). For an excellent overview, see Alan Bloom, "Toward a History of Homelessness," *Journal of Urban History* 31, no. 6 (September 2005): 907–17.

2 Kusmer, *Down and Out, on the Road*, 111–12.

3 There is an enormous literature, particularly in human geography, on the attempt in the late nineteenth century to "know" populations. Much of it builds, as I do, on the Foucauldian idea that the modern state controls not by brute power, but by the panopticonic power of making populations transparent, knowable, and observable, otherwise known as "governmentality." For the best recent scholarship on maps, knowledge, and human geography, see Pamela K. Gilbert's *Mapping the Victorian Social Body* (New York: State University of New York Press, 2004).

4 For more, see Joel E. Black, "Space and Status in Chicago's Legal Landscapes," *Journal of Planning History* 12, no. 3 (2013): 228–32; and Gilbert, *Mapping the Victorian Social Body*.

5 Kusmer, *Down and Out, on the Road* and Cresswell, *The Tramp in America*, 10.

6 Cresswell, *The Tramp in America*, 70–74.

7 Cresswell, *The Tramp in America*, 15.

8 Seth Rockman, *Scraping By: Wage Labor, Slavery, and Survival in Early Baltimore* (Baltimore: Johns Hopkins University Press, 2009), 161.

9 For more on the ties between laboring men and domestic rhetoric, see Paul Michel Taillon, "'What We Want Is Good, Sober Men': Masculinity, Respectability and the Railroad Brotherhoods, c. 1870–1910," *Journal of Social History* 36, no. 2 (Winter 2002): 319–38.

10 Cresswell, *The Tramp in America*, 92–97.

11 Martin, "The Life of a Lumber Camp Cook." This was a common construction of manhood in itinerant working conditions. For instance, one miner in late nineteenth-century British Columbia wrote that "generally gold diggers are not marrying men. They work, spend their money on drink, and work again." A Returned Digger cited in Adele Perry, *On the Edge of Empire: Gender, Race, and the Making of British Columbia, 1849–1871* (Toronto: University of Toronto Press, 2001), 30.

12 For demographics of the nineteenth-century vagrant population, see Mary Wyman, *Hoboes: Bindlestiffs, Fruit Tramps, and the Harvesting of the West* (New York: Hill and Wang, 2010); and Kusmer, *Down and Out, on the Road*. Higbie differs in his interpretation and insists that a much smaller percentage of the vagrant poor were women. Higbie, *Indispensable Outcasts*.

13 Journal of Frederick C. Mills, as quoted in Gregory R. Woirol, "Men on the Road; Early Twentieth-Century Surveys of Itinerant Labor in California," *California History* 70, no. 2 (Summer 1991), 198.

14 *Illinois Farmer V*, November 11, 1860 as quoted in Higbie, *Indispensable Outcasts*, 25. The bird metaphor is a running thread—for instance, the *Virginia Enterprise* of Virginia, Minnesota, reported on March 29, 1907, that "with the return of the robins the festive lumberjack and his roll are again in evidence."

15 Hill, "Life in a Logging Camp," 702; "Lumberjacks Coming West," *Evening Times* (Grand Forks, North Dakota), March 8, 1906.

16 This is not to say that no one *tried* to control the tide. While this chapter will focus primarily on the geographic methods of containment, it's worth noting that other, harsher methods existed, including imprisonment and even the whipping post. Heather Tapley, "The Making of Hobo Masculinities," *Canadian Review of American Studies* 44, no. 1 (2014): 24–43.

17 "Lumberjack Rush on Cities Begins," *Minneapolis Star*, April 3, 1906.

18 Higbie, *Indespensible Outcasts*, 117.

19 Frank A. Johnson, Diary, May 14, 1871, Frank A. Johnson Papers, P2217, Minnesota Historical Society, St. Paul, Minnesota.

20 Brotherton, "Early Logging Days."

21 Kromer, "Thorpe, 1968"; Nelligan, *The Life of a Lumberman*, 109; *Virginia (Minn.) Enterprise*, March 29, 1912.

22 Maud Garlick interview with Hope Mineau, Forest History Oral History Project, Minnesota Historical Society, St. Paul, Minnesota.

23 Grattan, "Dear Little Diary"; for more on outsiders' views of the spree, see "Amacoy Lake: Reminiscences of Lillian M. Granger" (unpublished manuscript, n.d.), Robert E. Inabit Papers, Wisconsin Historical Society, Eau Claire Area Research Center, Eau Claire, Wisconsin.

24 "She Made Him Move," *Times Herald* (Port Huron, Michigan), November 2, 1891.

25 Hill, "Life in a Logging Camp," 702.

26 Catherine Lee, "*Prostitution and Victorian Society* Revisited: The Contagious Diseases Acts in Kent," *Women's History Review* 21, no. 2 (2012): 301–16; for more on the ways the same ideology was enacted outside the Contagious Diseases Acts, see Phillip Howell, "A Private Contagious Diseases Act: Prostitution and Public Space in Victorian Cambridge," *Journal of Historical Geography* 26, no. 3 (July 2000): 376–402. For more on the equivalence between moral and physical diseases, see Gilbert, *Mapping the Victorian Social Body*.

27 In taking seriously the metaphoric use of language to describe lumberjacks as either natural disasters or moral contagions, I am building on the work of Edmund Russell in *War and Nature: Fighting Humans and Insects with Chemicals from World War I to Silent Spring* (Cambridge: Cambridge University Press, 2001) as well as the excellent synthetic work of Gerald V. O'Brien who draws together the language of several "alarm periods" using metaphor theory to examine how and why the language of contagion is so often used to characterize marginalized groups in *Contagion and the National Body: The Organism Metaphor in American Thought* (New York: Routledge, 2018). While O'Brien focuses on decay within what Americans conceive of as "the national body" and organism, and Russell focuses on the destruction of outside threats to that body, both argue that the use of metaphorical language and imagery was not simply descriptive. Metaphor primes us to make further connection points and directly paves the way for policies that treat people as the metaphors we use to describe them.

28 For more on the careers of prostitutes in the lake states, see Joel Best, *Controlling Vice: Regulating Brothel Prostitution in St. Paul, 1865–1883* (Columbus: Ohio State University Press, 1998); Joan M. Jensen, "Sexuality on a Northern Frontier: The Gendering and Disciplining of Rural Wisconsin Women, 1850–1920," *Agricultural History* 73, no. 2 (Spring 1999): 136–67; Penny A. Peterson, *Minneapolis Madams: The Lost History of Prostitution on the Riverfront* (Minneapolis: University of Minnesota Press, 2013); K. A. Ketz, E. J. Abel, and A. J. Schmidt, "Public Image and Private Reality: An Analysis of Difference in a Nineteenth-Century St. Paul Bordello," *Historical Archaeology* 39, no. 1 (2005): 74–88; and Mara L. Keire, "The Vice Trust: A Reinterpretation of the White Slavery Scare in the United States, 1907–1917," *Journal of Social History* 35, no. 1 (Autumn 2001): 5–41.

29 Bonne Shucha, "White Slavery in the Northwoods: Early U.S. Anti-Sex Trafficking and Its Continuing Relevance to Trafficking Reform," *William and Mary Journal of Women and the Law* 23 (2016): 94.

30 Melissa Hayes, "Sex in the Witness Stand: Erotic Sensationalism, Voyeurism, Sexual Boasting and Bawdy Humor in the Nineteenth-Century Illinois Courts," *Law and History Review* 32, no. 1 (February 2014): 149–202.

31 Shucha, "White Slavery in the Northwoods," 81–84.

32 "The Sexual Enslavement of Woman," *Fair Play* (Valley Falls, Kansas), November 23, 1888.

33 "Crimes Against Women," *The Woman's Tribune* (Beatrice, Nebraska), February 2, 1889; "The Wisconsin Lumber Dens," *Vigilance* (New York, New York), Issue 12, December 1888; "The Horrors of the Wisconsin Lumber Camps," *Vigilance* (New York, New York), Issue 11, November 1888.

34 "North Woods Dens," *Jackson Citizen*, June 19, 1888, quoted in Shucha, "White Slavery in the Northwoods," 89. For a thorough description of such reports, see Jensen, "Sexuality on a Northern Frontier," 152–53.

35 Shucha, "White Slavery in the Northwoods," 91. Fielding also admitted privately to Dr. Bushnell and Governor Jeremiah Rusk that he only ever visited one brothel, so his investigation can hardly be considered comprehensive.

36 State of Wisconsin and Howard Teasdale, "Report and Recommendations of the Wisconsin Legislative Committee to Investigate the White Slave Traffic and Kindred Subjects" (Madison, WI: Democrat Printing Company, 1914).

37 Shucha, "White Slavery in the Northwoods," 80–86, and Hayes, "Sex in the Witness Stand," 149–60.

38 "Social Crimes," *Ashland* (Wisc.) *Weekly News*, January 16, 1898.

39 Letter from James Fielding to Jeremiah Rusk (December 20, 1887), quoted in Shucha, "White Slavery in the Northwoods," 90–91.

40 *Report of the Vice Commission of Minneapolis to His Honor, James C. Haynes, Mayor* (Minneapolis, 1911), 26.

41 *Report of the Vice Commission*, 26.

42 State of Wisconsin and Teasdale, "Report," 15.

43 *Report of the Vice Commission*, 75.

44 "Gov. Hoard in His Office," *Milwaukee Sentinel*, February 1, 1889, quoted in Shucha, "White Slavery in the Northwoods," 90.

45 Goff, *Shantytown, USA*, 79.

46 For an overview of the demographic development of Northwoods cities, see John R. Borchert, *America's Northern Heartland* (Minneapolis: University of Minnesota Press, 1987).

47 For more on the vagrancy laws that worked to police "degenerate" manhood by isolating vagrant men to a particular section of town, see Black, "Space and Status in Chicago's

Legal Landscapes." There is an interesting change in the idea of separating out vice districts, particularly red-light districts, in the early twentieth century as attitudes toward capitalism among reformers experienced a sea change. While regulatory structures of the late nineteenth century saw vice as something to be separated out, Progressive Era women from the 1910s onward began to reframe the question of prostitution. No longer blaming individual women for their moral degeneracy, the language of red-light district reform increasingly focused on the role of pimps and the "Vice Trust," mirroring antitrust language (and antisemitic language) to blame capitalists for the victimhood of prostitutes. Keire, "The Vice Trust."

48  For more on the policing of lumberjack areas, see Kilar, *Michigan's Lumbertowns*, 113–23. The extent to which the law was willing to look the other way was, in some places, surprising; in 1877 the marshall of Muskegon, Michigan, was reprimanded when he was caught, after hours, in a brothel.

49  For more on the larger cities, see Kilar, *Michigan's Lumbertowns*; Faue, *Community of Suffering and Struggle*; and Matthew J. Friday, *Among the Sturdy Pioneers: The Birth of the Cheboygan Area as a Lumbering Community, 1778–1935* (Victoria, B.C.: Trafford, 2006).

50  "Hugo's Position," *Labor World* (Duluth, Minnesota), January 13, 1900.

51  Cox, *The Lumberman's Frontier*; Ray Allen Billington, *Frederick Jackson Turner: Historian, Scholar, Teacher* (New York: Oxford University Press, 1973); Kilar, *Michigan's Lumbertowns*.

52  For more on Hurley, see Julie Kenyon, "'Little Girl Bay,' Frontier, and Folklore: Fitzgerald's Use of Regional History in *The Great Gatsby*," *F. Scott Fitzgerald Review* 16 (2018): 109–26.

53  J. C. Ryan Papers, Minnesota Historical Society, Forest History Center, Grand Rapids, Minnesota.

54  "Seney," *Northern Tribune* (Cheboygan, Michigan), May 28, 1885.

55  Nevue, "'Incredible' Lumberjack Stories Debunked by Veteran of Camps."

56  Zetterstrom, "The Story of a Logging Town." For more on Seney and the smaller boomtowns culture, see Nelligan, *The Life of a Lumberman*; Lewis C. Reiman, *Incredible Seney* (AuTrain, Mich.: Avery Color Studios, 1982); "Gay Days in the Woods," *Milwaukee Journal*, March 2, 1947; Porter, "Northwoods Pioneers"; Kromer, "Thorpe, 1968"; and William S. Crowe, "A Lumberjack" (unpublished manuscript, 1952), Bentley Historical Library, Ann Arbor, Michigan.

57  "The Wisconsin Lumber Dens," *Vigilance* (New York, New York), Issue 12, December 1888, 2.

58  Holbrook, *Holy Old Mackinaw*; "The Wisconsin Lumber Dens," *Vigilance* (New York, New York), Issue 12, December, 1888, 2.

59 Gills, "Navigating the Landscape of Assimilation," 68–70.

60 Monthly Report for June 1881, Mackinac Indian Agency, RG 75, Letters Received by the Office of Indian Affairs, 12613: 1881, National Archives, Great Lakes Region, Chicago, cited in Gills, "Navigating the Landscape of Assimilation," 70.

61 Rockman, *Scraping By*, 2.

62 For excellent overviews of the ideological draw of the home and the reaction to the threat posed by tramps, see Depastino, *Citizen Hobo*; Cresswell, *The Tramp in America*, esp. 14–17; and Ted Grossardt, "Harvest(ing) Hoboes: The Production of Labor Organization through the Wheat Harvest," *Agricultural History* 70, no. 2 (Spring 1996): 283–301.

63 Higbie, *Indispensable Outcasts*, 4.

## SIX. FIVE HUNDRED DRUNKS IN THE STREET

1 For a very good recent example of this work, see Martin, "'So Nobly Struggling for Their Manhood.'"

2 Mark Walker, "'Manliness is the Backbone of Our Nature': Masculinity and Class Identities among Nineteenth Century Railroad Workers in West Oakland, California," *SCA Proceedings* 25 (March/April 2011): 1–11. The need to blur the lines and realize the instability of the categories of "rough" and "respectable" has been a central theme of labor historians who pay attention to the construction of late nineteenth-century masculinity. For more on the tensions between late nineteenth-century working-class masculinities, see Peter Way, "Evil Humors and Ardent Spirits: The Rough Culture of Canal Construction Laborers," *Journal of American History* 79, no. 4 (March 1993): 1397–1428; Taillon, "'What We Want Is Good, Sober Men'"; Gregory L. Kaster, "Labour's True Man: Organized Workingmen and the Language of Manliness in the USA, 1827–1877," *Gender & History* 13, no. 1 (April 2001): 24–64; Winter, *Making Men, Making Class*; Meyer, "Rough Manhood"; and Baron, "Masculinity, the Embodied Male Worker, and the Historian's Gaze."

3 For more on the choice to tramp and "opt out" of the industrial capitalist system, see Kusmer, *Down and Out, on the Road*, 9.

4 Way, "Evil Humors and Ardent Spirits," 1401.

5 For an excellent example of this method of understanding seemingly irrational violence, see Moore, "'Them's Fighting Words.'"

6 Paul Michael Taillon, *Good, Reliable, White Men: Railroad Brotherhoods, 1887–1917* (Urbana: University of Illinois Press, 2009); and Winter, *Making Men, Making Class*.

7 Here I am building off the work of Paul Michael Taillon who suggests the inadequacy of this dichotomy in "'What We Want Is Good, Sober Men.'"

8 Higbie, *Indispensable Outcasts*, 1. For more on laborers' attitudes toward work, see Michael Kaplan, "New York City Tavern Violence and the Creation of a Working-Class Male Identity," *Journal of the Early Republic* 15, no. 4 (Winter 1995): 591–617.

9 Fitzmaurice, *The Shanty Boy*, 115.

10 For more on the larger cities, see Kilar, *Michigan's Lumbertowns*; Faue, *Community of Suffering and Struggle*; and Friday, *Among the Sturdy Pioneers*.

11 Anette Atkins, "At Home in the Heart of the City," *Minnesota History* 58, no. 5/6 (Spring–Summer 2003): 302.

12 "Gay Days in the Woods" *Milwaukee Journal*, March 2, 1947; Nelligan, *The Life of a Lumberman*, 185; "Funny 'Lumberjack' . . . His Spring Vacation," *Minneapolis Journal*, April 13, 1901.

13 The story, though a slow starter, takes quite a good turn from here. The lady in question seems to be obeying and walks as far as the swinging doors before grabbing the cop and starting a fight that eventually earned her, in that bar at least, the right to drink. Nelson, "Reminisces."

14 For instance, John Nelligan remembers the somewhat unfortunately named Nina Mould of Florence, Wisconsin, best of all, claiming that "the name Nina Mould was well known and heard in the mines, in the woods, everywhere." Nelligan, *The Life of a Lumberman*, 185.

15 Roy Rosenzweig, *Eight Hours for What We Will* (Cambridge: Cambridge University Press, 1983), 35–39; and Jon M. Kingsdale, "The 'Poor Man's Club': Social Functions of the Urban Working Class Saloon," *American Quarterly* 24, no. 4 (October 1973): 472–89. For a distinctly less laudatory take on saloon life, see Way, "Evil Humors and Ardent Spirits."

16 Rosenzweig, *Eight Hours for What We Will*, 38.

17 Baron, "Masculinity, the Embodied Male Worker, and the Historian's Gaze." For more on brotherhoods, see Anna Clark, *The Struggle for the Breeches: Gender and the Making of the British Working-Class* (Berkeley: University of California Press, 2005).

18 Grossardt, "Harvest(ing) Hoboes," 292. For more on the creation of communities and collective identity around the working-class space of the saloon, see Michael Ripmeester, "Mines, Homes, and Halls: Place and Identity as a Gold Miner in Rossland, British Columbia, 1898–1901," *Canadian Geographer* 38, no. 2 (1994): 98–110. Ripmeester notes that while any communal space can help foster identity, what particularly creates a cohesive internal identity for a community is the networking of several oft-visited spaces. For lumberjacks, their mobility made this all that much stronger: their network of spaces stretched from the cities into the woods, linking together multiple work cities, small towns, and urban slums on a regional scale.

19 The lumbermen—a term used not for the laborers within the industry but rather its owners—found their own version of fraternity in the Concatenated Order of the Hoo-Hoo, formed in 1893 to "engender among members of the lumber craft a spirit of understanding and to build health, happiness, and long life among them." It was founded in Arkansas but drew membership from across the country, holding its

conventions predominantly in the Northwoods. The full minutes of these conventions, led by the ceremonial leader, The Snark, are preserved at the University of Wisconsin and have all the usual delights of fraternal orders, mostly including mayors welcoming gentlemen to drink freely in their cities and, annually, pages upon pages of complaints about the weather. Other offices included the Senior and Junior Hoo-Hoo, the Bojum, Srivenoter, Jabberwock, and Arcanoper. *The Bulletin: A Monthly Journal Devoted to the Hoo-Hoo* (Nashville, Tenn: Concentrated Order of the Hoo-Hoo, 1897–1915); for more, see Farrar Newberry, "The Concatenated Order of the Hoo-Hoo," *Arkansas Historical Quarterly* 22, no. 4 (Winter 1963): 301–10.

20 Jack London, *John Barleycorn* (New York: Century, 1914), 84. Rosenzweig, *Eight Hours for What We Will*, 62, 60. For examples of coincidental meetings, see Fitzmaurice, *The Shanty Boy*; Nelligan, *The Life of a Lumberman*; Dye, *Lumber Camp Life in Michigan*, 43–45; Hill, "Life in a Logging Camp"; Kuarala, "Memoirs"; and Kromer, "Thorpe, 1968," among others.

21 Griffin, "Forests and Logging in the Vicinity of Hibbing, Minn." For more descriptions of logging saloons, see Fitzmaurice, *The Shanty Boy*; Nelligan, *The Life of a Lumberman*; and Kilar, *Michigan's Lumbertowns*, 71–75.

22 Frank A. Johnson, "Memoirs" (unpublished manuscript, n.d.), Frank A. Johnson Papers, Minnesota Historical Society, St. Paul, Minnesota.

23 "Early Justice," WPA article for *Grand Rapids Herald Review*, unedited manuscript in WPA notes, Minnesota Historical Society, St. Paul, Minnesota. For more on excessive drinking, see Kilar, *Michigan's Lumbertowns*; Nelligan, *The Life of a Lumberman*; "Funny 'Lumberjack' . . . His Spring Vacation," *Minneapolis Journal*, April 13, 1901; Hill, "Life in a Logging Camp," 700; "Those Days of Yore," *Princeton (Minn.) Union*, February 18, 1897; Rose Conklin, "Reminiscences" (1969), S133, Beltrami County Historical Society, Bemidji, Minnesota.

24 Ceylon Childs Lincoln, "Reminiscences, 1910" (unpublished manuscript), SC2270, Wisconsin Historical Society, Madison, Wisconsin; Interview of Alton Van Camp and John Boyd by Dennis East and Joe Smith.

25 Hill, "Life in a Logging Camp," 714.

26 In thinking about the purpose and shape of violence I'm grateful to the work of southern and western historians who have previously explored this, especially Lorien Foote, who took the question of violence for honor outside of the South in *The Gentlemen and the Roughs*. For more on honor and violence, see Bertram Wyatt-Brown, *The Shaping of Southern Culture: Honor, Grace, and War, 1760s–1890s* (Chapel Hill: University of North Carolina Press, 2001); Daniel J. Herman, *Hell on the Range: A Story of Honor, Conscience, and Culture in the West, 1880–1930* (New Haven, Conn.: Yale University Press, 2010); and Moore, "'Them's Fighting Words.'"

27 Kilar, *Michigan's Lumbertowns*, 123–28; Nelligan, *The Life of a Lumberman*, 61; Dye, *Lumber Camp Life in Michigan*, 43–45; Kelly, "An Observer in the Woods."

28 As previously noted, while I found no records of violence toward Anishinaabe men by their coworkers in camps, outside of camp violence against Native men by Euro-American jacks was constant. But even by these standards, Nelligan's casual violence toward Native Americans never fails to astonish. The story this time was as simple as it seems: he saw several Native American river hogs standing on a dam and, for no reason whatsoever, took it upon himself to push them off. Nelligan, *The Life of a Lumberman*.

29 For more stories of violence, see Herman Bayne, *Memories of Herman Bayne* (Benzonia, Mich.: Benzie Area Historical Society, 1988), 11–28; Dan Carey, *Tales of a Michigan Lumberjack* (Mount Pleasant, Mich.: self-pub., 1950), 10; Ellis, *Pick-Ups and a Horse*, 11; Lynde Hartt, "Notes on a Michigan Lumber Town"; "Gay Days in the Woods" *Milwaukee Journal*, March 2, 1947.

30 *Times Herald* (Port Huron, Michigan), April 17, 1908; "Two Men Are Clubbed to Death," *Escanaba (Mich.) Morning Press*, April 27, 1911.

31 Johnson, Diary, May 14–28.

32 "Gay Days in the Woods," *Milwaukee Journal*, March 2, 1947.

33 Ira Bellaire, "Tales of Old Seney," *Escanaba (Mich.) Daily Press*, June 8, 1930, 8; Kilar, *Michigan's Lumbertowns*; W. W. Bartlett, "Glimpses into Early Day Wisconsin Logging Camps," 11 (unpublished manuscript, n.d.), Bartlett Papers, Wisconsin Historical Society, Madison, Wisconsin.

34 Lynde Hartt, "Notes on a Michigan Lumber Town," 103.

35 Grattan, "Dear Little Diary."

36 This same reporter goes on to give, for example, the following story from the Sawdust Flats of Muskegon: "Black Jap, one of the Flats girls, was waltzing with a handsome lumberjack when one of the imported sisters cut in. Black Jap resented the method her co-worker had used—a hefty wallop to the jaw—and the two rivals were soon tearing at each other's hair and ripping clothing. The other dancers stepped politely aside until the fracas was over. Then the party resumed." "Gay Days in the Woods" *Milwaukee Journal*, March 2, 1947.

37 Nelligan, *The Life of a Lumberman*, 27–28 (emphasis mine).

38 Nelligan, *The Life of a Lumberman*, 156.

39 Nelligan, *The Life of a Lumberman*, 158.

40 J. C. Ryan, *Early Loggers in Minnesota* (Minnesota Timber Producers Association, 1976), 40.

41 "Gay Days in the Woods," *Milwaukee Journal*, March 2, 1947.

42 Nelligan, *The Life of a Lumberman*, 185.

43 Grattan, "Dear Little Diary."

44 Ruth Rosen, *The Lost Sisterhood* (Baltimore: Johns Hopkins University Press, 1983), 5.

45 Interview of Alton Van Camp and John Boyd by Dennis East and Joe Smith.

46 Grossardt, "Harvest(ing) Hoboes," 292.

47 London, *John Barleycorn*, 30.

48 "Gov. Hoard in His Office," *Milwaukee Sentinel*, February 1, 1889.

## PART III. IN MEMORY

1 I am deeply indebted to the theoretical framework of Christine M. DeLucia's *Memory Lands: King Philip's War and the Place of Violence in the Northeast* (New Haven, Conn.: Yale University Press, 2018). Her work roots memory, something that can seem abstract, to place, bridging the gaps between environmental history and the study of cultural memory.

## SEVEN. THE ONLY AMERICAN HERO

1 Suzanne Robinson, "Popularization or Perversion? Folklore and Folksong in Britten's *Paul Bunyan* (1941)," *American Music* 34, no. 1 (Spring 2016): 1, 3; Richard M. Dorson, "Paul Bunyan in the News, 1939–41 (Part I)," *Western Folklore* 15, no. 1 (January 1956): 33; Richard M. Dorson, "Paul Bunyan in the News, 1939–41 (Part II)," *Western Folklore* 15, no. 3 (July 1956): 179–93; Edmonds, *Out of the Northwoods*. For methodology and an understanding of how and why folklore deviates from the stories at its roots, I am indebted to Scott Reynolds Nelson, *Steel Drivin' Man: John Henry, the Untold Story of an American Legend* (Oxford: Oxford University Press, 2006).

2 Dorson, "Paul Bunyan in the News, 1939–41 (Part I)," 26.

3 In what surely must have been a wrenchingly irritating move, the publishers of Richard M. Dorson's *American Folklore and the Historian* (Chicago: University of Chicago Press, 1971) adorned the cover of his book—which included his essay on "fakelore"—with a picture of none other than Paul Bunyan. Alan Dundes, "Nationalistic Inferiority Complexes and the Fabrication of Fakelore: A Reconsideration of Ossian, the Kinder- und Hausmärchen, the Kalevala, and Paul Bunyan," *Journal of Folklore Research* 22, no. 1 (April 1985): 11.

4 Dorson, "Paul Bunyan in the News, 1939–41 (Part I)," 26. I have used Dorson here as shorthand to stand in for the almost absurd amount of ink spilled on the question of Paul's authenticity. The best and most authoritative conclusion (which is that, essentially, he was based on folk stories in the Northwoods but drastically changed by commercial presses) is in Michael Edmonds's exhaustively researched *Out of the Northwoods*. For more, see Dorson, "Paul Bunyan in the News, 1939–41 (Part I)"; "Paul Bunyan in the News, 1939–41 (Part II)"; and "Paul Bunyan in the News, 1939–41 (Part

III)," *Western Folklore* 15, no. 4 (October 1956): 247–61; Edith Fowke, "In Defence of Paul Bunyan," *New York Folklore* 5 (Summer 1979): 43–51; Daniel Hoffman, *Paul Bunyan: Last of the Frontier Demigods* (Lincoln: University of Nebraska Press, 1983); Ellen J. Stekert, "The False Issue of Folklore vs. 'Fakelore': Was Paul Bunyan a Hoax?," *Journal of Forest History* 30, no. 4 (October 1986): 180–81; Dundes, "Nationalistic Inferiority Complexes and the Fabrication of Fakelore"; Rebecca Tisdel Rapport, "Paul Bunyan: Hero of the North Woods," *Language Arts* 56, no. 4 (April 1979): 394–99.

5 *Pioneer Press* (St. Paul, Minnesota), August 1, 1941, quoted in Dorson, "Paul Bunyan in the News, 1939–41 (Part III)," 253.

6 There are far too many excellent works on American historical memory to cite them all, but for some excellent starting points, see Stephen H. Browne, "Remembering Crispus Attucks: Race, Rhetoric, and the Politics of Commemoration," *Quarterly Journal of Speech* 85, no. 2 (1999): 169–87; David Blight, *Race and Reunion: The Civil War in American Memory* (Cambridge, Mass.: Harvard University Press, 2002); William Blair, *Cities of the Dead: Contesting the Memory of the Civil War in the South, 1865–1914* (Chapel Hill: University of North Carolina Press, 2004); Mitch Kachun, *Festivals of Freedom: Memory and Meaning in African American Emancipation Celebrations, 1808–1915* (Amherst: University of Massachusetts Press, 2003); Karl Jacoby, *Shadows at Dawn: An Apache Massacre and the Violence of History* (New York: Penguin, 2009); Monica Perales, *Smeltertown: Making and Remembering a Southwest Border Community* (Chapel Hill: University of North Carolina Press, 2010); Caroline Janney, *Remembering the Civil War Dead: Reunion and the Limits of Reconciliation* (Chapel Hill: University of North Carolina Press, 2013); Janice Hume, *Popular Media and the American Revolution: Shaping Collective Memory* (New York: Routledge, 2013); Ari Kelman, *A Misplaced Massacre: Struggling Over the Memory of Sand Creek* (Cambridge, Mass.: Harvard University Press, 2014); Lisa Tetrault, *The Myth of Seneca Falls: Memory and the Women's Suffrage Movement, 1848–1898* (Chapel Hill: University of North Carolina Press, 2014); David W. Grua, *Surviving Wounded Knee: The Lakotas and the Politics of Memory* (Oxford: Oxford University Press, 2015); DeLucia, *Memory Lands*; Adam Domby, *The False Cause: Fraud, Fabrication, and White Supremacy in Confederate Memory* (Charlottesville: University of Virginia Press, 2020); Hattem, *Past and Prologue*.

7 Both *Scribner's* and *The Atlantic* were cornerstones of well-read coastal households at the turn of the century, and unsurprisingly their writers often came from the same well-educated audiences they served. The *National Cyclopedia of American Biography* (New York: J. T. White, 1900), 17:273.

8 Lynde Hartt, "Notes on a Michigan Lumber Town," 102; Hill, "Life in a Logging Camp," 699.

9 Hill, "Life in a Logging Camp," 704–5.

10  Lynde Hartt, "Notes on a Michigan Lumber Town," 102, 105.

11  Hill, "Life in a Logging Camp," 713; Lynde Hartt, "Notes on a Michigan Lumber Town," 105.

12  Lynde Hartt, "Notes on a Michigan Lumber Town"; Hill, "Life in a Logging Camp," 702. In contrast, a much earlier version of local color from 1860 lingers on the beauty of nature and the work itself. While the "simple charm" of the camp is mentioned and illustrated, there is no mention of the bonds of brotherhood, nor of the emotional honesty and simplicity of the men themselves. Most noticeably, while the author clearly admires lumberjacks, he displays no longing for their fraternity. Charles Hallock, "Life among the Loggers," *Harper's New Monthly Magazine*, December 1859, 437–54.

13  Miles Orvell, *The Real Thing: Imitation and Authenticity in American Culture, 1880–1940* (Chapel Hill: University of North Carolina Press, 2014), 80–99. For more on authenticity in American culture, see Jonna Eagle, "Introduction: Power, Pain, and the Cultural Work of Authenticity in American Studies and Beyond," *American Quarterly* 73, no. 1 (March 2021): 123–33; Kaylan C. Schwarz and J. Patric Williams, "Introduction to the Social Construction of Identity and Authenticity," in *Studies on the Social Construction of Identity and Authenticity*, ed. Kaylan C. Schwarz and J. Patric Williams (New York: Routledge, 2020), 1–24.

14  For more, see Louis S. Warren, *Buffalo Bill's America: William Cody and the Wild West Show* (New York: Knopf, 2005), 417–25. For Cody's insistence that he was so authentic he could not act nor read a script, see his bizarre self-penned chapter in one of the dime novels written in his honor: Prentice Ingraham, *Adventures of Buffalo Bill from Boyhood to Manhood*, Beedle's Boy's Library of Sport, Story and Adventure 1, no. 1 (New York: Beadle and Adams, 1882).

15  Jackson Lears, *No Place of Grace: Antimodernism and the Transformation of American Culture, 1880–1920* (Chicago: University of Chicago Press, 1994), 36.

16  Erik Larson, *The Devil in the White City* (New York: Vintage, 2004).

17  Orvell, *The Real Thing*, 40, 144.

18  Charles Lindholm, "The Rise of Expressive Authenticity," *Anthropological Quarterly* 86, no. 2 (Spring 2013): 369–70. For a full exploration of the "unreality" of modern life, see Lears, *No Place of Grace*.

19  Henry James, *The Bostonians* (Baltimore: Penguin, 2001), 290.

20  Hill, "Life in a Logging Camp," 703.

21  "Logging Camp Life," *Democratic Northwest and Henry County News* (Napoleon, Ohio), March 5, 1896.

22  John F. Kasson, *Houdini, Tarzan and the Perfect Man: The White Male Body and the Challenge of Modernity in America* (New York: Hill and Wang, 2001), 32. For more on the interest in outdoorsmanship and the connection between sports, athletics, and

citizenship in the turn-of-the-century mind, see Malcolm McLaughlin, "American Recreation: Sportsmanship and the New Nationalism, 1900–1910," *Journal of American Studies* 54, no. 5 (2020): 839–69.

23 Nelligan, *The Life of a Lumberman*, 27–28.

24 This was true even at a young age. Educational reformer G. Stanley Hall obsessed over presenting boys only with idealized white, male bodies in his curriculum development. Exposure, without explicit disavowal, to "weaker" bodies might, he theorized, lead to moral and physical wreckage. Mickenzie Fasteland, "Reading the Antimodern Way: G. Stanley Hall's *Adolescence* and Imperialist Reading for White American Boys," *Journal of the History of Childhood and Youth* 12, no. 1 (Winter 2019): 13.

25 Anxieties about being identified as homosexual were so widespread that men could be fired from work in camps—far from the emerging gay life in New York—for smoking cigarettes, nicknamed "fairy sticks," rather than pipes. Kevin Murphy, *Political Manhood: Red Bloods, Mollycoddles, and the Politics of Progressive Era Reform* (New York: Columbia University Press, 2010), 11–20; George Chauncey, *Gay New York: Gender, Urban Culture and the Makings of the Gay Male World, 1890–1940* (New York: Basic Books, 1994).

26 Jonathan D. Martin, "'The Grandest and Most Cosmopolitan Object Teacher': *Buffalo Bill's Wild West* and the Politics of American Identity, 1883–1899," *Radical History Review*, no. 66 (Fall 1996): 94.

27 Jennifer Moskowitz, "The Cultural Myth of the Cowboy, or, How the West Was Won," *Americana: The Journal of American Popular Culture, 1900 to Present* 5, no. 1 (Spring 2006): https://americanpopularculture.com/journal/articles/spring_2006/moskowitz.htm.

28 Murdoch, *The American West*, 22. For more on the invention of the western myth, see Moore, *Cow Boys and Cattle Men*; Richard M. Dorson, "The Lumberjack Code," *Western Folklore* 8, no. 4 (October 1949): 358–65; Moskowitz, "The Cultural Myth of the Cowboy"; Richard W. Slatta, "Making and Unmaking Myths of the American Frontier," *European Journal of American Culture* 29, no. 2 (July 2010): 81–92.

29 Jefferson D. Slagle, "The Heirs to Buffalo Bill: Performing Authenticity in the Dime Western," *Canadian Review of American Studies* 30, no. 2 (2009): 119–38.

30 For a wonderful exploration of this phenomenon in a more modern context, see Gordon, *Time Travel*.

31 Nelligan, *The Life of a Lumberman*, 27–28, 178, 135; Federal Writers' Project, "Grand Rapids: The Story of a Logging Town" (unpublished manuscript, 1938), WPA Notes, Minnesota Historical Society, St. Paul, Minnesota. There is a parallel that almost blends into a sameness in the way that folklorists and admirers described both cowboys and lumberjacks. Both were described as chivalrous knights, as clean, innocent, open, and honest. John Lomax said that cowboys had a "certain wholesome strength, cleanliness and variety in [their] profanity," a statement that rings true of the romanticized image

of lumberjacks put forward by his fellow folklorist Richard Dorson, who described the fighting of his subjects as "honest." Lomax cited in Moore, *Cow Boys and Cattle Men*; Dorson, "The Lumberjack Code," 35; and Simon J. Bronner, ed., *Manly Traditions: The Folk Roots of American Masculinities* (Bloomington: Indiana University Press, 2005).

32 Landsberg, *Prosthetic Memory*.

33 J. Dwight Hines, "In Pursuit of Experience: The Postindustrial Gentrification of the American West," *Ethnography* 2, no. 2 (June 2001): 292. For more on anthropological and ethnographical understandings of the search for authenticity, see R. Handler and W. Saxon, "Dyssimulation: Reflexivity, Narrative and the Quest for Authenticity in 'Living History,'" *Cultural Anthropology* 3, no. 3 (August 1988): 242–60; and Carol J. Steiner and Yvette Reisinger, "Understanding Existential Authenticity," *Annals of Tourism Research* 33, no. 2 (April 2006): 299–318.

34 For more on Hall's ideas about boyhood education, see Bederman, *Manliness and Civilization*, 77–121; Fasteland, "Reading the Antimodern Way"; and Thomas Fallace, "Recapitulation Theory and the New Education: Race, Culture, Imperialism, and Pedagogy, 1894–1916," *Curriculum Inquiry* 42, no. 4 (2012): 510–33. Fallace, in particular, explores the widespread impact of Hall's ideas and the broad acceptance of recapitulation theory as a key underpinning of boys' educational models.

35 Deloria, *Playing Indian*, 95–100. For more on recapitulation, see Bederman, *Manliness and Civilization*, chap. 3.

36 G. Stanley Hall quoted in Fasteland, "Reading the Antimodern Way," 7.

37 Ingraham, *Adventures of Buffalo Bill from Boyhood to Manhood*, 5–8, 15.

38 Peter Hobbs, "Epistemology of the Bunkhouse: Lusty Lumberjacks and the Sexual Pedagogy of the Woods," in *Queering the Countryside: New Frontiers in Rural Queer Studies*, ed. Mary L. Gray, Colin R. Johnson, and Brian J. Gilley (New York: New York University Press, 2016), 203–22.

39 Levi Parker Wyman, *The Golden Boys with the Lumberjacks* (New York: A. L. Burt, 1916), 26–29. Wyman wrote dozens of books for A. L. Burt, a New York publisher of boys' adventure stories. The Golden Boys also variously hunted treasure, visited a haunted camp, were "Rescued by Radio," and had an adventure with "Their New Electric Cell," which, while I have been unable to obtain it, seems to be an engine; the story has two stars on Goodreads.

40 Stewart Edward White, *The Adventures of Bobby Orde* (New York: Grosset & Dunlap, 1911), 36.

41 Lears, *No Place of Grace*, 36–42. Lears's analysis of antimodernism among the Gilded Age elite, while now over thirty years old, remains indispensable and influential enough that in 2021 the *American Historical Review* published a reappraisal of the book that argued it served as a turning point in modern historical writing. Andrew Seal, "AHR Reappraisal:

'The Vanished Power of the Usual Reign': Jackson Lears, *No Place of Grace*, and the Struggle for Hegemony in History," *American Historical Review* 126, no. 2 (April 2021), 665–69.

42  Andrew Headbrooke, "Individual Continuity," *The Atlantic*, August 1888, 264. For more on wilderness and out-of-doors exercise as a cure for the ills of turn-of-the-century middle-class ailments including neurasthenia, see Rotundo, *American Manhood*, 185–93 and 227–32; Karen R. Jones, *Epiphany in the Wilderness: Hunting, Nature, and Performance in the Nineteenth-Century American West* (Boulder: University of Colorado Press, 2015), 33–70; Bederman, *Manliness and Civilization*, 82–92; Deloria, *Playing Indian*, 95–118; and E. Anthony Rotundo, "Middle-Class Men and the Solace of Fraternal Ritual," in *Meanings for Manhood: Constructions of Masculinity in Victorian America*, ed. Mark C. Carnes and Clyde Griffen (Chicago: University of Chicago Press, 1990), 37–52.

43  Grace Elizabeth Hale, *A Nation of Outsiders: How the White Middle Class Fell in Love with Rebellion in Postwar America* (Oxford: Oxford University Press, 2011), 3.

44  Peattie, "A Michigan Man."

45  Peattie, "A Michigan Man." For another excellent example, see Ralph Connor's *The Man from Glengarry*, brought to my attention by Hobbs, "Epistemology of the Bunkhouse," 219–20.

## EIGHT. PAPERING OVER A WASTELAND

1  M. M. Gambrill, "Logging in Wisconsin: Experience of an Eastern Kentuckian in Northern Lumber Camps," *Big Sandy News* (Louisa, Kentucky), June 17, 1910. Here there has to be some question of whether this story was Gambrill's or whether he stole it, since a nearly identical story attributing the tales to northern Minnesota appeared in the *Cincinnati Enquirer* nearly six months earlier. Of course, he might have published both. Either way, it hardly matters—both clearly trace the myth as coming from the Northwoods and tell the story the same way. "Frozen Snakes Used as Skids," *Cincinnati Enquirer*, February 5, 1910, 11.

2  Silver Jack, like Paul Bunyan, was an amalgam of stories about various men working in the woods. James Stevens, author of one of the most influential Paul Bunyan books, recalled that "when [he] spent a couple years in Michigan, there were seven or eight Silver Jacks . . . just names that were hung on able fighters." Elwood R. Maunder interview with James Stevens, Seattle, Washington, November 12, 1952, Forest History Society Archives, Durham, North Carolina. For more on Silver Jack, see Holbrook, *Holy Old Mackinaw*. There are dozens of theories as to where the actual *name* Paul Bunyan comes from, although one I have not seen elsewhere is that a man actually named Paul Bunyan lived in the lumbering center of Bemidji, Minnesota, around the turn of the century. The sum total of his existence I can trace, however, is a mention in 1901 that "Paul Bunyan arrived from Minneapolis today" in the *Bemidji (Minn.) Daily Pioneer*

(November 7, 1901), and a record of a laborer by that name living in Milwaukee in the 1910 census. Or equally likely was that he had traveled in the opposite direction to North Dakota and was the Paul Bunyan whom the *Ward County Independent* reported on as, along with Charley Seeley, "building them a neat little bungalow up near the mine and will soon have a comfortable little home in which to entertain their friends." Not much to go by, even by the standards of origins shrouded in time. U.S. Census Bureau, 1910 Federal Census, Milwaukee Ward 16, District 0176; *Ward County Independent* (Minot, North Dakota), September 23, 1915.

3 Gambrill, "Logging in Wisconsin."

4 For the rise of scientific forestry, see Char Miller, *Seeking the Greatest Good: The Conservation Legacy of Gifford Pinchot* (Pittsburgh: University of Pittsburgh Press, 2013).

5 Meier, *Bring Warm Clothes*, 7.

6 Julie Anderson, *I Married a Logger: Life in Michigan's Tall Timber* (New York: Exposition Press, 1951), 3.

7 Walter F. Benjamin, "Reminiscences, 1912" (unpublished manuscript, 1912), Benjamin Papers, P939, Minnesota Historical Society, St. Paul, Minnesota.

8 John Esse interviewing Don Benson, February 5, 1976, Talmoon, Minnesota, Forest History Oral History Project, OH 142.1, Minnesota Historical Society, St. Paul, Minnesota.

9 Tellingly, in the immediate aftermath of the fire, the lumber companies were not mentioned at all as culprits. In the *New York Times* the headlines for the fire mentioned rumors that "enemy agents" had been reported as responsible for the fires. "500 Lives Lost in Forest Fires," *New York Times*, October 18, 1918. For more on the firestorm, see Carroll and Raiter, *Fires of Autumn*.

10 Asher E. Treat, "Kentucky Folksong in Northern Wisconsin," *Journal of American Folklore* 52, no. 203 (January–March 1939): 1.

11 Fermin to A. L. Ainsworth, September 21, 1916, American Immigration Company Correspondence, September 1–30, 1916, 141.I.814 F, Box 1, BB1.A512i, American Immigration Company Papers, Minnesota Historical Society, St. Paul, Minnesota.

12 American Immigration Company, "The Upper Wisconsin" (pamphlet, n.d.), American Immigration Company Files, 145.I.8.14F, Box 1, Minnesota Historical Society, St. Paul, Minnesota.

13 Land papers and advertisement records book, BB1.H765, P2928, Box 19, Homeseekers Land Company Papers, Minnesota Historical Society, St. Paul, Minnesota.

14 J. A. Stransky to American Immigration Company, November 15, 1912, and M. W. Balfour to American Immigration Company, n.d., American Immigration Company Correspondence, 1909–1912, 141.I.814 F, Box 1, BB1.A512i, American Immigration Company Papers, Minnesota Historical Society, St. Paul, Minnesota.

15  Homeseekers Land Company Papers, Minnesota Historical Society, St. Paul, Minnesota.

16  American Immigration Company, "The Upper Wisconsin"; To F. E. Weyerhaeuser, June 25, 1908, American Immigration Company Correspondence 1900–1907, BB1.A512i, Minnesota Historical Society, St. Paul, Minnesota.

17  American Immigration Company, "The Round Lake Country" (pamphlet, Chippewa Falls, Wisc., n.d.), Colonization Company Records, Wisconsin Historical Society.

18  H. C. Strivers, *Grand Rapids, Deer River, Cohasset: A Guide for Home Seekers and Investors* (n.p., 1900), Minnesota Historical Society, St. Paul, Minnesota.

19  Walsh, "The Last Resort," 50.

20  American Colonization Company to Frederick von Pilis and George W. Claussenius, June 6, 1907, American Immigration Company Correspondence 1900–1907, BB1.A512i, Minnesota Historical Society, St. Paul, Minnesota; American Immigration Company, "The Upper Wisconsin"; Kapten Keyl to Alexander Reggi, January 21, 1907, American Immigration Company Correspondence 1900–1907, BB1.A512i, Minnesota Historical Society, St. Paul, Minnesota.

21  C. B. Hanson to American Immigration Company, December 28, 1912, American Immigration Company Correspondence, 1909–1912, 141.I.814 F, Box 1, BB1.A512i, American Immigration Company Papers, Minnesota Historical Society, St. Paul, Minnesota.

22  Villas County, Wisconsin, Board of Immigration, "For the Homeseeker" (pamphlet, n.d), Wisconsin Colonization Company Records, 1916–1938, Wisconsin Historical Society. For more on the image colonization companies attempted to project, see Aaron Shapiro, *The Lure of the North Woods: Cultivating Tourism in the Upper Midwest* (Minneapolis: University of Minnesota Press, 2013), 9–12.

23  "Man in the Cutover," Wisconsin Agricultural Experimental Station Research Bulletin #139, 1941; Michael J. Gox, "The Wisconsin Dust Bowl," *Wisconsin Magazine of History* 73, no. 3 (Spring 1990): 162–201.

24  Shapiro, *The Lure of the North Woods*, 11. See also Aaron Shapiro, "Up North on Vacation: Tourism and Resorts in Wisconsin's North Woods, 1900–1945," *Wisconsin Magazine of History* 89, no. 4 (Summer 2006): 3–13.

25  Elwood R. Maunder interviewing George W. Dulany Jr., La Jolla, California, September 21, 1956, Forest History Oral History Project, OH 142.1, Minnesota Historical Society, St. Paul, Minnesota.

26  For more on theft of land and woods from the Anishinaabe and federal government, see chapter 1.

27  The image of lumberjacks as not only accepting but reveling in the filth of older camps is echoed in later stories. The *Bemidji Pioneer* joked in 1915 that men threatened to strike when electricity was installed and were equally furious when efficient heat appeared.

The article was titled "Lumberjacks Are Now Taking Baths," Bemidji *(Minn.) Daily Pioneer,* December 24, 1915; E. O. Olund interviewed by Frederick Kohlmeyer. For more, see Loomis, *Empire of Timber.*

28  Seward D. Allen, *The Boy and the Man* (New York: Lyon's, 1915), 20–26.

29  Editorial, *Princeton (Minn.) Union,* April 26, 1894.

30  Harold Titus, *Timber* (Boston: Small, Maynard, 1922), 2–3.

31  Hill, "Life in a Logging Camp," 703; and Blakeman, *Report of a Truant,* 14.

32  Elwood R. Maunder interview with George W. Dulany, September 21, 1956, Forest History Foundation Papers, Minnesota Historical Society, St. Paul, MN, 36; Benjamin, "Reminiscences, 1912."

33  "Palmy Days Are Over," *Detroit Free Press,* January 14, 1907. The insistence that Scandinavian lumberjacks were completely untrained and unprepared for the job is one of the more baffling aspects of this myth, given the pervasiveness of lumbering in Scandinavia. For more, see Andrew A. Stromberg, "Pioneers of the Northwest" in *Swedes in America 1638–1938,* ed. Adolph B. Benson and Naboth Hedin (New Haven, Conn., 1938), 92–106; Johansson, "Beautiful Men, Fine Women and Good Work People"; Ingrid Semmingsen, *Norway to America: A History of the Migration,* trans. Einar Haugen (Minneapolis: University of Minnesota Press, 1978); and Gjerde, *The Minds of the West.*

34  There were rare dissenting voices on this topic. A "prominent logger," who, based on his description of camps, was likely the owner of at least two or three separate operations, told the *Escanaba Morning Press* in 1910 that "the modern woodsman takes more care of his physical health than his old daredevil brother. They are the new order steady, hard working men, with a view of something. They have succeeded the old timer, who carried his peaky in his bag, and his fortune on his back, and who worked just so long as the excitement pleased him and then quit." "Logging Is Much Changed," *Escanaba (Mich.) Morning Press,* January 28, 1910.

35  Kelly, "An Observer in the Woods," 51.

36  "Picturesque Lumberjack of Former Days Disappearing," *Detroit Free Press,* July 22, 1906.

37  For more on strikes, see chapter 3.

38  Hunt Taylor to Rudolph M. Weyerhaeuser, October 21, 1919, Frederick W. Kohlmeyer Research Files, Minnesota Historical Society, St. Paul, Minnesota.

39  Tripp and Tripp, *Life in a Lumber Camp,* 8.

40  Edmonds, *Out of the Northwoods,* 166–69.

41  For more on the ways in which Paul changed in the hands of writers, see Edmonds, *Out of the Northwoods,* 95–97. Edmonds is particularly thoughtful in picking apart what it was that made the written legend of Paul so different from the oral legend. Paul as a lumber camp story was a private tale created by a group, exchanged among working-class men. Paul as a national hero was instead in the hands of single authors, aimed at children and

produced not for personal reasons of expression or even venting frustration, but strictly for commercial gains.

42 David K. Vaughan, "The Au Sable River Lumberman's Monument: William B. Mershon's Struggle to Create a Meaningful Memorial of the Michigan Lumbering Era," *Michigan Historical Review* 43, no. 2 (Fall 2017): 16–17. Vaughn's interpretation of Mershon's monument differs strongly from my own: while he sees Mershon as attempting to rescue history from myth, as a "survivor of the old lumbering days trying to pass along his vision of the past to a world for which that past was increasingly modified by revisionist images of myth . . . or denigration" (21–22), I see Mershon's focus on the lumbermen who were "robust, short in stature, laughing eyes and smiling face" (21), next to their "higher type" boss as propagation of his own revisionist mythology.

## NINE. THE PASSING OF THE PINES

1 Dan Barry, "In an Era of Hyperbole, Paul Bunyan Is as Tall as Ever," *New York Times*, September 23, 2016.

2 Edenville, Michigan's Lumberjack Festival began in 1935 in competition with Shawnoo, Wisconsin's, where "Log Rollers Will Compete at Festival," *Herald-Palladium* (Benton Harbor, Michigan), July 31, 1935.

3 Herbert Lefkovitz, "Bumper Corn Crop Cheers the North West," *New York Times*, October 15, 1939.

4 "Gate Bigger at Muskegon," *The Billboard*, August 7, 1937.

5 For an overview of funding mechanisms for tourism, see Shapiro, "Up North on Vacation."

6 Shapiro, *The Lure of the North Woods*, xiii.

7 "Vacation Days, 1921" (pamphlet), Minnesota Historical Society, St. Paul, Minnesota.

8 For no clear reason I can discern, 1934, a fairly random seventeen years after the last log drive, was the boom year for starting festivals. In addition to Stillwater's successful festival, a "Lumberjack Picnic" that year was "the first pioneer lumberjack picnic ever staged in the Upper Peninsula" and brought over 10,000 people in 3,500 cars, while the Edenville, Michigan, Lumberjack Festival purportedly, if not particularly credibly, attracted 20,000 visitors that same summer. "Lumberjack Picnic a Great Success," *Ironwood (Mich.) Times*, August 17, 1934; "Old-Time Lumbering Days Will be Recalled at Edenville August 23," *Herald-Palladium* (Benton Harbor, Michigan), July 31, 1935.

9 Speech to the St. Paul Saints' fans at Lexington Park, John J. Sullivan Papers, 1933–1937, P1952, Minnesota Historical Society, St. Paul, Minnesota.

10 Programs for the second, third, fourth, sixth, and seventh Lumberjack Days festivals, Washington County Historical Society, Stillwater, Minnesota.

11 Letter from Stillwater Association to City Clerks, September 11, 1939, Washington County Historical Society, Stillwater, Minnesota.

12   Photographs of Lumberjack Days, Washington County Historical Society, Stillwater, Minnesota.

13   Stephanie E. Yuhl, *A Golden Haze of Memory: The Making of Historic Charleston* (Chapel Hill: University of North Carolina Press, 2005), 6.

14   *Eau Claire (Wisc.) Leader-Telegram*, July 15, 1937; *Herald-Palladium* (Benton Harbor, Michigan), July 3, 1937; *Escanaba (Mich.) Daily Press*, July 13, 1937.

15   "Muskegon's Centennial Advertised," *Herald-Palladium* (Benton Harbor, Michigan), July 1, 1934.

16   *Eau Claire Leader* (Eau Claire, Wisconsin), July 15, 1937.

17   "With the Editors in Michigan," *Eau Claire (Wisc.) Leader-Telegram*, July 28, 1937.

18   Murdoch, *The American West*, 19.

19   Deloria, *Playing Indian*, 137.

20   Bill Nichols, "Documentary Reenactment and the Fantasmatic Subject," *Critical Inquiry* 35, no. 1 (Autumn 2008): 72–89; Alex W. Bordino, "Antimodernism and Indigenous Reconstruction: Proto-Ethnographic Attractions in Early Cinema, 1894–1914," *Journal of American Culture* 45, no. 1 (March 2022): 38–39.

21   For more on the connection between folk heroes, like lumberjacks, and authenticity, see Joseph Feinberg, *The Paradox of Authenticity: Folklore Performance in Post-Communist Slovakia* (Madison: University of Wisconsin Press, 2018).

22   Muskegon Citizens Centennial Association. *Muskegon Centennial & Lumber Jack Festival [Muskegon, Michigan, July 17–31, 1937] Official Program* (Muskegon, Mich.: Earle Press, 1937).

23   For more on the spread of lumber sports and their modern cultural meanings, see Kate Kruckemeyer, "'You Get Sawdust in Your Blood': 'Local' Values and the Performance of Community in Occupational Sport," *Journal of American Folklore* 115, no. 457/58 (Summer/Autumn 2002): 301–33. Kruckemeyer's work is particularly interesting on the development of timber sports as a reaction to the modernization and mechanization of lumbering. As one interviewer noted, the noise of chainsaws and pace of modern work meant there was no longer a sociable aspect to work; instead it was a mechanized and lonely process. C. Frank Zarnowski similarly argues that occupational sports often allowed workers to have more dignity in their work, demonstrating that it required skill. That said, he also notes that occupational sport contests were often sponsored by companies themselves, perhaps as a piece of corporate paternalism aimed as distracting workers from how menial and repetitive their jobs had, in fact, become. C. Frank Zarnowski, "Working at Play: The Phenomenon of 19th Century Worker-Competitions," *Journal of Leisure Research* 36, no. 2 (2004): 273–78. Similarly, Catharine Anne Wilson argues that plowing competitions formed a key component of shoring up skill as a central part of rural manhood in response to the growing mechanization of farming. Both these

sports (timber sports and plowing competitions) as well as their more famous brother, the rodeo, are still alive and well today, despite the anachronistic nature of some of the skills they celebrate. Catharine Anne Wilson, "A Manly Art: Plowing, Plowing Matches, and Rural Masculinity in Ontario, 1800–1930," *Canadian Historical Review* 95, no. 2 (June 2014): 157–86.

24 Frank Zarnowski, *American Work-Sports: A History of Competitions for Cornhuskers, Lumberjacks, Firemen and Others* (Jefferson, N.C.: McFarland & Company, 2013). For more, see Zarnowski, "Working at Play"; James P. Leary, *Wisconsin Folklore* (Madison: University of Wisconsin Press, 1999); and Lew Freedman, *Timber! The Story of the Lumberjack World Championships* (Madison: University of Wisconsin Press, 2011). It is outside the purview of this book to provide a full analysis of the development of lumberjack games, but it is hard not to see a parallel with the escapism middle-class men found in camping and the outdoors, and the similar attempt to glorify an imagined past of glorious labor that is played out in lumberjack games.

25 Zarnowski, "Working at Play," 263.

26 Daniel J. Rypma, "Mourning the Forest: Logging and Public Memory in West Michigan," *Michigan Historical Review* 41, no. 1 (Spring 2015): 14, 2.

27 "Collective," "communal," "public," and "cultural" memory are all contested terms. Alicia Barber and others make the helpful distinction that collective memory consists of the actual memories of a group of people's own life experiences, whereas communal memory is the imagined shared memory of a group. However, cultural studies theorists tend to define collective memory as the narratives that "help to create, sustain and reproduce the 'imagined communities' with which individuals identify"—in other words, what Barber and other historians mean by "communal memory." Public memory is the term most commonly used by historians, but I believe it misleadingly implies that there is a single, uncontested public. In using "cultural memory," I am purposefully borrowing from cultural studies theorists, who posit that cultural memory is "imbued with relations of power." Alicia Barber, "Local Places, National Spaces: Public Memory, Community Identity, and Landscape at Scotts Bluff National Monument," *American Studies* 45, no. 2 (Summer 2004): 35–64; Chris Weedon and Glenn Jordan, "Special Section on Collective Memory: Introduction," *Cultural Studies* 25, no. 6 (November 2011): 843–47.

28 "Log Burler King to Defend Title," *The Times-News* (Hendersonville, North Carolina), August 28, 1934.

29 For a comprehensive and thoughtful history of Northwoods tourism, see Shapiro, *The Lure of the North Woods.*

30 For more, see Barber, "Local Places, National Spaces."

31 David Strauss, "Toward a Consumer Culture: 'Adirondack Murray' and the Wilderness Vacation," *American Quarterly* 39, no. 2 (Summer 1987): 270–86.

32 Cindy S. Aron, *Working at Play: A History of Vacations in the United States* (Oxford: Oxford University Press, 2001), 4–6.

33 Aron, *Working at Play*, 166–69.

34 Shapiro, *The Lure of the North Woods*, 15–20.

35 Shapiro, *The Lure of the North Woods*, 43–47. For more on the creation of natural spaces, and its attendant destruction of older land uses, see Karl Jacoby, *Crimes against Nature: Squatters, Poachers, Thieves, and the Hidden History of American Conservation* (Berkeley: University of California Press, 2001).

36 Elizabeth Outka, *Consuming Traditions: Modernity, Modernism, and the Commodified Authentic* (Oxford: Oxford University Press, 2008), 4. Film scholar Alex Bordino notes that the same tension existed in, and was central to, the pleasure of early filmed reenactments of "primitive" societies. Bordino, "Antimodernism and Indigenous Reconstruction," 35–38. For a more local example of the nearly impossible line between modernity and "authentic" history, see Jeffrey T. Manuel's treatment of the plan to restore Minnesota's Calumet to a 1920s "frontier" town for tourists in *Taconite Dreams: The Struggle to Sustain Mining on Minnesota's Iron Range, 1915–2000* (Minneapolis: University of Minnesota Press, 2015), 196–98.

37 Camden Burd, "Imagining a Pure Michigan Landscape: Advertisers, Tourists, and the Making of Michigan's Northern Vacationlands," *Michigan Historical Review* 42, no. 2 (Fall 2016): 44–45.

38 For more on the history of the uses of Native American images and imitation by white Americans, see Deloria, *Playing Indian*; for more on the continuing salience of primitive or antimodern cultures as a tourist attraction, see Susan L. Trollinger, *Selling the Amish: The Tourism of Nostalgia* (Baltimore: Johns Hopkins University Press, 2015).

39 "Paul Bunyanland Auto Tour Map" (pamphlet, 1957) and "Paul Bunyan, Vacationland! Vacation in Northern Minnesota: Land of the Sky Blue Waters" (pamphlet, n.d.), F614. A22, Pamphlet Collection, Minnesota Historical Society, St. Paul, Minnesota.

40 "Scenic Minnesota" (pamphlet, 1959), Pamphlet Collection, Minnesota Historical Society, St. Paul, Minnesota.

41 For an excellent analysis of American national identity and tourism, see Marguerite S. Schaffer, *See America First: Tourism and National Identity, 1880–1940* (Washington, D.C.: Smithsonian Institution Press, 2001). For more on the growth of tourism specifically designed to show Americans their own past, see Katrina M. Phillips, *Staging Indigeneity: Salvage Tourism and the Performance of Native American History* (Chapel Hill: University of North Carolina Press, 2021), 7–15, and Shapiro, *The Lure of the Northwoods*.

42 Phillips, *Staging Indigeneity*, 5–27.

43 Cynthia Culver Prescott, *Pioneer Mother Monuments: Constructing Cultural Memory* (Norman: University of Oklahoma Press, 2019), 43.

44 In reference to the ways tourists at the Oklahoma City and 9/11 Memorials consume a version of history that emphasizes American innocence, Marita Sturken has called this kind of tourism "comfort culture." Sturken, *Tourists of History*, 8–12.

45 "The Heart of Lake Land" (pamphlet, n.d.), Pamphlets Related to Minnesota Travel, 1887–, F604.1, Minnesota Historical Society, St. Paul, Minnesota.

46 Grand Rapids Civic and Commerce Association, *Carefree Days in Itasca County, Minn: The County of a Thousand Lakes* (Grand Rapids, Minn., n.d.), Pamphlets Relating to Itasca County, F612.I8, Pamphlet Collection, Minnesota Historical Society, St. Paul, Minnesota.

47 "Minnesota Welcomes You With a Smile" (pamphlet, 1951), F604.1.M6 1951, Minnesota Historical Society, St. Paul, Minnesota.

48 "Motoring in Minnesota: A Week in the Land of the Sky-Blue Water," *Buick Magazine*, August 1959, 4–8; "Minnesota . . . Has Everything" (n.d.), F604.1, Minnesota Pamphlets Collection, Minnesota Historical Society, St. Paul, Minnesota.

49 "Come to Paul Bunyan's Playground" (n.d.), Minnesota Pamphlets Collection, Minnesota Historical Society, St. Paul, Minnesota. The idea of Paul Bunyan's Playground was appealing enough to be featured beyond the pamphlets the association itself produced. A 1950s pamphlet by Shell invited motorists to visit the home of the hero "born in the mind of some long-forgotten, grizzled old woodsman," whose tales had been passed on "through the last century . . . by the light of a thousand flickering camp fires and bunkhouse stoves"; they identified his home as "Paul Bunyan's Playground," which was "equally as fine a place to play for the modern nature-lover as it was for the great woodsman." "Shell Tour Tips: Minnesota" (pamphlet, n.d.), Pamphlets Related to Minnesota Travel, 1887–, F604.1, Minnesota Historical Society, St. Paul, Minnesota.

50 Manuel, *Taconite Dreams*, 172–85. It was a particularly doomed endeavor to try to draw tourism with mining given that the crowds the Iron Range boosters were hoping to tap into were those on their way to visit Voyageurs National Park, a space premised entirely on the idea of nature untouched since the romantic preindustrial traders for which it is named.

51 Joseph Whitson, "Monumental Mines: Mine Tourism, Settler Colonialism, and the Creation of an Extractive Landscape on Minnesota's Iron Range," *Public Historian* 41, no. 3 (2019): 49–71.

52 Rebecca Cawood McIntyre's *Souvenirs of the Old South: Northern Tourism and Southern Mythology* (Gainesville: University Press of Florida, 2011) provides a particularly good portrait of the ways in which consuming tourist attractions shaped both the identity of (northern) tourists, and their understandings of the (southern) history they were consuming.

53 Landsberg, *Engaging the Past*, 7.

54 Prescott, *Pioneer Mother Monuments*, 43. Re-created logging camps with varying levels of verisimilitude still operate across the Northwoods (the most accurate is the Minnesota Historical Society's Forest History Center in Grand Rapids, Minnesota). Here festivals echo the effect of living history museums, whose commercial imperatives often lead to a "Disneyfied" past, as well as living history museums' creation of physical artifacts of a mythic past. For more, see Gordon, *Time Travel*, 6–8. For more on Historyland and its bizarre pseudo-historical landscape, which, according to Scott Magelssen, offered "a simulated past which became more authoritative than its referent," see Scott Magelssen, "The Stating of History: Theatrical, Temporal and Economic Borders of Historyland," *Visual Communication* 2, no. 1 (2016): 10. For more on the ability of ersatz re-creations to bear more authority than actual history, see the introduction of Paul Connerton, *How Societies Remember* (Cambridge: Cambridge University Press, 1989), 1–5.

55 Feinberg, *The Paradox of Authenticity*, 21.

56 For an excellent analysis of the feedback loop between heritage tourism and folk mythology, see Kirk Neigarth, "In Search of Authenticity: Public Memory, Living History, and Folk Art in Modern Canada," *Acadiensis: Journal of the History of the Atlantic Region* 41, no. 1 (Winter/Spring 2018): 243–56.

57 This transformation is particularly impressive, and particularly startling, in northern Minnesota, where the timber industry gave way not to the dust bowls of northern Wisconsin, but rather to the industrial mining of taconite on the Mesabi Iron Range. Taconite mining was environmentally disastrous, and ultimately could not halt the slow postindustrial decline in the region. There were even attempts on the Iron Range to revere the history of mining the way others did logging, eventually resulting in Ironworld, a roadside historical attraction. Yet, by two decades into the twenty-first century, much of the Iron Range is now included in the larger, vaguer "Northwoods" or "up North" not defined by industry.

58 Kromer, "Thorpe, 1968."

## CONCLUSION

1 Georgia Arndt, *Lumberjack's Daughter* (Dallas: Brown Books, 2003).

2 Brady Dennis, "In Fast-Warming Minnesota, Scientists Are Trying to Plant the Forest of the Future," *Washington Post*, April 29, 2020.

3 Duluth Trading Company, "Free Swingin' Flannel," YouTube, August 28, 2015; Alexandra Marvar, "Our Lives in the Time of Extremely Fancy Axes," *New York Times*, December 18, 2019; CBC Comedy, *This Is That*, "Maker Series: Artisanal Firewood," YouTube, September 9, 2015.

4 Nevue, "'Incredible' Lumberjack Stories Debunked by Veteran of Camps."

5 Nevue, "'Incredible' Lumberjack Stories Debunked by Veteran of Camps."

6 Lewis Beeson, letter to Wilfred Nevue, November 1954; Bruce G. Bell, letter to Wilfred Nevue, November 1954, IN 634.98, "Lumber and Lumbering—Lumberjacks" Pamphlet file, Marquette Regional History Center, Marquette, Michigan.

7 "Gay Days in the Woods," *Milwaukee Journal*, March 2, 1947.

8 Nelligan, *The Life of a Lumberman*, 135.

# INDEX

9/11 memorials, 291n44

accidents, 40–41. *See also* hospital tickets; risk; violence
achievement, 54–55
Adirondacks, 218
adventure novels, 179–80
*Adventure of Bobby Orde, The* (White), 180
advertising, xxxi, 165, 172, 203, 220, 222; landscape and, 219; nature tourism and, 226
advice manuals, 54
African-Americans, 261n45. *See also* Blacks
Agricultural Workers Organization, 86
agriculture, 14, 187. *See also* farmers
agropelters, xxi, 52
A. L. Burt publishers, 282n39
alcohol, 72, 147, 150; brotherhood and, 149; memory and, 234. *See also* saloons; temperance
alienation, 139–40
Allen, Seward D., 194
*Alpena News,* 30–32, 34–35; doubts about, 249n45
America, idea of, 165–67, 170, 172–74, 176–80

Americana, 165
American Colonization Company, 190–91
*American Folklore and the Historian* (Dorson), 278n1
*American Historical Review,* 282n41
American Immigration Company, 187–89, 191, 193
*American Progress* (Gast painting), 116
American Realism, 173
American West, ix, xxix
Ames, James H., xii
*A Michigan Man* (Peattie), 163
Anderson, Julie, 185
Andrews, Thomas, 101–2
Anglo-Americans, 39, 70
animism, 54
Anishinaabe, ix, xi, xvi, 2; 1837 treaty with, 15; advertising and, 222; Anglo-Americans and, 39; Anshnaabemowin and, 102; capitalism and, xvii, 104–5, 107; community resources and, 17, 106; Euro-Americans and, 79–80, 99; evolution and, 262n60; fictionalized version of, 205; fighting and, 150; footpaths of, 102; harvesting and, 266n43; Indian agents

and, 16; isolation and, 135; land theft and, 13, 18, 194; Mishibizhiw and, 101, 253n18; Nelson Act and, 15; "noble savage" and, 103; racialized hierarchies and, 70; smaller lumber towns and, 136; tourism and, 207, 219; traits versus skill and, 76; United States policy and, 14; violence and, 81, 261n52; whiteness and, 75; wilderness myth and, viii. *See also* Ojibwe

antimodernism, 181, 213, 282n41. *See also* modernity

antiracism, 73. *See also* race

aristocracy, 172–73, 176–77

Arndt, George, 231

Arthurian legend, 177

*Ashland Weekly News,* 127

assimilation, 14–15, 103

Atlanta, Michigan, 58

*Atlantic, The,* xxix, 30, 168, 279n7; chivalry and, 153; identity questioned in, 182; ruggedness in, 216

Auden, W. H., 165

Au Sable River, 203

authenticity, xxvi, xxviii, 165, 170–72; adventure novels and, 180; Buffalo Bill and, 280n14; effeminacy and, 176; festivals and, 210, 213; folk culture and, 173; Lumberjack Days and, 209; masculinity and, 193; Paul Bunyan and, 184, 278n4; perfect simulation and, 179; reality and, 177; role-playing and, 173; romanticism and, 167; self and, 182

ax-throwing, 232

bad jack myth, xxvii

"bad" jacks, 92

Bae, Youngsoo, 243n23

Balfour, M. W., 189

"Ballad of Harry Dunn, The" (song), 40, 60

ballads, 45–49. *See also* songs

barbarity, 50, 78. *See also* savagery

Barber, Alicia, 289n24

Baron, Ava, 146

Bartlett, William, xi, 152

Beard, Native, 179

Beaton, Jack, 87–89, 108, 200

Beaver Island (Lake Michigan), xxi

Beck, Earl Clifton, 45, 58

Bederman, Gail, xxviii, 63, 254n24

Beecher, Lyman, xix

Beef Slough, Battle of, 11, 13, 108

Beef Slough Manufacturing, Booming, Log Driving and Transportation Company, 10–11, 13

Beeson, Lewis, 233–34

Bell, Bruce G., 234

Bemidji, Minnesota, 90, 161

*Bemidji Pioneer,* 90, 285n27

Benjamin, Walter F., 185, 198

Benson, Barbara, 13, 36, 262n5

Benson, Don, 185–86

Berg, Jhalmer, 72–73

Berkhofer, Robert F., 76

Big Delia (prostitute), 154

"Big Two Hearted River" (Hemingway), 133

*bimaadiziwin* (pursuit of the good life), 102

biology, 76, 78

bird metaphor, 270n14

Black Jap (Sawdust Flats dancer), 277n36

Blacks, 73, 261n45; as cowboys, 234

Blakeman, C. E., 27, 197

bodies, 48–50; contagion and, 271n27; control and, 55, 58; curriculum development and, 281n24; Gilded Age fascination with, 173; homosociality and, 174; mastery and, 64; men's changing roles and, 256n7;

muscular Christianity and, 217; violence and, 53, 60

booms (river storage areas), 10–11

boomtowns, 83–84, 157–58, 269n67; geography of, 248n30; prostitution and, 124; sprees and, 144; tramps and, 137; violence and, 138

Boone, Daniel, 177; Sons of Daniel Boone, 179

boosters, xv, xxix, 162; Lumberjack Days and, 209; mining and, 226; narrative and, 222; tourism and, 217

Bordino, Alex, 290n36

*Bostonians, The* (James), 173

boundaries, 61–62, 65, 73, 75–76, 87, 123–24; belonging and, 39; management and, 33; prostitution and, 124; between public and private, 256n10; race and, 73; skill and, 65; whiteness and, 75; wildness and, 76

Bourgeois, Euclid J., xxii, xxiv, xxv, 19, 97–98

*Boy and the Man, The* (Allen), 194

Boyd, John, 72

boyishness, 168–69

Brainerd, Minnesota, 161

*Brainerd Daily Dispatch,* 85

bravery, 46–47, 60

Brawny paper towels, 166

Brazil, 64

Bremer, Frederika, 71

Britain, 113, 219

British Contagious Disease Acts, 123

Britten, Benjamin, 165

brochures, 222, 224

brothels, 128, 131, 135, 139, 142–43, 272n35; policing of, 273n48. *See also* prostitution

brotherhood, 146–47, 149–50, 152, 169, 197, 280n12; skill and, 68, 70; violence and, 157. *See also* camaraderie; fraternity

Brotherton, R. A., 119

Brown Brother's Lumber Co., 265n37

Buffalo, Paul, 70, 79–81, 261n52

Buffalo Bill (William Cody), 170, 177; adventure novels and, 180; authenticity and, 227, 280n14

Buffalo Bill's Wild West Show, 170

*Buick Magazine,* 224

bull cooks, xiii, 34, 36, 194. *See also* cooks

bums, 117. *See also* tramps

bunkhouse, 33–34

Bureau of Indian Affairs, 17, 103

Bureau of Labor Statistics (Minnesota), 245n42, 251n2

Bushnell, Kate, 126–27, 129, 272n35

Calgary Stampede, 216

California, 65, 261n45

camaraderie, 84, 146, 152, 169; saloons and, 157; sprees and, 143. *See also* brotherhood; fraternity

Canada, xi, xx, 97, 99, 113, 198

cant hooks, 68

capital, 52, 55, 145; Marx's formulation of, 243n23. *See also* profit

capitalism, xv, xvi, 4, 234; Anishinaabe and, xvii; communal property and, 105; critiques of, 242n23; cultural memory and, 166; decolonial theory and, 247n15; fires and, 4, 6; folklore and, 165; homelessness and, 137; identity and, 172; irrationality of, 103; mixed economies and, 14; modernity and, 171; nature and, 107; reformers attitudes towards, 273n47; rejection of, 145; resistance to, 104; second contradiction of, 266n43; self-made man and, 21; self-ownership and, 255n29; smaller lumber towns and, 135; tourism and, 207;

unskilled workers and, 140; vagrancy and, 139; wealth consolidation and, 191; whiteness and, 243n25

Carlisle Indian Industrial School, 17

cattlemen, 60. *See also* cowboys

censuses, 96, 114; poverty maps and, 113

census of 1890, 71, 176; closing of frontier and, xxix; frontier and, 245n47; pay and, 89

*Century* (magazine), 117

chambers of commerce, xv

chance, 54, 56. *See also* luck; risk

Charleston, South Carolina, 211

chastity, 124, 128

cheap labor, 26, 193

cheap nature, xvi, xvii, 26, 266n43, 266n43

Cheyenne Frontier Days, 216

Chicago, Illinois, xxi, 4, 23. *See also* Great Chicago Fire

*Chicago Tribune,* 111

Chi Inaakonigewn (laws of relationships between humans and nonhumans), 102–3, 107

Chippewa Log and Boom Company, 25

Chippewa Lumber Company, 24

Chippewa River, 8–11

Chippewas, 15, 70, 107, 209. *See also* Anishinaabe; Menominee

chivalry, 153–54, 158, 177

chore boys, xiii, 34, 36, 194. *See also* cooks

Christianity, 32; gentleman ideal and, 55; muscularity and, 217

Christie, Sam, 99, 152

*Cincinnati Enquirer,* 283n1

cities, 171–72; aggressiveness and, 254n24; ethnic enclaves and, 38; identity of, 136; lumber industry and, 130; marketplace interactions in, 54; nature tourism and, 218; prostitution and, 129; resorts and, 205; unreality and, 183.. *See also* towns; urban life

citizenship, 200

Civilian Conservation Corps, vii, x, 231

civilization, xxvii, 50–51; chivalry and, 158; evolution and, 179; femininity and, 232; markets and, 104; national expansion and, 194; pageants and, 222; prostitution and, 124; race and, 77; racism and, 78; savagery and, 71, 81; shantytowns and, 252n9; untainted/untamed masculinity and, 180; valorization of skill and, 63; whiteness and, 75

Civil War, xv, 113, 166; demographic changes and, 23; nature tourism and, 217

class, 30–33, 172–73; bosses and, 196; boy-ishness and, 169; civilization and, 76; economic advancement and, 57; foremen and, 33; hierarchy and, 65; lumber camps and, 194; lumber camp structure and, 21; mining and, 254n21; Paul Bunyan and, 201; stratification by, 108–9; whiteness and, 74, 78; working class identity and, 140

clear-cutting, 4, 7, 13, 185; agriculture and, 14; wilderness restored from, 231. *See also* cutover; cutover land

climate, 6

*Clinging to Mammy* (McKelya), xv

Cloquet Firestorm of 1918, xi, 4, 186

Cody, William (Buffalo Bill), 170, 177; adventure novels and, 180; authenticity and, 227, 280n14

collective memory, 289n24

colonialism, 222, 247n15

colonization companies, xxix, 187–90, 192

Columbian Exposition (1893), 170, 172, 176

commercialism, 165

commodities, xxix; community resources as, xvii

communal memory, 289n24

communal property, 105

communism, 108

community, 103, 140, 157, 228; bunkhouse as, 33–34; cohesive identity of, 275n18; imagined communities and, 289n24; respectability and, 142; saloons and, 146

community resources, 14, 17–18, 75, 105–7; as commodities, xvii; nature and, 102

company men, 25, 27

Concatenated Order of the Hoo-Hoo, 193, 275n19

Confederacy, 166

confidence men, 54, 171–72, 182

Connaught, Con, 152

conservation, 185, 219, 232; nature tourism and, 218, 226

conservation policy, ix

consumerism, xv

contagion, 84, 122–24, 130, 133–35, 138, 271n27; prostitution and, 135; smaller lumber towns and, 133–34

*Contagion and the National Body: The Organism Metaphor in American Thought* (O'Brien), 271n27, 272n35

containment, 270n16

control, 53–54, 56, 58; hierarchy and, 81; luck and, 253n21; types and, 254n22; walking patterns and, 102

cooks, xxii, xxiii, 34, 36, 65; women as, 250n57

Cornell, Ezra, 10, 24

corporations, xv, xxix; advertisers and, 203; company men and, 25; domesticity and, 200; identity and, 172; mixed economies and, 187; myth and, 184, 193, 197, 228;

paternalism of, 288n23; resistance and, 108; romanticism and, 227. *See also* industry; lumber barons

Costley, Leonard, 68

Cott, Nancy, 256n10

cowboys, xxvi, 178; Blacks as, 234; cultural values and, 177; dime novels and, 180; distastefulness of violence and, 256n9; dude ranches and, 215; festivals and, 211, 213, 216; folklore and, 281n31; myth and, xxix, 8; Paul Bunyan and, 203; popularity of, 182; romanticism and, 176

Cox, Thomas R., ix, xviii; resistance and, 262n5

craft union movement, 139

Cresswell, Tim, 114–15

Crookston Lumber camp, 90

Cross, Gary, xv

crosscut saws, x; alternating tooth innovation of, 21–22

cruising, xxv, 2, 101

cultural amnesia, 246n3

Cunnion, T. C., 152, 234

Cushing, Franklin Hamilton, 181

cutover land, 191–92, 205. *See also* clear-cutting

*Daily Virginian,* 108

danger, 41–42, 44, 50; ballads and, 47; capital gain and, 52; constant presence of death and, 45; pay and, 241n15; protecting workers and, 252n8; wilderness and, 51. *See also* risk

Dawes Act (1887), 17, 104

"dead and down" trees, 15

Deadman, Richard Hector, 111

death, 41–42, 44–45; ballads and, 46–47; bodies and, 60; itinerancy and, 98;

lumber camps and, 252n6; risk and, 56; skill and, 57; transformation and, 49; worker safety and, 251n2

"Death of Harry Bradford, The" (ballad), 49

de Beaumont, Gustave, 50

decolonial theory, 247n15

Deer Lake, Minnesota, vii, 232

Deer River, Minnesota, 133, 269n67; *Democrat* newspaper of, 196; prostitution and, 135

degeneracy, xxviii–xxix, 117, 123, 208, 229; heroism and, 229; itinerancy and, 84; red-light districts and, 273n47

DeLucia, Christine M., 278n1; roots memory and, 262n1

democracy, 34, 113, 176

*Democrat* (Deer River, Minnesota), 196

demographics, 23, 111, 113, 240n10

*Detroit Free Press,* 92, 198–99

*Devil in the White City* (Larson), 172

Dietz, Myra, 248n31

difference, 73–74; ethnicity and, 259n32; natural predispositions and, 80; social geography of, 114

dignity, 64, 288n23

dime novels, 179–80

Disneyification, xxxi

Domby, Adam, xiv, 166

domesticity, 116–17, 137, 200

Dorsey, Bruce, 63

Dorson, Richard, 72, 165, 278nn3–4, 282n31

drifters, 92, 94. *See also* itinerancy

Dulany, George W., 193, 197

Duluth, Minnesota, xxv, xxvi, 84, 132; extractive industries and, 191; heritage and, 226; lumber barons and, 25; mills and, 130; refugees from fire and, 4

Duluth Trading Company, 232

Dunn, Harry, 46

Dust Bowl, 6, 192, 246n4

*Dust Bowl* (Worster), 246n4

Dye, Rex J., 150

easterners, 20, 158, 167, 182; nature tourism and, 218; romanticism and, 168; standards of manliness and, 254n21; urban life and, xxix; wildness and, 253n15

Eastern Europe, 193, 198

Eau Claire, Wisconsin, 8, 10–11

*Eau Claire Leader-Telegram,* 25, 211

ecology, 2. *See also* environment

Edenville, Michigan, 216, 287n8

Edmonds, Michael, xix, 286n41

education, 27–30; class and, 31–32; curriculum development and, 281n24; economic advancement and, 57

effeminacy, 54, 173–74, 176, 180, 198. *See also* femininity

egalitarianism, 146, 152; myth of, 18, 20–21

Ellingson, Ter, 76

Engberg, George, 101, 263n14

Enstad, Nan, 242n23

environment: degradation of, 185, 229; Dust Bowl and, 246n4; harvesting and, 266n43; industrial constraints and, xxi; labor strife and, 229; Oregon and, 232; study of masculinity and, xvi; transformation of, ix, 2; violence and, 41, 60; Walleye Wars and, 107

environmental history, 262n1, 278n1

*Escanaba Morning Press,* 286n34

escapism, 174, 181–82, 219–20, 226, 289n24

Esse, John, 25–26, 248n30

ethnicity, 39; blending of, xxi; civilization and, 71; effeminacy and, 198; enclaves of, 38; fighting and, 151; historiography of,

250n59; natural predispositions and, 80; small differences and, 259n32; violence and, 150; whiteness and, 73–75

ethnography, 77, 221; films and, 213

eulogies, 45–47

Euro-Americans, 75–77; Anishinaabe and, 99; measuring progress of, 78; skill and, 79–80

Europe, ix, xxvii; aristocracy and, 172; market systems in, 14; poverty maps and, 113

evolution, 75–76, 78, 179, 262n60

extractive industries, xxix, 6, 14, 116, 191; bodies and, 48; cultural memory and, 166; hierarchy and, 65; landscape and, 220; mixed economies and, 187; modernity and, 224; romanticism and, 193; tourism and, 207; vagrancy and, 139; West and, 60; white settlement and, 226; wilderness and, 185; workscapes of, 101

Exxon, 107

fakelore, 165–67, 173, 204, 278n3

*False Cause, The* (Domby), xiv

family, 115, 145, 194

family camps, 8–9, 19, 97; historiography and, 18; industry and, 193; myth and, 89, 198; Paul Bunyan and, 201; Timber Barons and, 13. *See also* logging camps

farmers, xi, xxix, 18, 103, 186; colonization companies and, 190; cutover and, 192; ethnic enclaves and, 38; grassbacks and, xxv; ideal of, 191; land theft and, 13; mixed economies and, 187; mobile workforce and, 137; national expansion and, 194; plowing competitions and, 288n23; stumpage and, 189; tourism and, 193; unions and, 89; wilderness and, 194. *See also* agriculture

Feinberg, Joseph, 227

femininity, 116, 153, 173, 232; men's changing roles and, 256n7

Ferguson, Roderick A., 259n39

Fermin, Mr. (Weyerhauser department head), 187–88

festivals, xxix, xxxi, 204, 210–14; 1934 as boom year for, 287n8; Disneyification and, 292n54; games and, 215; heritage and, 221, 226; historiography and, 227; memory and, 205; narrative and, 222; nostalgia and, 208–9, 216; resorts and, 212

Fielding, James, 127–28, 272n35

fighting, 150–52; memory and, 234; prostitution and, 154; sprees and, 143. *See also* violence

Finnish Socialist Opera, 86–88, 90, 200

Finns, 72–73, 198; Anishinaabe and, 81, 261n52; civilization and, 71; communism and, 108; racialized hierarchies and, 70; resistance and, 90; Socialist Opera and, 86–88, 90; Weyerhauser and, 200

fires, xi, xvii, 3–4, 6–7, 96; 1871 firestorms and, 186; cultural amnesia and, 246n3; lumber companies and, 284n9; lumber industry reverence and, 205; purposefully starting, 268n58

Fitzgerald, F. Scott, 133

Fitzmaurice, John W., 142

Florence, Wisconsin, 155

Flynn, Francis, 62

folklore, xvi, xxix; authentic heroism and, 184; authenticity and, 172–73; circulation and, 101; cowboys and, 281n31; development of, xxvii; effeminacy and, 176; fakelore and, 165–67, 204, 278n3; heroism and, 182; initiation and, 65; Paul Bunyan and, 163; working class and, xxviii

Foote, Lorien, 63–64, 254n22

foreignness, 199–200. *See also* immigration

foremen, 25, 27, 34–35; ballads and, 47; class and, 33; class structure and, 31–32; constant presence of death and, 45; hierarchical camp structure and, 30; living quarters and, 250n48; protecting workers and, 252n8

Forest History Center (Grand Rapids, Minnesota), 61, 91, 162, 226, 232, 255n1; Disneyification and, 292n54

Forest History Society, xxxiii

Forsyth, Hannah, 243n25

Foss, Bart, 4

Foucault, Michel, 260n40, 269n3

Fournier, Joe, 152

fraternity, 34, 146, 180, 280n12. *See also* brotherhood; camaraderie

French-Canadians, 70–71. *See also* Canada

frontier, xix, 172, 176–78; Census of 1890 and, 245n47; closing of, xxix; festivals and, 211; "lumberman's frontier" and, xviii; middle class and, 260n43; mimesis and, 215; popularity of, 182; prostitution and, 124

fur trade, 14, 70, 104

gambling, 53–54, 56, 132

Gambrill, M. M., 184, 283n1

games, 21, 52, 214–16, 289n24; constant presence of death and, 45; danger and, 51; skill and, 67; violence and, 68

Gast, John, 116

"Gay Days in the Woods" (*Milwaukee Journal*), 155, 234

gender, 63–65, 68, 70; authenticity and, 173; boundaries and, 256n10; class divide and, 53; ideals of, 55; identity and, 138; language and, 102; study of masculinity and, xvi

generosity, 169

gentleman ideal, xxvi, xxvii, 234; Christianity and, 55; festivals and, 209; frontier and, 178; Paul Bunyan and, 201; popularizing of, 162

geography, 129–30, 132; attempt to "know" populations and, 269n3; of boomtowns, 248n30; containment and, 270n16; difference and, 114; roughness and, 140; smaller lumber towns and, 136

Gilded Age, xxi, xxviii, 111, 113, 115–17; adventure novels and, 180; antimodernism and, 282n41; bodies and, 48, 173; contagion and, 122; management and, 32; masculinity crisis in, 56; meritocracy and, 248n26; morality of, 140; poverty maps and, 114; progress and, 222; prosperity and, 136; reality and, 172; risk and, 54; self and, 182; self-made man and, 21; urban life and, 167; white slavery and, 125

Gillmor, Frank, 98

Gitchi Manito (Great Spirit), 14

Gjerde, Jon, 71; ethnic enclaves and, 250n59; (space) on space, 244n33

Glenn, Horace, 27–30, 37, 71–72, 81

Goff, Lisa, 130

Golden Boys, 282n39

*Golden Boys with the Lumberjacks, The* (Wyman), 180

Goldstein, Eric L., 73–74, 260n40

"good" jacks, 92, 200

government, 269n3

Grand Canyon, 218

Grand Rapids, Minnesota, 178; famous jacks in, 99; festivals and, 205; Forest History Center and, 61; nostalgia and, 232;

saloons and, 148; Tall Timber Days and, 162, 216. *See also* Forest History Center

*Grand Rapids Herald,* 198

grassbacks, xxv, 83, 89. *See also* farmers

Grattan, Josephine, 45, 121, 153; mail-order brides and, 155–56

Great Chicago Fire, 4, 23; cultural amnesia and, 246n3

Great Depression, 192

Great Hinckley Fire (1894), 3–4, 96

Green Bay Commercial Business College, 27

greenhorns, 50, 52, 61, 66

green timber, 15–17

Griffin, Richard, x, 102, 146

Grossardt, Ted, 157

Hale, Grace, 73, 182, 260n39

Hall, G. Stanley, 281n24; recapitulation and, 179

Hanes, J. Dwight, 179

Hanson, C. B., 191

*Harper's Weekly,* xxix, 6

"Harvest(ing) Hoboes" (Grossardt), 157

Hayes, Rutherford B., xix

Hayward, Wisconsin, 162

Haywood, "Big" Bill, 87

hazing, 30, 68. *See also* initiation

Hemings, Sally, xv

Hemingway, Ernest, 133

Herbert, Christopher, 254n21

heritage tourism, 220–21, 226

Herman, Binger, 104

hermaphroditism, 174

heroism, 162–63, 165–67, 180, 182; degeneracy and, 229; fake folk culture and, 167; festivals and, 208, 213; folklore and, 184; foreign labor and, 199; forestry and, 216; labor and, 197; lumber industry and, 224;

national project of expansion and, 193; nature tourism and, 218; Paul Bunyan and, 200–201; reputation and, 183

Hicks, Steve, 152

hierarchy, 30, 32, 35, 63–65; lumber barons and, 39; power and, 81; skill and, 261n45; violence and, 150, 256n9; whiteness and, 75, 78; working class and, 73

Higbie, Frank, 119, 137, 142, 251n59, 270n12

Hill, Arthur, 36, 44–45, 168–69, 173

Hinckley, Minnesota, 96

history, xiii, 71; of capitalism, 243n23, 243n25; egalitarian myth and, 21; erasure and, 226; ethnic enclaves and, 250n59; festivals and, 227; heritage tourism and, 221; itinerancy and, 96; of labor, 138, 274n2; loss and, 267n46; memory and, xiv, xv, 166, 260n43; modern writing of, 282n41; mythic storytelling and, xxxi; obscuring of, xxxiii; oral history accuracy in, 269n67; popular literature and, xix; respectability and, 141; revisionist mythology and, 287n42; roots memory and, 262n1; of rough culture, 139; small family camps and, 18; strikes and, 86, 89, 263n14; study of masculinity across, xvi; women and, 63; of working class, 140

Historyland, viii, ix, 226, 292n54

Hobbs, Peter, 180

hobos, 64, 96, 117, 136, 146, 157. *See also* tramps

hodags, xxi, 52, 99–101; origins of, 253n18; Paul Bunyan and, 265n37

Holbrook, Stewart, xxxiii, 178

*Holy Old Mackinaw* (Holbrook), xxxiii, 178

homelessness, 113–15, 117, 137. *See also* itinerancy

Homeseeker's Land Company, 189, 191

*Homes of the New World* (Bremer), 71

Homestead Act (1862), ix

homosexuality, 174, 281n25

homosociality, 63, 144–45, 174

honor, 64

hospital tickets, 41–42, 251n3

Howden, Julia, 126

*How the Other Half Lives* (Riis), 170

Hurley, Wisconsin, 133

identity, 172, 182–83; class and, 140; gender and, 138; mass media and, 178; memory and, 179; Northwoods and, 162; tourism and, 291n52; violence and, 60

illness, 50

imitation, 172. *See also* mimicry

immigration, 70–71; Americanization and, 32; crossing over types and, 261n60; cutover land and, 191; ethnic enclaves and, 38; heroism and, 229; itinerancy and, 92; Lumberjack Days and, 209; racialized hierarchies and, 70; whiteness and, 74

"'Incredible' Lumberjack Stories Debunked by Veteran of the Camps" (Nevue), 264n19

Indian agents, 15–17, 106; Bureau of Indian Affairs and, 17; Mackinac report (1881), 135

Indian commissioners, 104–5

Indians. *See* Native Americans

Indigenous people. *See* Native Americans

*Indispensable Outcasts* (Higbie), 251n59

industrialization, 183, 222

Industrial Revolution, 111, 113

Industrial Workers of the World (IWW), 86–90, 108–9, 200; brotherhood and, 146; community and, 157; newspaper accounts of, 85, 108; Pacific Northwest and, 262n1; "real" jacks and, 198

industry, 4; conservation and, 232; identity and, 172; lumber camps and, 21; mobile workforce and, 137; modernity and, 224; premodern memories and, 205; rehabilitating image of, 193; romanticism and, 216; shift from agriculture to, 14; tourism and, 185. *See also* corporations; lumber barons

inequality, 260n39

infestation, 119, 123. *See also* contagion

initiation, 30, 52, 63; stories and, 65; violence and, 33

innocence, 291n44

innovation, 21–22

*Internationalist Socialist Review*, 87

Iron Range. *See* Mesabi Iron Range

Ironworld, 292n57

Irving, Washington, 32

isolation, 135–36

Itasca County, 222

itinerancy, xii, 25, 92–96, 98, 234; degeneracy and, 84; Gilded Age morality and, 140; hiring practices and, 97; labor and, 27; networks of, xxi, xxvii, 110, 157; quarantine and, 117; resistance and, 109; respectability and, 139; roving ways and, 108; rural/urban separation and, 251n59; skill and, 64; sprees and, 119; strikes and, 86, 90; vice districts and, 158; walking out of camps and, 107; working class and, 257n10; working conditions and, 270n11

jackalopes, xxi

Jack Pine Lumberjack Shows, 162

Jacobsen, Charles, 86–88, 200

Jacobsen, Matthew Frye, 73

"Jam on Gerry's Rocks, or the Ballad of Young Munroe, The" (ballad), 45–47, 50, 58, 60

James, Henry, 173

"James Whalen" (ballad), 47

January 6th coup attempt (2021), xiii

Jay Gatsby (*Great Gatsby*), 133

Jefferson, Thomas, xv, 176, 253n15

Jennings (Indian agent), 17

Jesus Christ, 50

Jim Crow system, 73

"Jimmie Jot" ("The Jam on Gerry's Rocks"), 45

Jimmy Powers (*The Adventure of Bobby Orde*), 181

jobbers, xi, 20. *See also* farmers

John Henry (folk character), 165

Johnny Inkslinger (folk character), 184

"John Robertson" (ballad), 46

Johnson, Abraham, xxvi

Johnson, Frank A., 42, 119, 152

Johnson, Susan Lee, 63

jokes, 52, 68, 72, 87, 168, 201; "Lena and Ole" books and, 259n32

jungles (tent cities), 140, 146

Kelly, C. C., 151, 198–99

Kelly, Hungry Pig Eye, 99

Kelly, Pig Eye, 152

Kelly the Cook, 152

Kett, Joseph, 248n26

key log, viii

"Kid, The" (ballad), 46

Kilar, Jeremy W., 150

*Killing for Coal* (Andrews), 101

Kingsdale, Jon, 144

kitsch, 203, 224, 232, 234

knighthood, 168–69, 177

Knights of Labor, 56

Knowlton, Wisconsin, 1

Kolchin, Peter, 73, 259n39

Kromer, Manita, 72, 228

Kruckemeyer, Kate, 288n23

Kuarala, Martin, 30, 72

Kusmer, Kenneth, 114

LaBeouf, Henri, xxii, xxiii

labor, 27, 110, 136–37; bosses and, 196; cheap labor and, 26, 193; citizenship and, 200; constant presence of death and, 45; environmental degradation and, 229; foreignness and, 199–200; heroism and, 197; histories of, 138, 274n2; honest forms of, 203; identity and, 172; indigenous source of, 15; itinerancy and, 27; management and, 201; reform and, 194; rights and, xxvii; romanticism and, 216; safety and, 56; sexual division of, 65; stratified sites of, 109; strike histories and, 263n14; study of masculinity and, xvi; traditional forms of, 21. *See also* strikes; unions

Laird, W. H., 32

Lake Superior, 25

land agents, 189

Landberg, Alison, 227

land-grabs, 13

Landsberg, Alison, 179

landscape, 205, 207; advertising and, 219, 222; degradation of, 6; extractive industries and, 220; fires and, 4; isolation and, 135; pamphlets and, 224; workscapes and, 101

land surveys, xvii

Landt, Sophronius Stocking, 1

land theft, 8, 13, 15, 18, 24, 194; capital and, 75

Lapham, Increase, 6–7

LaPoint Agency, 15

La Prairie, Henry, 80

Larson, Agnes M., 89, 94, 97

Larson, Erik, 172

Laughead, William B., 163, 201

Lears, Jackson, xxviii, 54, 57, 182; antimodernism and, 282n41

Leech Lake Band, 17

Leech Lake Reservation, 15

*Legend of Sleepy Hollow* (Irving), 32

"Lena and Ole" joke books, 259n32

Le Seur, Meridel, xxvi

"lesser" jacks, 197–98

Levy, Jonathan, 255n29

"Life in a Logging Camp" (*Scribner's Magazine*), 168

*Life of a Lumberman* (Nelligan), 161

lifeways, 103–4, 107

Lincoln, Ceylon, 149

Lindholm, Charles, 172

literacy, xi, 28

Little, Norman, 6

Little Falls, Minnesota, 40

logging camps, 18–21, 25, 27, 29–32; brotherhood of, 280n12; class and, 194; class structure of, 30–32; daily pattern of, 36; death in, 252n6; filth of, 285n27; games and, 214; hierarchies in, 35; labor and, 196; Lumberjack Days and, 209; mixed backgrounds in, 37; networks of, 25; recreations of, 227, 292n54; saloons and, 146; tourism and, 204; White Earth Tragedy and, 15. *See also* family camps

*Logging Town: The Story of Grand Rapids* (WPA), 166

log jams, xxiv, xxv, 10, 42; ballads and, 47; death and, 56

logrolling, 80, 214–15

Lomax, Alan, 58

Lomax, John, 281n31

London, Jack, 146, 157

longing, 169

Lost Forty (Minnesota State Forest), vii

Loy-Wilson, Hannah, 243n25

luck, 56–57; nature and, 59; risk and, 253n21; songs and, 60. *See also* chance; risk

lumber barons, xi, xii, 10–11, 194–95; centralization and, 36; cheap nature and, xvii; concentration and, 25; consolidation by, 57; end of small camps and, 13; government backing of, 25–26; hierarchy and, 39; management and, 32; memory and, 203; resistance and, 107; romanticism and, 228; self-made man and, 21; strikes and, 87; *Timber* and, 196; Weyerhauser as king of, 24. *See also* corporations; industry

lumber boom, xii, xxiv, 36; vice and, 131. *See also* boomtowns

lumber industry, vii, xvi; Battle of Beef Slough and, 11, 13; centralization of, 36; cities and, 130; colonization companies and, 189; conservation and, 185; distribution and, xxi; festivals and, 216; fires and, 284n9; heroism and, 224; mixed economies and, 187; myth of, viii, ix; national expansion and, 194; as national endeavor, xviii; natural history and, 227; ownership concentration and, xii; pace of growth of, 6; Paul Bunyan and, 201; reverence for, 205; strike histories and, 263n14; tourism and, 207

Lumberjack Days, 209, 216

Lumberjack Festival, 211, 216

Lumberjack Fight on the Flambeau River (mural), 8

lumberjack picnics, 31, 161, 287n8

lumberjacks, vii–xi, ix; fascination with, xxvi; folk heroism of, xvi; geographic origins of, xi; myth and, xix, xxix, xxxi; sources on, xxxiii. *See also* masculinity

*Lumberjack's Daughter* (Arndt), 231

*Lumberjack's Life, A* (Nelligan), xxxiii

"Lumberjack Song" (Monty Python), xxvi

Lumberjack Steam Train and Forestry Museum, 162

Lumberjack World Championships, 162

Lumberman's Monument (Michigan), 162, 203

lumbersexuals, xxvi

Lunden, Francis, 72

Lynde Hartt, Rollin, 30–31, 168–69

Mackinac Indian Agency report (1881), 135

Mackinaw City, Michigan, 162

Magelssen, Scott, 292n54

*Making Whiteness* (Hale), 73, 260n39

Malinowski, Bronislaw, 176–77

Mall of America, 161

management, 32–33; company-men and, 27; labor and, 201; resistance and, xxi

manganese, 220

manhood. *See* masculinity

*Manliness and Civilization* (Bederman), 254n24

Mann, Geoff, 261n45

Manoomin (wild rice), 106–7

mapping, 113–15, 119, 122; formalized spatial strategy and, 157

markets, 14; 1929 crash and, 246n4; cities and, 54; cutover land and, 191; increased demand and, 23; lifeways and, 104; marketplace men and, 142; risk and, 55; sprees and, 143

Marples, Eldon, 61

Marquette, Michigan, 133, 135

Marquette County, 233; contagion and, 134

Marx, Karl, 243n23

Marxism, 73, 259n39

masculinity, xvi, xxvi, xxvii; achievement and, 55; aggressive forms of, 254n24; authenticity and, 193; beauty and, 174; bodies and, 48, 53; boundaries and, 62; changing roles and, 256n7; childhood reform and, 179; civilization and, 71; class identity and, 140; crisis in, 56; curriculum development and, 281n24; Eastern standards of, 254n21; effeminacy and, 176; ethnicity and, 198; families and, 115; femininity and, 173; "good" jacks and, 200; heroism and, 182; hierarchy and, 63–64; homelessness and, 117; hyperbolic forms of, 232; idealized forms of, 211; ideals of, 2; itinerancy and, 95; Paul Bunyan and, 201; primal traits of, 169; redefining of, 162; reputation and, 65; respectability and, 124, 139, 141, 152; restraint and, 168; risk and, 54, 60; roughness and, 70, 140; rural life and, 288n23; saloons and, 147, 149, 158; self-made man and, 21; self-ownership and, 255n29; sprees and, 143; untainted/untamed version of, 180; vagrancy laws and, 272n47; violence of nature and, 41; whiteness and, 75, 229; women's space and, 116; working conditions and, 270n11

mass media, 165, 178

masterless men, 113, 115, 117

mastery, 48–50, 54, 56–58; bodies and, 64; saloons and, 254n23

Mayo Clinic, 220

McDonald, Pig-Foot, 155

McKelya, Micki, xv

McLeod, Laura, 14

mechanization, 288n23

*Memorials of the Minnesota Forest Fires in the Year 1894* (Wilkinson), 3

memory, xiv, xv, xxix, 161, 233, 260n43; extractive industries and, 166; fakelore and, 204; festivals and, 205, 211, 216; historiography and, 166; history obscured by, xxxiii; itinerancy and, 92; mass media and, 178; memoryscapes and, 84; myth and, 234; nostalgia and, 217; pamphlets and, 222; prosthetic form of, 179; prostitution and, 124; public memory and, 289n24; roots memory and, 262n1, 278n1; tourism and, 227

*Memory Lands: King Philip's War and the Place of Violence in the Northeast* (DeLucia), 278n1

Mencken, H. L., xxvi

Menominee, xi, 2; capitalism and, 104; community resources and, 17, 106; land theft from, 13, 18; racialized hierarchies and, 70; tourism and, 219; violence and, 80–81

Mercer, W. A., 15–18, 104

meritocracy, 21, 248n26

Mershon, W. B., 203, 287n42

Mesabi Iron Range, 71, 191, 226, 291n50; histories of, 263n14; Mesabi strike and, 90; taconite and, 292n57; tourism and, 207

métis culture, 70, 78, 105

Mexicans, 65

Meyer, Melissa, 105

Michigan, vii, ix, xviii, xxix, 3, 19; clear-cutting and, 7, 185; festivals and, 205, 211, 213; Gilded Age in, xxi; impenetrability of, 1–2; Lumberman's Monument in, 162, 203; nature tourism and, 218; Paul Bunyan and, 161; railways and, 22; resort towns and, 212; songs and, 45, 58; "white slavery" and, 127, 135

Michigan Historical Commission, 233

"Michigan Man, A" (Peattie), 183

Michigan State Conservation Commission, 204

middle class, 2, 218, 229; achievement and, 55; attitudes towards nature and, 52; bodies and, 48, 53, 60; boomtowns and, 158; camp hierarchy and, 30; emotional distance and, 130; escapism and, 289n24; families and, 115; frontier and, 260n43; homosociality and, 174; mastery and, 58; men's changing roles and, 256n7; nature and, 193; prostitution and, 124; rejection of, 145; respectability and, 141–42; restraint and, 56; risk and, 54; saloons and, 254n23; self and, 182; self-ownership and, 255n29; tramps and, 117; tramp scares and, 157; vice districts and, 84; women's space and, 116

Midwest, xix, xxi; demographic changes in, 23; ethnic enclaves and, 38; festivals and, 216; historiography of, 250n59; mixed backgrounds and, 37; nature tourism and, 218; space and, 244n33; Upper region as rational grid, xvii. *See also* Northwoods; Upper Midwest

migration, 21–22; population boom and, ix

mills, ix, xxi; cities and, 130; seasonal round and, 245n42; strikes and, 86; summer work in, xxv

*Milwaukee Journal,* 155, 234

mimicry, 179, 181. *See also* imitation

*Minds of the West* (Gjerde), 71, 251n59

Mineau, Hope, 121

mining, 86–90; boosters and, 226; clear-cutting and, 185; Exxon and, 107; freedom of, 102; gendering of skill and, 65; gold and, 270n11; manganese and, 220; restrained manliness and, 254n21; taconite and, 292n57; tourism and, 291n50; working conditions and, 270n11

*Mining Journal,* 233

Minneapolis, Minnesota, 84, 118–19; mills and, 130; Vice Commission report (1911), 128

*Minneapolis Journal,* 15–16; tourism and, 207

*Minneapolis Star Tribune,* 85; "Lumberjack Rush on Cities Begins," 118

Minnesota, vii, xviii, 1–2; brochures and, 224; Bureau of Labor Statistics in, 245n42, 251n2; Census of 1890 and, 71; control of rivers and, 8; cultural circulation and, 99; farmland and, 187; festivals and, 205; Forest History Center and, 61; Gilded Age in, xxi; itinerancy and, 98; land stewardship and, 7; land theft and, 13; nature tourism and, 218; Office of Indian Affairs in, 105; Paul Bunyan and, 161; tourism and, 207; virgin forest and, 185; warming and, 231; wilderness, 220

Minnesota Scenic Highway Association, 219

Minnesota State Forest, vii

*Minnesota v. Mille Lacs Band* (1999), 15

Mishibizhiw (water-panther), 101, 253n18, 265n36

Mississippi River Logging Company, 24

mixed bloods, 268n58. *See also* métis culture

mixed economies, 14; extractive industries and, 187; sustainability and, 17

modernity, 171–72, 181, 213, 282n41; American Realism and, 173; antimodernism and, 181; festivals and, 213; health and, 286n34; homosexuality and, 174; nature and, 183; prehistory and, 221; prehistory dichotomy with, 219; premodern

memories and, 205; primitivism and, 220; tourism and, 185

modernization, 288n23

money, 142, 155

Monroe, Young, 45, 47

Montgomery, David, 242n23

Monticello, xv

Monty Python, xxvi, 162

Moore, Jacqueline M., 60, 256n9

Mormons, xxi

Morrison, Daniel, 80

Moskowitz, Jennifer, 176

*Motley Register* (Little Falls, Minnesota), 40–41

Mould, Nina, 275n14

Munro, John, 73

Murdoch, David Hamilton, 177, 213

Murphy, Kevin P., 174

muscularity, 21, 60, 116, 173–75, 217, 228

Muskegon, Michigan, 84, 211; brothels and, 273n48; festivals and, 208, 211, 213; Lumber Queen status of, 212; *Passing of the Pines* pageant and, 205; prostitution and, 135; resorts and, 216; Sawdust Flats in, 234, 277n36

Muskegon Citizens Centennial Association, 212

mysticism, 54

myth, xxix, 8; Buffalo Bill and, 176; capitalism and, 185; circulation of, 99; corporations and, 184, 193, 197, 228; danger and, 51; degeneracy and, 229; Disneyification and, 292n54; East and, 158; egalitarianism and, 18, 20–21; fakelore and, 204; family camps and, 89, 198; festivals and, 213; frontier and, 260n43; history obscured by, xxxiii; itinerancy and, 94; lumber industry and, viii, ix, 224; lumberjacks and, xix, xxxi; memory and, 234; national consciousness and, 249n45; Nelligan and, 245n2; nostalgia and, 232; revisionism of, 287n42; salvage tourism, 227; self-made men as, 54; social charter function of, 177; sprees and, 119; two strains of, xxvi, xxvii; whiteness and, 260n40

narrative, 179, 221; heritage and, 226; Lumberjack Days and, 209; national forms of, 217; pageants and, 222; pamphlets and, 224; primitivism and, 219
national expansion, 193–94; nature tourism and, 226
nationalism, 220
national narratives, 217, 219, 224. *See also* narrative
national parks, 220
Native Americans, 247n15; authenticity and, 227; brochures and, 224; casual violence towards, 277n28; dispossession of, 222; erasure and, 226; Euro-Americans working with, 79–80; festivals and, 213; land surveys and, xvii; land theft from, 8, 13, 15; levels of evolution and, 75; "naturalness" of, viii; pageants and, 221; race and, 78; reenactments and, 213; stereotypes and, 232; traits versus skill and, 76; violence and, 81; Woodcraft Indians and, 179. *See also* Anishinaabe; Menominee
natural disaster metaphor, 84, 118, 121, 271n27
naturalist image, 166, 205, 232; narrative and, 222; tourism and, 207
nature, 8, 49–52; advertising and, 222, 226; ballads and, 47–48; capitalism and, 107; chance and, 56; cheap form of, xvi,

xvii, 26, 266n43, 266n43; community resources and, 102; crimes against, 6; escapism and, 182, 219; festivals and, 213; industry and, 227; living parts of, 102; luck and, 59; lumber industry and, 224; middle class veneration of, 193; premodern framework of, 183; resorts and, 216; romanticism and, 291n50; tourism and, 217; violence and, 40–41, 53, 57, 60; whiteness and, 76. *See also* wilderness
Nelligan, John Emmett, xxvi, 6, 27, 42, 67; casual violence of, 277n28; cowboys and, 177–78; editing of, 245n2; fighting and, 150, 154; itinerancy and, 98; *Life of a Lumberman,* 161; *A Lumberjack's Life,* xxxiii; masculine beauty and, 174; Nina Mould and, 275n14; resistance and, 107; saloons and, 144; sprees and, 120–21; violence and, 80; white slavery and, 155
Nelson, Miles, 96, 144, 275n13
Nelson Act (1889), 15
Nevue, Wilfred, 92, 94, 233–34, 263n19; contagion and, 134
Newton, Jason, 26
*New York Times,* 205, 252n6; fires and, 284n9
Nguyen, Viet Than, xv
Nixon, Rob, 263n10
Norrgard, Chantal, 261n52
North, 291n52
Northern Paper Mills, 234
Northwest Territory, 212
Northwoods, vii, xviii, xix, xxi; entry costs to logging in, 13; environmental degradation and, 185; environmental transformation and, ix; firestorms in, 3–4; gentleman ideal and, 178; idealized versions of, viii; identity and, 162; image control and, 207; impenetrability of,

1–2, 96; nature tourism and, 218–19; oral histories and, 99; primitivism and, 220; prostitution and, 157; regulation and, 158; resistance to exploitation in, xvii; single cooperative in, 24; transformation of, 6, 8, 11; whiteness and, 70. *See also* Midwest

Norwegians, 72; savagery and, 81

nostalgia, xv, xxviii, 162, 176, 205, 208–9; collective memory and, 217; festivals and, 211, 214; itinerancy and, 94; myth and, 232; Paul Bunyan and, 224; romanticism and, 216; saloons and, 158; sprees and, 143

*Nothing Ever Dies* (Nguyen), xv

Nott, J. C., 78

Nowlin, John, 50

Obernauer, Mrs. (WCTU leader), 126, 156

O'Brien, Gerald V., 271n27

O'Connor, James, 266n43

Odawa Anishinaabe. *See* Anishinaabe

Office of Indian Affairs, 105

Ojibwe, 2, 107; advertising and, 222; civilization and, 71; Euro-Americans working with, 79; whiteness and, 75. *See also* Anishinaabe

Oklahoma City, 291n44

Old Lou (brothel madam), 234

"Old Tamarack Dam, The" (ballad), 47, 49

Olund, E. O., 194

Olund Employment Service, 194

*Omaha World-Herald,* 193

"One Big Union" motto, 86–87, 108

O'Neill, Maggie Orr, 68

Ontario province, Canada, 107

"On the Beau Shai River" (ballad), 50

oral history, xxxiii, 52, 89, 97–98, 155, 193; circulation of, 99; written legends and, 286n41

Oregon, 232

Oregon Trail, 217

Orvell, Miles, 172

*Oscoda Press* (Oscoda, Michigan), 200

Outka, Elizabeth, 219

*Out of the Northwoods* (Edmonds), xix

Pacific Northwest, xviii, xxix, 13; 1917 strikes and, 262n1; clear-cutting and, 185; extractive industries and, 6; festivals and, 214; songs and, 45; stumpage and, 187

pageants, 205, 214, 216, 221–22, 224

Palmer, Bryan, xvi, xvii

pamphlets, 54, 139, 224; primitivism and, 222

Panic of 1873, 97, 113

panopticon, 269n3

Park Falls, Wisconsin, 8

*Passing of the Pines, The* (pageant), 205, 214, 216

patriotism, 220

Paul Bunyan, ix, xix, xxvii, xxxi, 161–63, 165–67; authenticity and, 184, 278n4; buffoonery of, 201; capitalism and, 185; conquest of nature and, 51; corporations and, 200; fakelore and, 204, 278n3; festivals and, 213; friendly portrayal of, 203; heroism and, 224; history obscured by, xxxiii; hodags and, 265n37; Nelligan's memoirs and, 245n2; *New York Times* on, 205; nostalgia and, 232; Silver Jack and, 283n2; statues of, 214, 227; written vs. oral legends of, 286n41

*Paul Bunyan* (Britten and Auden), 165

Paul Bunyan Land, 161

"Paul Bunyanland," 220

Paul Bunyan's Playground, 291n49

Paul Bunyan's Playground Association, 224

pay, xii, xiii, xxv, 97; danger and, 241n15; economic autonomy and, 89–90; winter and, 94

Peattie, Elia, 163, 182–83, 260n43

Pelton, E. H., 143–44

Peshtigo Fire, 4; cultural amnesia and, 246n3

Phillips, Katrina M., 221

Pinchot, Gifford, 185

Pine, Minnie, 126

pine barrens, xviii

pioneers, 63, 177–79, 211, 218, 234; Lumberjack Days and, 209; statues of, 222

place, xvii, xviii; "fugue" as rejection of, 111; memoryscapes and, 84; roots memory and, 262n1

plains, xxi; ethnic enclaves and, 38; space and, 244n33. *See also* prairies

plantation museums, 226

planting, 7, 203

*Playing Indian* (Deloria), 213

*Police Gazette,* 28

policing, 67, 88, 106, 131, 138, 154–55; brothels and, 273n48; vagrancy laws and, 272n47

*Political Manhood* (Murphy), 174

popular imagination, xxi. *See also* myth

popular literature, xix. *See also* stories

population boom, ix

Port Huron, Michigan, 151

poverty, 139–40, 231; Gilded Age prosperity and, 136; representation and, 170; women and, 270n12

power, xv, 63–65; cultural memory and, 289n24; hierarchy and, 81; panopticon and, 269n3; unskilled workers and, 140

prairies, xix; ethnic enclaves and, 38. *See also* plains

pranks, 30, 52; skill and, 67. *See also* initiation; jokes

preachers, 32–33, 66, 218

Prescott, Cynthia Culver, 222

primitivism, 182, 220; filmed reenactments and, 290n36; modernity and, 224; narrative and, 219; pamphlets and, 222

*Princeton Union,* 196

profit, 6, 26–27; fires and, 4. *See also* capitalism

progress, 50; Gilded Age ideal of, 222

Progressive Era, 114, 122, 126, 273n47; white slavery and, 125

property, xvii, 105

prosperity, 136–37

prostitution, 123–27, 132, 135; femininity and, 153; fighting and, 154; memory and, 233; Northwoods and, 157; Progressive Era and, 273n47; saloons and, 144; smaller lumber towns and, 134; violence and, 155; white slavery and, 128–29. *See also* brothels; saloons

Protestantism, 54

public land, 13; survey maps of, xvii, xviii

Quan-Wickham, Nancy, 65

quarantine, 117, 122, 129, 157. *See also* contagion

race, 14, 39; American ideas of, 71; Anishinaabe and, 105; boundaries and, 73; civilization and, 77; diversity and, 240n10; heroism and, 229; hierarchy and, 65, 70, 261n45; levels of evolution and, 75; lumber camps and, 37; masculinity and, 63; natural predispositions and, 80; quasiracial other and, 119; roughness and, 141; scientific racism in, 78; smaller lumber towns and, 135; traits and, 76; Walleye Wars and, 107

railways, ix, 22; respectability and, 141

Ramsey, Alexander, 7

rationality, 54; capitalism and, 103; mastery and, 58

reality, 170–73; authenticity and, 177; unreality and, 183

"real" jacks, 197–98

recapitulation, 179

recklessness, 59; violence of nature and, 41. *See also* danger; risk

Red Cliff Band, 103

redistribution, 259n39

red-light districts. *See* vice districts

Red River Lumber Company, 163, 187; Laughead and, 201

red sash brigade, 150, 169; sprees and, 143

redwood forests, xviii

reenactment, 179, 227

refinement, 250n48

reforestation, 7, 203

Reitman, Ben, 114, 129; Vagrants Isle of, 139

religion, 54. *See also* preachers

"Reminisces" (Nelson), 275n13

*Report on the Disastrous Effects of the Destruction of Forest Trees* (Wisconsin State Forestry Commission), 6–7

representation, 170, 222; lumber industry and, 224

reputation, 64–65, 154; heroism and, 184

reservations, 103–4

resistance, 86, 89–91, 107–10, 262n5; capitalism and, xvii, 104; history of, xvi; IWW and, 200; land theft and, 15; management and, xxi; psychological resilience and, 267n46; smaller lumber towns and, 135; strike histories and, 263n14

resorts, 205, 211–12, 216–17; nature tourism and, 218; tourism and, 207

resources, 14, 75, 105–7; as commodities, xvii; Indian agents and, 17; land theft and, 18; mixed economies and, 187; nature and, 102

respectability, 139, 141–42; prostitution and, 123–24, 135; reputation and, 154; risk and, 54; roughness and, 152; saloons and, 158; stable categories of, 274n2; women and, 156

restraint, xxvi, xxvii, 6; adventure novels and, 180; aggressiveness and, 254n24; bodies and, 53; gambling and, 56; lack of, 168; men's changing roles and, 256n7; profit and, 6; propriety and, 2

Riis, Jacob, 170, 177

Ripmeester, Nanette, 275n18

risk, 53–57; brotherhood and, 157; hierarchy and, 63; luck and, 253n21; masculinity and, 60; self-ownership and, 255n29; skill and, 64; songs and, 59; sprees and, 143. *See also* danger

river drives, xii, xxv, 9–10, 22, 80; control of rivers and, 8; death and, 47; hospital tickets and, 42; sprees and, 121

river pigs, xxv, 10, 42, 45, 47

road monkeys, xii–xiii, 41, 70, 241n15, 242n23

Robertson, Mike, 61–62

Rockman, Seth, 136

rodeos, 289n23

Roediger, David, 260n39

role-playing, 172–73

romanticism, viii, xxvii, 21, 37, 168; authenticity and, 167; corporations and, 227; industry and, 193; labor and, 216; landscape paintings, 176; nature and, 291n50;

"noble savage" stereotype and, 103; pamphlets and, 222, 224; Paul Bunyan and, 201; savagery and, 228; tourism and, 207; virgin forest and, 220

Ronning, Gerald, 90

Roosevelt, Teddy, 185

Rosen, Ruth, 156

Rotundo, Anthony, 55, 142

roughness, 139, 141, 234; culture of, 116; idea of, 153; masculinity and, 140; respectability and, 141, 152; saloons and, 158; stable categories of, 274n2; violence and, 70

Round River Drive, 200

Rousseau, Jean-Jacques, 76

rugged individualism, 105, 215–16, 227

rural life, 96, 99; authenticity and, 173; conservation and, 219; historiography of, 250n59; manhood and, 288n23; respectability and, 139; role-playing and, 173

Rusk, Jeremiah, 272n35

Russell, Alexander Alger, 26

Russell, Edmund, 271n27

Ryan, J. C., 133

Saginaw, Michigan, 18, 50

saloons, 144–48, 157; brotherhood and, 149–50; mastery and, 254n23

salvage tourism, 221, 227

Sandow, Eugene, 173–74

San Francisco Chronicle, 165

Santos, Martha, 64

Saunders, E. N., Mrs., 3–4

savagery, xxvii, 104; adventure novels and, 180; Anishinaabe and, 81; civilization and, 71; evolution and, 179; narrative and, 222; noble image of, 76; quasiracial other and, 119; romanticism and, 103, 228; skill and, 79; strikes and, 90; valorization of

skill and, 63; whiteness and, 74, 78. See also barbarity

Sawyer, Philetus, 20

scalers, 27, 32, 66; living quarters and, 250n48

Scandinavians, 68, 70–73, 198–99; "Lena and Ole" joke books and, 259n32; myths of, 286n33

Schoolcraft County, 233

scientific forestry management, 17, 203

Scribner's Magazine, 20, 279n7; Hill and, 36, 44, 197; "Life in a Logging Camp," 168; ruggedness in, 216; vice and, 173

seasonal year, xxii–xxvi, xxvii; mills and, 245n42; rounds of, 102–3, 105

second-growth forest, vii, viii, 162; natural history and, 227; tourism and, 207; warming and, 231

"See America First" campaigns, 220

Seeley, Charles, 284n2

self, 48–50, 182; control and, 55; labor and, 197; masculinity crisis and, 56; ownership of, 255n29; violence and, 60. See also mastery

self-made men, 21, 36, 54, 89, 248n26

Seney, Michigan, 133–35, 155, 264n19; saloons and, 144; sprees and, 120; women's population and, 269n67

Seton, Ernest Thompson, 179

settlement, 117; patterns of, xix, xxi

settler colonialism, 13–14; community resources and, 17; violence and, 226

seven-generation rule, 106

sexuality, 260n40. See also homosexuality; prostitution

shanty boys, 20, 169; shantytowns and, 252n9; songs of, 45; violence and, 33

"Shanty Boys Alphabet" (song), 99

shantytowns, 130 252n9. *See also* jungles (tent cities)

Shapiro, Aaron, 207

Shaw, Daniel, xi, 36, 248n30

"sheep," game of, 67–68

Sheppard, Eugene, 99, 101, 253n18

Shoppenagon, David, 103

"Significance of the Frontier in American History" (Turner), 176

Silver Jack, 152, 283n2

Sioux, 209

Sirotiak, John, xxvi

skid rows, 25, 111, 131–32, 158; prostitution and, 124. *See also* vice districts

skill, 60–62, 70, 76, 168; death and, 57; dignity and, 288n23; Euro-Americans and, 79–80; fighting and, 152; gender and, 68, 70; greenhorns and, 66; hierarchy and, 63, 70; itinerancy and, 64; power and, 65; racial hierarchies and, 261n45; roughness and, 139; songs and, 59; tall tales and, 67; technology and, 215; temperance and, 141; unskilled workers and, 140; whiteness and, 75

sky pilots, 32–33, 66, 218. *See also* preachers

slavery, xv

small camps, 8–9, 19, 97; historiography and, 18; industry and, 193; myth and, 89, 198; Paul Bunyan and, 201; Timber Barons and, 13. *See also* logging camps

Smithsonian Institution, 99

snake rooms, 102, 146

snipes, xxi

social capital, xi

social charter theory, 177

socialism, 90

society, 177

*Something for Nothing* (Lears), 53–54

*Song of Hiawatha, The* (Longfellow), 219–20

songs, 52; circulation of, 99; constant presence of death and, 45; danger and, 51; risk and, 59; violence and, 58, 60

*Songs of the Michigan Lumberjacks* (Beck), 138

Sons of Daniel Boone, 179

South, 6, 73, 211, 291n52

South region: pine barrens in, xviii

spaces, 33, 144–45; boyishness and, 169; ethnicity and, 244n33; femininity and, 115; men's changing roles and, 256n7; networks of, 157, 275n18

Spanish Flu epidemic (1918), 122

sports, 232, 288n23. *See also* games

sprees, xiii, 110, 119–21, 137, 141–44, 146; saloons and, 158

spring, xxiv, 117–20

Srole, Carol, 56

stability, 92, 94; employment and, 257n10; of whiteness, 260n40

Stanchfield, Daniel, x

*Star Trek,* 259n39

State of Maine camps, 18, 20, 22, 97; songs and, 45

state-owned lands, 13

St. Croix boom, 24

St. Croix valley, 97

stereotypes, 103, 177, 210, 227, 232. *See also* types

Stevens, James, 283n2

Stile, Johnny, 59–60

Stillwater, Minnesota, 205, 208–10, 216, 287n8

stock figures, xv

stories, 51–52, 65–66; boys' adventure and, 179–80; constant presence of death and, 45. *See also* tall tales

Stott, Richard, 256n7

*St. Paul Pioneer Press,* 7, 165

Strang, James, xxi

strikes, 109; 1916 strike, 85–87, 90, 108, 200, 262n60; 1917 strikes, 56, 85–86, 88, 90–91, 262n1, 263n14; 1937 strikes, 86. *See also* labor; unions

stumpage, 185–86, 188–90; corporations and, 187

Sturken, Marita, 291n44

Sullivan, Hungry Mike, 99

Sullivan, John J., 208–9

summer, xxv

Superior, Wisconsin, 4

supernatural beings, 52. *See also* hodags

sustainability, x, 185; farmers and, xxix

Swedes, 71–72

Synnott, J. J., 251n3

Tacoma, Washington, 108

taconite, 226, 292n57

tall tales, 39, 52; circulation of, 99; skill and, 67; woods as character in, 51. *See also* stories

Tall Timber Days (Grand Rapids, Minnesota), 162, 205, 216

Tarzan, 77

Taylor, Hunt, 200

technology, 21–23, 171–72, 174; resistance and, 108; skills and, 215

temperance, 126; respectability and, 142; skill and, 141; unmanliness of, 174. *See also* alcohol; saloons

tent cities, 140

terrors, 2–3. *See also* myth

*The Tomahawk* (White Earth Reservation newspaper), 17–18

*This Is That Show* (television program), 232

Thoreau, Henry David, 253n15

*Timber* (Titus), 196

timber barons. *See* lumber barons

*Times Herald* (Port Huron, Michigan), 151

*Tomahawk, The* (newspaper), 105–6

Tomczik, Adam, 21

Tom's Historic Logging Camp and Trading Post, 226

top loaders, 41, 61–62

tourism, viii, xxix, xxxi, 162, 220–24, 226–27; boosters and, 211, 217; clear-cutting and, 185; colonization companies and, 192; comfort culture of, 291n44; escapism and, 219; farmland and, 193; kitsch and, 234; landscape and, 207; lumber camps and, 204; lumber industry and, 216; Lumberjack Days and, 209; memory and, 227; mining and, 291n50; nature and, 226; regional identity and, 291n52; stumplands and, 188

towns, 133–34; isolation and, 135; prostitution and, 135. *See also* cities; urban life

traits, 63, 76, 78, 169, 180

*Tramp in America, The* (Cresswell), 114

tramping, 140

tramps, 111, 137, 234; alienation and, 139; quarantine and, 129; tramp scares and, 113–17, 157. *See also* vice; vice districts

transcendentalism, 52

transformation, 2, 6; ballads and, 47–48; environment and, ix; labor and, 197; logging industry and, 11

transportation, 108

Treat, Asher, 187

treaty rights, 107; theft by, 18

Tripp, Florence, 63

truth, 170

Turner, Frederick Jackson, xix, 133; Census of 1890 and, 245n47; "Significance of the Frontier in American History," 176

"'Twas on the Napanee" (ballad), 46

types, 174, 210, 254n22; crossing over of, 261n60; "Typofications" as, 213. *See also* stereotypes

*Types of Mankind: Or, Ethnological Researches* (Nott), 78

Uintah Reservation, 17

unemployment, xxiii

Union Pacific Railroad, 216

unions, 86–90; brotherhood and, 146; class and, 196; craft union movement and, 139; false idealism and, 194; safety and, 56; strike histories and, 263n14; "suckers" and, 34

United States: Anishinaabe policy of, 14; aristocracy and, 172; capitalism and, 103; meritocracy and, 21; millionaires per capita and, 25; poverty maps and, 113; Swedes acceptance in, 71

United States Department of Agriculture, 190

United States Supreme Court, 14

*United States v. Cook (1873)*, 14

unskilled workers, 139–40

Upper Midwest: lumberjack myth in, 20; myth in, xxix. *See also* Midwest; Northwoods

Upper Peninsula, Michigan, 26; extractive industries and, 191; itinerancy and, 98; mining and, 185; songs and, 45; sprees and, 119; tourism and, 207

Upper Peninsula Development Bureau, 192

urban life, xxi, xxii, 96; American Realism and, 173; ax-throwing and, 232; boyishness and, 169; East region and, xxix; folk heroes and, 167; gender ideals and, 55; historiography of, 250n59; homelessness and, 114, 137; homosociality and, 174; isolation and, 135; prostitution and, 157; representation and, 170; respectability and, 139, 158; retreat from, 207; shantytowns and, 252n9; sprees and, 119; ties between rural and, 99; wealth and, 182

"Vacation Land" brochures, 222

vagrancy, 113, 139–40, 272n47. *See also* itinerancy

Van Camp, Alton, 36, 72, 79, 92, 94, 157

Van Sant, Samuel, 16

Vaughn, David K., 287n42

venereal disease, 123, 251n3

"vibrant visibility," xvi

vice, 122, 173; contagion of, 133; lumber boom and, 131; restraint and, 168. *See also* prostitution; tramps

vice districts, 127–31, 136, 138–39, 157–58, 234, 273n47; prostitution and, 122, 154

Victorian age, 6; aggressiveness and, 254n24; chastity and, 124; prostitution and, 123, 135

Vikings, 224

Vinette, Bruno, 11

violence, 50, 234; alcohol and, 150; Anishinaabe and, 80–81; brotherhood and, 157; within camps, 261n52; casual forms of, 277n28; distastefulness of, 256n9; employment and, 257n10; establishing power and, 64; gendering skill and, 65; hierarchy and, 63; luck and, 58; narrative and, 222; nature and, 40–41, 52–53, 57; prostitution and, 154–55; roughness and, 70; savagery and, 76; settler colonialism and, 226; sexual forms of, 115; skill and, 62, 67; slow form of, 263n10; songs and, 60; valorization of skill and, 63; whiteness and, 75; women and, 156. *See also* fighting virgin forests, vii, xxix, 2, 185–86, 207, 227; advertising and, 220, 224; last stand of, 22–23

Virginia, Minnesota, 6; sprees and, 121; strikes and, 85, 87–88, 108

Virginia and Rainy Lake Lumber Company, 6, 86, 98

"voting with their feet," xxi, xxiii, 91, 95, 97. *See also* itinerancy; resistance

Voyageurs National Park, 291n50

voyeurism, 126

*Wages of Whiteness* (Roediger), 260n39

Walker, Mark, 139

walking bosses, 25, 27, 34; fighting and, 154

walking patterns, 101–2. *See also* itinerancy

Walleye Wars, 107

*War and Nature: Fighting Humans and Insects with Chemicals from World War I to Silent Spring* (Russell), 271n27

Ward, Willis, 52

*Ward County Independent,* 284n2

*Washington Post,* 204

Way, Peter, 140

wealth, 173, 182, 191. *See also* capitalism; lumber barons

West, 177; Census of 1890 and, 245n47; democracy and, 176; dispossession and, 222; domesticity and, 116; extractive industries and, 60; festivals and, 211; gentleman ideal and, 178; heroism and, 182; identity and, 178; land markets and, 191; migration to, 21–22; nature tourism and, 226; prostitution and, 124; reenactments and, 213; savagery and, 179; tourism and, 207; Wild West Show and, 170

Westerns, 227

Weyerhauser, Frederick, xi, 13, 24, 36, 187, 189

Weyerhauser, J. P., 108, 188

Weyerhauser Timber Company, 187, 200

Whalen, Jimmy, 46

"When You and I Were Young, Maggie" (song), 58

White, Stewart E., 180

White City (Columbian Exposition), 170, 172

White Cloud, 268n58

White Earth Band (Anishinaabe), 78

White Earth Reservation (Anishinaabe), 15–17, 105–6

White Earth Tragedy, 15, 107

White Hair, Chief, 105

whiteness, 70–71, 73–77; capitalism and, 243n25; curriculum development and, 281n24; hierarchy and, 78; Marxism and, 259n39; masculinity and, 198, 229; myth and, 240n10; Paul Bunyan and, 201; redefining masculinity and, 162; tenuous stability of, 260n40; violence and, 81

*Whiteness of a Different Color* (Jacobsen), 73

white pine, ix, x, 4; last virgin stand of, 22–23; virgin forest and, 185; warming and, 231

*White Pine Industry in Minnesota, The* (Larson), 89, 94

"white slavery," 124–27, 129, 135; mail-order brides and, 155–56; Nelligan on, 155. *See also* prostitution

Whitson, Joseph, 226

widowmakers, 41, 56

wilderness, viii, xv; advertising and, 220; changing attitudes towards, 253n15; danger and, 51–52; decolonial theory and, 247n15; degraded land and, xxix; Early American settlers and, 50; escapism and, 226; extractive industries and, 185; farming and, 194; levels of evolution and,

75; lumber industry and, 224; national expansion and, 194; naturalist image and, 166; nature tourism and, 218; tourism and, 193, 207; untamable nature of, 56; virgin forests and, 227. *See also* nature

wildfire. *See* fires

"Wild Mustard River, The" (song), 58

wildness, 75–76; changing attitudes towards, 253n15; savagery and, 78. *See also* wilderness

wild rice (Manoomin), 106–7

Wild West shows, 176, 221. *See also* Buffalo Bill (William Cody)

Wilkinson, William, 3

Wilson, Catharine Anne, 288n23

winter, xxii, 91–92, 96–97; pay and, 94; sprees and, 121

"Winter Desires" (song), 138

Wisconsin, vii, xviii, xxix; 1871 fires in, 186; agriculture and, 187; chastity laws and, 124; clear-cutting and, 7, 185; control of rivers and, 8; cultural circulation and, 99; cutover and, 191–92; festivals and, 204–5; Gilded Age in, xxi; impenetrability of, 1–2; itinerancy and, 98; legislature report on "white slavery" and, 127–29; nature tourism and, 218; Paul Bunyan and, 161, 184; respectability and, 158; "white slavery" and, 135

Wisconsin State Forestry Commission, 6

women, 152–53, 155; cook role for, 250n57; heroism and, 229; history and, 63; homelessness and, 113; idealized forms of, 210–11; mail-order brides and, 155–56;

Northwoods stories about, xxi, 2; permeable boundaries and, 124; poverty and, 270n12; prostitution and, 135; sacred space of home and, 115; sprees and, 143. *See also* prostitution

Women's Christian Temperance Union (WCTU), 126, 129

Woodcraft Indians, 179

worker safety, 56, 251n2. *See also* danger

working class, xvi, 30, 33; floating of, xxi; folk culture and, xxviii; gendered identity and, 138; hierarchy and, 73; identity and, 172; manhood ideals and, 256n10; masculinity crisis and, 56; mastery and, 48; nature tourism and, 218; permanence of, 108; reputation and, 65; respectability and, 141; risk and, 54, 60; safety and, 251n2; saloons and, 158; spaces for, 144–45; study of, 139; valorization of skill and, 63; violence of nature and, 41

Works Progress Administration (WPA), xxxiii, 99, 148, 152

World's Fairs, xxxi

World War I, 39

Worster, Donald, 246n4

Wyman, Mark, 282n39

Yankees, 71

Yellowstone National Park, 218

YouTube, 232

Zarnoski, C. Frank, 288n23

Zeterstrom, John, 133

Zunis, 181

WILLA HAMMITT BROWN is a historian, speaker, and writer based in Minneapolis, Minnesota. She holds a PhD in American history from the University of Virginia and has taught history, gender studies, and analytical writing at the University of Virginia, onboard Semester at Sea, and at Harvard University. Her writing has been published in *The Atlantic, Western History Quarterly,* and *Environmental History.* She has spoken about masculinity and memory on the CBC's Q show, National Public Radio, and *Drinking with Historians.* She first had her picture taken in Paul Bunyan's hand at four years old and still spends every moment she can in the Northwoods with her husband and their excellent dog.